THE DANGER
IMPERATIVE

"Based on rigorous observation and insightful analysis across three police departments, *The Danger Imperative* is a sobering journey into the 'soul' of U.S. public law enforcement—one that reveals police violence not as the product of 'bad apples' but as an expected outcome born out of an organizational fixation on death and danger. Carefully attending to police culture on its own terms without losing sight of the broader inequalities that policing reflects and reproduces, Sierra-Arévalo reveals the largely obscured and unappreciated stamp of the 'danger imperative' in the everyday rituals of policing as it amplifies officers' fears of vulnerability, exacerbates the perceived likelihood of violence, and crowds out other orientations toward policing. Necessary and troubling, *The Danger Imperative* shifts the conversation from how police make violence to how violence makes police—and in doing so, invites us to reimagine the relationship between officer safety and public safety in ways that move beyond superficial reforms—and encourages us to rethink our own investment in the danger imperative."

—Jennifer Carlson, author of *Merchants of the Right: Gun Sellers and the Crisis of American Democracy*

"Through deep immersion in the worlds of police, Sierra-Arévalo shows how policing continually re-creates a worldview of acute danger in every civilian encounter. From this sense of constant threat comes a justifying ideology that privileges the possibility of violence toward the policed—sometimes preemptive and often racialized—to ensure officer survival. *The Danger Imperative* skillfully locates officers and the public within the institutional and social worlds of policing and reveals the situated exchanges that sustain officers' fear and justify their practices. This remarkable book should be read and taught in criminology and sociology and, importantly, throughout the police profession."

—Jeffrey Fagan, Isidor and Seville Sulzbacher Professor of Law, Columbia Law School

"Violence against the police is at a historic low, and it is hard to find evidence of a 'war on cops.' Indeed, police work is usually routine and uneventful. But in this powerful ethnography, Sierra-Arévalo shows us how police departments create a culture where 'officer safety' is the organizing principle—the 'soul'—of police work. Clearly written and nuanced, *The Danger Imperative* should be read by anyone concerned with policing today."

—Annette Lareau, author of *Unequal Childhoods: Class, Race, and Family Life*

"From the first day at the academy to the last call at the retirement banquet, a preoccupation with violence and survival runs like a blue thread through American policing. With painstaking research and firsthand observation, Sierra-Arévalo brilliantly traces this 'danger imperative' in police training, operations, and seldom seen rituals. A masterful contribution, from its harrowing opening pages to its clear-eyed conclusion."

—Christopher Uggen, coauthor of *Locked Out: Felon Disenfranchisement and American Democracy*

"*The Danger Imperative* showcases how danger becomes routinized as an organizing principle of policing through training and the day-to-day practices of officers. Sierra-Arévalo convincingly captures the heart of policing as an institution, and we are left with an understanding of why current proposals for reforming the police often overlook the heart of the problem. The significance of this contribution cannot be overstated."

—Brittany Friedman, University of Southern California

THE DANGER IMPERATIVE

VIOLENCE, DEATH, AND
THE SOUL OF POLICING

MICHAEL SIERRA-ARÉVALO

Columbia University Press   *New York*

Columbia University Press
Publishers Since 1893
New York   Chichester, West Sussex
cup.columbia.edu

Library of Congress Cataloging-in-Publication Data
Names: Sierra-Arévalo, Michael, author.
Title: The danger imperative : violence, death, and the soul of policing /
Michael Sierra-Arévalo.
Description: [New York] : [Columbia University Press], [2023] |
Includes index.
Identifiers: LCCN 2023022359 | ISBN 9780231198462 (hardback) |
ISBN 9780231198479 (trade paperback) | ISBN 9780231552646 (ebook)
Subjects: LCSH: Police brutality—United States. |
Police-community relations—United States. |
Danger—United States. | Equality—United States.
Classification: LCC HV8141 .S533 2023 | DDC 363.20973—
dc23/eng/20230829
LC record available at https://lccn.loc.gov/2023022359

Cover design: Milenda Nan Ok Lee
Cover art: BIJILAPIS / Shutterstock

CONTENTS

Preface   *vii*

Acknowledgments   *xvii*

Introduction   1

1 Survival School   29

2 Ghosts of the Fallen   77

3 The Threat Network   115

4 Going Home at Night   157

Conclusion   223

Methodological Appendix and Reflection   *243*

Notes   *267*

Index   *329*

PREFACE

I n July 2014, Eric Garner was choked to death by New York City police officer Daniel Pantaleo, one of several officers attempting to arrest Garner for allegedly selling untaxed cigarettes. Video of Pantaleo's fatal chokehold and Garner's labored cries of "I can't breathe" spread across the country, drawing widespread condemnation. Less than a month later, Michael Brown was shot and killed by Officer Darren Wilson in Ferguson, Missouri. Protests in the wake of Brown's killing were met with a shockingly militarized response. Police deployed multiple armored vehicles, including a nearly 18,000-pound BearCat—a Ballistic Engineered Armored Response Counter Attack Truck—equipped with gunports and blast-resistant floors. Officers dressed in military-style fatigues, ballistic helmets, and gas masks pointed their rifles at peaceful protestors. Police dogs snarled and barked at Black residents of Ferguson, a modern reflection of the police dogs that tore the flesh of children and civil rights protesters in Birmingham, Alabama, more than half a century before.

In the days and months after Ferguson, the shift in public sentiment that we now describe as policing's crisis of legitimacy was palpable. Many—including me, then a twenty-four-year-old graduate student—were shocked by the callous violence, the injustice streaming to their smartphones in high definition. Black Lives Matter erupted into the public consciousness seemingly overnight. Cable news programs rushed to produce breathless exposés on police misconduct and a broken criminal legal system. Mass incarceration, police brutality, and racial inequality were ripped out of ivory tower seminar rooms and placed in the center of mainstream discourse. The upswell of attention and calls for action seemed to mark a seismic shift in mainstream public consciousness. The feeling of the moment was tangible; the possibility of real change was inspiring.

It was amid the tumult of 2014 that I began to ride along with police officers. I began my ridealongs on the east coast, in a small city that I call Elmont. My initial questions centered on community policing, a pervasive but ill-defined strategy that revolves around building and leveraging cooperative police-community relationships to, hopefully, reduce crime. The origins of this policy prescription can be traced back to the turmoil of the 1960s and calls to institutionalize "community relations" programs in the hope of building trust in Black neighborhoods.[1] President Barack Obama's Task Force on Twenty-First Century Policing, convened in the wake of Ferguson, revitalized this tradition and called for community policing to build "positive relationships with members of the community" to address "crime, social disorder, and fear of crime."[2]

What I found when I began riding with officers in Elmont was both more quotidian and more crushing than I could ever have imagined. Unlike the romanticized depictions of policing in television and film, calls for service were seldom about life-threatening violence. Instead, officers' daily calls were for an endless stream of disputes, whether between siblings, spouses, neighbors, friends, or lovers. Simultaneously, structural disinvestment made manifest in poverty, mental distress, physical illness, and substance abuse were so common as to be unremarkable in the professional lives of police.

Arrests were rare. Far more often, calls for service were resolved with little more than a short conversation, a written report, advice to file an order of protection, or a suggestion to take an argument to small claims court. When arrests did occur, they were usually for small amounts of narcotics, theft, drunken fights, or outstanding warrants for similarly low-level offenses. In all of this, the promise of community policing fell exceedingly short in its street-level implementation. As much as the Elmont Police Department (EPD) touted its commitment to community policing, and as much as officers spoke of trust, respect, and cooperation, the daily grind of shuffling about the symptoms of social inequality left little room or incentive for nourishing police-community relationships. While there were community meetings between police and Elmont residents, and some officers did check in on a store owner or chat with someone sitting on their front porch, time not spent answering calls for service was far more often used for writing reports, eating lunch, or stopping residents to search them and their property for drugs and guns. In practice, community policing was the exception, not the rule.

As the ideals of community policing faded into boilerplate rhetoric and the rigamarole of patrol, the dominance of danger in officers' worldview became especially stark. When I asked officers about how and why they performed their work as they did, "officer safety" repeatedly rang out as their central concern. Where they parked for lunch, how they stood when interacting with citizens, and why they chose to use violence were all justified on the grounds of ensuring their own survival. Across rookie officers and salty veterans, from the street to the offices of department leadership, in the academy and on a memorial wall erected in honor of fallen officers, survival was a powerful and unerring concern. Of course, the EPD was only one police department. To see if the focus on danger and violence I observed in Elmont was present in other locales, I expanded my research to two additional cities: a city on the west coast, which I call West River, and a city in the southwest, which I call Sunshine.

These departments, located across the country, showed remarkable consistency in the contrast between their day-to-day work and the preoccupation with violence that suffused departmental culture and officer behavior. Indeed, even "hot" calls about violence or weapons hewed more toward bureaucratic routine than heart-pounding danger. Racing to reports of an armed home invasion in Sunshine did not result in any arrests; it did lead to several hours in a dark parking lot guarding two victims until detectives arrived to interview them. A mass police response to a triple shooting near a street festival in West River turned into hours of directing residents around a perimeter marked with yellow police tape. Suspects were never found.[3] But while I never saw an officer in a knock-down, drag-out brawl, much less a full-blown firefight, officers' concern that they might be ambushed while eating lunch in their car or gunned down at a call for service was ever present. Across each department, officers' preoccupation with violence and potential death was the same, reflected in their words and behavior as much as the symbols and routines of the organizations they inhabited.

All the while, the "war on cops" narrative that rose to prominence after Ferguson was perpetuated by pundits, politicians, and police leaders alike.[4] A *Washington Times* op-ed warned that a "growing anti-cop campaign" of "public rants, violent protests, excessive lawsuits, political posturing, and unflattering portrayals in popular culture" was causing deadly violence against police. Dr. Ron Martinelli, a retired officer turned police trainer and legal consultant, wrote in *Police Magazine*: "Make no mistake about it. The law enforcement community is under attack. . . . America is at a critical turning point. We can either be destroyed by ISIS and Al Qaeda terrorists from outside of our borders; or we can be destroyed from within by lawless criminal predators and society's violent criminal activists and police haters. You choose."[5]

Nowhere was the growing power of the "war on cops" narrative more apparent than in Donald Trump's campaign for the presidency of the United States. In the lead-up to the 2016 election, Trump explicitly courted aggrieved police officers and aligned himself with Blue Lives Matter, a countermovement and cultural riposte to the rise of Black Lives Matter.[6] He praised the NYPD's unconstitutional stop-and-frisk tactics.[7] He won endorsements from the National Fraternal Order of Police, state FOP lodges across the country, the National Border Patrol Council, and local police unions in Philadelphia, Chicago, and Cleveland.[8]

While accepting the endorsement of the New England Police Benevolent Association, he was greeted with cheers when he promised: "That anybody killing a policeman, a policewoman, police officer—anybody killing a police officer: death penalty. It's going to happen, OK."[9] At the Republican National Convention, he declared: "An attack on law enforcement is an attack on all Americans. . . . I have a message to every last person threatening the peace on our streets and the safety of our police: When I take the oath of office next year, I will restore law and order to our country."[10]

Buoyed by increased voter turnout among police, Trump made good on that promise and swiftly moved to revitalize tough-on-crime policies from decades past and roll back Obama-era efforts to reform policing.[11]

Now, nearly a decade after I set out to understand policing from within, it is clear to me that the fires in Ferguson—in all their furor and possibility—marked only the newest chapter in a cycle of repression, outrage, reform, and regression as old as the nation itself. As articulated by the historian Elizabeth Hinton, "Racial hierarchy, inequality, and violence are among the oldest American stories."[12] While smartphones and social media have forced many to bear witness to police brutality for the first time, the contemporary struggle for racial justice is inextricably linked to Black rebellion against generations of state exclusion, and violence.

These injustices, for me as for so many well-intentioned progressives, were and remain a world away. I was spared the psychic tax of wondering when I would be stopped and searched by a police officer. I never received "the talk" that Black parents give their children in the hope of ensuring their survival when—not if—they encounter a police officer. That America, existing alongside but segregated from my own, was hidden in plain sight. Even as a Latino man and the son of immigrants—someone who had been stopped by police, followed by campus security, and required to identify myself or submit to a pat down while others entered spaces unquestioned—I did not understand these arrangements of state power as anything more than a historical accident when I began to study police. I did not yet see that every stop, every killing, and every protest was the sum of countless infringements on liberty, the product of injustice borne in the memory and bones of a people. It was only with time, after opening myself to the violent tradition of policing and the American project, that I could understand the present as a consequence of a past that is always prologue.

Then, in the summer of 2020, amid the COVID-19 pandemic that has killed more than 6.5 million people worldwide and more than a million in the United States, George Floyd was murdered by Minneapolis police officer Derek Chauvin. Like seventy others in the past decade alone—including Eric Garner in Staten Island, New York; Willie Ray Banks in Granite Shoals, Texas; Balantine Mbegbu in Glendale, Arizona; and Fermin Vincent Valenzuela in Anaheim, California—Floyd pleaded for air.[13] For more than nine minutes, Chauvin kneeled on Floyd's neck, crushing his life away as he begged for mercy and cried out to his children and dead mother. For more than nine minutes, Floyd gasped for breath just six miles from where Philando Castille, another Black man, was fatally shot by an officer four years prior. In response to Floyd's desperate terror, Chauvin smirked, "It takes a heck of a lot of oxygen to talk."[14]

The fire this time was of unprecedented scale. From coast to coast, massive protests marked the largest social movement in the history of the United States and thrust the concepts of police abolition and "defunding" squarely into the public arena.[15] The upswell of criticism and protest was met with extreme force, even in cases where there was no violence directed at police. Journalists were shoved, pepper sprayed, hit with batons, shot with "less lethal" projectiles, and arrested.[16]

Following protests just a few miles from my home in Austin, Texas, a group of physicians penned a letter to the *New England Journal of Medicine* that described how the use of "less lethal" beanbag munitions by the Austin Police Department had resulted in skull fractures, intracranial bleeding, and brain damage.[17] An elderly man in Buffalo, New York, was shoved to the ground by two officers wearing riot helmets and holding batons. Footage of blood seeping from the unconscious seventy-five-year-old's ear quickly went viral on social media, joining the flood of videos showing unrestrained police violence in cities across the country.[18] As has come to be expected, those two officers faced no legal accountability. All charges against them were dismissed by a grand jury. When asked about the grand jury's choice, Erie County district attorney John Flynn said that "society made the decision, not me."[19]

But unlike in the many police killings that came before, Derek Chauvin was, one year after Floyd called out for mercy beneath his knee, found guilty of third-degree murder, unintentional second-degree murder, and second-degree manslaughter. During his trial, multiple Minneapolis officers took the stand to condemn the actions of one of their own. The chief of the Minneapolis Police Department, Medaria Arradondo, in full uniform with four gold stars on each side of his collar, testified that Chauvin's actions were "not part of our training and is certainly not part our ethics or values."[20] The blue wall, it seemed, was cracking.

In a year marked by the ravages of COVID-19 and a violent insurrection at the U.S. Capitol encouraged by President Trump, Chauvin's conviction was a small and merciful reprieve from an endless refrain of chaos and injustice. As I sat alone in my home watching the judge read out the jury's decision, I let out a breath I hadn't realized I had been holding. With the memory of the previous summer still so fresh, part of me was afraid of the rage that might be unleashed and the state violence that would inevitably follow if Chauvin were shielded by the system that had protected so many officers before him. Another part of me, I think, feared losing hope altogether.

But even in the relief of the guilty verdict, it was plain just how miraculous this triumph over policing's violent inertia was. Less than a year before, the Minneapolis Police Department had not been so quick to sacrifice Chauvin on the altar of the court. On May 26, 2020, the day after Floyd was murdered, the MPD released an investigative update on the incident. Though the report confirmed that the officers' body-worn cameras were activated, the report made no mention of Chauvin's brutality. Instead, it said only that Floyd "physically resisted," that officers believed he was "suffering medical distress," and that he was transported to a hospital where he later died. Not one of the other officers present reported Chauvin for excessive force after he killed Floyd. If not for the prescient bravery of Darnella Frazier, the seventeen-year-old girl who recorded Floyd's murder on her phone and posted it online, the story would likely have ended there.

This dynamic continues to play out in departments across the United States. Complaints—a clear underestimate of the totality of officers' misconduct—rarely result in formal discipline. When punishment is meted out, it is often minimal.[21] Criminal charges are rarer still thanks to a phalanx of legal and cultural shields that insulate police from accountability.[22] As a case in point, Floyd was not Chauvin's first victim. Over his career, Chauvin was the subject of twenty-two complaints or internal departmental investigations. Multiple citizens recalled being brutalized by Chauvin, including a fourteen-year-old boy whom he beat with a flashlight, choked, and then pinned to the ground with his knee in 2017. Like Floyd, the boy cried out that he couldn't breathe.[23]

Today, Floyd's memory is preserved in murals and statues; Chauvin is in a cage. This outcome is a necessary modicum of accountability. But it is not justice. It is not justice because the system that constructed Floyd's murder, that trained, paid, and protected a brutal officer for years, is all but unchanged. Despite claims that the "defunding" of police departments caused increases in crime and violence across the

United States, most cities did not markedly reduce police funding after Floyd's murder.[24] Those that tried quickly reversed course when a historic rise in homicide pressured city leaders to pour even more money back into the policing apparatus.[25]

At the federal level, President Biden attempted to appease both sides of the political divide. For progressives, he announced billions of dollars for "community-based prevention and intervention programs" that do not depend solely on arrests and incarceration. For those more inclined toward the age-old strategy of punitive enforcement, he promised billions more in support to police departments across the country.[26]

And so the cycle continues: violence to crisis to piecemeal reform that fails to address our nation's collective predilection for punishment. This is our bloody inheritance, proof that our current moment is neither novel nor accidental. It is the persistence of a policing institution repeatedly empowered and expanded to more efficiently surveil, control, and coerce the public. Today's police, including the officers with whom I spent time in Elmont, West River, and Sunshine, are tied to the same history. It is certainly true that officers today are part of a system not entirely of their own making, saddled with the weight of a history wrought long before a badge was pinned to their chest. But while any one officer cannot be held responsible for the decisions of decades past, they must be understood as a product of a policing institution that is wholly culpable for its present policies, practices, and errors.

Over many days and nights on patrol, through countless conversations in the steady glow of an in-car computer or the red-and-blue flicker of a patrol car's light bar, I became familiar with officers' vision of their world and work. This same vision connects them to our shared heritage of violent struggle over an incomplete and imperfect society. At a time when calls to abolish or defund police are rebutted with "Blue Lives Matter" banners and claims of a "war on cops," it is apparent that our present debates are about more than how to improve or reform policing. We are reckoning with fundamental questions about what this powerful institution *is* and what it *should* be. This book, through an account of policing's structure, culture, and practice across three police departments from 2014 through 2018, provides a view of policing as it is and likely will remain.

ACKNOWLEDGMENTS

When I began riding along with police almost a decade ago, I could not fathom the intellectual and emotional challenges that this research and the writing of this book would present. I am deeply thankful to the many who helped me stay the course, especially when I didn't think it possible.

I am grateful to the advisors who supported and guided me. Thank you to Tracey Meares, Frederick Wherry, Joscha Legewie, and Jacob Hacker for your intellectual generosity and encouragement. I am especially indebted to the mentorship of Andrew Papachristos. As much as you've taught me about asking and answering questions, you have taught me even more about being a teacher, son, father, and friend. From me and my family: thank you.

I owe a debt of gratitude to a long list of colleagues who believed in me and always made my thinking better. My thanks to Brittany Friedman and Samantha Simon, my staunch writing partners and dear friends. Thanks also to Sarah Brayne, Matthew Clair, Thomas Abt, Jordan Conwell, Forrest Stuart, Sarah Lageson, Andrew Selbst, Sara Wakefield, Bob Apel, Abena Mackall, Stuart Craig, Jennifer Wu, Kyle Peyton, Nicholas Occhiuto, Heba Gowayed, Tony Cheng, Jooyoung Lee, Josh Page, Letta Page, Justin Nix, and Seth Stoughton. You have shaped this book through your comments, suggestions, and, above all, kindness.

To my oldest friends, my chosen family—Derron, George, Kevin, Cameron, Chris, JD, Scott, Rigo, Anu, Skylar, Julien, Mario, and Patrick—thank you for being in my life and letting me share in yours. It has been a great privilege to watch you persevere in your pursuit of happiness. Thank you, too, for always giving a broke graduate student a hot plate, cold beer, and a place to stay.

Este libro es, ante todo, un testamento del amor y apoyo de mi familia. También es prueba del esfuerzo de los que vinieron antes y soñaron con crear una nueva vida lejos de su patria. A Lyda Consuelo, mi Mami, nunca podré repagar tu cariño y respaldo. Cada página de este libro plasma tu dedicación como madre, maestra, y mentora. Leslie, mi hermana y constante amiga, gracias por siempre creer en mi más de lo que yo puedo. Mo, Rafik, Sabi, y Lucho, gracias por siempre estar a mi lado, sus gritos de emoción en cada graduación, y su constante apoyo. Luis Felipe y Lyda, mi Nonito y mi Nonita, gracias por ser los cimientos de nuestra familia. La profundidad de su amor por nosotros y todos a nuestro alrededor ha sido el más maravilloso obsequio y ejemplo. Aunque siento orgullo de haber logrado esta meta, ese orgullo palidece al lado del honor de ser su hijo, hermano, sobrino, primo, y nieto. Desde lo más recóndito de mi corazón, mi querida familia: gracias.

And to Asia, thank you for being my partner in all things. Someday, the indefinite toil of this book will be a distant memory. But your grace when my doubts loomed large, your gentle but unyielding faith in me, will never dim in my memory. Thank you for lifting me up, for filling my life with joy, and for taking care of Shiner and me. I love you.

Finally, my thanks to the officers of the Elmont, West River, and Sunshine police departments without whom this book would not have been possible. It is no small thing to trust someone with your memories and beliefs, much less when that person is a stranger. Though some of you will disagree with my critiques of policing, I am hopeful that you will recognize this book as a true and informed account of your work. Thank you for sharing your experiences and views of the world—I have tried to represent them so others might better understand them.

THE DANGER
IMPERATIVE

INTRODUCTION

THE WAR AT HOME

On the afternoon of December 20, 2014, New York City's holiday season was in full swing. The famous Christmas tree in Rockefeller Center, a Norway spruce from Danville, Pennsylvania, rose eighty-five feet into the air. Nearby, teeming crowds perused the dazzling window displays of Fifth Avenue. Across the East River in Bed-Stuy, Brooklyn, a smaller twenty-five-foot Canadian spruce twinkled at the corner of Marcy Avenue and Fulton Street, a festive reminder of the holiday bazaar and musical performances that had accompanied the tree-lighting ceremony a few weeks earlier. A little over a mile north of Marcy and Fulton, adjacent to the Tompkins Houses, NYPD officers Wenjian Liu and Rafael Ramos sat in their police car, on loan from the Eighty-Fourth Precinct in downtown Brooklyn.

In all likelihood, Liu, the son of Chinese immigrants who emigrated to New York when he was twelve, and Ramos, a lifelong Queens resident, were engaged in one of the infinite mundane tasks of patrol work. They may have been writing paperwork on their in-car computer or asking about each other's families; they may have just been taking shelter from the winter chill before getting back to the job of reducing violence that had prompted their assignment to a CRV (Crisis Response Vehicle) outside the Tompkins housing development.[1] But the violence that would strike the corner of Myrtle and Tompkins Avenues on December 20, 2014, would not be the kind that Liu and Ramos were there to address. Instead, at about 2:45 P.M., Ismaaiyl Brinsley, a twenty-eight-year-old Baltimore man angered by the police killings of Michael Brown and Eric Garner, followed through on threats he had made alongside his Instagram post of a stainless-steel handgun: "I'm Putting Wings On Pigs Today. They Take 1 Of Ours . . . . . . Let's Take 2 of Theirs #ShootThePolice #RIPErivGardner #RIPMikeBrown . . . I'm Putting Pigs In A Blanket."[2]

After telling two bystanders to "watch what I'm going to do," Brinsley walked up to the passenger side, where Liu was seated, and opened fire, shooting both officers in the head at point-blank range.[3] Neither had a chance to draw his own weapon. After executing the officers, Brinsley fled into a nearby subway station. As officers closed in on him, he took his own life with the same weapon he had used to kill the NYPD veterans.[4]

Later that night, from outside the Woodhull Medical Center where the officers' bodies were transported, Patrick Lynch, the president of the Patrolmen's Benevolent Association (PBA), blamed Liu's and Ramos's deaths on anti–police brutality activists "who incited violence on the street under the guise of protest." He also blamed Mayor Bill de Blasio, stating, "There's blood on many hands tonight. . . . That blood on the hands starts on the steps of City Hall, in the office of the mayor."[5] Soon after, the PBA released a dire memo that recalled "the 1970s when police officers were ambushed and executed on a regular basis." It proclaimed ominously, "We have, for the first time in a number of years, become a 'wartime' police department. We will act accordingly."[6]

On the heels of the nationwide outrage and protests following the police killings of Eric Garner, Michael Brown, and Tamir Rice, the murders of police officers like Liu and Ramos bolstered the increasingly popular narrative that America's police were under attack, both ideologically and literally. This "war on cops," its proponents argued, was fueled by growing scrutiny and criticism of police by liberal factions among the public, politicians, academics, and the news media. This criticism was at the root of pervasive disrespect and violence against police officers.[7] The former NYPD commissioner Howard Safir declared that widespread criticism of police was poisoning police morale and empowering "murderers, drug peddlers, rapists, [and] thieves."[8] Milwaukee sheriff David A. Clark—the controversial Black lawman known for his western-style hat and the decorative pins on his dress uniform—put it more bluntly, "War has been declared on the American police officer."[9]

This vision of police under siege featured prominently in testimony given to President Barack Obama's Task Force on Twenty-First Century Policing, which was convened to chart a path forward through the growing policing crisis. The sixth and final day of testimony to the task force focused on officer safety and wellness. As part of this listening session, a Voices from the Field panel centered the perspective of law enforcement officers and advocates. Via Skype, Yousry "Yost" Zakhary, the director of public safety for Woodway, Texas, and a former president of the International Association of Chiefs of Police (IACP), called for renewed funding of the Bulletproof Vest Partnership program by emphasizing the increased danger facing contemporary police officers: "Being a law enforcement officer has always been a stressful and dangerous job. But currently the law enforcement community is up against even greater pressures, challenges, and violence. Police officers face and witness profound danger on a daily basis." Later in the session, Chuck Canterbury, the national president of the Fraternal Order of Police, reminded the task force of his prior testimony calling for new legislation to make the killing of a police officer a federal hate crime. To highlight the need for enhanced punishment, he declared, "Now, more than ever, we see our officers in the crosshairs of these criminals."[10]

The danger that police face is very real. Putting aside simplistic comparisons between policing's fatality rate and that of other occupations—loggers, fishermen, roofers, sanitation workers, farmers, truck drivers, farmers, lawn service workers, and others have higher rates of lethal workplace injury than police officers—policing stands apart in how often officer injury and death come at the hands of another person. Nationally, patrol officers were nonfatally injured at a rate of 371.4 nonfatal injuries per 10,000 employees in 2018, more than 3.7 times the national average and more than 30 percent higher than the rate for the next most injurious occupation, nursing assistants (272.4 per 10,000). About 10 percent of officers are assaulted in the line of duty each year, accounting for tens of thousands of these nonfatal injuries.[11] Bureau of Labor Statistics data show that policing has a violent injury rate of 121.7 per 100,000, more than 16 times the national average for all occupations.[12]

Available data on violence directed at police, however, do not support claims of a "war on cops." Since the emergence of this narrative in late 2014, multiple studies have empirically tested whether the police killing of Michael Brown in Ferguson, Missouri, kicked off a wave of violence against police officers. These studies have drawn on data from a range of sources, including the FBI, the Officer Down Memorial Page (ODMP), and the Gun Violence Archive (GVA). These data, in turn, have been used to measure subsets of violence against police in varied ways, including not only coarse distinctions such as fatal and nonfatal assaults but also more fine-grained distinctions such as fatal ambushes and both fatal and nonfatal firearm assaults. Regardless of the data or definitions used, no study to date has found empirical support for the sharp and sustained increase in violence claimed by proponents of the "war on cops."[13]

As is often the case with matters of crime and violence, however, perception remains stubbornly resistant to statistical reality.[14] Buoyed by the voices of conservative media pundits and police leadership sounding the alarm of this new and bloody "war," the "war on cops" narrative took hold among the public and police. One nationally representative study found that 63 percent of the U.S. public agreed with the statement "There is currently a war on police," and 59 percent agreed that "the police are currently under siege in the country."[15] A Pew Research Center survey administered in the summer of 2016 found that 70 percent of the public believed that policing was more dangerous than five years prior; 93 percent of police reported that "high-profile incidents involving blacks and the police" had spurred increased concern with officer safety in their department.[16] The same perceptions are common among police leadership.[17]

While entertainment and news media emphasize the rarest, most heroic police activity—car chases, gunfights, and innocents snatched away from certain death—officers' days are largely consumed with mediating and shuffling an array of social problems that they are woefully equipped to address. Every day, 911 calls are placed by residents and local businesses, routed to a dispatcher who distills the contents of the call, and then beamed to officers' in-car laptops. The overwhelming majority of these calls are for petty disputes, varied signs of "disorder," or some low-level property crime. Poverty, substance abuse, and mental illness, even if not listed in the descriptions of calls sent by dispatchers to officers, are unremarkable features of life on patrol.[18]

It is against this largely invisible background of police work that officers' attunement to danger and violence stands out so starkly. Officers know better than most how unlikely it is that they will become involved in a life-or-death fight while on patrol. They are, after all, the ones driving from call to call, triaging an endless stream of small crises, and writing endless boilerplate reports. But as one officer wrote for *Police Magazine* more than twenty-five years ago, "the vast majority of [police] can readily identify with the old law enforcement cliché that police work is 99 percent sheer boredom and 1 percent sheer terror."[19]

Despite work that far more often resembles armed social work than valiant crime fighting, it was this 1 percent that loomed especially large in officers' minds. As put by the former Baltimore police officer and sociologist Peter Moskos, "The most important part of your job is that you go home. Everything else is secondary."[20] No matter the empirical probability of being shot or killed on patrol, police officers' core concern is survival.

This seeming paradox—a police institution consumed with violence and survival despite historic decreases in officer mortality—is at the heart of this book. To understand how and why policing continues to orient itself around danger, I rode along with officers in three urban police departments across the United States from 2014 through 2018. Drawing on more than a thousand hours observing officers, more than a hundred interviews, and countless interactions with officers in their cars, at calls for service, and inside police facilities, I provide a sociological account of how the cultural preoccupation with violence and officer safety—what I term the "danger imperative"—anchors the culture, perception, and practice of the contemporary policing institution. I detail how the danger imperative is reconstructed through formal and informal mechanisms at the police academy, within the police department, and among officers themselves. Crucially, this frame operates in an ostensibly color-blind way, omitting discussion of race in lieu of a single-minded focus on threat, weapons, violence, and officer safety. Without relying on bigotry or overt racism, this frame privileges the survival of officers over the well-being of the public, re-creating long-standing inequalities in police violence.

VIOLENCE, CULTURE, AND THE STATE

Violence shapes culture. This is not a phenomenon restricted to the police. For decades, social scientists have tried to understand how and why violence persists. And significant attention has been paid to the violence that the state seeks to control, often discussed as "violent crime." In communities that contend with poverty, ineffective schools, and a lack of employment opportunities, the threat of criminal victimization often looms large.[21]

These same communities are the ones most likely to experience the brunt of inequitable police stops, searches, arrests, and violence used by the state to address crime and disorder.[22] Some community members, in turn, adopt norms, values, and behaviors—that is, a culture— in response to the simultaneous problems of insecurity and an ineffective, predatory state. Estranged from the state, its agents, and security, individuals operating within a cultural framework informed by these structural conditions respond to their environment in ways understood to increase their physical safety.[23] One such response is violence.[24] Crucially, this culture does not exist distinct from or outside of those it affects; it is continually maintained by people. Over time, individuals experiencing similar conditions and responding to them in similar ways re-create the culture that collectively shapes their perception and action.

By comparison, our understanding of the interplay among structure, culture, and violence within the state itself is limited. There is, of course, a wide range of scholarship attending to the *distribution* of state violence performed by the state's most visible and contacted agents: police. This work asks where, to whom, and under what conditions police violence occurs.[25] Police culture, however, receives short shrift. When it is examined, it is treated as a static, a priori phenomenon spawned by the structural conditions commonly confronted by officers across disparate police organizations, including the threat of violence.[26]

Rather than being continually re-created through the perception and action of officers, this top-down model views culture as something which acts upon officers and exists external to them; officers are treated as products of culture, not producers. This framework limits our understanding of how violence and culture interact within the organizational infrastructure of the state, within precisely the institution whose coercive power is trained on its own citizens. So, too, do we lose sight of the state agents whose experience and action are both consequence and cause of a culture consistently linked to the violent control of the body politic.[27] As a result, though we know a great deal about the continued existence of a culture that shapes state violence, our view of its reproduction within the walls of police departments and through the actions of police officers is markedly less clear.

This book explores the function of contemporary policing in order to shed light on how culture and violence intersect within the state. More pointedly, I show that the privileged position of danger in police culture depends on the daily and often quotidian operations of the police organization and the officers tasked with street-level policing. I argue that the preoccupation with violence and officer safety constitutes a cultural frame through which officers' experiences are filtered. This frame, the "danger imperative," amplifies officers' attention to the possibility of violence and potential death in the line of duty, in turn shaping their perception and action in ways designed to maximize the likelihood of their survival. The danger imperative is neither accidental nor undesired. Instead, it is the intended and logical outcome of socialization within the police department that begins the moment an officer enters the police academy and is reinforced every day they are on patrol.

The salience of physical harm in police work is by no means a novel observation. Since the earliest studies of police behavior and culture, scholars have noted the prominence of danger, violence, and the potential of an untimely death in how officers understand and practice their work.[28] But while past inquiry into the world and work of police has treated danger as one of many occupational pressures, vying with the constraints of finite time, limited resources, and administrative scrutiny, this book places danger and the threat of violence against officers at the center of its analytic focus. Rather than treat danger as one of many occupational challenges or the use of violence as the defining feature of the police role,[29] I delineate how the occupational environment and institutional structure of policing repeatedly defines the danger of police work as officers' central concern on patrol.

I argue that the danger imperative is policing's governing institutional frame. More simply, the danger imperative is the "soul" of policing. I do not use this term to imply that the danger imperative is an essential or immutable feature of policing. As resistant as police culture and the institution writ large are to change, policing's operations, power, and meanings are continually contested.[30] Nor does "soul" necessitate that the danger imperative has always existed in its current form or in the ways I describe it was recreated across Elmont, West River, and Sunshine. This book is not a historical account of the genesis of policing's preoccupation with violence and officer safety, nor is it a prolonged normative account of what policing should or should not be.

Instead, my description of policing's "soul" encapsulates what sociologist Anne Swidler has described as a "style or ethos of action" organized by the social structure in which individuals exist.[31] The danger imperative is such an ethos. But it is more than one of several ethics that could operate within the police institution. It is policing's governing ethic, structuring officer perception and behavior across the institution and taking precedence across the varied situations which police encounter. This soul—the danger imperative—concisely distills the "how" and "why" of policing as it is experienced by police officers themselves. The structure and practice of policing is not driven by justice or honor or any of the other laudable ideals codified in departmental mottos or emblazoned on patrol car doors. The daily production of policing, much of it hidden from view or unnoticed in its mundanity, revolves primarily around one thing: survival. The danger imperative is the collective manifestation of this unyielding institutional problem and is the organizing framework of officers' work.

The danger imperative is a distinct concept from a raft of police archetypes advanced by scholars since the 1960s. Danger and violence—whether against or by police—are central to several of these policing archetypes. The "hard charger," unlike the feminized "station queen," rejects emphasis on police-community relations in favor of pursuing dangerous criminals.[32] The "enforcer" is comfortable using violence, especially when it is against a "them" that threatens the moral "us."[33] In contrast to the "guardian," who values respect, patience, and inclusiveness, the "warrior" sees the public as a source of threat that must be controlled or conquered.[34]

The warrior is the most recent policing archetype conceptualized to explain the damaging manifestations of policing's preoccupation with physical danger. This archetype is especially instructive for outlining how the danger imperative differs from prior research on the intersection of danger, culture, and behavior in policing. The concept of the warrior officer was first popularized as part of critiques focused on militarized police tactics and equipment, most notably the proliferation of paramilitary police units (PPUs) more commonly known as SWAT (special weapons and tactics) teams. These units and their aggressive tactics were originally justified as necessary to enhance officer safety when confronting especially dangerous situations. Unlike the modal officer with a patrol car and a blue uniform, this new "warrior" was equipped with battle dress uniforms (BDUs) and specialized weaponry formerly reserved for the military. As we now know, SWAT teams quickly expanded outside their original mandate and became a common tool for drug enforcement in an ongoing war on drugs.[35]

Following the police killing of Michael Brown and the violent, militarized police response to protestors in Ferguson, Missouri, discussion of the "warrior" expanded from specialized units to include the realm of routine police work. This scholarship contends that modern police officers are socialized to understand members of the public as potential threats. As a result of training geared toward inculcating officers with a warrior mentality, these officers come to see themselves and to engage in their work as being "locked in intermittent and unpredictable combat with unknown but highly lethal enemies."[36] In turn, this warrior mentality and warrior policing frustrate efforts to enhance police-community trust and public safety.

Contemporary discussion of the warrior is limited in three ways. First, it emphasizes formal training in the academy as the primary means by which the warrior officer comes to be.[37] Academy training is doubtless a vital point in police officers' socialization. The academy marks recruits' formal introduction to the assumptions, values, tools, and techniques of policing. But focus on the earliest and most formal point of police socialization relies on a unidirectional, "download" model of culture.[38] In this model, socialization is a discrete period of time during which individuals acquire "the requisite orientations for satisfactory functioning in a role."[39] Like a piece of software, these orientations—described by the legal scholar and former police officer Seth Stoughton as "a coherent set of principles that pervade modern policing"[40]—are downloaded by police recruits in the academy. Upon hitting the street, officers then put these principles into practice.

This download heuristic, while concise, fails to account for the actions and agency of individual officers who re-create police culture through their contextually situated cognition and behavior. Rather than treat culture as something that is maintained and reinforced by individuals operating within a particular social context, a download model treats officers as "passive by-products of a culture and organization that exist independent of them and outside of their control."[41] As a result, how and why officers choose to re-create culture in particular ways is treated solely as a symptom of seemingly total and permanent academy socialization.

Second, this download conceptualization of police culture is limited in its attention to only the shortest part of an officer's career. On average, municipal police officers receive 977 hours of training—about six months. Across all state and local agencies, the average falls to 833 hours.[42] While academy training is certainly formative, a focus on formal socialization to explain the continued existence of the warrior mentality fails to ask how it is maintained once officers leave the academy. Given that officers will spend far more of their professional lives as fully fledged police officers than as recruits, it is crucial to understand how the routine processes of departmental life are implicated in the re-creation of police culture. And because a focus on academy training relegates police socialization to a discrete and relatively short time period, we have little view of how the police department interacts with and mediates the wider sociopolitical environment in which policing operates.[43] In short, current inquiry on danger and police culture obscures the role of the police organization that sets the bounds for how the shared problem of physical danger is understood and addressed by officers.[44]

Third, along with its lack of focus on the wider police organization and outsize attention to the role of academy training, discussion of the warrior mentality tends to focus on its most overt or damaging consequences. This includes the aesthetic of the warrior—camouflage, tactical equipment, and armored vehicles—and the catastrophic effects of warrior policing run amok, such as SWAT raids, car stops, and calls for service that result in the death of innocents. It is necessary to name and understand these manifestations of warrior policing. But just as emphasis on academy training limits our understanding of how danger is maintained at the center of police culture, focusing on the most damaging behavioral consequences of the warrior mentality misses the quotidian, often hidden ways that danger shapes police culture and officers' lived experience. To fully apprehend how the centrality of danger in police culture is perpetuated by and among officers, it is necessary to look beyond the unreasonable shootings and wanton brutality, which are its rarest and most extreme manifestations.

In comparison to the warrior and other police archetypes, my analysis of the danger imperative provides important theoretical and substantive strengths. First, the danger imperative is not fate. Unlike a typology that deterministically associates a set of outcomes with particular subsets of officers—whether "warriors" or "bad apples"—cultural frames do not directly or universally cause individuals to behave in particular ways.[45] Rather, they mediate how individuals perceive, understand, and navigate the social world, making certain perceptual and behavioral outcomes more or less likely given the content of the frame and an individual's environment.

In turn, the danger imperative provides room to account for officers' agency on patrol. Unlike robots programmed with a culture that is then re-created as if it were computer code, officers make choices in response to their perceptions of the world around them. What the danger imperative does is constrain the realm of the possible and the acceptable within the occupational environment of police work. The danger imperative is not fate. But its emphasis on violence increases the likelihood that officers will search for, perceive, and respond to what they understand as emergent threats.

My analysis also emphasizes that police culture is continually re-created through a combination of individual- and organizational-level processes. Like other scholars, I point to the academy as an important site and period of police socialization. However, my account of police culture vis-à-vis danger also attends to the routine, unquestioned processes that operate outside the academy and that structure the lived experience of officers for their entire careers. By exploring how the preoccupation with violence is reflected within the police department and among officers long after their introduction to the norms, values, and practices that form police culture, my analysis also shows how the danger imperative is intentionally and iteratively reproduced by officers and the organization they inhabit. The danger imperative is not simply downloaded; it is continually re-created through the routine operations of the police department and the behavior of officers responding to the shared problem of potential violence.

Finally, I argue that the danger imperative operates as a color-blind frame that supports the preservation of racial inequalities in police violence. Whereas a large and growing body of research details persistent and pervasive racial inequalities in policing,[46] concerted attention to race and structural racism is conspicuously lacking from much empirical research on police culture.[47] My account of the danger imperative looks to address this troubling limitation of prior research by considering how the danger imperative, constructed and practiced with a single-minded emphasis on ostensibly race-blind criteria of violence and officer safety, encourages behaviors that nonetheless perpetuate racial inequalities in policing.

Crucially, I do not approach the problem of racial inequalities within policing as driven by "bad apples" or "warriors" or other subsets of officers. This book eschews a sole focus on individuals or their characteristics to reveal the organizational structures that continually reinforce a shared preoccupation with violence and officer safety. In turn, I show that these organizational processes, devoid of overt racism and often any mention of race at all, reify the danger imperative and resulting officer practices designed to ensuring their survival. Like the organizations they inhabit, officers' safety-enhancing strategies do not depend on racial animus. In fact, the danger imperative provides concise, color-blind motivations and justifications whereby officers can motivate and justify the very actions that, regardless of intent or immorality, reproduce persistent racial inequalities in police violence. I turn now to a dedicated consideration of policing's vital role in the "mutual constitution" of race, danger, and policing.[48]

DANGER, RACE, AND COLOR-BLIND POLICING

Danger's role in police culture and practice is inextricable from its historical development and its role in constructing conceptions of race, crime, and violence. The existence of a dangerous "other" that threatened the property and power of the ruling class dates to at least the late nineteenth century. At this time, early policing in England and France was spurred by the rise of the "dangerous classes," largely composed of poor émigrés from rural areas into new cities.[49] Across the Atlantic, formal policing in the antebellum South evolved out of militias and slave patrols used to terrorize enslaved people and mitigate the threat of violent slave uprisings.[50] Following the end of the Civil War, these groups transitioned into more organized policing bodies that continued to preserve white dominance through the enforcement of Black Codes and Jim Crow segregation.[51] In the North, police, which began as loosely tied watchmen influenced by the English "night watch," coalesced into the first urban police departments in the late nineteenth and early twentieth centuries. These early police departments were used as a cudgel against a variety of "dangerous" groups, including southern Blacks who migrated to western and northern cities, European and Latino immigrants, and a burgeoning labor movement.[52]

Simultaneously, the advent of prison and crime data at the close of the nineteenth century spawned the "scientific" discourse on crime and violence that continues to justify the conflation of Blackness and threat in the American consciousness.[53] The establishment of the Uniform Crime Reports (UCR) in 1930 formalized local and state police as the chief producers of local crime data that remain central to social science research, policy making, and public understandings of Black criminality.[54] In the decades since, police coercion focused on Black communities, and the data produced by these practices entrenched fear of what sociologist Elijah Anderson calls the "iconic ghetto," a stereotypical schema in which poverty, crime, and violence are inextricable from Black people and where they live.[55] The power of the iconic ghetto, in turn, manifests in what cognitive scientists describe as the "implicit association" of Black men with criminality, aggression, violence, and danger.[56]

But Black criminality and violence were not the only threats used to continually justify the expansion of policing over the past century. The Chicano movement, communists, antiwar college students, and Islamic terrorism have all been pointed to as existential threats to society and police alike.[57] To protect officers against this fearsome and ever-growing range of threats, military tactics, organizational arrangements, and cultural values honed in foreign theaters of war were imported for use on U.S. soil throughout the twentieth century.[58] Beginning in the 1960s, unprecedented federal infrastructure and funding were created to support the expansion of U.S. police to fight the "war on crime," which included early financial incentives for states to acquire military equipment such as rifles, tanks, radios, and bulletproof vests.[59] SWAT teams modeled after elite military units, though originally formed in the late 1960s and early 1970s to address rare events such as "civil riots, terrorism, barricaded suspects, and hostage situations," became de rigueur for the execution of low-level search and drug warrants in minority communities.[60]

With bipartisan support for massive investment in the criminal legal system over the past fifty years,[61] policing has continually expanded in scope, technology, and practice to fight against limitless enemies on home soil.[62] This forever war, evolving seamlessly through a focus on crime, drugs, and terror, has now taken the form of the "war on cops." In this newest manifestation of policing's forever war, officers are purportedly besieged not only by violent criminals[63] but also by a cabal of antipolice politicians and academics whose critiques of police are responsible for crime and the murder of police officers. Of particular concern to today's police are antifascist groups and Black Lives Matter activists that, as described in a document distributed by the International Law Enforcement Educators and Trainers Association (ILEETA), plan to use "extreme violence" to "overthrow the U.S. government."[64]

Against the backdrop of this racialized history, decades of social science research document pervasive and persistent racial inequalities in U.S. policing. Whom police stop, search, arrest, and subject to state-sanctioned violence is structured by race and place, with poor minority communities bearing the brunt of police power.[65] These inequalities have persisted despite a century of local, state, and federal commissions tasked with addressing the abuse of police power.[66]

What's more, new evidence shows that administrative police records and even federal vital statistics are likely to *underestimate* measures of racial bias and police violence.[67] Inequalities in police contact and coercion, in turn, have effects that echo far beyond the bounds of the criminal legal system, including damaged mental and physical health, diminished school performance, avoidance of key social institutions, and estrangement from full participation in democratic life.[68] Across decades, departments, and the policing outcome of interest, the weight of the evidence shows that policing actively perpetuates social inequality and structural racism. This is a social fact.

It is equally undeniable that the ugliest, most overtly racist attitudes are still found among police. The FBI has warned for years of the danger posed by white supremacist infiltration of law enforcement. One FBI memo detailed policy changes within the FBI to address the fact that "domestic terrorism investigations focused on militia extremists, white supremacist extremists, and sovereign citizen extremists often have identified active links to law enforcement officers."[69] A different FBI report warned in no uncertain terms of "self-initiated efforts by individuals, particularly among those already within law enforcement ranks, to volunteer their professional resources to white supremacist causes with which they sympathize."[70] Police officers who are members of white nationalist and secessionist groups like the Ku Klux Klan, the Proud Boys, and the League of the South have been identified in multiple departments.[71] Far more common than avowed members of white supremacist organizations are racist, sexist, violence-glorifying posts by thousands of current and former police officers in police-focused Facebook groups and online forums.[72] Multiple studies have found that biased racial attitudes are more common among police than in the general public.[73]

Of course, avowed white supremacism and explicit bigotry represent only the most extreme cases of racism in today's police departments. In lieu of overtly racist intent that runs afoul of departmental policy and law, contemporary policing and society writ large are increasingly characterized by "color-blind" logics that minimize, deny, and naturalize racial inequality.[74] This was the case in my own field sites. Rather than point to the inherent criminality or immorality of racial minorities, they sometimes invoked "culture" or "parenting" as root causes of crime and dislike of law enforcement. Officers were quick to deny that they engaged in or had ever witnessed disparate treatment by officers in their department, though all three departments' own data showed marked disparities in police stops, searches, arrests, citations, or violence.[75] At most, officers deployed the language of "bad apples," minimizing the issue of racism and biased policing to the immorality of a small number of officers. Still others claimed to have a keen ability to distinguish the "sketchy" or "suspicious" person from the law-abiding by engaging in "criminal" or "behavioral" profiling based on things as unremarkable as riding a bike on a sidewalk, loitering, failing to use a turn signal, or wearing a sweater when the weather was warm.

These color-blind explanations for how and why policing operates as it does highlight that the perpetuation of social inequality does not depend on individual-level bigotry. As part of organizations embedded within broader networks of institutions and prevailing understandings of race, officers' daily practices contribute to the re-creation and "mutual constitution" of racial categories and assumptions about race, crime, violence, and danger.[76] Across the labor market, medicine, banking, education, and housing,[77] neither individual behavior nor organizational rules need explicitly cite race or other demographic characteristics to re-create inequitable outcomes.[78] Within policing, this means that officer behaviors do not need to be illegal, against policy, or intentionally motivated by racial animus to inequitably distribute police contact and coercion across the population. Indeed, advances in surveillance technology and predictive analytics provide unprecedented means by which to "hide both intentional and unintentional bias in policing" behind a veil of mathematized impartiality, allowing organizational decisions and officer behaviors to be justified as purely data-driven.[79]

The danger imperative aligns with the increasingly color-blind logic of contemporary policing. The officers with whom I spent time did not draw direct equivalences among racial minorities, danger, and violence. Departmental policies and training materials made no mention of race beyond articulating that officers were to perform their duties "impartially" or that there was zero tolerance for any racial, ethnic, gender, or religious discrimination. Instead, the danger imperative is re-created through mechanisms that elide any mention of race. In the police academy, for example, recruits are introduced to the aseptic legalese of constitutional law that governs their use of violence. Police, they learn, respond only to empirical "threats," such as firearms. After the academy, race is mentioned only as an objective description, such as during daily reviews of recent crimes and suspects, intended to arm officers with information necessary to ensure their survival. Even in cases of high-profile and highly racialized police killings, race is superseded by color-blind discussion of tactics or individual responsibility, decoupling police violence from even the suggestion of racial bias.

Even if one were to achieve a police institution utterly devoid of racist officers, the danger imperative would continue to shape policing outcomes. Further, even if one were to achieve wholesale change within policing itself, the landscape of overlapping inequalities in education, housing, health, and employment to which policing has contributed would also remain. The intergenerational transmission of this structural disadvantage would, in turn, continue to generate concentrated crime and violence in historically segregated and disenfranchised communities. So long as policing remains the default institution for addressing these social problems, officers operating within the danger imperative will inevitably concentrate in these same communities, as will the consequences of their unerring preoccupation with violence and officer safety.[80]

FIELDWORK

My account of the danger imperative relies on ethnographic observations and interviews gathered between 2014 and 2018 in three police departments: the Elmont Police Department (EPD), the West River Police Department (WPD), and the Sunshine Police Department (SPD) (see table 1). In the style of classic ethnographic studies of policing,[81] my observations focused on the patrol officers who are involved in more than 61 million yearly contacts with the public. Observations took place mostly in the course of "ride-alongs" during which I accompanied officers as they engaged in their varied duties. Shifts were dominated by reactive work (i.e., answering calls for service) but also included proactive activities (i.e., stops of pedestrians and cars). Other observations were gathered at police in-service training, inside police facilities like substations and the police academy, an award ceremony, a retirement banquet, and a memorial service. I also reviewed training documents, departmental policies, department-produced media, and local news coverage during and after my time in the field.

In lieu of structured interviews poorly suited to the start-and-stop nature of patrol, I audio recorded my conversations with officers as they drove around between calls, patrolled their beat, ate lunch, or completed boilerplate reports. These free-flowing conversations were approached in the style of the "ethnographic interview."[82] In contrast to interviews conducted according to a predetermined protocol,

TABLE 1 DATA COLLECTED PER DEPARTMENT

Department	Observation hours	Interviews
EPD	315	29
WPD	380	36
SPD	325	43
Total	1020	108

ethnographic interviews allowed for conversation to move in and out of focused questions, providing space to build rapport with officers and to allow their unique experience and identities to inform my questions. The flexibility of ethnographic interviews also allowed for questions generated by my immediate observations. Who officers were and what situations emerged while we were together helped inform my questions on patrol.

Tables 2 and 3 provide descriptive information on the three departments and cities in which I collected data. The departments that I observed differ in size. The EPD is the smallest, with some five hundred officers in a small city of approximately 150,000 in the northeast. The SPD is the largest, with approximately nine hundred officers patrolling a city of around 500,000 under the blazing sun of the southwest. The WPD lies in between, with about seven hundred officers patrolling a city of about 400,000. Similarly, these departments differ in terms of their racial and ethnic composition (see table 2). The SPD is the least racially diverse department, with a police force that is approximately 70 percent white. The remainder of the SPD is

TABLE 2 DEPARTMENT CHARACTERISTICS

Department	Region	Officers	% White	% Black	% Latino	% Asian	% Female
EPD	Northeast	500	50	25	20	0.5	15
WPD	West	700	40	15	25	15	12
SPD	Southwest	900	70	2	25	2	15

TABLE 3 CITY CHARACTERISTICS

City	Population	% White	% Black	% Latino	% Asian
Elmont	~130,000	30	35	25	5
West River	~400,000	25	30	25	15
Sunshine	~500,000	45	5	40	3

largely Latino, with a handful of Black and Asian officers. In contrast, the WPD is markedly more diverse, with a police force that is 60 percent nonwhite, including 15 percent of officers who identify as Asian. The EPD falls in the middle, with a force that is 50 percent white. Of the three departments, it has the largest share of Black officers (25 percent) but has almost no Asian officers.

These differences notwithstanding, the EPD, WPD, and SPD are more similar than they are different when considered in the context of the wider police institution. Though they are orders of magnitude smaller than oft-studied mega departments like those in New York, Chicago, and Los Angeles, they are still within the top 1 percent of police departments by number of officers.[83] All three departments operate in an urban setting with a strict hierarchy and rank system modeled after the military. All have a range of divisions and units tasked with unique work: in addition to patrol officers who handle 911 calls for service, these departments have a range of specialized units that include motorcycle patrol, horse-mounted patrol, boat patrol, bomb squad, underwater search and recovery, helicopter unit, gang and firearms unit, special weapons and tactics (SWAT), and many more. These departments also run their own police academies with full-time instructors, have their own internal affairs divisions, and are monitored by a civilian review board (CRB) that examines cases of police misconduct.

To be sure, these departments and their officers are embedded in distinct local contexts that shape some contours of the danger imperative in site-specific ways. For example, EPD officers frequently described incidents of violence against police in nearby cities, such as Philadelphia, New York, and Boston. In contrast, Sunshine's proximity to the U.S.-Mexico border informed SPD officers' worry over drug cartels and narcotrafficking-related violence. The long-standing concern with street gangs in West River informed how WPD officers understood the danger of the streets they patrolled. But there was no department in which police administrators, instructors, line-level supervisors, or officers summarily discounted the possibility of being killed on duty. Regardless of the specific threat to which they pointed, individual officers and the organizations in which they were embedded provided clear evidence that violence and officer safety were dominant concerns.

Similarly, though there is variation across my field sites in terms of officers' racial and ethnic composition, all three departments are less racially diverse than the cities they patrol (see table 3). This lack of minority representation is reflective of the wider policing institution, which, despite some improvement in terms of racial and ethnic diversity, remains largely white.[84] Police departments are also whiter than the places they patrol. This pattern is particularly pronounced in urban areas like those policed by the EPD, WPD, and SPD.[85]

The lack of racial representation in policing continues to have negative consequences for Black and Latino officers, including racial discrimination within their departments.[86] This hostile environment within policing pushes minority officers to assimilate into a shared institutional identity that privileges "blue" over officers' racial or ethnic identity.[87] As a result, attachment to features of police culture—including the belief that policing is a dangerous occupation—cuts across officers of different races.[88]

All three departments are also overwhelmingly male. This gender imbalance is a long-standing feature of policing. Despite thirty years of gender diversity efforts, policing remains less than 13 percent female.[89] Unsurprisingly, policing operates as a deeply gendered institution that actively re-creates assumptions and arrangements of policing as inherently (even ideally) male.[90] Masculine imagery and ideals consistently create a vision of dangerous crime fighting as "men's work."[91] It is a mistake to assume, however, that the danger imperative is restricted to or only reproduced by male officers. Just as prior research has shown that women in policing adapt their behavior to align with a masculine conception of police work as "action-oriented, expedient, violent and risky,"[92] policewomen are expected to prioritize their safety and that of other officers at all costs.[93]

Recognizing that the frame of the danger imperative allows for individual agency, my analysis focuses on phenomena and processes common across my field sites and the officers I spoke with rather than the variations among them. Though quantitative research on police culture emphasizes variation in what features of police culture officers subscribe to most strongly,[94] ethnographic accounts of policing over the past seventy years consistently note the prominence of danger in police culture and behavior.[95] Recent experimental evidence shows that officers' assessments of danger are remarkably consistent across gender, race, age, experience, and prior military service.[96] Police are not an undifferentiated mass inculcated with a culture that perfectly predicts their behavior, but no officer I spoke with denied or wholly disregarded the possibility of being injured or killed in the line of duty. It is this shared understanding of perilous police work to which the danger imperative speaks.

By describing common processes, symbols, logics, and practices across officers and departments in disparate locations, this book provides a parsimonious account of how and why police understand and practice their work as they do. Though there is undoubtedly variation in a population of nearly 18,000 departments and some 780,000 officers,[97] my observations and interviews across Elmont, West River, and Sunshine show that the danger imperative operates with remarkable consistency across police departments and officers. In lieu of individual or organizational idiosyncrasy, this book reveals the unifying mechanisms that re-create the preoccupation with violence among officers, within departments, and across the wider police institution. By extension, it shows that the danger imperative is neither an aberration nor an accident. It is, instead, the intentional and defining institutional ethos—the soul—of policing.

BOOK OUTLINE

My description of the danger imperative and policing across Elmont, West River, and Sunshine is broken into four empirical chapters. Chapter 1 attends to the police academy where recruits are formally introduced to the life-or-death stakes of their chosen profession. This socialization begins immediately and persistently reiterates to recruits that they must always keep survival at the forefront of their minds. Instructors already versed in the contours of the danger imperative teach officers to understand their own violence as a righteous, moral tool necessitated by the profound danger of their work. Graphic videos of calls "gone wrong," in which officers are attacked, injured, or killed, underscore the police adage that any interaction could devolve into violence at any moment. Defensive tactics and weapons training are used both to assess recruits' willingness to use violence in defense of their lives and to rudely remind them of their vulnerable mortality. Virtual "shoot/don't shoot" simulators require officers to rehearse the identification and neutralization of perceived threats, as well as the justification of their use of lethal violence within the constraints of law and departmental policy.

Chapter 2 begins after recruits graduate from the academy and enter an organizational environment filled with reminders of the rarest, most catastrophic possibility of their dangerous work: death in the line of duty. From memorial walls to tattoos, fallen officers are immortalized in the stone and skin of the department and its officers. Each face, name, and "end of watch" date is irrefutable proof that the violence at the heart of the danger imperative is all too real. These commemorative artifacts help maintain the danger imperative and maintain an organizational memory within the EPD, WPD, and SPD that centers violence and death. The commemoration of fallen officers is not restricted to a department's own. Officers killed in other jurisdictions and in decades past are also commemorated within police departments, linking the EPD, WPD, SPD, and their officers to an occupational history and culture that emphasizes violence and death. The danger imperative connects discrete departments and their officers across time and space, uniting them in a common struggle for survival in defense of the law, order, and the nation itself.

Chapter 3 shifts focus from the commemorative artifacts that immortalize rare line-of-duty deaths to the ritual operations of the police department that amplify information about threats to police. Some of these danger signals originate from within the department itself, such as information about incidents of violent crime disseminated to officers at daily lineup meetings in the form of "hotsheets." Officer safety bulletins are printed on paper or displayed in police facilities to warn officers about any number of threats, be they suspects in violent crime, low-level theft, or the debunked urban legend of overdose by fentanyl exposure. Besides signals generated locally, a vast "threat network" of local, state, and federal agencies shares information about a vast array of enemies and weapons that pose a threat to police anywhere and everywhere. Access to a bottomless supply of articles and videos about violence against police via YouTube, social media, and policing websites further expands the channels through which danger signals can enter a contemporary police department, which then amplifies and transmits them to officers.

Chapter 4 describes how the danger imperative is reproduced in the minds and actions of police officers. Officers on patrol foster a "tactical imagination" by visualizing potentially deadly scenarios and how they would react to them. The danger imperative also informs their use of "tactical color-blindness" in assessments of police violence. Instead of considering or confronting the overtly racialized context of high-profile police killings of unarmed Black people, officers omit race in favor of discourse centered on raceless tactics and individual responsibility. The danger imperative shapes a range of officer behaviors: where officers park their cars, where they eat their lunch, and how they stand when interacting with the public are all tailored to maximize their advantage in a potential fight and increase the likelihood of their survival.

But though some of these safety-enhancing behaviors incur few costs, others undermine police legitimacy, public well-being, and even officer safety. A situation in which officers are intent on maintaining "command presence" to dissuade violent resistance can quickly devolve into one of aggression and disrespect. Officers may disregard departmental policies requiring seat belts and restricting high-speed driving in the name of officer safety, unintentionally increasing the possibility of injury or death for themselves and an unsuspecting public.

Other behaviors motivated and justified on the grounds of officer safety, even if squarely within the law and departmental policy, can anger the public or physically harm them. Worse, the danger imperative's preoccupation with violence can encourage unconstitutional policing in the name of safety while increasing the likelihood of violent catastrophe during police-public interactions. None of these outcomes are dependent on overt or conscious racial animus; all of them are bound to concentrate in communities characterized by generations of structural disadvantage and reliance on police to address symptoms of social inequality.

The book concludes with consideration of policing's violent future. Despite the tremendous institutional inertia of the danger imperative, there are concrete policy changes that should be implemented. Enhanced local and state-level oversight of training curricula within and outside the formal academy setting can help mitigate the unchecked dissemination of the danger imperative in U.S. policing. Of course, even successful training reforms would only dull the sharpest edge of the danger imperative. They do nothing to address the social conditions that support policing's preoccupation with violence and officer safety, be it deepening economic inequality or ubiquitous firearms. Reform, though necessary, will not save us. The danger imperative is not an aberration to be excised. It is the governing ethos—the soul—of the institution. There is little reason to believe that policing can ever be decoupled from that soul. To minimize policing's damaging consequences, we must fully consider alternatives to using armed state agents as the default mechanism for enhancing public safety.

1

SURVIVAL SCHOOL

Seen from the road, the Elmont Police Academy is an unremarkable, flat-roofed building of red brick. It could be mistaken for a post office or a small school. The surrounding area is residential and predominantly Black. To the east, streets lined with multifamily homes are dotted with a handful of churches, and the local high school is within sight of the academy's small parking lot. The glass doors that lead into the academy are embossed with the words:

> The police at all times should maintain a relationship with the public that gives reality to the historic tradition that the police are the public and the public are the police; the police are the only members of the public who are paid to give full-time attention to duties which are incumbent on every citizen in the interest of community welfare.[1]

These words reflect the Elmont Police Department's stated philosophy of "community policing," a policing ethos qua strategy that, since 1995, has been funded by the U.S. Office of Community Oriented Policing Services to the tune of more than ten billion dollars. At its core, community policing aims to build cooperative police-public relationships through initiatives like community meetings, walking patrols, summer camps for local youth, and popular Coffee with a Cop meet-and-greets.[2]

For decades, the EPD and departments across the country have pointed to these activities as evidence of their commitment to working hand in hand with the communities they serve. But within the walls of the academy, a very different vision of policing is on display. Instead of compassion and collaboration, the academy is awash in military imagery and bellicose language. Murals with painted battle helmets, crossed swords, and screaming eagles in black and yellow line the hallways. Academy classes are given monikers like Sentinels, Centurions, and Knights. Instead of an idealistic, aspirational view of policing in which "the police are the public and the public are the police," the academy is designed to promote a singular vision of police as valiant protectors besieged on all sides by infinite threats.

According to Dave "JD Buck Savage" Smith, a former officer who is now a police training consultant and commentator, "Perhaps as much as any profession we know death and injury stalk us in multitudes of forms, many springing at us unexpectedly and with terrible malice and while we cannot keep that from happening many times, we can harden the target . . . and that's us!"

To stay alive, officers must be part of what Smith terms a "conspiracy of safety." For Smith, this conspiracy is quite literal. Based on the Latin *conspirare*, which means to "to breath together," Smith's conspiracy requires that officers "breath[e] safety together" to ensure they all return home alive. "Day-to-day, hour-by-hour, minute-by-minute," officers must be ready to defend their lives and that of their fellow officers. "Every building search, field interview, alarm call, domestic, accident with injuries on a busy roadway, whatever you're doing, you must think, 'Not today, not now, I will not be caught unawares!'"[3]

Although modern academy curricula in well-resourced departments include training on mental illness, de-escalation, procedural justice, and implicit bias, the core lesson of the academy is neither compassion nor service—it is survival.[4] Despite the statistical rarity of mortal peril in police work, the academy selectively foregrounds discrete incidents of violence that provide the raw material for the construction of the danger imperative among would-be officers. To prepare recruits for the violence to come, academy instructors mold recruits' minds and bodies through classroom instruction, fistfights, and real-world and virtual scenario training. This training, beyond inculcating officers with a shared preoccupation with their safety, is designed to shift how recruits understand and practice violence. Alongside the specific tools and techniques of violence, officers are taught how to understand and justify their violence as both legal and moral. In the hands of a well-trained officer, they learn, violence is just and necessary, a righteous intervention to ensure their own survival and protect the innocent from those who would do them harm.

THE ACADEMY AND DISCRETIONARY DESIGN

The perpetuation of the danger imperative's focus on violence and officer safety is supported by the design of academy curricula across the United States. On average, police academies require 843 hours of classroom-based instruction. Training is remarkably diverse, covering topics ranging from domestic violence and elder abuse to crime mapping. But of the myriad topics that recruits must master in the course of their training, weapons and violence receive special attention. Per the Bureau of Justice Statistics' most recent Census of Law Enforcement Training Academies, academy training on "weapons/defensive tactics" receives an average of 172 academy hours. About 10 percent (18 hours) is dedicated to de-escalation, a set of interactional and tactical strategies to prevent situations from escalating to violence. Though such training is popular with the public and shows promise for reducing police violence and injury to officers, a 2021 investigation of state training requirements found that twenty-one states still do not require de-escalation training for officers.[5]

The remaining 90 percent of weapons and defensive tactics training is focused on nonlethal weapons like batons, OC spray, and

TASERs (20 hours), physical combat using punches, kicks, and grappling (61 hours), and firearms (73 hours). Indeed, no other academy topic receives as many raw hours of instruction in the police academy as firearms and defensive tactics. The next closest subjects are patrol procedures (52 hours), criminal/constitutional law (51 hours), and health and fitness (50 hours), while cultural diversity (14 hours), community building (11 hours), ethics and integrity (12 hours), and professionalism (12 hours) lag far behind force-related training.[6]

Minimum standards that dictate the structure and content of academy training are not federally regulated. Instead, they are overseen by each state's Police Officer Standards and Training body (POST), leading to marked variation in the minimum hours of training required in each state. For example, Sunshine's POST requires a minimum of nearly 590 hours, while the WPD's and EPD's require approximately 660 and 870 hours, respectively. What's more, academies regularly exceed the POST-required hours, so that the SPD's 880 hours of academy training are in line with the national average but 40 percent more than the state-mandated minimum. This disparity is more marked in the EPD, with more than a thousand hours of academy training (nearly 20 percent higher than the required hours), and the WPD, whose 1,164 hours roughly double the state's POST requirement.[7]

So long as academies meet state minimums, decisions about the focus of any additional training hours are largely within departmental control. This discretion is necessary, to some degree, to allow departments to tailor their academies to their organizational context, including training on department-specific equipment and policies. A clear example is training related to body-worn cameras (BWCs). Not only do the types of cameras and software differ across departments, but departmental policies differ on when and how cameras are to be used by officers on patrol. For instance, the WPD's BWC policy states that officers need not activate their cameras when initially talking to victims of sexual assault. In contrast, the SPD policy mentions only "victims" and that officers "may" consider a victim's request to not be recorded. EPD's policy has no such considerations. And all three departments use different BWC technology.[8]

Discretionary training has two other benefits for departmental academies. First, it allows academies to adapt their curricula to cover topics specific to a department's local challenges and existing institutional relationships. For example, the EPD contends with markedly higher rates of violent crime, including gun violence, than the vast majority of agencies in the state. In response, the EPD academy collaborates with a local university to train officers on trauma-informed responses to children exposed to violence. It also mandates training on a citywide gun violence prevention strategy that builds and leverages relationships among the police department, social service providers, and other community organizations.

Second, discretionary training allows departments to include instruction that, even if in line with best practices, is not yet part of the state-mandated curriculum. Crisis intervention and de-escalation training, for instance, are supposed to help officers resolve conflicts without coercive force, including during interactions with people suffering from mental illness or substance abuse disorders. The public often demands this sort of training, and it is recommended by professional bodies like the International Association of Chiefs of Police, but it is not yet part of the EPD's state POST requirements.[9] The discretion afforded to the EPD allows its academy curriculum to mandate that training for its new recruits.

At the same time, departmental training discretion operates within the broader framework of the danger imperative. This preoccupation with violence and officer safety often results in academy curricula designed to focus disproportionately on teaching officers how to think about and use violence, overcome resistance, and eliminate threats. For example, although the EPD does include crisis intervention and de-escalation training that is not required by the state—two hours on crisis intervention and eight hours on de-escalation—defensive tactics, firearms and other weapons, use of force, and "officer safety/ mechanics of restraint and control" account for more than 16 percent of EPD training (170 hours).

This emphasis on officer safety and force-related topics is also present in the SPD and WPD academies. SPD's recruits receive 23 percent more firearms training than the average American police recruit, and 57 percent more than is required by the state. The West River academy's attention to combat-related topics is even more pronounced. At 151 hours, firearms and chemical agents training is more than double the 72 hours required by state standards; its 160 hours of "arrest and control" training (which includes defensive tactics) is 100 hours more than the state's requirement. Regardless of the state in which they operate and the variations in their curricula, the academy training in all three of these departments is designed to hone officers' survival skills above all else.

PROOF OF PERIL

Although tabulations of academy training hours provide some sense of what topics and skills are most central to the socialization of academy recruits, they provide only a glimpse of the powerful and unquestioned assumptions of deadly police work that justify the academy's heavy focus on firearms and physical violence. Though unlisted in official breakdowns of academy curricula, recruits are exposed to material that is specifically designed to drive home the horror of violence and death in the line of duty. These graphic videos, which show police being punched, stabbed, shot, and killed on patrol, serve as visceral proof that justifies the danger imperative's unerring preoccupation with violence and officer safety.

The ability of contemporary academies to marshal this sort of grisly evidence is unprecedented in the history of policing. Whereas police of the past relied largely on local stories passed down across generations of a department's offficers, today's academies show videos from across the country.[10] The internet provides an endless, easily accessible supply of violent videos from which to choose. With a few keystrokes, anyone can find dozens of videos on YouTube or Facebook that show officers being attacked in rural areas and urban centers, in broad daylight and in the dead of night, during traffic stops, during evictions, and while gassing up their patrol cars.

Policing-focused social media pages and websites aggregate and distribute these videos to a sizable audience. *Law Enforcement Today*, which has more than 850,000 followers on Facebook, regularly posts videos of attacks on police and stories of officers attacked or killed in the line of duty. *Police1* provides violent videos and other officer survival content to more than two million monthly visitors and more than 749,000 registered police members.[11] Sunshine's academy even lists *Police Magazine*'s website as a helpful resource for trainees. Across these various platforms, the aggregate lesson is that a police officer's life is always in danger—anytime, anywhere.

A seven-year EPD veteran with a penchant for stopping cars and pedestrians to look for guns, Officer Estacio recalled the impact of seeing such videos during academy training. "You're hearing their last breaths, their last words. It hits home," he said. One infamous video has been shown to officers for more than twenty years and is "forever seared into the minds of law enforcement officers across the world".[12] Officers in the EPD, WPD, and SPD remembered the exact video. Officer Shepard, who shows the video to his Sunshine recruits, recalled the video with mournful reverence, "You're watching a cop get murdered. You hear it. You can *feel* it." One West River officer, years after seeing the video in the academy, recalled the sound of dripping blood. The video, recorded by dashboard camera on the evening of January 12, 1998, captures the murder of twenty-two-year-old deputy Kyle Dinkheller.

———

The January evening in rural Georgia was still wrapped in Southern winter, windy and cloudy with a chilly, periwinkle sky. Deputy Dinkheller was a half hour from the end of his shift when he spotted an eastbound pickup truck flying by on the interstate outside Dudley, a town of around 500. Dinkheller's radar display flashed 98 mph—a good stop, any day of the week.

The deputy pulled onto the highway and gave chase. He caught up to the speeding white Toyota Tacoma, lights flashing as he initiated a traffic stop. The truck turned onto Whipple Crossing, two lonely lanes alongside the interstate, and came to a stop on the right side of the road. Dinkheller stopped about 15 feet behind the truck and exited his vehicle. The driver also exited his vehicle and stood by the drivers-side door. A dog moved around in the cabin of the truck as Dinkheller called out, "Driver, step back here to me. Come on back here for me." The driver, a bearded white man wearing a hat, large glasses, and a military-issue jacket, answered, "Okay," but stayed put.[13]

The driver was Andrew Howard Brannan—a decorated Vietnam veteran who served in the Army Reserves after returning home. Brannan suffered from combat-related mental illness, including severe depression and post-traumatic stress disorder (PTSD). Unknown to Dinkheller, Brannan had run out of his psychiatric medication five days before.[14]

Dinkheller called out again, "Come on back. How you doin' today?" Brannan responded, "Good. How you doin'?" and took a few steps toward the back of his truck, adjusting his jacket and placing his hands in his pockets as he drew even with the left rear taillight of his truck.

Dinkheller's training kicked in and he commanded firmly, "Keep your hands out of your pockets, sir." Hidden hands could be holding a weapon. When Brannan asked why, Dinkheller simply repeated the order. Brannan began to turn away as if to go back to the truck's cab. Dinkheller stepped forward, right hand wrapped around the pommel of his holstered pistol. In the space of a moment, the situation escalated. Brannan exclaimed, "Fuck you, goddamn it! Here I am! Shoot my fuckin' ass!" and began dancing from one foot to the other, waving his hands in the air. "Here I am! Here I am! Shoot me!"

"Sir, come here." But Brannan continued to dance, calling out "Here I am! Here I am! Shoot me!"

As Dinkheller radioed for backup, Brannan charged toward Dinkheller, stopping within arm's reach.

"Sir, get back!"

Brannan's hands clenched into fists by his sides and his chest puffed out with defiance: "Who you calling, motherfucker?!" Again and again—a total of nine times—Dinkheller commanded that Brannan get back. Brannan only grew more enraged. He challenged the deputy, "Fucking do it, man!" Dinkheller commanded him to get back again, and Brannan screamed defiantly, "Noooooo!" Brannan continued, incensed, "I am a goddamn Vietnam combat veteran! Fuck you!" and moved towards his truck. Dinkheller commanded him to stay away from the truck and got back on the radio to tell his backup to pick up the pace.

Dinkheller resumed verbal commands as Brannan rummaged in the truck's cab. Momentarily, the man pulled his head out of the Toyota and pointed an angry, accusatory finger at Dinkheller. "I am in fear of my fucking life!"

Dinkheller responded in kind: "I am in fear of my life! Get back here now! Step away from your vehicle."

And then Dinkheller saw the rifle—a .30 caliber carbine like those issued to U.S. soldiers during the Vietnam War.[15] Dinkheller's voice shifted. Alarm punctuated his words. "Put the gun down!" He was breathing hard now, out of breath from screaming and charged by adrenaline as he radioed for help again. "I got a man with a gun, I need help!" He then commanded Brannan again, "Put the gun down!

"No!"

"Put it down now! Put the gun down! Drop the gun, now!"

Finally, Dinkheller opened fire. He missed. Brannan returned fire, the cracks of his rifle splitting the evening air as Dinkheller took cover behind his patrol car. Some of Brannan's rounds hit the windshield of Dinkheller's cruiser, spiderwebs of cracked glass blooming as Dinkheller returned fire.

One of his rounds just missed, smashing the window of the open door by which Brannan crouched.

During a moment's lull, Brannan broke from cover and skittered to the back of his truck. Keeping the deputy's car between them, Brannan raised his rifle and methodically stalked around the patrol car's right side, laying down a steady stream of fire. A scream ripped from Dinkheller's throat, all fear and pain, as a bullet shattered his leg.[16] In anguished desperation, Dinkheller continued to issue commands: "Stop now!" Wounded and panting, the deputy reloaded his pistol. Brannan moved back around to the front of the vehicle and did the same with his rifle.

Peering around the edge of the vehicle, Brannan ducked reflexively at the sound of another shot from Dinkheller's pistol. A moment later, he leveled his rifle and calmly returned fire, testament to his time in combat. He marched forward, firing round after round. Dinkheller's screams no longer formed words, only terror. He had been shot nine times—in both legs, both arms, buttocks, chest, and head. The guttural screams faded to quiet, rasping gasps.

Brannan paused only a moment, touching a gunshot wound in his right side, then moved forward once again. Standing over Dinkheller, he shouted "Die fucker!" and shot the deputy through the eye. Brannan then ran to his truck and fled the scene. Dinkheller's radio crackled with voices, but there was no response from Dinkheller, only a soft, bloody gurgle as his life seeped out onto the pavement.

The dash cam's timestamp read 5:37 pm—barely three minutes after Brannan was stopped on that lonely Georgia road. When the first deputy arrived on scene, Dinkheller's radar display still flashed 98.[17]

———

Just over seventeen years after Dinkheller's murder, and three days after Andrew Brannan was executed by lethal injection for the heinous crime, I sat next to Officer Michaelson while he completed one of countless reports he'd written in his two years on the streets of

Elmont.[18] The temperature plummeted outside as he documented a largely administrative affair from earlier in his shift: a man had come to the district substation to report that his ex-wife was in violation of a court-ordered custody agreement. There was little Michaelson could do to enforce the custody agreement, but, as he explained to the father, having a police report to document the incident might help him in court.

While filling out that report, Michaelson recalled being shown the Dinkheller video in the academy. He remembered details of the video with remarkable accuracy—Brannan's "dancing" in the roadway, the rifle, how Brannan reloaded before executing Dinkheller—testament to how effectively such gruesome videos are engrained in the minds of recruits. He reflected gravely on the more than twenty-year-old video, "It was crazy." As Michaelson explained, graphic, real-life footage taught recruits to "not let your guard down." Such videos, he said, were designed "to show us how bad things can go, and how quickly things can happen. Not to underestimate people just because they look a certain way or are a certain age." The statistical improbability of a car stop going bad was far less important to Michaelson and his fellow officers than the possibility that any interaction *could* turn lethal.

The Dinkheller video and others like it also warn recruits of the fate that awaits them if they hesitate to use force. Recalling how Brannan danced around in the street before charging at Dinkheller, Michaelson commented, "He gets up in the officer's face, screaming at him. If you get up in my face like that, being aggressive, I'm going hands on. But this officer didn't, and the suspect goes back to his car and starts loading a rifle." For Michaelson, Dinkheller's sin was not that his first shot missed or that he did not take cover more effectively; it was Dinkheller's *inaction* that allowed the situation to spiral out of control.

In the decades since Dinkheller's murder, this lesson has taken on a life of its own, mixing shades of truth with outright fiction in the manner of many urban legends. One common narrative holds that Dinkheller's inaction was a result of departmental discipline for excessive force that made him wary of using violence in defense of his own life. Officer Casillas, a Latino officer in his early thirties with salt-and-pepper hair and acne scars dotting his face, was taught this lesson when he was shown the video of Dinkheller's murder in the academy. "He was told by his sergeant he was way too strict and he used too much force on people," he recalled. The discipline was so severe, Casillas said, that Dinkheller, a father of one with another on the way, would lose his job if another incident occurred. "So, when he made this car stop," he went on, "he was, I guess, scared to use force on this guy." Fearful of running afoul of his superiors and losing his livelihood, he hesitated to use violence against a clear and present threat.

In reality, Dinkheller had not been formally disciplined for excessive force prior to his murder. Rather, according to some of his coworkers at the time, he had been made to write and hand deliver a letter of apology for speaking harshly to a motorist who had failed to yield to emergency vehicles.[19] To this day, some believe that this informal punishment, unrecorded in his official disciplinary record, is what caused Dinkheller's fatal hesitation on that empty Georgia road.[20]

Despite the factual discrepancy between the narrative Casillas was taught and what actually occurred, the fundamental lessons about perilous, violent policework encapsulated by the video of Dinkheller's murder are the same. A deadly threat can materialize at any moment; an officer who is unable or unwilling to use violence decisively is gambling with their own life. In policing, Casillas explained, "Your sergeant's going to come down on you, people are going to come down on you. But doesn't mean . . . it's gonna stop you from doing your job. If you have to do something, if you have to use force on someone, then you gotta use the force. You gotta do whatever is appropriate. If you have to shoot somebody, unfortunately you gotta shoot somebody."

Casillas's explanation is echoed in a well-known phrase used by several officers I spoke with to describe the primacy of their own survival, even if it results in calamitous error: "It's better to be tried by twelve than carried by six."[21] This axiom, also commonly understood within the military and among gun owners, is an outgrowth of the danger imperative constructed with examples of extreme violence like the murder of Deputy Dinkheller.[22] Recruits who are repeatedly shown that the stakes of police work are a matter of life and death also learn that grievous errors are an acceptable and even necessary price to ensure that they are not murdered on the side of the road. Criticism, discipline, even trial and potential imprisonment are eclipsed by the danger imperative and its single-minded emphasis on survival.

"EVERYONE IS TRYING TO MURDER YOU"

Whereas videos of officers being attacked and killed in the line of duty provide recruits concrete substantiation of policing's deadly possibilities, these warnings are abstract. As potent as videos of officers being injured and killed are for evidencing the life-or-death stakes of police work, even the most harrowing examples of on-duty violence cannot hope to re-create the experience of an interaction suddenly spiraling out of control. While some scenarios are focused on overtly dangerous situations like an armed robbery in progress or an active shooter in a school, others involve ill-defined disturbances or routine car stops that recruits will perform many times on patrol. No scenario is excepted from the danger imperative and the preoccupation with violence. As put by Officer Diggler, an SPD veteran and academy instructor, reality-based training repeatedly imparts a powerful message to recruits: "Everyone is trying to murder you."

The night Diggler explained this feature of academy training, I'd met him and Officer Alonzo, another SPD veteran and longtime friend of Diggler, at a local brewery. After graduating from the academy and cutting their teeth on patrol, the two officers had worked undercover narcotics together for years before returning to the daily grind of answering calls for service. Alonzo, a tall, bald Mexican American man with a dark mustache, didn't speak Spanish but was "fluent in South Side," a skill that he credited with his success impersonating a drug dealer during narcotics investigations. In contrast, Diggler's thin build and white skin (along with a long goatee and a "dirty ass wife beater") helped him pose as a drug user while building a case one undercover buy at a time.[23]

After they recounted tales of excitement from their time working undercover, our conversation wound its way to patrol and its dangers. To prepare recruits to confront violence that might erupt at any moment, reality-based scenario training persistently emphasizes the possibility of attack and the cost of not taking all steps necessary to ensure officer safety. He recalled a training scenario in which he played a driver being pulled over by a recruit. The recruit was not told that there would be a "sims gun"—a training firearm that fires paint or plastic rounds—in plain view. To complete the exercise successfully, the trainee should do a proper scan of the vehicle and identify the firearm. They should then address the firearm's presence by, for example, taking possession of the sims gun until the conclusion of the vehicle stop.

It's when the recruit fails to identify and address the firearm that the exercise's true lesson is clearest. Diggler explained bluntly, "If the trainee doesn't see the gun, you kill the cop. He walks up to the car . . . 'Hi, sir, how's it going?' And if he doesn't see the gun, when he walks back to his car, you get out and you fucking murder him." Alonzo, seated across from Diggler and me nodded and concisely distilled this "mindset": one mistake, one wrong move, one moment of lapsed vigilance, and "You're gonna die."

To aid recruits in learning to identify threats before an attack occurs, reality-based scenario training also stresses that recruits must constantly assess those they interact with for signs of potential violence. Though there is vanishingly little evidence that body language or facial expressions are reliable predictors of violence, recruits are trained to be on the lookout for a wide range of "pre-assault" indicators.[24] These behavioral indicators were listed in West River training documents and are widely described in policing publications aimed at enhancing officer safety.[25]

Some are uncontroversial and obvious, such as a person shifting their weight to assume a boxerlike stance with one foot forward and one back. Other so-called indicators, however, such as sweating, hesitation, darting eyes, an averted gaze, a clenched jaw, fidgeting, and changes in blinking or breathing, are just as likely to be signs of what social psychologists term "stereotype threat."[26] This concern with being negatively judged because of context-specific group stereotypes is especially salient in the context of policing, where racial minorities are far more likely than whites to be distrustful of police, whom they fear will perceive them as suspicious or threatening.[27] Still other purported indicators, such as being "overly compliant," are simply paradoxical, suggesting that someone who too quickly or completely cooperates with police is actually a threat.

By continually emphasizing to recruits that every interaction or call for service is suffused with the possibility of lethal violence, training designed as an approximation of "reality" constructs police work as synonymous with survival. To ensure that they are prepared to survive when they begin to take calls on patrol, recruits are taught that the practice of their work must always center officer safety. Failure to do so, regardless of the situation at hand, is a recipe for disaster.

VIOLENCE EXPERTS

The implementation of academy training that re-creates the danger imperative's collective preoccupation with violence is controlled by academy instructors. These instructors are responsible for meeting state training requirements and producing recruits versed in department policy and the criminal code. Most importantly, they are entrusted with preparing the recruits in their charge to survive. The officers selected for this vital task are not selected at random. Like enforcement-minded officers who are selected for specialized units that focus on gangs or narcotics, academy instructors who successfully apply for limited instructor positions often have expertise in the firearms and fighting heavily emphasized in the academy. By the same token, these instructors tend toward an understanding of police work that is closely aligned with the danger imperative and the maximization of officer safety. Instructors, over the course of hundreds of hours in the academy, serve as key conduits for the tenets of the danger imperative. As experts on the theory and use of violence, instructors mold recruits' minds and bodies to both use violence and survive the violence that awaits them after graduation.

In an environment and occupation in which survival is sacrosanct, officers skilled in the use of violence are held in high esteem by their colleagues and superiors. Officer Cisneros, an academy instructor in Elmont, was a paragon of consummate violence. Compared to other officers, including former soldiers who had seen active combat, the fervor with which Officer Cisneros approached officer survival and the mastery of violence stood out. Among other EPD officers, Cisneros had a reputation as someone with tremendous knowledge about defensive tactics, firearms, and all things "tactical."

In policing, "tactical" is shorthand for describing the techniques and specialized equipment that officers use to ensure their survival. SWAT officers learn special tactics for clearing buildings; all officers learn tactics for safely undertaking a vehicle stop or responding to a burglary in progress. Tactical equipment denotes weapons, clothing, and other gear that maximizes functionality, durability, and effectiveness in the harsh conditions that soldiers, police, and other first responders might encounter.

Lean and light-skinned with a shiny, shaved head, Cisneros lived and breathed all things tactical. When I sat down to talk with him at the Elmont academy, he sported a dark navy hat, emblazoned with a centurion helmet over crossed swords, and a large, rubberized Casio G-Shock watch. A folding knife with a specialized glass breaker—useful for shattering car windows—poked from the right pocket of his abrasion-resistant tactical pants, and a braided paracord keychain hung from the left. Though not especially large, his sharp jawline and the ripple of muscles and veins in his arms were evidence of his dedication to fitness and a clean diet, both of which he assiduously documented via social media.

Training was not just a hobby for Cisneros; it was a matter of life and death. The caption under one video of him lifting weights read, "You can't train hard enough for a job that will kill you." Beyond fitness, he also trained in Brazilian jiujitsu, kick boxing, and knife fighting in his spare time. All of this, he told me, was to be ready to win. "I train all the time, regularly shooting, jujitsu, martial arts, CrossFit," he said. "That's just a lifestyle for me—to be prepared. Victory favors the prepared."

This belief in the necessity of training to ensure victory over violent criminals was reflected across departments and is common within policing more broadly. In Sunshine, for example, a picture taped to the wall outside a substation weight room showed a prison cell with a hulking bald man in an orange prison jumpsuit standing with his hands balled into fists. The image was captioned, "Every day you don't workout someone else does." Poster-size versions of the same image can be easily purchased online and customized with any agency's name and insignia.[28]

Whereas some officers fell into policing for mundane reasons like an attractive pension or no requirement of a college degree, Cisneros told me he'd always wanted to be a police officer. He recounted to me that his mother once had to punish him for handcuffing his brother to the bed for being a "bad guy." He applied to be a police officer as soon as he turned twenty-one because, he explained, he believed in "good versus evil." When I asked whether the world was that simple, he affirmed, "Morally, it's right or wrong."

From the day he hit the street in Halbrook, one of Elmont's more violent districts, Cisneros was, as he put it, "full of piss and vinegar," a case study in the enforcement-focused, adrenaline-fueled policing associated with being a "hard charger."[29] He quickly developed a reputation as an officer who engaged in a high number of walking and traffic stops and was selected to work a dedicated crime-suppression detail. He recalled those years fondly: "I had a blast doing that. The goal every night was to get a gun." Though working the overnight shift in Halbrook, which had a high concentration of Latino and undocumented residents, required shifting his sleep patterns, the odd hours were worth it given the ease with which he could make arrests. "Like shooting fish in a barrel," he said.

Now, as an academy instructor, Cisneros trained new generations of EPD officers. He viewed this role as a great responsibility and was well aware of the power he held to shape the EPD through the training of its officers. He remarked, "I think Hitler actually said, 'If I can control the youth of a nation, in turn I'll control the nation itself,' right? Investing in the future—the future of this department are the recruits that come through here."[30] He continued, "I think I can effectively make change if I can make more officers of the same mindset as me, and other officers that are on this department that share the same mindset, that really care about the war about good and evil, who care about the little things."

It seemed lost on Cisneros that his pedagogy was informed by the wisdom of a fascist leader who used Germany's police forces to carry out the extermination of more than 6 million Jewish people.[31] Or that the Nazi blueprint for ethnic cleansing was informed by prominent American eugenicists and the system of U.S. slavery.[32] Whether Cisneros knew this history or not, his view of policing through the danger imperative in the present took precedence and informed his description of policing as a "war." In this war, police are understood as "warriors," what law professor and former police officer Seth Stoughton describes as "soldiers on the front lines in the never-ending battle to preserve order and civilization against the forces of chaos and criminality."[33]

Cisneros, bedecked in tactical apparel and committed to honing himself for the fight to come, embodied this vision of policing in body and spirit. For him, being a police officer was a vocation, something approaching a divine mission. With their weapons and training, Cisneros and those whom he could mold in the vision of the danger imperative were duty bound to protect the weak from monsters who lurked in the shadows. "Bad things happen in the dark," he warned. "Evil looks for dark places."

(ANTI)HEROES

Along with concise narratives of good and evil that reify police as the "thin blue line" between order and anarchy, the vision of police wielding righteous violence in pursuit of justice was reflected in a common affinity for the Punisher, a hyperviolent Marvel comics antihero who eschews the rule of law in favor of torture and murder. Cisneros's Snapchat account (username: punisher_epd22) once featured a collection of Punisher comic books. An old picture of Cisneros from his time on a federal task force showed him with a long beard emblematic of the rough, masculine aesthetic heavily influenced by the elite special forces operators he so revered. Next to where a rifle slanted across his chest, a black Punisher skull patch was stuck to one of the pouches attached to his armor carrier. To commemorate his time with the task force, he also kept a quote pinned to the wall of his office at the academy. Next to an image of an officer hefting a rifle, the quote, taken from Ernest Hemingway's *On the Blue Water*, reads: "There is no hunting like the hunting of man, and those who have hunted armed men long enough and liked it, never care for anything else thereafter."

The Punisher transcends policing. The violent antihero was also admired by Chris Kyle, a Navy SEAL whose 160 confirmed kills across four tours in Iraq earned him the honorific of "the deadliest sniper in U.S. military history."[34] Like Cisneros, Kyle hewed to a starkly binary view of human nature and the stakes of his violent work—good versus evil. In his autobiography, Kyle connected this moral binary to why he and his fellow soldiers revered the Marvel vigilante:

> We all thought what the Punisher did was cool: He righted wrongs. He killed bad guys. He made wrongdoers fear him.
>
> That's what we were all about. So we adapted his symbol—a skull—and made it our own, with some modifications. We spray-painted it on our Hummers and body armor, and our helmets and all our guns. And we spray-painted it on every building or wall we could. We wanted people to know, *We're here and we want to fuck with you.*
>
> It was our version of psyops.
>
> *You see us? We're the people kicking your ass. Fear us. Because we will kill you, motherfucker.*
>
> *You are bad. We are badder. We are bad-ass.*[35]

The Punisher's creator, Gerry Conway, has warned that police officers who identify with the Punisher are embracing an "outlaw mentality." He also stated that the use of the Punisher's insignia—a foreboding skull sometimes customized with an American flag pattern or a single, thin blue line—is akin to flying a Confederate flag on a government building. "Whether you think the Punisher is justified or not, whether you admire his code of ethics," he explained in one interview, "he is an outlaw. He is a criminal. Police should not be embracing a criminal as their symbol."[36]

Nonetheless, police-focused online stores are awash with Punisher-themed police paraphernalia, and officers across the country continue to identify with the Punisher's hyperviolent persona.[37] In Sunshine, one officer used the Punisher logo as a cellphone background, another decorated his aluminum water bottle with a thin blue line Punisher sticker, and still others had Facebook profile pictures that featured the Punisher skull. Even when not specifically a Punisher skull, the hypermasculine ideal exemplified by the Punisher is reflected in

FIGURE 1.1 Sunshine officer's water bottle with a Punisher sticker that combines the American flag with a thin blue line motif. The infamous skull of the hyperviolent anti-hero is also displayed by soldiers and a range of right-wing groups.

content produced and sold by any number of police-focused entities. Instagram accounts like @thinbluelinebeasts and @policeposts feature images of armored centurions and snarling dogs alongside videos featuring heavily muscled men, firearms, and martial arts training. Relentless Defender, along with "Patriotically Correct" and "Second Amendment" apparel lines brimming with U.S. flags and firearms, also has dedicated "Law Enforcement" merchandise available for purchase: mugs, T-shirts, window decals, and keychains showing "thin blue line" emblazoned skulls, war helmets, centurions, and depictions of the archangel St. Michael.[38]

Cisneros's kinship with the Punisher meshed well with his affinity for the more violent, militaristic facets of policing. Though he had never served in the armed forces, he was prone to military analogies

FIGURE 1.2 "Centurions" academy class logo painted on the wall of the Elmont police academy's central hallway. Other symbols in the EPD academy included eagles and swords.

and references when discussing police work. In reference to the Sandy Hook Elementary School massacre, he told me we need police who are "quiet professionals"—a nickname for the Army's Green Berets—who can mete out swift violence to save innocents. "There's an old saying," he added. "*Si vis pacem, para bellum*: If you want peace, prepare for war."

Violence, from Cisneros's point of view, was not an inherently bad or evil thing; violence was a professional necessity and a moral good. What mattered most was who, how, and why violence was being used. When used judiciously, violence was the means to ensure peace and safety. Like the soldiers he emulated in dress and manner, Cisneros understood that his work as an officer and an academy instructor came with the obligation to be an expert in the use of violence.

This viewpoint was especially clear on his public Instagram account. Under the tagline "God, Family, Country," Cisneros posted dozens of images and videos of himself engaged in combat training using firearms, knives, and his own body. Hashtags used to label his posts and make them more easily discoverable included popular police-focused hashtags like #thinblueline, as well as others focused on violence, survival, and the military.[39]

In the caption of one post, he articulated a relativistic understanding of the morality of violence. Rather than being inherently bad, violence is a tool whose ethics depend on its intended use and effect: "The characterization of violence as being good or bad is incumbent upon the intent of the one(s) employing said violence. Violence used unlawfully and immorally is evil. However, when used legally and ethically with the intent of thwarting unlawful and unethical violence, it is not only acceptable but commendable."

In one video on his social media, Cisneros stood in front of a punching bag as rap lyrics played over the stylized, black-and-white video. In an instant, he sprang into action: after two quick palm strikes to the punching bag, he drew a concealed knife from his waistband and stabbed at eye level. As his left arm completed the knife strike, he drew a concealed pistol from his right hip and aimed at the bag. The video is captioned with the words of Jordan Peterson, the Canadian psychologist turned conservative YouTube star and best-selling author: "A harmless man is not a good man. A good man is a very dangerous man who has that under voluntary control."[40] To be unskilled in the use of violence, then, is not only an abdication of one's duty as a police officer. It is also a failure to live up to a violent, masculine ideal necessary to defend innocent life and ensure one's own survival.[41]

Cisneros's valorization of violence, in turn, found its way into recruits' training. A PowerPoint lecture that he designed—titled simply "Combat"—began with the words of Scott Mattison, a former chief deputy of the Swift County Sheriff's Department in Benson, Minnesota.[42]

> Until technology enables me to handcuff you from afar, I will need to arrest you, face-to-face, man-to-man. This means that, when we fight, when I call upon those elements of the warrior within, I will be close enough to smell you, to touch you, to strike you, to cut you, to hear you, to plead with you, to wrestle with you, to shoot you, to handcuff you, to bleed on you and you on me, to tend to your wounds, to hear your last words. Our meeting may be brief, but I will have had a more intense contact with you, my unwanted adversary, than with most of my loved ones.

Whereas some officers view violence as an unfortunate but sometimes unavoidable reality of police work, Mattison's words, selected by Cisneros and shown to EPD recruits, present police violence as an intimate affair bordering on the sexual. To fulfill their mandate as police, officers must embrace "the warrior within" and engage in a primal exchange of sweat and blood and bodies with another man. This confrontation is similar to the "edgework" undertaken by extreme sports enthusiasts who balance control and chaos to achieve a "magnified sense of self."[43] It is through violence that police attain the same.

These words, shown to generations of EPD recruits and read by innumerable other officers across the country, are drawn from the broader ecosystem of violent, militaristic content that lionizes police as righteous warriors in a battle for society itself. The same words used by Cisneros in his academy PowerPoint are written in a book that Cisneros recommended to me, titled *On Combat: The Psychology and Physiology of Deadly Conflict in War and Peace.* The book, an international bestseller, was placed on the U.S. Marine Corps commandant's required reading list. Along with Loren Christensen, a retired police officer and defensive tactics instructor, the book was written by retired Lt. Col. Dave Grossman, the self-proclaimed inventor of "killology" and one of the most in-demand police trainers in the United States.

KILLOLOGY

For more than twenty years, Dave Grossman has taught soldiers, police officers, and the public how to embrace violence and think like killers. The former West Point psychology professor and founder of the Killology Research Group (KRG) is nothing short of a celebrity in law enforcement circles. He's on the road nearly three hundred days a year, traveling across and outside the United States to teach about the "Bulletproof Mind," described on the KRG website as "psychological preparation for combat."[44] To date, tens of thousands of law enforcement officers from hundreds of agencies across the country have undergone this training in police academies, college classrooms, churches, and hotel ballrooms.

In his trainings and his books, Grossman divides society into three distinct groups: sheep, wolves, and sheepdogs. Most people are sheep—hardworking citizens neither inclined nor trained to use violence. Sheep are the natural prey of wolves—predators comfortable with the use of violence to subjugate and harm the sheep. And then there are the sheepdogs, the "police officers, soldiers, and other warriors" who are "blessed with the gift of aggression."

In this paradigm, violence is a useful, even necessary tool to uphold social order and safeguard civilization.[45] In the hands of "modern paladins" and "knights" like police officers, Grossman writes, violence is a righteous instrument to defend a public that is ignorant of the dangers that prowl in the shadows. But to emerge victorious from their battle with the wolf, officers must embrace the "warrior mindset." It is this mindset that allows the sheepdog, even when bitten by the wolf, to stay in the fight, to confront, combat, and triumph over evil. "A warrior," he says, "meets the predator and survives."[46]

The 2016 film *Do Not Resist* features a Bulletproof Mind seminar held by Grossman in a Ohio hotel ballroom. Pacing back and forth in front of the assembled officers, microphone in hand, Grossman exudes the intensity of a true believer. With decades of these seminars under his belt, he eschews notes while constructing a deadly, zero-sum vision of the communities that police are sworn to safeguard. While citizen sheep may be naïve to violence and their own weakness, police cannot afford this complacency. Addressing the officers seated in front of him, he makes the true calling of today's police officers patently clear.

"You fight violence," he declares, and immediately follows up with a question, "What do you fight it with?" After a pregnant pause, he looks up at the audience and grins, "Superior violence. Righteous violence, yeah?" Nodding knowingly, he continues, "Violence is your tool. Violence is your enemy. Violence is the realm we operate in. You are men and women of violence." Once again, a smile turns the corners of his mouth, and he concludes, "You must master it, or it will destroy you."

In Grossman's seminars, the world is constantly poised on a knife's edge, a moment away from carnage should there be no one there to stop the predators that prowl among us. Only the vigilant and the true of heart will survive. He asks the officers, "What does a predator do?" He answers himself and then concludes dramatically, "They kill. Only a killer can hunt a killer."

This deceptively simple statement captures a foundational building block in Grossman's ideology, an unwavering truism that is something approaching natural law. Violence and evil are very real. Those who choose to deny or ignore them are courting disaster, and they will not survive when their adversaries strike. Any who are unprepared to kill are destined to fail at the moment of truth. He then poses a grim question to the room full of officers: "Are you emotionally, spiritually, psychologically prepared to snuff out a human life in defense of innocent lives?" For those who are not, there is only one logical conclusion: "You need to find another job."

Grossman's violent orthodoxy does more than provide quotable passages for academy instructors to use in their training slides. His violent ideology also explicitly shapes the state-approved training curricula of modern police departments. As with academy curricula in other states, Sunshine's POST allows certified instructors to design new courses and submit them for approval by a state-level committee. The lesson plan for the POST-approved course Psychology of Survival cites Grossman and other police consultants whose teachings were used to create the course.[47]

Grossman's teachings are prominently featured in course materials. Just as officers in his seminars are told to harness the predator's violence and aggression in defense of the sheep, the course section titled "Be the Predator" teaches recruits the importance of emulating their adversaries' intuition, tactics, aggressiveness, and cunning. Each recruit must become a "paladin," "a paragon of chivalry; a heroic champion" that embodies the "warrior spirit." To survive, recruits must harness the violence of the predator and turn it against them. "Warriors are the predator," the lesson says. Warriors, though willing to extend "the olive branch of piece to all you meet," must "be prepared and have a plan to use force."

Policing, the lesson reads, is a constant fight for survival that must be won at all costs. Drawing on the work of the former police officer turned trainer Brian Willis, the lesson's section on "The Winning Mind" stresses that every situation is a contest to be won. To do so, officers must focus on "Offense, *not* defense. . . . By thinking *offensively* we are able to maintain control—make things happen rather than reacting to them." This lesson, rather than encourage recruits to defuse violence, teaches them they can and should maintain constant control over situations on the street.[48]

As one policing columnist wrote, offensive tactics necessary to "communicate to everyone present that you are in charge—not just now, but right the [bleep] now. Not just sort of in charge, but totally and completely [bleeping] in charge."[49] Any officer who fails to maintain control risks losing their life.

THE SCIENCE OF VIOLENCE

Academy training need not explicitly discuss Grossman's teachings to perpetuate the danger imperative. Within their first few days at the academy, Sunshine recruits sit through a lesson titled "Game Day in Law Enforcement: Enhancing Officer Performance Under Pressure." The class is loosely based on the POST-approved Psychology of Survival curriculum and frames violence as a rational matter of physiology, perception, and action. The class was designed by Officer Shepard, a SWAT officer and K9 handler who, in his own words, has "been around the block a few times" when it comes to the use of violence. He shared his class materials with me and walked me through how he teaches the class.

Despite his comfort with violence, he disagreed with the zero-sum, warrior policing espoused by Grossman. He explained to me that while the concept of the sheepdog speaks to the more noble features of policing, the rhetoric of "predators" has no place in police training. "I'm not one of those officers that buys into the idea of the thin blue line and we go home safe no matter what," he told me. "There's a greater good here, and it's important we get this right." He did not glorify violence, and he recognized that the probability of being killed on duty is low. "You're not likely to die on a traffic stop," he said. "We do billions of traffic stops over our career. . . . Like, very, very rarely does a traffic stop turn into a shooting."

Shepard was no zealot. But neither was he naïve to the violence police must face and that is inherent to their work. As put by Jonathan Rubinstein in his study of the Philadelphia Police Department in the early 1970s, "The use of force is not a philosophical issue for a policeman. It is not a question of should or whether, but when and how much."[50] Shepard shared this unvarnished pragmatism and used his class to rationalize the chaos of combat for recruits. For police, violence is neither unknowable nor unlikely; it is a harsh but necessary feature of police work that must be studied and mastered.

This class, designed by Shephard, is not a how-to on force; it does not cover defensive tactics or firearms and is not focused on teaching recruits the particulars of using violence. Instead, Shepard focuses on what he calls the "human element" of decision making and violence. "We have to understand how our brain works when we deal with stress," he explained to me. "You have to be exposed to levels of stress and be coached and take those lessons, those training points, and turn them into behaviors. . . . We want to understand how stress affects the body. We want to understand the ways that our perception, our memory, our judgment are fallible, so that we can contextualize our training to account for them."

As a preface to months of physical training on fighting and shooting, Shepard's lessons on violence encouraged recruits to see themselves as biological entities that respond in predictable ways to external stimuli. For instance, he presented them with a host of empirical studies on officers' physiological responses to on-duty shootings, such as the racing heart, sweating, and perceptual distortions that come with fight-or-flight sympathetic nervous system arousal.[51] Training is the key to overcoming these reactions and ensuring that officers do not panic under stress and use violence incorrectly. "What we want, in a perfect world," Shepherd explained, "is [for] an officer who, when things are getting kind of hairy, to be cool, calm and collected and be able to see a way out of the panic, the 'Oh-shit-BANG' kind of scenario."

To illustrate the danger of letting emotion override clear thinking, he showed recruits videos of officers engaging in a variety of what he described as poor decisions under stress. In one such video, an Arkansas Game and Fish Commission officer is engaged in a high-speed chase of an armed robbery suspect. While chasing the suspect vehicle against the flow of traffic, the officer takes both his hands off the wheel to aim his pistol at the fleeing vehicle. Eventually, the suspect is run to ground. As soon as the suspect exits his vehicle, the officer grabs him by the hair, throws him to the ground at gun point, and screams in the terrified man's face, "I will kill you!"

"On no planet can you tell me that guy's acting reasonably," Shepard said. "That guy is completely out of control. It's insane to me." The video served as a cautionary tale for recruits. Emotion, when unchecked and unmastered, can hijack an officer's decision making. In Shepard's eyes, this officer's shocking behavior was not a case of immorality or malintent. This officer's lack of control and the danger in which he placed himself, other officers, and the public were a product of inadequate training. Whereas a properly trained officer would have been able to fall back on ingrained skills and critical thinking in the midst of a vehicle pursuit, this officer reverted to a primordial, knee-jerk reaction. Without the proper training, he said, "Your emotions get the best of you."

Rather than react emotionally, recruits should aspire to dispassionate, rational violence. "A scared cop is a dangerous cop," he said. "I have to teach cops how to turn off their fight-or-flight response—like, the actual fear, you know?" In the heat of the moment, a poorly trained officer is liable to panic and either freeze or overreact. If they fail to use violence to stop a threat, they or someone else might be harmed. If they overreact and use disproportionate violence, they are liable to, as Shepard put it, "get famous on YouTube." That an overreaction might also injure or kill an innocent was not explicitly mentioned. It is only through "deliberate practice, getting out of [their] comfort zone and training," Shepard said, that recruits can learn to calm their minds and make crucial decisions.

Clarity is particularly important in the context of the OODA loop, a cognitive concept developed by Air Force colonel John Boyd in the late 1970s based on his experience in air-to-air combat. As Shepard teaches his recruits, the OODA loop is a four-step decision-making process: Observe, Orient, Decide, Act. First, an individual must observe their surroundings. They then orient themselves to address what they are observing, make a decision on how to act, and execute that decision. As a general decision-making framework, the OODA loop has wide appeal outside of the military. Since its introduction, it has been adopted by both city governments and large corporations that must make decisions in uncertain and evolving circumstances.[52]

For police officers, efficient cognitive movement through the OODA loop is a matter of life and death. The "tighter" an officer can make their OODA loop, the faster they are able to adapt to a threat on the street. If they act fast enough, they can interrupt their opponent's ability to move through their own OODA loop. Speed kills.[53] "In a life or death situation," writes one officer survival instructor, "you need to be able to process through the OODA loop as quickly and effectively as possible in order to increase your odds of survival and triumph." Decisive action trumps reaction; the officer who hesitates will be outmaneuvered and killed.

But for all his efforts to rationalize violence for recruits, Shepard is not immune to the gallant rhetoric attached to policing and the violence at its core. Near the end of his class, Shepard presents recruits with a quote by Fisher Ames, a member of the First United States Congress and a Federalist Party leader. Under a statue of Lady Justice holding scales aloft and the words "Tyranny" and "Anarchy," the quote reads: "Liberty is not to be enjoyed, indeed it cannot exist, without the habits of just subordination; it consists, not so much in removing all restraint from the orderly, as in imposing it on the violent."

Shepard believed that recruits enter law enforcement, as he did, for honorable reasons. He recalled that he tells them, "You guy are not here for money. It's not a fortune and fame thing. You're here because you want to do the right things, for all the right reasons." That some might enter policing for the wrong reasons, or wield power based on flawed conceptions of the good, is unmentioned. Their profession, he tells recruits is part and parcel of a country and history rooted in revolution. "It was not so many years ago," he reminds recruits, "that the people of this county decided to revolt against their government and do their own thing." This noble history of patriotic resistance is their inheritance. When recruits become sworn officers, they will join the ranks of the most contacted and adversarial arm of local government. Without a commitment to use violence in defense of order, they risk chaos. Without calculated restraint, they flirt with tyranny. "It falls on us," he said, "to find that balance." Violence is the tool with which officers find it.

SURVIVAL SKILLS

Pushing Through Pain

From the moment they enter the academy, recruits are under siege. Like more than 80 percent of academies across the United States, the EPD, WPD, and SPD use "stress-based" training based on a military model specially formulated to induce physical and psychological stress.[54] Physical exercise is an especially popular method, and recruits are made to perform endless calisthenics. Whether to build camaraderie or as a form of collective punishment, the effect on individuals is predictable: recruits are disoriented, exhausted, and forced to make decisions under duress.[55]

In West River, academy recruits can be spotted running in formation through the city's streets, all dressed in white T-shirts and gray shorts with their class flag flying at the front of the column. On a beach near town, Elmont recruits are forced to turn themselves into what Navy SEALs call "sugar cookies"—after rolling around in the frigid surf, recruits throw sand onto their sweat-soaked and water-logged uniforms before continuing with endless fireman carries and wheelbarrow races. Sunshine's recruits run up and down a seventy-five-foot tower used for Sunshine Fire Department rescue training, even in summer heat that averages well over one hundred degrees Fahrenheit.

In a local news story on the Sunshine academy, an instructor wearing a wide, round-brimmed drill sergeant's hat said, "This job, this profession is very stressful." Several dozen recruits behind him were suffering through an exercise that required each to hold a jug of water at chest level with outstretched arms while instructors yelled at them. He continued, "It's extremely stressful on the street. And this is a controlled environment, but we try to bring the stress to see who can think on their feet and who can get the job done when they're under pressure."

The need to push through and "get the job done" is central to training that forces recruits to experience the havoc of physical violence. Besides dedicated instruction on how to strike, wrestle, and physically control a suspect, academy training includes a wide variety of ritualistic drills that force recruits to undergo intense discomfort, even pain. These drills, repeated across successive generations of academy classes, bind officers together in the shared conviction that they can and must fight back at all costs.

One especially agonizing rite of passage is OC spray exposure. OC is named for its active ingredient, oleoresin capsicum, an oily substance containing capsaicin (the compound responsible for the telltale heat in spicy food). Purified OC is mixed with a solvent and pressurized into handheld cans that disperse the caustic mixture in a spray or stream. Skin contact results in an intense, burning pain that lasts around half an hour, with hours of sensitivity to follow; inhalation causes respiratory distress and violent coughing; and ingestion can cause nausea and vomiting.[56]

Similar to how recruits are made to endure a TASER's 50,000 volts, they must suffer through a shot of OC spray to the eyes, nose, and mouth. And while some OC exposure exercises simply make recruits bear the pain, others require them to take a direct spray to the face before shooting firearms, striking with their bodies and batons, and handcuffing suspects. Officer Manchaca, another instructor interviewed by the local Sunshine news, said OC exposure was crucial in showing recruits "they can work through the discomfort and get through the situation and be able to carry out whatever job is necessary." Pain cannot be a barrier to doing what is necessary to survive.

Under a bright blue sky in early spring, Elmont recruits' OC exposure drill began with a race to tire them out before they got sprayed. In a video recorded by Officer Cisneros on his cellphone, two recruits, both sporting buzzed haircuts and blue T-shirts with their last name in yellow letters on the back, took off running toward a trashcan set up forty meters away. Instructors harassed them with a mixture of commands and encouragement. "Fast!" "Run!" "Let's go, Chuckles!" Officer Cisneros continued to record and snarked to another instructor, "Hey, I'ma hit this one [with OC]. I *owe* him," getting a sharp laugh in response. Cisneros screamed, "Hurry up! It's a race!" Then, he warned, "Last one back gets a double dose!"

When the recruits finished their run, Cisneros took charge of the recruit nearest to him, a young man named Pacenko, and led him to a table. He gave Pacenko a few seconds to look into a cardboard box and memorize its contents: a dental floss pick, staples, a battery, a bobby pin, coins, a rubber band, a wide-mouthed paper clip, and other knickknacks. Next, he had Pacenko stand with his back to a stack of blue plastic barrels and commanded him to recite his date of birth and social security number. As soon as Pacenko began speaking, Cisneros sprayed the OC directly into the recruit's eyes, nose, and mouth. Pacenko's eyes clamped shut. He grimaced and gasped as the OC burned his nasal cavity, throat, eyes, and skin.

While Pacenko burned, Cisneros called out commands, encouraging the recruit to take cover behind the barrels as he began the firearms portion of the exercise. Pacenko pawed ineffectively at his burning eyes with his left hand, pistol gripped in his right. "Keep your eyes open! Let's go, Pacenko! Let's go, Pacenko!" Pacenko struggled, but he was finally able to insert a new magazine and take cover behind the blue barrels. He racked the slide of his pistol and opened fire on the paper target positioned about five meters away. After three successful hits, it was on to the next station.

Pacenko holstered his pistol and ran to where another recruit stood waiting with a black foam pad. Whipping open his expandable baton, Pacenko executed three strikes. Each hit thudded with a dull "whumph" against the pad as he practiced issuing commands, yelling, "Get on the ground!" With the baton station completed, and still blinded by the OC spray, Pacenko collapsed his baton and stored it on his duty belt before moving on. This time he handcuffed another recruit while issuing commands. Next, he kneeled down to simulate radioing for assistance. With his eyes clenched and breathing heavily, Pacenko fumbled to clip his handcuff key to his belt and cried out, "99! Shots fired at 107 Sheridan! I've been exposed to pepper spray!" Though he had given his location and correctly used the "99" code to signal that all other radio traffic should cease, he'd forgotten to relay other crucial information. Cisneros prompted, "What unit is this?" and Pacenko responded, "Unit B229!"

Having successfully pushed through to shoot, strike, handcuff, and radio for assistance, Pacenko's final task was to clear his mind, choke back his coughs, and recall the contents of the cardboard box. He gasped out, "A penny, a dime, a blue paper clip, a black paper clamp thing, a battery." With that, Pacenko was released to the main academy building where other recruits were already doing their best to mitigate the burn of the OC. Some fanned their eyes with scraps of cardboard, others jumped into the academy showers, fully clothed, to flush the oily chemical out of their eyes and nose. Still others jammed their heads into the open door of a freezer. Cisneros, camera still rolling, quipped, "Yo, stickin' your head in a freezer ain't gonna do shit for you, homie!"[57]

Fight for Your Life

Training in the chaos of physical combat starts almost immediately for academy trainees. Officer Baker, a heavyset officer and SPD academy instructor in his early fifties, told me about the drill that takes place within the first few days of the academy. As an Air Force veteran who took up policing as a second career in his forties, Baker was at home in the bureaucracy of the SPD and the militaristic environment of its academy.

As he drove me around the academy training grounds, he pointed to an open area of dry, brittle grass. That sunbaked field, he explained, is where recruits are made to run and do calisthenics to tire them out before they are ushered into a nearby building for the "fight for your life" drill. Once inside, they are led into a room retrofitted with padded walls and floor where they don gloves and foam sparring helmets. Pairs of recruits are then ordered to drop to their knees and, on the command of an instructor, as Baker put it, "beat the shit out of each other for two minutes."

Much like fights in the real world, the "fight for your life" is messy and imprecise. The drill is designed not to forge skillful strikers so much as to force recruits into a brawl that approximates the raw emotion and physical stress of the violence that awaits them on patrol. Baker told me that the drill helps calibrate recruits' understanding of the brutality of police work: "It's all one thing that's really cool on the TV—to see people fighting. And it's really cool to think, 'Yeah, I'm going to be a cop,'" he said. "But when you get a right hook to the jaw and you start seeing Tweety Birds, that's kind of the 'Holy shit, this is real. I'm getting the shit kicked out of me.'" For the instructors watching, the drill is "just kind of to see who's going to curl up into a ball, who's got what it takes." After all, he continued, "you can't just curl up in a ball when you're out on the street," far from the padded floors of the academy and the watchful eye of instructors.

Another fighting drill used in the police academy is the "red man," named for the bright red protective padding worn by an instructor playing the role of a combative suspect. Unlike the "fight for your life," the "red man" (also referred to as a "padded assailant") centers around a scenario dreamed up by academy staff. As in other scenario-based training, recruits receive some basic information about a call for service to which they must respond, usually a seemingly mundane report of trespassing or a disturbance in a gas station or other local business. They must then try to navigate the encounter using their verbal and physical skills, either alone or in pairs.

Whereas "fight for your life" has recruits fight one another, the "red man" pits them against experienced instructors with extensive training in jiujitsu, Krav Maga, or boxing. While the vast majority of suspects that recruits will encounter on the street will not violently resist, the "red man" is designed to have recruits confront a skilled and motivated assailant who is intent on doing anything but complying with their commands.

The fights can be intense. There are body slams, takedowns, punches, and kicks; knees and elbows fly. And though the "red man" instructors eventually allow themselves to be taken into custody, the exercise is specifically designed so that recruits do not dominate the fight. On the contrary, Officer Baker told me, the "red man" is intended to show recruits that no one, no matter their training and tools, is guaranteed to walk away from a fight on the street. He explained bluntly, "No matter how much of a badass you are, there are other people out there that might be a little badder than you."

In this sense, "red man" shows recruits the benefits of preemptive tactics to ensure officers safety. Ideally, well-trained officers can tip the scales in their favor early, calling for backup before approaching a volatile situation, sizing up a suspect and how a fight might go, well before they find themselves in a life-or-death fight, miles and many minutes from help. Of course, the street is inescapably uncertain. No officer is guaranteed backup on every call, and even the best-trained officer can be laid low. The controlled combat used in the academy inculcates recruits with an understanding of the harsh and potentially fatal nature of their work and a powerful certainty: If they hope to survive, they can never, ever give up the fight.

The Good Shoot

In addition to training that solidifies the danger imperative's preoccupation with officer safety among recruits and stresses the necessity of their commitment to using violence, modern academies also employ virtual simulations to train recruits how to use and justify that violence. Using high-resolution video and simulation firearms, extensive libraries of scenarios provide a plethora of visual and auditory stimuli to which trainees must adapt on the fly. Often referred to as "shoot/don't shoot" training, these video simulations, which are given not only to academy recruits but also to sworn officers during periodic in-service training, disproportionately feature suspects attacking officers with fists, knives, blunt object, and guns. These scenarios force trainees to make split-second decisions about whether a suspect poses a threat that justifies the use of lethal force. They also provide opportunities for recruits to learn and practice justifications for the use of their firearms in line with policy and law that resonate with the danger imperative.

The Sunshine academy's PRISim simulator was set up in a squat building adjacent to a 250-foot shooting range. The system comes

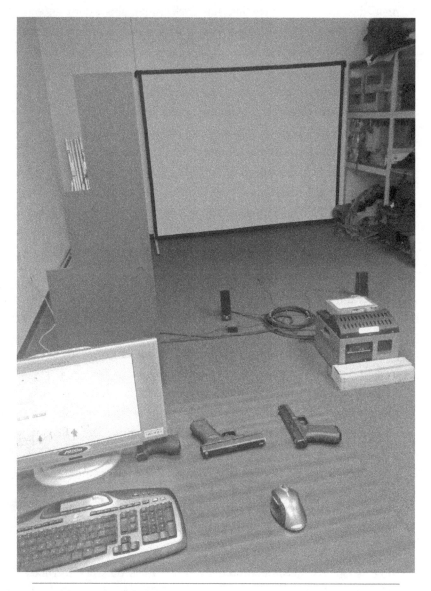

FIGURE 1.3 Virtual force simulation training setup and infrared pistols at the Sunshine police academy. During virtual training, an academy instructor sits at the monitor and controls the video scenarios shown to trainees.

preloaded with more than five hundred unique shoot/don't shoot scenarios that can be projected onto a flat screen. According to the PRISim's manufacturer, this technology can re-create the "judgement calls, indecision, sudden fear, partial understanding, blind side surprise and eye-blink response . . . that conditions the trainee for survival."[58] While some scenarios capture common calls for service like disturbances at homes or stores, others are the stuff of nightmares: an active shooter in a school, an infant held at knifepoint, or a fellow police officer held hostage by a gunman. Across these hundreds of scenarios, there is one constant: any of them might turn deadly in the blink of an eye. Though most officers will never be shot or shoot their weapon in the line of duty, such virtual scenario training requires officers to confront and practice their reactions to these rare, deadly confrontations again and again.[59]

During a day of firearms in-service training, Officer Baker, dressed in a red, long-sleeved instructor's shirt, was charged with administering PRISim training. From where he sat behind the officers going through the training, Baker could manipulate the encounter by selecting from various video "branches" to change how on-screen subjects behaved. Unlike a purely linear video with a single outcome, these branches allow instructors to change the simulation and force trainees to readjust based on whether a suspect surrendered, fled, or fought.

Officer Stuart was up last that day, and Baker allowed me to act as his "partner" in the simulation. Baker stipulated that I allow Stuart to take "primary" on the calls since I had seen the scenarios play out a dozen times. I agreed and awkwardly stuffed an infrared pistol in my right pocket to simulate a holster, taking up a position to Stuart's left. As the simulation began, we arrived on scene to what radio dispatch described as a "fight brewing" between a tenant and their landlord. Two white men were shouting at each other outside a neat, white house on a clear blue day. Snatches of their argument carried, with words like "rent" and "pay" becoming clearer as we drew closer. The man closer to us appeared to be the tenant and was standing at the foot of the front porch, shouting up at the presumed landlord on the porch.

Stuart called out, telling everyone to calm down and then asking the tenant to step away from the porch and come with him—separating arguing parties is a common strategy to create space for tempers to cool. The landlord barked angrily, "Deal with this guy, because if you don't deal with him, I will!" then stormed back into the house. That caught Stuart's attention, and he ordered the landlord to come back outside. When the man emerged from the house, he held a black-barreled shotgun. The tenant fled as Stuart drew his pistol, took aim, and yelled, "Put it down! Drop it!" Moments later, before the landlord could drop the shotgun or raise it to fire, Stuart let off two shots, striking him squarely in the chest.

FIGURE 1.4 Two SPD officers, armed with infrared simulation pistols, take part in virtual force simulation training during in-service training.

The video in the PRISim simulator froze, two blue dots shining on the landlord's chest where Stuart's infrared pistol shots landed. I asked Stuart what he was thinking when he shot, and he walked me through his perceptions of threat and how they justified his decision to use deadly force. "Our presence is already there," he began. "We talked to him before he went back in the house. He made the choice to go back in and back out with a gun. Him walking out with a gun is already a threat. I gave him a verbal command to drop it, he didn't, and at that point I would fear for my life."

Without explicitly invoking it, Stuart's justification was aimed at fulfilling the legal standard set in *Graham v. Connor*, the 1989 Supreme Court case that enshrined the perception of the "reasonable officer on the scene" as the benchmark by which to judge the constitutionality of police violence. Under this "reasonableness" standard, Stuart's perception (or that of any officer) is compared to what a prototypically reasonable officer would have perceived in identical circumstances. The question at hand is not whether that perception is accurate—the Court explicitly wrote that officer perception must not be judged "with the 20/20 vision of hindsight." Whether a person shot by an officer was, in fact, a threat is superseded by the altogether different question of whether a reasonable officer would have perceived that person as a lethal threat.[60]

Drawing on this underlying logic of reasonableness, Baker began his debrief of Stuart's performance. "I don't have a real problem with that one," he said, even though he had selected a scenario branch in which the man would *not* raise and fire the weapon at Stuart. The fact that the suspect came out with a weapon was, in and of itself, justification for the use of lethal force. "The idea on this scenario is that the guy doesn't pick the gun up at you," Baker continued. "But then again," he asked rhetorically, "who walks in when two cops are standing out there, grabs a shotgun, and walks back out again? With a gun?"

From Baker's perspective, the presence of a weapon represents a lethal *possibility* that any reasonable officer would be justified in addressing with lethal force. "[The scenario] can go two different ways. When he pulls the shotgun up, how long does it take? Not even a half a second. It's about a quarter to a half a second for him to go from that position to getting that shotgun downrange. I won't critique that shot. That was reasonable."

Unlike in the real world, where it is impossible to know whether someone holding a firearm will or will not try to shoot at an officer, Baker knew that the gunman on screen would not raise the weapon. That the landlord did not raise his weapon—that he *wouldn't* have, if Stuart waited a few moments longer—does not change that he *could* have fired at any moment. This scenario and others like it teach recruits and experienced officers alike that the very possibility of a firearm being raised justifies their use of lethal force.

Similar training was used in the Elmont Police Department. The EPD's simulation training takes place in a portable, forty-eight-foot tractor trailer retrofitted with a bullet trap and soundproofing. Unlike the SPD's simulator, this "shoot trailer" enables officers to shoot live rounds at a paper screen onto which prerecorded video scenarios are projected. The combination of video and live fire, the shoot trailer's marketing materials boasted, allowed trainees to answer two questions that are core to the legal and practical reality of every deadly force decision: "Am I justified?" and "Can I make the shot?" I observed Detectives Kelly and Tomlinson go through several scenarios under the watchful eyes of Officers Cisneros and Ochoa, both academy instructors with experience in narcotics enforcement and SWAT.

Kelly stood on the left, about six feet in front of me, in a pantsuit and ponytail. Tomlinson, a broad-shouldered man whose purple tie was the only splash of color in his all-black outfit, stood to her right. Both were wearing over-the-ear hearing protection and ballistic glasses. The lights in the trailer were turned off, leaving only the bright glow of the screen some twenty feet ahead of the detectives. Unlike other firearms and use-of-force training I observed, both detectives drew their firearm before the start of each video scenario.

Though preemptively drawing a firearm is not the standard response to the vast majority of service calls, shoot trailer training intentionally confronts officers with situations that can (or should) be addressed with lethal force. Knowing this, Kelly and Tomlinson unholstered their weapons well before they observed any potential threats.

The first scenario was a traffic stop. In the video, the on-screen officer explained to the driver that there was a warrant for his arrest. When the driver questioned, "You sure you got the right guy?" he was asked to step out of the car. He grumbled but otherwise complied. As he exited the vehicle, Kelly spotted the grip of a pistol in his waistband. She called to Tomlinson, "Weapon in his back, weapon in his back." Tomlinson commanded the driver to put his hands over his head at the same time that the on-screen officer told the driver to turn around. The driver asked if he was going to jail. When the on-screen officer confirmed that he was under arrest, the interaction shifted sharply. "I don't think so!" shouted the driver defiantly as he grabbed for his pistol. Kelly and Tomlinson opened fire.

In the enclosed trailer, each gunshot filled the trailer with a bright muzzle flash and a tangible, momentary increase in pressure. The video simulator, designed to pause the video after a predetermined number of shots, was now frozen, with five black holes punched through the paper screen by the detectives' bullets. Three had hit the suspect, all below the chest where officers are trained to place their shots. Two shots missed.

After instructing the detectives to holster their weapons, Ochoa began a quick debrief. In addition to telling the detectives that they should yell much louder when calling out "Gun!" or other threats, Ochoa suggested they be sure to fire at vital areas to ensure the suspect is "neutralized." He praised the detectives for striking the suspect in the lower extremities three times but said, "He's still in the fight at that point. You want to go center mass to make sure you neutralize the threat effectively."

Like officers who discuss deadly force as "shooting to stop" instead of "shooting to kill," Ochoa's use of the word "neutralize" is little more than a euphemism to distance officers from the brutal consequences of their decision to use deadly force. There is no practical distinction between "neutralize" and "kill" when shooting bullets at a human's "center mass," home to the heart, the lungs, and the dense network of arteries and nerves that keep the body running.[61]

Kelly and Tomlinson's final scenario was also a traffic stop. Though not explicitly stated, the scenario hearkened to the infamous Dinkheller video shown to EPD recruits and in police academies across the country. The scenario began, and almost immediately the driver exited his red pickup truck, palpably angry. "I'm fucking telling you, I'm fed up with this shit!" he cried out. "Back off. Fuck you. I'm telling you right now, I'm gonna, I'm gonna fucking get you!" Tomlinson told the man to relax, then shouted to Kelly, "He's going back to the car!"

"Watch his hands! Watch his hands!" she replied as the driver reached into the back of his truck's cab and struggled with something. For only an instant, what appeared to be the wooden stock of a rifle or shotgun peeked out through the car door. Kelly and Tomlinson opened fire, each getting off two rounds.

"Good," said Ochoa as the lights came on. His first question was standard shorthand for the legal and ethical test that hums in the background of every police shooting: "Was it a good shoot?" Neither detective hesitated to say it was, and Ochoa earnestly agreed: "Good shoot." Then he detailed all of the evidence—the articulable facts—that supported the objective reasonableness of the detectives' decision to shoot. "The guy gave you all the tells in the world. He was loud, he was being aggressive, he made direct threats, and then he went into the car." Even so, the video had paused before the driver could finish pulling out the object stuck in the back of his truck. Ochoa posed a crucial question that highlighted the uncertainty inherent to split-second force decisions: "What if that was a Gibson guitar, not a rifle?"

Tomlinson laughed: "Fuck, if someone came at me with a guitar, I'd shoot them, too!" Ochoa chuckled back: "Well, for what it's worth, it's an M870 [shotgun]."

Ochoa knew the eventual outcome of the video scenario: the driver would pull out a shotgun and attack the officers. From his perspective, Tomlinson's decision was a correctly calculated gamble. But for Tomlinson, a veteran officer who had gone through academy and in-service training throughout his career, the fact that the driver was armed with a shotgun was incidental. A guitar—and really any other object—can be used to attack an officer. As recruits learned in the academy and sworn officers were reminded through in-service training, officer perception is reality.

GRADUATION

Recruits who convince instructors of their ability and willingness to use violence are allowed to graduate the police academy. In 2016, local reporting described an EPD graduation ceremony that took place in the auditorium of a local high school located just a few blocks from the academy. Throughout the ceremony, police executives and local politicians spoke of the great promise shown by the soon-to-be police officers, all seated in full uniform complete with hat and ceremonial white gloves. An assistant chief congratulated the graduates on joining the great profession of policing, and a member of the Elmont Police Commission said they looked forward to new officers connecting with the local community, including students in schools. A U.S. senator urged the graduating class to be role models in the communities they would serve, and a state representative reminded them of their duty to commit themselves to the ideals of community policing.[62]

Along with celebration and optimism, there was recognition of the danger that the newest class of EPD officers would face. In her remarks, the mayor of Elmont praised the EPD for recent progress in forging relationships with the Elmont community. She also noted that police officers had been targets of senseless violence and assured the graduates seated behind her that she and those present all recognized the immense responsibility they took on when they donned their uniform. After she concluded, the audience was treated to a video that took them inside the police academy where their sons and daughters had been for the past seven months.

That year's video, shot and edited by academy staff, began with a voiceover taken from *American Sniper*, the Hollywood biopic about Chris Kyle, the infamous sniper whose autobiography detailed his fondness for the ultraviolent Punisher antihero esteemed by many police. The words were inspired by *On Combat*, the book written by Lt. Col. Dave Grossman that made its way into EPD academy presentations. They laid out the violent, romantic typology of defenseless sheep, predatory wolves, and the noble sheepdogs whose ranks the newly minted EPD officers would join.

There are three types of people in this world: sheep, wolves, and sheepdogs.

Some people prefer to believe that evil doesn't exist in the world. And if it ever darkened their doorstep, they wouldn't know how to protect themselves Those are the sheep.

And then you've got predators who use violence to prey on the weak. They are the wolves.

And then there are those who've been blessed with the gift of aggression and the overpowering need to protect the flock. These men are a rare breed that live to confront the wolf. They are the sheepdog.[63]

The academy class's logo came after to solidify their newfound status as valiant protectors. Two snarling dogs flanked a police shield topped with the words "With It or On It," a phrase drawn from the ancient, war-loving Spartans popularized in the 2006 film *300*.[64] Beneath the shield, which was edited to resemble that carried by King Leonidas and his troops in the film, was the class's moniker: Sheepdogs.

The next eight and a half minutes of the video were a whirlwind of heavy metal music, hip-hop, and the most extreme facets of recruits' training: high-speed driving, hand-to-hand combat, and grueling workouts flashed on-screen. The crash of drums and distorted guitar from Disturbed's *Indestructible* blared over footage of firearms training shot via officer-mounted cameras and remote-controlled drones. The song's lyrics, which describe an invincible and righteous warrior who triumphs over his terrified and broken enemies, boomed in step with the violent ethos woven through the entirety of the academy. Though there were brief glimpses in the video of community policing and service emphasized in the EPD's public messaging—seventeen seconds, to be exact—it was the use of violence that defined it. Similar videos were shown at WPD graduations and used in the EPD and SPD's recruitment programs to attract new generations of officers.

Rather than being secreted away or hidden from view, violence was openly celebrated at the EPD graduation in front of community members, local politicians, and the news media. For recruits' family and friends, the video was also proof that their loved one— an untrained recruit only months before—was now transformed. Through the burn of OC spray and the fire of physical combat, they had learned the skills and mindset necessary to hold the thin blue line between order and chaos. Now, armed with the myriad tools and techniques of violence, they were ready to ensure they returned home from their noble work. They were ready to survive.

2

GHOSTS OF THE FALLEN

Each of Elmont's police districts has its own substation—a holdover from a push for community policing to address distrust of police in the 1980s and 1990s. But the heart of the EPD's operations is its hulking headquarters near the city's downtown. A remnant of brutalist architecture that fell out of fashion by the 1980s, the building's sharp corners and wide, windowless walls loom over the surrounding streets. The bland, tan façade of the building is undecorated save for a ten-foot-tall re-creation of the EPD shield affixed to the wall adjacent to the main entrance.

During the day, a steady stream of visitors walks beneath that shield and through the swinging glass doors at the building's front. Once someone enters the lobby, they wait in a line to speak to an officer through an intercom embedded in a wall of bulletproof glass. Some residents come looking for a copy of a police report. These petitioners are usually directed to a phone affixed to the wall left of the intercom; the phone has no number pad because it automatically dials into the department's records division when it's taken off its hook. Others come to inquire about how they can acquire a pistol permit. They are informed of the next time a folding table will be set up in the lobby so that residents can be fingerprinted by a private company as part of their permit application. Still others come to the lobby to report being victims of a crime or to inquire about an ongoing case.

They may be met in the lobby by an officer who will take their report, or they may be not so subtly dismissed with the vague promise that a detective will reach out to them.

At night, the visitors disappear and the walk up the wide steps to EPD headquarters is a lonely one. Some areas outside the EPD are illuminated with harsh floodlights. Where their light doesn't reach, the shadows are especially deep. I made my way through the shadows and up the steps into the lobby of EPD headquarters on a clear, cold evening in early 2015. I settled onto the same wooden bench where I'd seen many residents wait under the buzzing glow of fluorescent lights. That night, the lobby was empty of any Elmont residents. Whereas the daylight hours were filled with the loud buzz and clack of security doors unlocking as officers moved in and out of the department's restricted area, the lobby was still and quiet. But like anyone who stepped into the lobby of EPD headquarters, I was not alone. I was watched by dead men.

Under the words "Above and Beyond the Call of Duty," the black-and-white portraits of every Elmont police officer killed in the line of duty were arranged in neat rows. For those fallen officers without a photograph on record, their frames displayed an image of the Elmont Police Department shield from the era in which the officer was killed. Beneath each name and face, a burnished plaque detailed the circumstances of their death, serving as reminders of the danger inherent to policing. Most had been killed in accidents since the inception of the department in the late nineteenth century: a fall down an elevator shaft claimed one officer and motor vehicle accidents killed several more.

Others had met with a violent end. Officer Collela was shot three times while pursuing a burglary suspect in 1935. Mortally wounded, he was rushed to a nearby hospital where he was able to identify his killer before expiring. St. Mark's, the hospital where he and other EPD officers breathed their last, still stands on Bishop Street, a handful of city blocks from the district's substation where officers type up reports on a desktop computer or use the bathroom during their shift.

Other plaques describe an officer's violent end in grisly detail. Officer Riccardo, who had died recently enough to be remembered by veteran officers in the present day, was shot in the face while attempting to interrupt a drug transaction. The bullet pierced Riccardo's cheek, tore through his esophagus, and then shattered the top of his spine. Though he survived the immediate aftermath of being shot, he succumbed years later to complications from his injuries.

Walls like the one in Elmont can be found across the country, in departments of all sizes. In Wake Forest, North Carolina, a town of just over 42,000, three slabs of stone stand outside the Wake Forest Police Department's main station. The middle slab is dark gray and is carved with a golden WFPD shield and a bible verse: "Greater love hath no man than this, that a man lay down his life for his friends." On the left, under "Dedicated to Those Who Made the Ultimate Sacrifice," the names of the three WFPD officers killed on duty are inscribed in softer, light gray stone.[1]

Chicago's memorial wall, a band of black granite on which fallen officers' names are written, is the centerpiece of a five-acre, $3.5 million memorial park nestled east of Soldier Field and Lakeshore Drive. A yearly candlelight vigil for fallen officers is held adjacent to the wall and the "sacrifice space" where their names are inscribed. The police memorial is dedicated to Gold Star Families, bearing the same name given to the honorific bestowed on the kin of soldiers killed while serving their country.[2]

But memorial walls are only the most evident commemorations of fallen officers. Within the halls of the police department, a diverse and largely hidden world of cultural artifacts—the tangible reflections of policing's orienting assumptions and values—are used by police to commemorate their dead.[3] Along with rituals like fundraiser barbecues, memorial 5k runs, and public monuments at the local, state, and federal level, a vast array of clothing, pictures, songs, poetry, and countless other commemorative artifacts pervade police officers' professional and personal lives. Difficult to see from anywhere but within the police department itself, these artifacts are crucial for mourning and healing after a violent death shreds the fabric of social life.

But the rituals and symbols of commemoration do more than honor the memory of the fallen. As much as commemorative artifacts valorize those who pay the ultimate price, they also provide grim and conspicuous evidence of the violence to which all officers, regardless of where they patrol, may fall prey. The curated images and words that make up these artifacts also re-create and reenergize the fraternity—the brotherhood knowable only to the initiated—that ties officers to one another within and across departments.[4]

This solidarity is central to a heroic vision of police as the selfless few chosen and trained to stand on the "thin blue line" between civilization and anarchy.[5] Regardless of the city or town name engraved on their badge, officers are united across space and time by the specter of violence that threads through the multigenerational wars on crime, drugs, and terror. Across departments, commemoration of the fallen is proof to the living that this endless struggle is not only a valorous sacrifice to safeguard the streets they patrol but also a noble and necessary fight for the survival of the nation. Surrounded by concrete proof that this deadly struggle against criminals and omnipresent threat continues unabated, today's police are conscripted into the same forever war that claimed the lives of their honored predecessors.

THE WALLS THAT BIND

Pursuant to a joint resolution of Congress in 1962, President John F. Kennedy proclaimed May 15 as Peace Officers Memorial Day. The entire week in which May 15 falls was designated as Police Week.[6] Beginning in 1982, a yearly memorial service was held in Washington, DC, to honor officers killed in the line of duty. Today, the memorial service, organized by the Fraternal Order of Police (FOP) and the Fraternal Order of Police Auxiliary (FOPA), takes place on the western lawn of the U.S. Capitol.[7] At night, tens of thousands gather within sight of the Washington Memorial's 555-foot obelisk for a candlelight vigil; after sundown, a sea of tiny flames dance across the National Mall, each one held in the hands of someone who came to honor the fallen.

Less than a mile away, the National Law Enforcement Memorial sits in the heart of Judiciary Square. The three-acre memorial is enclosed by two 304-foot-long marble walls; the names of more than 22,000 local, state, and federal officers dating back to 1786 are carved into the blue-gray stone. The wall, guarded by massive bronze lions, is a dramatic physical record of the officers killed in the line of duty for more than two hundred years, uniting their sacrifice under a shared and sacred banner.

The national memorial was born in violence. In 1991, the year the memorial was dedicated, the U.S. homicide rate reached its historical zenith.[8] At the memorial's dedication ceremony, President George H. W. Bush spoke at length about the nation's police as "forgotten heroes," lauding their profound sacrifice. He recalled the words of President Calvin Coolidge, "The nation which forgets its defenders will itself be forgotten." He promised, "We will not forget. America will not forget."

But remembrance of the fallen was not enough. He also warned of the of the war raging on American streets. To win that war and protect the officers fighting it, he declared, new, more severe punishment for lawbreakers was required.

> There is a war going on out there, a war between criminals and a good society. We know that war will not end as long as evil dwells in men's souls. But we can work to lock up those who are too violent to live in civilized society. And we can support the law enforcement officers who are on the front lines saving us every single day of our lives. And we can put new laws on the books to keep new names off of these walls.[9]

Echoes of this never-ending war and proof of its bloody toll reverberate in the present. Like the stone or wood stelae used in ancient societies to commemorate the dead, police memorial walls across Elmont, West River, and Sunshine venerate officers killed in the line of duty. They also connect these disparate deaths across space and time into a cohesive history of violence.[10]

The purpose of these walls extends beyond remembrance. On its surface, every wall is an homage to the departed, a small token of gratitude and respect for those who have lost their lives in public service. It is also a cautionary totem of that department's organizational memory and a reminder of the sacrifice made by those officers who came—and died—before. Assistant Chief Altidore, a round man with salt-and-pepper hair trimmed high and tight, explained to me that memorial walls served as both a commemoration and a warning of the danger that no officer can afford to forget.

"I think in a lot of ways, it stands there to remind you . . . that your job is a dangerous job and that the end result can be the ultimate sacrifice, the sacrifice of your own life," he told me. "It serves as a reminder. Not just to remember them, but to also remember the job and the dangers and how to carry yourself as a police officer, how to make sure that you're safe and that your partners are safe and that you end up going home at night and not end up in a casket."

West River's wall has no faces. Alongside a short flight of stairs that leads down into the bowels of the department, the WPD's memorial wall is a stark expanse of black marble topped by a large-scale WPD shield. A black mourning band permanently crosses it. Under the shield and the words "In Tribute to West River Police Officers Who Have Given Their Lives in the Line of Duty," the wall is engraved with the name and "end of watch" date of every WPD officer killed in the line of duty since the department's founding more than 150 years ago. The contrast between dark marble and white lettering bears a striking resemblance to the Vietnam War Memorial in Washington, DC.

The day I arrived in the WPD, an American flag was draped over a small podium at the foot of the wall. Taped to the wall were four red flowers, a gift from a local woman who for decades had brought flowers to WPD headquarters to honor fallen officers. On the right side of the wall was a large wreath of white flowers with a blue "In Loving Memory" ribbon cutting across it. The wreath was placed there a few weeks before, during the yearly memorial service that brought hundreds of WPD officers, friends, family members, and city residents to the foot of the wall. During the service, a children's choir sang renditions of Josh Groban's "Thankful" and Rascal Flatts's "I Won't Let Go" to an audence of officers wearing dress uniforms and snowy white gloves.

For Lt. McWilliams, an experienced SWAT officer and academy instructor well versed in tactics and the practical concerns of officer survival, the wall was a means to honor the fallen and remind officers of the infinitely high price their work may exact. The wall, he said, "is really to kind of pay homage to those that made that type of sacrifice. It's respecting so that they're not forgotten." At the same time, the wall was also a tangible link between the WPD's dangerous past and present. "It's not just for the fellow officers or the people that knew them," he said. "There is a historical perspective. It's one of the things we talk to our academy classes about. As you're getting your head wrapped around doing this job, you need to realize that it's not going to be all sunshine and daisies. Take a look at that wall. Those were all good folks that started off sitting in a chair just like you did." Should any recruit or officer need a reminder of just how dangerous their chosen profession is, they need only gaze upon the dozens of names carved into the WPD.

Two names on the WPD wall, Emmanuel Randolph and Timothy Daiyo, were especially meaningful to McWilliams. Randolph, a beloved department veteran, and Daiyo, a rising young star, were murdered during a SWAT operation to apprehend an armed and barricaded suspect. As a member of the SWAT team himself, McWilliams was as close as one possibly could be to Randolph and Daiyo's deaths, both personally and professionally. In the years following their deaths, McWilliams took it upon himself to honor his friends' sacrifice by providing training to WPD recruits, officers, and other police agencies on the events and tactical decisions that preceded his friends' murders.

"[You find a] silver lining in the tragedy," he explained to me. "You try to assign some meaning to their deaths, because the short version is the entire thing could have been prevented. . . . Here is the sacrifice they made and here is what we can do to try to honor that with the idea that it won't happen again, or at least we can try and mitigate the odds of it happening if people listen to this debrief."

Lessons were also taken from the honored dead in Sunshine. Academy instructors recount to SPD recruits how Officer Harold Patterson was ambushed and killed when he continued to pursue a suspect of whom he'd lost sight, and the department's foot pursuit policy was amended to prevent such deaths in the future. In addition to his name being inscribed in the SPD's main memorial—a public plaza anchored around bronze statues paid for by local donations and grants from the Bureau of Justice Assistance—one of the SPD's sub-stations is named after him.

Inside that substation's lobby, Patterson's death was front and center. A large color portrait hung on a wall in the waiting area above a plaque that read "It Is Not How This Man Died That Made Him a Hero, It Is How He Lived His Life." But it was in an adjacent hallway that his death lived on most starkly. The hallway itself was nonde-script—fluorescent lighting and unremarkable gray carpet that could have been in any office building. The walls, however, were covered in vivid reminders of the pain that rocked the SPD when Patterson was killed. Every four feet, framed newspapers chronicled Patterson's murder and its emotional toll. The images were heart-wrenching. In one, an SPD officer leaned on a chain-link fence near where Pat-terson died, forehead resting on one arm in grief or disbelief. Articles covering Patterson's funeral immortalized the sorrow of the day: an officer wiped tears from his eyes, Patterson's mother wept on her hus-band's shoulder, and two officers embraced in mourning.

Another article placed Patterson's death in the broader history of death in the SPD, listing him alongside other SPD officers who had been killed in the line of duty over the course of a century. Patterson's death, like theirs, was a reminder that, as the chief of the SPD at the time put it, "we, too, may have to make the ultimate sacrifice to ensure the safety of this great city." The president of the SPD union echoed the sentiment: "It's a reminder to us that you leave home every day, kiss your wife goodbye, and think you'll come home, and your family thinks the same thing."[11] Like all those that came before and all that would come after, Patterson's death laid bare that some never return home. For any who doubt the gravity of their chosen profession, they need only look to those enshrined on the walls of the department.

PERSONAL EFFECTS

Memorial walls are the most evident artifacts created to commemorate the fallen and remind the living of policing's life-or-death stakes. They are publicly accessible and can be viewed by passersby. Whether or not someone has a personal connection to the department or its officers, anyone can look upon those who died in the line of duty. But these walls are only the most conspicuous memorials used by police to honor their dead. Besides the static marble and framed portraits of memorial walls created and maintained by the department, officers curate their own commemorative artifacts that tie them to the fallen, their department, and the omnipresent threat of death.

These commemorations are not visible to the public. They are displayed in the depths of the department and rarely seen except by police themselves. Lieutenant Karlson, a tall, balding man who joked about how politically liberal he was compared to most officers in the department, had an office in a cramped hallway on the third floor of EPD headquarters. A sign in honor of two officers killed on duty was displayed outside his office.

The white sign was unassuming. The names of two fallen officers—Officer Denali and Officer Riccardo—were written below flowery blue script that read "In Memory Of" between two EPD shields. The bottom third of the sign is taken up by "Never Forget," also in blue. Karlson had saved the sign after a memorial fundraiser or "Signal 4" in honor of the fallen officers, an allusion to the EPD's radio code for "officer needs assistance." Similar fundraisers are held across the country by individual departments, police unions, and nonprofits to raise money for the families of officers killed in the line of duty.[12]

The two officers named on the sign died for unrelated reasons. Denali, just a few years away from being eligible to retire with a full pension, was killed after being struck by a car while he directed traffic. Riccardo, a second-generation EPD officer, died from medical complications stemming from the gunshot wound he had sustained years earlier during a narcotics investigation. At the time I saw the sign, both officers had been dead for more than a decade. Nonetheless, both of these officers' deaths—one an accident and the other a slow-motion murder—attested in the starkest possible terms to the unpredictability and potential lethality of policing. Several years after his death, Riccardo's nephew Matthew became the third generation of his family to wear an EPD badge. He continues to walk the halls his uncle once did, a living, breathing reminder of the Riccardo whose name and face were displayed on the wall of police headquarters.

Besides displaying the sign outside his office, Karlson also carried tangible reminders of death and the danger of policework everywhere he went. On his wrist, he wore two bracelets. The first was a black-and-blue silicone bracelet modeled on the "thin blue line" frequently featured on flags, T-shirts, hats, dog tags, bumper stickers, and other accessories sported by officers and their supporters.[13] Every year, he would place a bulk order for around fifty bracelets from the National Law Enforcement Memorial to give out to other EPD officers who wanted one, he told me. "Guys like 'em," he said. "As a kind of . . . reminder." I asked him of what they were a reminder. He responded, "People that have died; the dangers of this profession."

Karlson's second bracelet was a nondescript steel cuff that he wore in honor of a fellow officer killed during a SWAT training exercise at the department where he began his career. Nearly twenty years after his friend's death, he told me that the memory of that day would always come with "an image and a smell and a sound" that was now a part of him. "To this day," he said, "if I hear a 308-caliber rifle go off, it sends chills down my spine." Though this death was an accident, it was still part and parcel of an occupation shaped by a preoccupation with violence and death. Karlson explained that the training during which his friend and colleague was killed "was preparing us for the worst. It was after 9/11. We were doing bus entries and he felt that if a terrorist attack would come, it would be at the schools or the busses the next time. . . . Even though it is friendly fire, he's still doing something to prepare his men . . . to be safe in their job." This death, though accidental, was still proof of the costs that police bear in their endless toil against violence.

Commemorative artifacts like bracelets were not worn exclusively by the "guys" in the department. Though women make up less than 13 percent of officers nationwide and continue to face gender discrimination and sexual harassment, they are not excluded from policing's cultural reverence for fallen officers or the danger imperative that this reverence solidifies.[14] Women like Assistant Chief Raynes, the only woman on the EPD's command staff at the time, also displayed artifacts, including bracelets, to commemorate the fallen. Raynes, a slight woman with dirty blonde hair always pulled back into a bun, grew up in Fulton, a small city of about sixty thousand located a thirty-minute drive from Elmont. Before joining the EPD, she worked at a hospital and had ambitions of becoming a nurse. While there, she came across a job ad put out by the EPD. A desire to help others and encouragement from her colleagues pushed her to apply. After joining the department in 1998, she worked her way from the patrol division through a wide range of roles, including investigations, internal affairs, and the training division, eventually being promoted to the rank of assistant chief more than twenty years after entering the academy.

Like other officers, Raynes spoke of fallen officers—including those who had died in the distant past—with a quiet but no less genuine respect. When telling me about her memorial bracelet, she explained that every officer killed in an EPD uniform died, in some way, in the service of others. She told me, "They're a hero, in a sense that they sacrificed their life trying to help other people. So, for that reason, I think that they should be remembered." After all, she said, "How many other people do you know that would give their life for a complete stranger?"

By the same token, every death honored by her bracelet highlighted the omnipresent possibility of her own death. "When someone dies in the line of duty, even if it's briefly, you think about your own mortality," she said. When walking into EPD headquarters building before starting one's shift, she said, "You realize that they were killed senselessly, usually for doing the exact thing that you're going to be asked to do in an hour, two hours, [or] tomorrow."

Along with artifacts that commemorate fallen officers en masse, others are created and displayed in memory of specific officers killed in the line of duty. In West River, WPD officers displayed a host of commemorative artifacts following the murder of officers Randolph and Daiyo. In an office space near the back of the WPD's eastern station, seized firearms were hung on the wall in custom wooden frames. Several were assault rifles like the one used to kill Daiyo and Randolph. Across from where the rifles hung, Sgt. Belmont had decorated his office with poignant reminders of his fallen friends. Two shadow boxes that a nearby agency had donated to the WPD in honor of Daiyo and Randolph hung on his office wall. Two ballistic helmets like the ones they wore on the day they were killed sat on the bottom row of a bookshelf. A shortened version of the fallen officers' first names—Emm and Tim—were painted in blue on the back of each helmet. Belmont told me that the helmets came from within the surviving ranks of the SWAT team of which he, Randolph, and Daiyo were part.

At several desks near Belmont's office, officers displayed the funeral pamphlets from Randolph's and Daiyo's funeral services. A commemorative postcard showed both officers' faces under the words "Heroes Live Forever." It also displayed a poem titled "The Wall" (author unknown), a reference to the memorial wall in the lobby of the WPD headquarters where Daiyo's and Randolph's names are engraved:

On this Wall are the names of heroic men
A sacrifice like no other, they fought until the bitter end

They are all heroes some were sons, some were fathers, husbands too
We won't forget what they did, they gave their lives for me and you

Everyday they go out to make it safe for you and me
And they know that today, might be the day they don't foresee

They all are heroes some were sons, some were fathers, husbands too
We won't forget what they did, they gave their lives for me and you

God bless the cops in uniform. God bless them every single day
May no more names go on this Wall is what we pray for on this day

No more heroes, no more sons, no more fathers, husbands too
We won't forget what they did, they gave their lives for me and you

Another desk displayed a collection of newspaper clippings and pictures of Daiyo and Randolph that had been combined into a memorial collage. The clipping at the top of the collage read "Duty, Honor." The officer's own words, printed and neatly cut from printer paper with scissors, framed the bottom of the collage: "Gone but never forgotten. Rest In Peace Brothers."

Commemorative artifacts can also be found in officers' homes. Nearly a decade after Randolph and Daiyo were murdered, Officer Summers's memory of that day—what she called "the longest day I've ever had"—was seared into her. She recalled the surreal haze that washed over her and other officers who gathered at the hospital to stand together amid the unthinkable. She remembered seeing officers drenched in Randolph's and Daiyo's blood and the sight of their lifeless bodies. Her voice broke as she remembered the sight of brain matter stuck in the boots of a surviving SWAT officer.

To remember her friends and heal from the pain of their loss, she erected a small shrine near the bar area of her home, adding slowly to it over the years. She placed the same memorial postcard displayed by other WPD officers inside a black frame decorated with "the boys!" in silvery script. Two rubber duckies in police uniform sat next to a black silicone bracelet inscribed with "Band of Brothers" and a commemorative coin engraved with the WPD shield and the fallen officers' badge numbers. Two small U.S. flags, a single yellow rose, and a flag from the National Police Unity Tour—a yearly cycling fundraiser in honor of officers killed in the line of duty—stood over a funeral pamphlet from Daiyo's funeral.

"I'll never forget that day. I'll never forget them," she told me. "And it's all of us. We all dealt with it. We felt like a family." Though the pain of Randolph's and Daiyo's deaths would never completely vanish, it had dulled with time. Her shrine, she explained, was no longer laden only with sadness. "Every once in a while, you just kind of glance over at it and it's, like, it makes me happy. It doesn't make me sad anymore to look at it. So, it just, you know, kind of reminded me of them in a good way." At the same time, the objects gathered and displayed to commemorate her friends are a reminder of the violence that may yet find her or her fellow officers, a cautionary message to, as she said, "Remember: Don't get complacent in this job. Remember to appreciate your friends and family because this could be the last day. You don't know."

Summers also commemorated Randolph and Daiyo in her flesh. She had a tattoo on her wrist, a small "thin blue line" banner with the date her friends were killed. She told me that other officers had similar tattoos; members of the SWAT team were tattooed with the WPD SWAT crest and the fallen officers' badge numbers. Sergeant Belano, still a member of the SWAT team when we met at a SWAT training day, tattooed his entire back in memory of his fallen friends and teammates. Some of the tattoos were more general symbols: an eagle for patriotism and bravery, a set of scales for justice. Others were specific to Randolph's and Daiyo's lives and deaths: arrows like those on the WPD SWAT crest, the date of their deaths, and a rose for each of them. Along with a metal commemoration bracelet he had worn every day for a decade, his tattoos helped him process the murders. "I wanted to remember it," he said. "Just for me personally, it helps me get past it a little better instead of just hide it away or bury it somewhere. So, after my grieving process, then it was more of remembering who they were and all the good things they did. That helped transform that grieving process into more of a way to deal with it, just remembering who they were." Where some might try to forget in the hope of escaping their pain, Belano's chosen commemorations preserved the memory of his friends among the living, moving with and connecting him to his fellow officers, the WPD, and its history of deadly violence.

BLUE BLOOD

Commemoration of officers killed in the line of duty reinvigorates the bonds among officers and helps assuage the pain of losing a friend and colleague. But the power of commemoration is not restricted to the department that has lost one of its own. Commemorative artifacts and the fallen officers for whom they are wrought also connect the living and their departments to the policing occupation, what sociologist Peter Manning has described as "the corporate body of policemen."[15] Though every officer wears the name of a particular town, city, or state on their uniform, the unique constraints of their work bind them to one another and set them apart from the public that threatens to do them harm.

In contrast to highly localized artifacts that emphasize a department's unique and painful loss, extralocal commemorations connect discrete, otherwise unrelated deaths across geographic space. Either by connecting a local death to the broader occupation of policing or by treating distant deaths as one of their own, these artifacts subsume all police deaths into the broader occupational assumptions of police work, including the danger and violence that may find any officer, anywhere, at any time. Every officer's death, be it in a rural backwater or in the heart of a metropolis, is understood as an assault on the institution of policing itself.

Shortly after arriving in Sunshine, I made my way toward the entrance of the SPD's southernmost substation. The building was a squat, one-story structure with plain walls the color of sun-bleached sand. The landscaping outside its walls matched the desert: spiky yucca plants and hearty bushes soaked up the sun while a handful of mesquite trees provided a small pool of precious shade. As I neared the front door of the station, I noticed that the state and U.S. flags were flying at half-mast.

I was there to meet with Lt. Pinelli, a short female officer who had begun her career on the south side of Sunshine nearly twenty years before. From a patrol officer taking calls for service, she'd worked her way up through the ranks, eventually returning to the south side as watch commander. After being buzzed into the secure area of the substation for our meeting, I saw that she had an elastic band wrapped around the police shield pinned to the left side of her chest. These bands—known as mourning bands—are worn by police after the death of an officer in the line of duty. Whereas other departments and officers used a solid black mourning band, Pinelli's was modeled after the "thin blue line," the black band split by a narrow blue stripe. Combined with the flags at half-mast—another common symbol to honor the fallen—it was clear that an officer had died.

When I asked about her mourning band and the flags outside, she explained that they were in honor of Officer Gary Danielson, a veteran patrol officer who had been fatally shot by a burglary suspect. Though he was being commemorated in Sunshine, Danielson had not died there; he was killed in Harrison, a town more than 125 miles away. Even though Danielson was not a member of the SPD, his death resonated with the emphasis on violence and death that pervades the policing occupation. Mourning bands and half-mast flags, Pinelli told me, were a testament to this exacting preoccupation and the grave sacrifice that officers understand every line-of-duty death to be. These artifacts, she said, were designed "to remember" and "to honor the officers that gave the ultimate sacrifice." Even though Danielson had not fallen on a Sunshine street, his death served as a powerful admonition to all officers, even in a distant department, that they must remain vigilantly attuned to violence. "I also think it's a reminder for all of us," she said, "every day, right, don't get complacent and go home to your family at the end of every day." That summer would provide yet more reminders of policing's inherent dangers.

———

The first week of July 2016 was full of blood and anger. A string of Black men killed by police had fueled a fresh surge of public outrage. On July 4, Delrawn Small was killed by an off-duty NYPD officer who claimed that he opened fire in self-defense after Small attacked him following a traffic accident. On July 5, Alton Sterling was fatally shot by police in Baton Rouge, Louisiana. The officers claimed that Sterling reached for a pistol in his pocket while they had him pinned to the asphalt outside the convenience store where he was known to sell CDs. And on July 6, Philando Castile was shot dead during a traffic stop in Falcon Heights, Minnesota. The officer, Jeronimo Yanez, shot Castile in front of his girlfriend and her five-year-old daughter when Castile reached for his wallet. He would later claim that the smell of marijuana in the car made him fear for his life.[16]

Unsurprisingly, protests against police brutality popped up in cities across the country, including Dallas, Texas. Around 7:00 P.M. on July 7, hundreds of protestors gathered in Belo Gardens, a public green space in the heart of central Dallas. As helicopters hovered overhead, protestors called out, "Black lives matter!" Others screamed, "Hands up, don't shoot!" Some stopped to take selfies with Dallas police officers who were present to provide security along the approved march route.

The protestors eventually left the gardens and began marching through downtown. Near the Dallas College–El Centro campus, just two blocks west of where the protest began, Micah Xavier Johnson sat in an SUV with hazard lights blinking. Johnson, a twenty-five-year-old Black man and Army veteran, was later described as a "loner." After he returned from Afghanistan, he worked transporting individuals with cognitive disabilities to and from medical appointments and shopping trips. Pushed to a breaking point by that week's string of other Black men killed by police, he had made his way to downtown Dallas to exact vengeance. He wore a tactical vest with heavy, rifle-resistant plates. His weapons included a 9mm Glock handgun, a .25 caliber semiautomatic pistol, and a Saiga AK-74 assault rifle equipped with a red dot scope. In the coming days, a search of his home by law enforcement would find even more firearms, stockpiled ammunition, and bomb-making equipment.[17]

Johnson exited his vehicle just before 9:00 P.M. and opened fire on police. Protestors screamed and ran for cover. Some tried to gain entry to a nearby courthouse, while one mother told her children to hide beneath parked cars.[18] Dallas police officer Michael Krol and Senior Corporal Lorne Ahrens were killed in this initial volley of fire. Nearby officers immediately began running toward the boom of gunshots echoing off the downtown buildings. Officer Patrick Zamarippa, a Navy veteran who *had served three tours in Iraq, was fatally shot as he ran toward the threat, bullets continuing to slam into the asphalt around him and fellow officers who took cover behind parked police vehicles. Officers Jorge Barrientos and Gretchen Rocha and Senior Corporal Ivan Salda were nonfatally shot, as were two civilians.[19]*

Johnson made his way toward an entrance to El Centro College and, taking cover behind a column, continued to let off controlled bursts of fire as he had trained to do in the Army.[20] He engaged several Dallas Area Rapid Transit (DART) officers who had left the nearby West End Station to lend aid. DART officers Misty McBride and Lee Cannon and Dallas police sergeant Giovanni Wells were nonfatally shot. Johnson then began shooting out the glass doors of El Centro but was rebuffed by campus police officers. El Centro corporal Brian Shaw was grazed by a bullet, and Officer John Abbott suffered injury from shards of flying glass.

While Johnson was focused on the doors of El Centro, DART Officer Brent Thompson attempted to flank him from the right. Thompson opened fire and Johnson whirled to face the incoming fire. Rather than scamper for cover, Johnson immediately executed a "combat glide" toward the column where Thompson had taken cover, keeping his weapon level and continuing to fire while he closed the distance between them. As he neared Thompson's position, he fired toward the left of the column, drawing Thompson's attention. Johnson then feinted to the right of the column and, finding Thompson's exposed back, fatally shot him. Thompson died just two weeks after celebrating his marriage to a fellow DART officer.[21]

Johnson turned away from Thompson's body and moved around to the north side of El Centro, gaining entry to the college after shooting out a set of glass doors. He traveled up the stairs to the second floor and into the library. He took up a new position at a window on the north side of the building and resumed fire. He shot and killed Dallas police sergeant Michael Smith as he exited his vehicle; DART officer Jesus Reitana was shot in the arm. Meanwhile, police were closing in on Johnson's position, following a trail of blood and broken glass through El Centro. As police neared his position, Johnson yelled out, "Black supremacy! Black liberation!" and opened fire on the approaching officers. Police commanded Johnson to come out with his hands up. Johnson responded, "No surrender!"[22]

A standoff ensued. Dallas police sergeant Larry Gordon attempted to de-escalate the nightmare. At one point, he told Johnson that he, too, was Black, and that he just wanted to talk and hear Johnson's story. Johnson was unmoved. "The talking is over," he said. "It's time for revolution, brother. If you are my brother," he told Gordon, "turn your weapon on those behind you."[23]

Hours later, with no end to the standoff in sight, Dallas police concocted an unprecedented plan: they would strap explosives to a bomb-disposal robot, maneuver it via remote control to where Johnson was hiding, and then detonate the device. Shortly after 1:00 A.M., Dallas SWAT followed through on the plan, detonating the robot-controlled bomb, killing Johnson, and marking the first time in history that a U.S. police department used a robot to kill a suspect.[24] Before he died, Johnson had killed five police officers and wounded an additional nine. July 7, 2016, remains the deadliest day for U.S. law enforcement since the terror attacks of 9/11.

———

I was entering SPD's eastern substation for the night shift when the initial reports of shots fired at the Dallas protest first came cross my Twitter timeline. I made my way to the lineup room with Sgt. Laroux, continuing to check my phone for more information. Laroux, now seated at the front of the lineup room, where officers were trickling in before the start of their shift, was doing the same. "You guys see about Dallas?" he asked. "Three dead." An officer seated near me told the sergeant that he and other officers had learned of it through a GroupMe thread that he and other officers were on. A little while later, Laroux asked the room whether the shooter, as yet unidentified, was dead. "He 10–15?" The officer who learned of the shooting via GroupMe responded, "No, it's a manhunt. He was open carrying an assault rifle in the crowd."

This early theory was incorrect. Dallas police had erroneously identified Mark Hughes, an unrelated Black man who had been legally open-carrying an AR-15 at the protest, as a suspect. This was only one of many pieces of false information rapidly disseminated during and after the attack. One security expert claimed that the attack was likely carried out by multiple shooters trained as part of a militia or domestic terrorist group. During the standoff between police and Johnson, Sean Parnell, an Army Ranger turned Republican political candidate, tweeted, "Heard 3 semi automatic rifles from 3 separate positions. Coordinated ambush. Fire was synchronized & focused. This was sophisticated." Dallas police chief David O. Brown also contributed to the spread of misinformation, claiming that officers were shot at by multiple suspects, including two snipers who coordinated to ambush officers more effectively.[25] None of these claims, we now know, were true.

That night on patrol, information came in trickles, sometimes from unexpected sources. Between responding to calls for service with Officer Tate, a four-year SPD veteran, we stopped at a gas station to grab a snack and use the bathroom a little before midnight. On our way in, a red-bearded man in a baseball cap turned to Tate and asked, "What the fuck is going on in Dallas, bro? Shit is crazy! Eleven shot, four dead."

"Everyone just needs to turn it down, man. Everyone," Tate responded.

Turning to leave, the man told Tate, "Be safe out there, brother," then walked off into the night.

At around 2:15 A.M., a message went out to officers via their in-car computers instructing them to be on the lookout for suspicious activity around police facilities because of the Dallas attack. The message made no mention of threats or any intelligence that suggested the Dallas ambush indicated any emergent threat to officers in Sunshine. Nonetheless, the message instructed officers to perform security checks that consisted, Tate told me, of "circulating the area and looking for anything suspicious." The message, sent by a captain from the Southern District, specifically mentioned the sighting of a "suspicious" vehicle, a silver Kia, in the public parking lot of another district's substation earlier that day. Why the vehicle was considered suspicious, how it was connected to the Dallas attack, and any specific information on the car besides its color and make were unmentioned.

In the coming days, departments across the country took steps to enhance officer safety. In Elmont, officers were assured that the department was deploying additional undercover officers and counterintelligence resources. Both there and in West River, patrol officers were mandated to work in pairs. Similar orders were given across the country. The NYPD mandated that officers work in pairs and issued an internal memo urging them to "maintain a heightened level of awareness." Departments in Washington, Chicago, Los Angeles, Philadelphia, Seattle, Cleveland, Las Vegas, Boston, and Burlington, Vermont, also instituted paired patrols.[26]

As was customary, the end of the shift saw officers gather at the station to finish their paperwork and debrief on the night's events. After this night shift, five officers sat watching news coverage of the Dallas attack that was playing on loop. They were quiet as they watched the TV. One white officer broke the silence by commenting wryly in response to the newscast's characterization of the protest: "*Mostly* peaceful." I left the station shortly after that and headed to the house where I was renting a room. When I arrived, around 7:30 A.M., the death count had risen to five.

Over the following weeks, officers in the EPD, WPD, and SPD donned black mourning bands across their badges in commemoration of the police who lost their lives in Dallas.[27] Officers from West River and Sunshine attended memorial services in honor of their slain brethren. One WPD officer who traveled to Texas sent me pictures of a makeshift shrine outside the Dallas Police Department headquarters. A lone DPD cruiser was almost completely covered in flowers, stuffed animals, balloons, U.S. flags, and the patches of departments from

FIGURE 2.1 Shrine outside the Dallas Police Department headquarters for officers killed during the July 7, 2016 attack at a Black Lives Matter protest.

across the nation. A handmade sign stuck to the rear passenger door read, "#BackTheBlue Because Someone I Call <u>Dad</u> Is on the Force!"

On July 12, the day after more than a thousand people gathered for a vigil outside Dallas City Hall, a memorial service was held for the five fallen officers. That day, the Morton H. Meyerson Symphony Center, located less than a mile from where the attack took place, was filled with mourners. Nearly a thousand police officers from departments near and far were present.[28] President Barack Obama, joined on stage by First Lady Michelle Obama, former president George W. Bush and Barbara Bush, and Vice President Joe Biden and Dr. Jill Biden, spoke at the service. Before remembering the life of each officer lost just a few days before, he reminded every officer present of the unique danger of their profession and the possibility that they might never return home to the family they kissed before heading on patrol. Looking out at the audience, a retinue of white-gloved Dallas police officers at his back, he told them, "Your work and the work of police officers across the country, is like no other. For the moment you put on that uniform, you have answered a call that at any moment, even in the briefest interaction, may put your life in harm's way."

Two weeks later, I found myself back in the substation where I had first learned of the Dallas attacks. While I waited for an officer with whom I had scheduled an interview, I noticed several funeral programs similar to those saved by West River officers in memory of their fallen friends. Upon closer inspection, I saw that the programs were not for SPD officers. They were pamphlets for officers killed in Dallas, brought back from their memorial services. A nearby desk had a Dallas Police Department badge on display. That these officers were killed in a distant state was immaterial. These five officers— victims of a man who specifically set out to murder police officers— were commemorated as if the SPD's own.

FIGURE 2.2 Three funeral pamphlets saved by an SPD officer who attended the memorial services for officers killed in the 2016 attack on police in Dallas.

In West River Officer Garner also saved funeral pamphlets throughout her career. Some of these pamphlets were for officers she knew personally; others were strangers to her but for their shared role as police. When I asked her why she kept these pamphlets carefully tucked away in a closet in her home, Garner explained that, for her, the pamphlets were both a warning and celebration of what policing was. On the one hand, she said, they "were a reminder to me that law enforcement is a dangerous job." Each pamphlet, she said, regardless of the officer named and pictured in its pages, served as a simple but no less dire admonition: "Don't end up on one of these programs." On the other hand, funeral pamphlets were a distillation of policing's most cherished values. "There's all this amazing honor in it as well, despite what the current narrative has out there," she told me. "There's all this amazing honor and dignity even in death when you are a police officer."

Despite what she saw as a critical and imprecise "narrative" about the many faults and excesses of policing, the officers who died—immortalized in pamphlets from the funerals held in their memory and honor—were sacred, above reproach. The blood of the fallen waters policing's most essential, unquestioned values. Regardless of where they died, fallen officers are hallowed proof of policing's deadly violence that reify the danger imperative. In death, officers achieve the vaunted status of hero, the policing ideal of the selfless, courageous officer willing to lay down their life in service to others. It is in the face of death that the living, those officers left behind to continue the watch, most clearly remember the stakes of their dangerous work.

A PART OF AMERICA DIED TODAY

The Officer Down Memorial Page, a nonprofit dedicated to recording line-of-duty deaths, was founded in 1996 by Chris Congriff to immortalize and honor fallen officers from across the nation. Then a James Madison University freshman who was too young to join the Fairfax County Police Department, he was angered and spurred to start his website when a man who killed two police officers was released from prison after serving seventeen years.[29] Twenty-five years later, Congriff's creation has become a key source for data on police mortality where friends, family, fellow officers, and police supporters can post words of remembrance in honor of the fallen.[30] The home page of the website spotlights Congriff's words: "When a police officer is killed, it's not an agency that loses an officer, it's an entire nation."[31]

This nationalistic bent is mirrored in the ritual and symbol of the commemoration of police deaths in departments across the country. During the same speech in Dallas in which President Obama underscored the unique danger of police work, he also assured the officers gathered before him that they were necessary for the survival of the nation. Rather than any expectation of fame or fortune, he said, the reward of being a police officer "comes in knowing that our way of life in America depends on the rule of law; that the maintenance of that law is a hard and daily labor; that in this country, we don't have soldiers in the streets or militia setting the rules. Instead, we have servants—police officers—like the men who were taken away from us."

Patriotic symbolism is ubiquitous in commemorations of officers killed in the line of duty. Just a few feet from the hallway lined with newspapers detailing the murder of Officer Patterson, the SPD officer killed during a foot pursuit, a collection of artifacts connected his death to the long history of officers killed across the United States. More than thirty years after President George H. W. Bush inaugurated the National Law Enforcement Officers memorial, his son, President George W. Bush, spoke at the Annual Peace Officers' Memorial Service in which Patterson was honored. A framed copy of his remarks hung next to Patterson's portrait; it bore Bush's signature and was addressed to Patterson's widow. Another frame displayed a pair of hands creating a pencil rubbing of the etching of

Patterson's name on the National Law Enforcement Officers Memorial in Washington, DC.

The display of localized artifacts alongside those created or brought back from the other side of the country was especially clear in a restricted area of the same substation where Patterson's portrait was displayed. A glass case near the officers' lounge contained a mix of artifacts from near and far. On one shelf was a small-scale version of the framed portrait in the substations lobby alongside two white teddy bears, each with SPD embroidered on its right foot and "Ofc. Patterson" over a police shield crossed by a black mourning band on its chest. On another shelf sat a plaque from the SPD's union, the Sunshine Police Officer Association (SPOA), that bore four metal challenge coins etched with the SPD shield, Patterson's name, and the words "Your Service to Sunshine Will Never Be Forgotten."

Next to these department-specific artifacts, objects saved and brought back from the National Law Enforcement Memorial physically tied Patterson's death to the hallowed ground where the deaths of police officers from across the country are honored. A T-shirt from Police Memorial Week showed Patterson's name alongside the name of every officer added to the memorial wall that year. The list was topped by a golden eagle and a splash of red, white, and blue stars. There were also pencil etchings of Patterson's name from the National Memorial wall, the pamphlet from that year's national memorial service, and a candle with its plastic drip protector that was lit at the nighttime vigil. A folded and framed U.S. flag sat on top of the display case next to a sign that explained its provenance:

> The flag that rests here was the flag that flew over midtown.
> It is the flag that covered our fallen officer.
> He will not be forgotten.

This mixture of artifacts combined the local and the national to honor Patterson's death as a sacrifice made not only for Sunshine, but for the United States. Having joined the ranks of those immortalized in stone within walking distance of the nation's capital, Patterson's death was part of a history and culture far bigger than that of the Sunshine Police Department. Safeguarded and brought across some two thousand miles from Washington, DC, the artifacts used to commemorate Patterson's death transformed his murder from a finite and localized tragedy into an attack on the nation. Amid eagles and stars and stripes, Patterson's death, like that of any officer, proves that the nation's legal, moral, and social order is under existential threat.

Artifacts that commemorated police killed in the September 11 terror attacks also connected individual departments and their fallen to the history and fate of the nation. Across the room from a plaque that commemorated fallen SPD officers, next to a string of blue tinsel and a small banner that read "Blue Lives Matter" and "Thank a Cop," two frames commemorated the single deadliest day in law enforcement

FIGURE 2.3 Commemorations of NYPD officers killed in the 9/11 attack on the World Trade Center, displayed adjacent to images of fallen SPD officers

history. The first frame showed the faces of twenty-three NYPD officers who died responding to the attack. "Our NYPD Heroes" was written at the top of the image. The NYPD's motto, "Fidelis Ad Mortem"—"Faithful Unto Death"—was written underneath.

"We Will Prevail," a rallying cry and promise repeatedly made by President George W. Bush in the wake of 9/11, topped the second frame in bold black letters.[32] Below were two images. The first was of the NYPD's memorial in Battery Park, just off the Hudson River a few blocks from where the World Trade Center once stood. The granite wall that bore officers' names and end-of-watch date, normally a dark gray, was pale, covered in the dust that billowed out over lower Manhattan when the towers collapsed in flame and fury. Two NYPD officers stood in front of the wall in an area called the Sacred Precinct, rubble covering the ground at their feet. The photo was dated Wednesday, September 12, 2001.

The second photo, dated Sunday, September 16, 2001, showed two workers cleaning the memorial, both standing in the Sacred Precinct now free of dust and debris. One of the workers used a hose to spray down the memorial wall, revealing the gleaming, dark stone. A makeshift plywood sign was propped against the edge of the memorial, spray-painted with "N.Y.P.D. Memorial." In addition to the twenty-three killed on September 11, 2001, the names of more than 250 officers who died of 9/11-related illness would be added to the memorial wall over the next twenty years.[33]

These artifacts, displayed alongside the SPD's fallen, is testament to officers' membership in an occupation whose value and valor transcend the bounds of their home department. Sergeant Dennis Veloso—a good-natured man who insisted I call him Denny when we first met—described this supra-organizational identity as "a second family" that was not dependent on direct ties to officers across the country. The "law enforcement family," he told me, was one that "extends beyond just, you know, actually having physically met them and having personal, you know, contact to draw from."

When I asked Lt. Pinelli about the 9/11 commemorations in her substation, she used similar familial language to explain the link between the SPD and NYPD officers who died on the other side of the country fifteen years earlier. "It's that public safety family," she told me. "You get NYPD officers and FDNY [New York Fire Department] who were all killed in 9/11—probably, I mean, in the largest terrorist attack in United States history. It affected everybody. And so, it goes to that, 'We will never forget.' We honor their sacrifice." As much as 9/11 shocked and shaped the United States as whole, it held unique meaning for police who saw officers lose their lives wearing a uniform much like their own. No matter where an officer falls, their death is a loss felt by every member of the policing family. She went on, "When you become a member of the law enforcement community, you become the part of a larger family and you bleed blue. So, when you lose somebody—whether or not they're in Dallas or Baton Rouge or New York—your heart breaks because they're a member of your family. They're a member of the law enforcement family."

Unlike the police deaths of September 11, the vast majority of officers killed in the line of duty are not claimed by an act of war. Nonetheless, the metaphor of war is re-created in police funerals across the country. The caskets of officers killed in the line of duty are draped in the Stars and Stripes. The surviving family members are presented with their own flag, crisply folded into a neat triangle, the same as the families of soldiers killed on a distant front. Military-inspired death rites extend to the crack of three-volley rifle salutes and the mournful peal of taps played on a lone bugle.[34] Together, these rituals and symbols honor police killed on home soil like those sent oceans away to fight and die under the standard of the United States.

Policing is explicitly equated to war in a popular poem displayed in West River. The poem, "A Part of America Died," is sometimes attributed to Harry Koch, a retired member of the Maricopa County Sheriff's Office. The poem can be found etched into the marble of police memorials and quoted in state legislation.[35] It reads:

A PART OF AMERICA DIED

Somebody killed a policeman today,
And part of America died.
A piece of our country he swore to protect,
Will be buried with him at his side.

The suspect that shot him will stand up in court,
With counsel demanding his rights,
While a young, widowed mother must work for her kids,
And spend many long, lonely nights.

The beat he walked was a battlefield, too,
Just as if he had gone off to war.
Though the flag of our nation won't fly at half-mast,
To his name they will add a gold star.

Yes, somebody killed a policeman today,
In your town or mine.
While we slept in comfort behind locked doors,
A cop put his life on the line.

Now his ghost walks a beat on a dark city street,
And stands at each new rookie's side.
He answered the call . . . of himself gave his all,
And a part of America died.

The fallen officer described in the poem did not die in service to a town, city, or state—he died protecting a nation. After a critical jab at a justice system that promises rights to cop killers while the officer's family grieves, police are equated to soldiers; the streets they patrol are battlefields. By extension, those who kill an officer are enemies, hostile combatants aligned against police and the United States. It

I never dreamed it would be me.
My name for all eternity,
Recorded here at this hallowed place.
Alas, my name, no more my face.
In the Line of Duty, I hear them say.
My family now the price to pay.
My folded flag stained with their tears.
We only had those few short years.
The badge no longer on my chest.
I sleep now in eternal rest.
My sword I pass to those behind.
And pray they keep this thought in mind.
I never dreamed it would be me.
And with a heavy heart and bended knee,
I ask for all here from the past...
Dear God, let my name be the last.

FIGURE 2.4 Commemorative poem of an unnamed officer, hung in the Elmont Police Department union office.

is only because of the price paid and sacrifice made by police that Americans can enjoy the safety of their homes. The death described might have been in West River, Elmont, Sunshine, or any town in between. Any officer's death, regardless of the city or town written on that officer's badge, is a national tragedy.

A faceless, nameless officer was also present in art displayed on the wall of the Elmont Police Union office, down the hall from the lineup room where officers gathered before their shift. Between a poster that read "Real heroes don't need capes" and a framed Iraqi flag captured during the Iraq War, the artwork depicted a male officer on one knee, covering his eyes with his left hand and holding a folded U.S. flag in the crook of his right arm. To the left of the image, a poem took the perspective of a fallen officer mourning their own death:

I never dreamed it would be me.
My name for all eternity,
Recorded here at this hallowed place.
Alas, my name, no more my face.
"In the line of duty" I hear them say.
My family now the price will pay.
My folded flag stained with their tears.
We only had those few short years.
The badge no longer on my chest.
I sleep now in eternal rest.
My sword I pass to those behind
And pray they keep this thought in mind.
I never dreamed it would be me.
And with heavy heart and bended knee,
I ask for all here from the past . . .
Dear God, let my name be the last.[36]

These artifacts in the WPD and EPD do not betray how an officer died or where they fell. Rather than commemorate a single death within a single department, they speak to the timeless specter of death that haunts departments across the country. The deaths commemorated in these images and poems are not circumscribed by place or time; they could have occurred yesterday or a century ago, in departments large or small, anywhere in the United States. The commemoration of this omnipresent, immortal threat connects officers from distinct departments to policing's pervasive preoccupation with violence It also proves that policing was, is, and will remain an occupation defined by the possibility of death.

THE FORGOTTEN

The 2016 Elmont Police Department award ceremony pulled out all the stops. The EPD rented out Antonelli's, a beautiful oceanside venue, for the celebration. Outside, the water was just a stone's throw from the patio and bar where officers and their families gathered before the ceremony. The sinking sun silhouetted distant sailboats and set the waves aflame as officers milled about in their dress uniforms. Detective Estacio, whom I had met years before when he was still a patrol officer, was wearing a gray suit instead of ceremonial blues. He had brought his young daughter, who squealed with delight, "Boats! Boats!" as she pulled her father behind her. Estacio, bent down to hold her tiny hand, responded in kind, "Boats! Let's go look at the boats!"

Estacio's tenderness belied the fact he was among the department's most proactive officers. That night alone, he would receive a total of ten awards for dangerous, adrenaline-fueled work: foot chases, fights, the recovery of drugs and firearms, and the apprehension of a murder suspect.[37] Over the course of the evening, other officers would stand again and again from the white-clothed tables at which they sat to shake the hands of the commanders standing at the front of the room and receive their framed awards. Officers Franklin Martienza and Andrew Deluca, partners who worked in one of Elmont's highest crime districts, received a combined twenty-six awards, including a Medal of Valor for each. This medal is awarded to an officer who "performs an outstanding act involving personal hazard and/or in cases of heroism involving combat with an armed adversary." Martienza and Deluca earned theirs for an incident in which they fought with an armed suspect who led them on a car chase when he fled from a traffic stop. When they were awarded their medal, the command staff made a special point of emphasizing that both officers were exposed to the suspect's blood during the struggle.

The names of these and every other officer receiving an award that night were catalogued in a color program placed at every chair in the main ballroom. As important as the night was to recognize the service of Elmont's finest, it was also an opportunity to remember the fallen. On the front of the program, a golden star bearing "Elmont Police" was surrounded by the words "Remembering those who have fought, those who have persevered, and those who have made the ultimate sacrifice." Two of the awards given that night were named after EPD officers who had died on duty; a third was named for an officer who, while off duty, had died trying to save someone from drowning. On the back page of the program, against a thin-blue-line background, were the same faces of fallen officers that are on the walls of the EPD's headquarters. Amid the faces, the words "Never Forget" served as both instruction and warning.

The keynote speaker for the ceremony was Don Elgin, a former state trooper turned attorney and use-of-force expert who advised departments across the country. He opened his speech by lamenting the "intense scrutiny" of policing in the years since Michael Brown was killed by police. This "criticism by a small percentage of society," Elgin said, was making officers worry about becoming "the next You-Tube sensation." In response, they were retreating from police work. The officers being honored that night, Elgin proclaimed, were the ones who persevered through the condemnation of the moment with hard work and dedication to the people of Elmont.

This sort of dedication, Elgin said, was necessary to "take back the narrative" from the media and those "vocal few" who were "quick to react and criticize law enforcement on a daily basis." It was through the sorts of heroic accomplishments for which officers were being honored that night that police could make the public see that they, the EPD, and police across the country were "dedicated to the protection and service of the community." By the same token, their tenacious pursuit of lawbreakers was necessary to restore pride in being a police officer. That pride, Elgin told the officers gathered before him, was the same sort that a new officer feels when they have their badge pinned to their chest during their academy graduation. Pride, he told them, was what "unites you all as police officers." Before turning it over to the EPD command staff to begin distributing awards, he told officers, "Until the next time that we meet, help those that need your help, protect those that need your protection, and most importantly, keep yourselves and others safe."

Over the next hour, commanders read the names of officers and a brief description of the acts for which they were receiving an award. The vast majority were for arrests, many of which involved proactive police work, foot chases, and the recovery of firearms. Heroism, courage, and danger were mentioned again and again.[38] Following each description, named officers made their way to front of the ballroom to receive their awards and shake hands with their commanders amid the applause from those still seated.

But there are officers whose deaths are unremembered, uncoupled from the celebration of officers who lived to fight another day and absent from the commemorations of fallen officers that cut across departments and decades. Whereas officers who survive their encounters with danger are exemplars of the crime-fighting ideal so central to policing's self-conception, those who commit suicide are excluded from memorials at the local, state, and national level. Their names are missing from the memorial walls in Elmont, Sunshine, and West River, just as they are missing from the walls of the National Law Enforcement Officers Memorial in Washington, DC. Their faces do not adorn the programs of departmental award ceremonies; no awards are named after them.

This omission is especially glaring since far more officers kill themselves than die at the hands of a suspect. Between 2017 and 2020, the Officer Down Memorial Page reports that an average of fewer than fifty officers were killed by gunfire each year. Blue H.E.L.P., the lone nonprofit in the United States that gathers data on police suicides, estimates that over the same time, more than three times as many officers took their own lives.[39] This number is undoubtedly an undercount.

These officers are the Forgotten, excluded from the place of honor reserved for those killed in the line of duty. The omission of police suicides from commemorations of the fallen is not accidental. These suicides, most of which are committed with the very firearms officers are issued to protect themselves from violence, lays bare the fragility and vulnerability of officers wholly at odds with a vision of the ideal officer who is wholly in control of themself and the dangers of the street.[40]

Their absence is an inverse reflection of the admiration for the officers who died heroes' deaths, cut down by the violence emphasized by the danger imperative. So, too, are they tragic reminders that, despite growing recognition of the need to support officers' mental health, policing's hypermasculine cultural emphasis on self-reliance and invulnerability perpetuates the stigma of mental illness. In a profession constantly attuned to threat, seeking help is understood by many as weakness. When vigilance and strength are a matter of life and death, such weakness is often seen as an inexcusable liability.[41]

Commemorative artifacts, besides uniting police in a shared understanding of their dangerous work, are testimony to the living that policing's most revered values—courage, heroism, sacrifice—endure. The fallen are remembered for their sacrifice; the living are recognized and rewarded for avoiding such an untimely fate in the pursuit of lawbreakers. Both are held up as proof of the enduring danger of police work and the necessity of brave police willing to hold the line against chaos. They are also a promise that, should any officer fall in the line of duty, their death will also be commemorated, their memory and valor immortalized among the honored dead.

But to commemorate officers killed by their own hand would prove that danger also lurks in the hearts and minds of officers. These dangers—stress, depression, substance abuse—cannot be arrested, wrestled to the ground, or shot. A bulletproof vest does not protect an officer from their own gun. To remember suicides alongside those killed in the line of duty would be to admit policing's continued powerlessness—even unwillingness—to protect officers from themselves and their chosen profession. Denying commemoration to victims of suicide excludes these officers from policing's hallowed values and tradition, safeguarding policing's heroic ideal and preserving the danger imperative's preoccupation with death and violence.

3

THE THREAT NETWORK

After they've buttoned their uniform shirt over their ballistic vest and secured their duty belt around their waist, officers leave the locker room and head to lineup. Also referred to as roll call or briefing, lineup is a daily ritual during which officers are counted and receive their assignments for that shift. It's also a staging ground of sorts, a haven for officers to spend time together away from the prying eyes of the public and the oversight of departmental leadership. Before the watch commander arrives to call the lineup to order, the room buzzes quietly with officers chatting about their families, a recent basketball game, or a string of days off to which they're looking forward. Coffee cups and various energy drinks dot the tables where officers sit with one another; some have insulated lunch bags that they hope to have a few minutes to dip into during their shift.

Naturally, the unvarnished experiences of police work also make their way into officers' conversations. Before one lineup in West River, two officers seated behind me spoke quietly to each other about a recent suicide attempt to which one of them had responded. "I've never seen that much blood," said the first officer. "Dude cut open both his wrists with a box cutter." He held up his thumb and index finger spaced about three inches part. "There was this much blood in the sink. It was all clogged up. And the guy was just sitting there

FIGURE 3.1 A WPD lineup room where officers gather before each shift.

crying." He laughed, "How're you not dead, dude?" The other officer exclaimed, "Welcome to West River!"

In Elmont, one lineup was run by Lt. Tantrelli, an early-to-mid-fifties white man with a clean-shaven head. At the strike of 4:00 P.M., the clang of a school bell marked the beginning of the shift. On cue, chair legs scraped the battered tile floor as officers stood and faced the front of the room. A sergeant roamed briskly around the outer edge of the lineup room, visually inspecting the officers' uniforms and equipment. When he finished the inspection, he called out to Tantrelli, "All good, L-T," and the officers were told to take their seats. Tantrelli took roll quickly, calling out officer surnames and, after an officer responded they were present, telling them where in the city they'd be patrolling that shift.

With assignments confirmed, lineup turned to its central purpose: disseminating information to officers about threats to their safety. After informing officers about an ongoing storm warning and the possibility of coastal flooding, he turned to a description of a stabbing that had occurred earlier in the day. The victim, he told officers, was a woman who was sitting in a car with a man from whom she was attempting to buy drugs. According to what officers gathered at the scene, the man's wife came up to the vehicle, saw her husband with another woman, then stabbed her. He described the stabbing suspect—"Black female, 5'6", 150 pounds, dark complexion, between 35 and 40 years old, and has dreadlocks"—and the "dealer"—"reported as a Jamaican, Black, male, tall, approximately 40 years old." Several pens clicked as officers took down the descriptions in their notepads.

The next threat Tantrelli warned them of concerned an explosive placed underneath a police vehicle in Boston. Earlier that week, he told officers, an "unidentified incendiary device," was ignited underneath a parked police vehicle. Though the initial explosion did not result in any injuries, a secondary explosion injured three officers who were clearing the area of traffic and pedestrians.[1] To guard against such an attack, Tantrelli told officers, it was important to carefully and repeatedly inspect their own vehicles. "Make sure you check your cruisers before your shift and during," he cautioned officers. "Make sure there's nothing suspicious around it." Though there was no information provided to indicate that the incident was tied to Elmont or the EPD, located more than 150 miles from Boston, the implicit link was clear: a threat to officers anywhere was a threat to officers everywhere.

After the conclusion of lineup, Elmont officers lined up along the eastern wall of the lineup room to get keys for their patrol cars. Following the end of a different lineup, standing with officers as they waited for their keys, I chatted with Officer Estacio, a tall, youthful officer with whom I'd ridden two years before. Since the first time we met, he'd grown out his dark hair, and his infant daughter was now a toddler. I asked how she was doing and he said she was fine, joking about the children's movies he'd been watching on loop: "I watched *Finding Nemo* three times today!"

Turning from home life, I asked how life on patrol was going. The timbre of the conversation shifted to a more dire tone as Estacio explained the nervous unease that haunted his hours on the street. He recalled being parked outside a Dunkin' Donuts with his partner on a recent shift. "I'm looking in the rear view, the side mirror, the rear view, out the front. And we're in the dark." After a few minutes of peering into the darkness, trying to look everywhere at once, he recounted to me, he fled from the shadowy lot and potential ambush. "I was like 'Fuck that. I'm not getting shot in the back today.'" He pointed specifically to the ambush that had left Jesse Hartnett, a Philadelphia police officer, seriously wounded exactly a week before, and he connected it to ambushes on police across the country. "It's so uneasy right now, man. So uneasy. I don't feel safe sitting in a police cruiser. Like that cop in Philadelphia; it's terrible. Fifteen officers were killed in ambushes last year. It's scary."

The number of ambushes cited by Estacio was reflected in a printed report stuck to a nearby wall with clear tape. Several parts of the report, produced by the National Law Enforcement Officer Memorial Fund (NLEOMF), a nonprofit dedicated to recording and honoring law enforcement officers killed in the line of duty, had been highlighted by hand: "ambush attacks," "disturbance calls," "during a traffic stop," and "suspicious persons" were all marked in bright orange. Another highlighted line noted: "Firearm-related fatalities increased 56 percent" from the previous year. This report, however, drew on data for 2014—*two* years prior. Though the report for 2015 had already been released by the NLEOMF, it was the report from the previous year that remained displayed in the EPD lineup room. Had the 2015 report been posted, it would have shown six ambushes—a 60 percent *decrease* from 2014—and a decrease in overall firearm deaths of 14 percent.[2]

The routine functioning of the police department persistently amplifies such information and reinforces the danger imperative in officers' working environment. Rather than being simply "downloaded" by recruits and then executed on the street by fully fledged officers, the danger imperative is iteratively energized by the intentional and conspicuous amplification of information "signals" about the danger of police work.[3] Some of these danger signals originate within the walls of the department itself: descriptions of recent violent crimes, mugshots of wanted suspects, and warnings of threats ranging from local gang members to "antipolice" protestors all reinforce the necessity of the danger imperative. Other danger signals originate outside the walls of the department. A diffuse network of institutions, including other law enforcement agencies at the local, state, and federal level, news media, police nonprofits, and the wider internet all produce and disseminate danger signals readily amplified by individual departments.

These signals are not powerful in and of themselves. They hold potent meaning because they *resonate* with the danger imperative and officers' shared understanding of their dangerous work. In the physical world, all systems have a natural frequency at which they vibrate when acted upon by an outside force, like a wineglass ringing at a particular pitch when tapped with a fork. When the frequency of that pitch matches the system's natural frequency, the resulting intensity of the system's vibration skyrockets—a phenomenon known as resonance. When an opera singer's pitch matches the natural frequency of their own vocal cords, their song can fill the house; were they to sing and hold a note that matched the natural frequency of the wineglass, the glass would vibrate with enough intensity to shatter.

The danger imperative is policing's natural frequency. Like an orchestra's sections combining into a cohesive piece of music, a diverse array of resonant signals coalesces into something greater than the sum of its individual parts. Shift after shift, officers are awash in a constant stream of danger signals that are deeply intertwined with the routine, unquestioned operations of the police department. In combination, signals from inside and outside the department reify a collective understanding of dangerous policing that transcends the particulars and probability of any one threat, amplifying the danger imperative's preoccupation with violence and the sanctity of officer safety.

ENEMIES

Danger signals amplified within the police department enumerate the individuals and groups whose violence poses a threat to officers' safety. Many of these are produced using information stemming from surveillance and enforcement activity, such as pictures of Black and Latino men arrested by police in the past or identified as being members of street gangs. An entire wall of the lineup room in West River's eastern substation, for example, was covered in dozens of mug shots of mostly Black and Latino men. Under each picture was the person's name, aliases, active warrants, and state department of corrections ID number. Some were grouped under labels like Money-Mobb and Band Boys, gangs of which the WPD said the pictured men were members.[4]

Other danger signals about gangs emphasized the geographic areas of the city where gangs were located. In Sunshine, a series of laminated posters in one of the SPD's lineup rooms displayed the names and locations of street gangs across the city. The posters, produced by the state's gang task force, showed a dizzying mix of shapes and colors that covered huge swaths of the map, especially on the south and west sides of the city where Sunshine's poor and working-class Latino communities were concentrated. While the map indicated that these areas of the city were especially dangerous because of gang presence, it also took care to reinforce the shared understanding that nowhere can ever be considered truly or totally safe. A special note at the top left of the poster warned officers that even areas not marked as gang territory could be home to dangerous gang members: "Map reflects traditional gang neighborhoods but members are not exclusive to these areas."

Mug shots and gang maps reify both the danger imperative and broad assumptions of criminality intimately tied to race and place without ever making those connections explicit. Overt discussion of race is replaced with images of Black and Latino men with criminal records, gang ties, and active warrants. The racial composition of neighborhoods denoted as gang territory is similarly undiscussed, naturalizing and normalizing the connections among place, race, violence, and danger.

These signals reinforce the danger imperative even though the information on which they are based can be hopelessly dated. For example, the gang intelligence posters in Sunshine were produced in 2008, nearly a decade before their being observed on the wall in the lineup room.[5] In addition to persistent inaccuracies in official gang lists and databases, the fluidity of gang membership makes such dated lists exceedingly unlikely to reflect current conditions on the street.[6] Inaccuracies aside, they were posted in areas where patrol officers—not officers who are part of specialized gang or firearm-focused units—gather every day. The fact that the vast majority of an officer's shift is spent doing little, if anything, related to gangs is superseded by the message that gang violence may strike almost anywhere at a moment's notice.

In the name of officer awareness and safety, the amplification of these danger signals constructs officers' work environment as one replete with fearsome Black and Latino street gangs. Without any explicit discussion of race, much less any recognition of the broader social forces that lead to the persistent geographic concentration of crime and violence over time, these signals simultaneously perpetuate assumptions of minority criminality and reinforce the danger imperative's preoccupation with violence and officer safety.[7]

Other danger signals extend the realm of policing's enemies to an ever-expanding cast of ideological foes whose politics pose a mortal threat to officers on the street. These signals, rather than being generated within the police department based on officers' surveillance and enforcement activity, emanate from outside institutions, often in the form of editorials and news stories. Commonly posted in and around the lineup room, they further amplify the danger of police work by connecting the omnipresent threat of physical violence to the broader sociopolitical context in which policing is situated.

In the hallway that EPD officers walk through every day when leaving the locker room to go to lineup, for example, a bulletin board reserved for notices from the police union displayed a mix of announcements, printouts, and newspaper clippings. Next to an op-ed about recent protests on a local university campus against racism (and the threat such protests posed to free speech), other articles focused on crime and violence. One op-ed pinned to the board, "The Danger of the 'Black Lives Matter' Movement," was penned by Heather Mac Donald, a fellow at the Manhattan Institute and high-profile proponent of the "war on cops" narrative.[8] The article was published by *Imprimis*, a magazine dedicated to "promoting civil and religious liberty" and operated by Hillsdale College, a Christian liberal arts college with strong ties to conservative politicians and political causes.

Building on the strawman that Black Lives Matter activists believe "racist police officers are the greatest threat facing young black men today," she claimed that social movement was responsible for "the murder and attempted murder of police officers." And because police were withdrawing from enforcement in the face of unprecedented "venom" from the public and the media, she wrote, Black Lives Matter was also responsible for increases in violent crime. The problem of police racism is a "canard," she wrote, claiming that "no government agency is more dedicated to the idea that black lives matter than the police." The real problem, she argued, was that more than twenty years of discussion about "alleged police racism" had avoided "a far larger problem—black-on-black crime." Black Lives Matter, the press, and politicians who remain critical of police were not only getting police killed, she concluded, but actively preventing police from saving Black people from themselves.

Still other articles focused on linking criminal justice reform to violence against police. On the same bulletin board, someone had highlighted an article from the *New York Times* that mentioned the Law Enforcement Leaders to Reduce Crime and Incarceration, a group of police chiefs, sheriffs, and prosecutors who advocate for decarceration through alternatives to arrest and an end to mandatory minimum sentences.[9] The article made a connection between these reforms and officer safety; that link was made explicit in the margins of the article through a handwritten note: "Is it possible that the people being arrested are the people committing the crimes? (See next article for the result of these 'reforms.'"

The next article pinned to the board came from a local news paper and detailed the 2015 murder of NYPD officer Randolph Holder. Holder was killed by Tyrone Howard, a thirty-year-old man who, at the time, was wanted in connection with another shooting earlier that year. In addition to Howard's lengthy criminal history, the article focused on the fact that he had been released into a drug-treatment diversion program instead of being incarcerated following an arrest for narcotics sales. At the time, NYPD commissioner Bill Bratton stated, "If ever there was a candidate not to be diverted, it would be this guy. There are people in our society who are criminals, who are violent criminals . . . who should be separated from the rest of society." Another handwritten note read "One of the 'reforms' they have in mind—", implying that Howard's release into a treatment program led to Holder's murder and not so subtly insinuating that further reforms would worsen the bloodshed. Similarly unsubstantiated claims that bail reform was driving violence against police would bubble up in 2021 as cities across the United States experienced a surge in shootings and homicides.[10]

These articles, painstakingly collected, annotated, and displayed by police for police, were signals amplified within the department to construct a world in which ideological or political enemies are tantamount to physical threats. The amplification of these danger signals supports a belief that critique and reform of policing are founded on libelous outrage about police violence and racism. Calls for accountability or alternatives to punishment pose an existential threat not only to the power of the police institution but also to the lives of individual officers. Those who agree with claims of police racism or consider also: "or are in alignment with. efforts. . . ." support efforts to curtail inequalities in policing—be they university students, academics, journalists, politicians, or fellow officers—are assumed to be complicit with those who would attack and kill police.

WEAPONS

Along with curated information about the people and groups against whom police must protect themselves at all times, police departments also collect and preserve information about a staggering array of weapons that might be used to injure or kill an officer anytime, anywhere. Weapon-related danger signals focus heavily on firearms. In an area of a West River station, for example, a range of framed firearms—including an AK-47 and AR-15 rifles—hung on the walls overlooking patrol sergeants' cubicles. Each of these weapons, I was told, was seized on the streets of West River; some were even used to shoot at officers. In another WPD station, a large board was displayed on the wall along the path by which officers frequently exited the facility to reach their patrol cars. The board was covered in pictures of firearms recovered by one of the WPD's crime reduction units (CRUs), a specialized unit that, unlike the vast majority of the patrol division, was not beholden to the radio and calls for service.

Illegal firearms, like drugs and cash, are prestige-laden prizes within the police department. Officers who seek out and find firearms are revered among their peers as dedicated, hardworking crime-fighters. Firearm recovery is frequently the topic of departmental awards and commendations, which, along with felony arrests, are a boon to any officer interested in being promoted to a CRU or other specialized gun, gang, or narcotics assignment.[11] At the same time, these mementos are conspicuous evidence that deadly firearms are a persistent and pervasive problem on the streets of West River.

Other danger signals focused on weapons are not produced by the departments in which they are amplified. I came across one such signal in the same lineup room in Sunshine that displayed gang maps on the walls. This was a report authored by Michael Chesbro, PhD, an Army veteran and former intelligence analyst for the Department of Defense, titled "Catalog of Unique, Concealed & Disguised Weapons, Concealments, Escape Techniques, Tactics & Tradecraft." The title page was marked "Officer Safety and Awareness" in red letters, and the report was tailored to provide officers with information they could use to ensure their survival on patrol. Its introduction read:

> Everyday law enforcement, security, and intelligence personnel are faced with potential threats from unique, concealed and disguised weapons. Contraband is hidden in concealment devices; escape techniques allow criminals to run free, and tactics and tradecraft are employed which make our jobs more difficult and our lives more dangerous. By being aware of what's out there it becomes easier to recognize a threat and take action to protect ourselves against it.

The report is replete with images and descriptions of tools that can be used against police. Some are focused on escape: lockpicks, handcuff keys disguised as bracelets or zippers, and guides for how to use these tools. Others are used to hide weapons, narcotics, or cash: fake, hollow cans of food, household cleaners, or toiletries can all be used to stash contraband. There are also books and online resources that provide instructions on clandestine surveillance, how to build smoke bombs, and an extensive guide on "eco-sabotage."

Officers are also warned of communication technologies used by protestors. Along with frequency-hopping walkie-talkies to communicate with one another or cell phone GPS jammers to prevent satellite tracking, the report mentions Vibe, an application that allows messages based on users' proximity to one another before deleting them automatically. The report notes, "This app was used frequently during the 'Occupy Wall Street' protests," suggesting that communication among protestors is, in and of itself, a threat to officer safety.

But the bulk of the report catalogs a litany of deadly weapons. Unsurprisingly, many of the listed weapons are firearms, the type of weapon most often used to kill police officers.[12] The FN Five-seven pistol, in addition to being concealable and "extremely accurate," the report reads, is "best known for firing armor-piercing rounds" commonly referred to as "cop killers."[13] The .32 and .380 caliber pistols produced by Seecamp, as described in the report, hold up to seven shots, are 4.25-inches long, and weigh less than a pound when fully loaded. Even smaller is the NAA .22 Long Rifle-HG (Holster Grip), a mini-revolver that holds five shots and can literally fold in half. Firearms, the report shows, are deadlier and more concealable than ever.

The report also described weapons that stray firmly into the fantastical. The report detailed butterfly-shaped throwing stars, a "Batman Batarang Shape Dark Knight" folding knife, and a chain whip like the one used by the Marvel superhero Ghost Rider. There was even a blowgun that shoots thin metal darts and a pistol-grip crossbow; an image of the crossbow was accompanied by a warning in red: "Note: Darts from this crossbow may penetrate body armor."

Such weapons are perishingly rare on patrol. The officers I observed across three cities recovered a handful of knives and firearms on patrol, none of which was used against them; nary a folding pistol, throwing star, or armor-piercing crossbow was seen, much less confiscated. But officers operating within the danger imperative cannot afford to dismiss out of hand the possibility of encountering these weapons, no matter how seemingly outlandish. To prove this, the report included hyperlinks to Amazon or other retailers where these weapons could be purchased. These links, the report warned, were evidence that the pictured items were easily accessible to the public: "Any item that can be easily found or purchased on-line should be considered commonplace and is something that may very likely be encountered in the field." That these weapons could be acquired with a few keystrokes and a credit card was irrefutable proof of their ubiquity.

Then there were weapons that showed officers how any mundane object might be used to kill them. Whereas the uninitiated might associate a walking cane with the elderly or infirm, the report showed that such an object could be a weapon in disguise. On the page after the image and description of a black steel throwing star, the report showed the Zap Cane™, a one million volt "stun gun cane." An umbrella was not just for staying dry in a downpour; it could also conceal a full-length sword that might be plunged into an officer's heart. Steel playing cards were potentially lethal projectiles or slashing instruments. Cell phone cases, belt buckles, necklaces, bracelets, and hair combs could be just what they appeared to be—or they could conceal a blade used to puncture an artery or slash an officer's throat.

In isolation, a single report might be assumed to be little more than a case of overzealous vigilance, one officer or one department overextending the danger imperative to the point of absurdity. But when considered alongside the wider occupational environment in which all threats must be identified, recorded, and mitigated, such reports are best understood as danger signals that are both product and component of the danger imperative. The creation and dissemination of such signals is interpretable as reasonable, useful, and necessary within policing because of the institution's persistent preoccupation with violence and officer safety. These signals, not to mention the time and resources required to obtain and display them, would make little sense in environments which do not encourage workers to understand themselves as involved in a constant struggle for survival. Once created, these signals are evidence of the very assumptions that motivated their creation, joining the endless stream of information that reifies the danger imperative.

The internet ensures that reports like the one kept in the Sunshine lineup room are instantly accessible to officers and departments across the country. Similar reports have been produced by employees of the Los Angeles County Sheriff's Department and the Brunswick Police Department in Maine. Although such reports are produced by individuals, they would not be possible without combining information on weapons drawn from other law enforcement agencies. In its front matter, for example, the Brunswick report expressed gratitude to federal law enforcement agencies, local and state departments, and even Canadian law enforcement who generated information included in the report.[14] Even without privileged access to law enforcement sources, information like that contained in these danger compilations is easily found online. The FBI's website describes knives hidden in coins, lighters, money clips, keys, and keychains, and police-focused forums hosted on sites like Officer.com allow for the crowdsourcing of danger signals, too.[15]

Though there is no way to draw a direct line from these danger signals to any one officer's actions, the predictable outcome of the logic that any object could be a lethal weapon is easily identifiable in acts of police violence. Some of this violence (and its justification) is tied to plentiful and easily accessible firearms in the United States. Police have shot citizens who were holding any number of mundane objects—sunglasses, a cologne bottle, a sandwich, underwear—that officers said they perceived as one of the more than 393 million firearms in circulation.[16] Following a foot pursuit stemming from reports of a man breaking car windows, the two Sacramento officers who fatally shot Stephon Clark claimed they mistook a cell phone for a firearm. The Sacramento County district attorney found the fatal shooting to be legally justified.[17] Richard Salazar was mistaken for a robbery suspect and then shot four times by police in Corpus Christi, Texas, when they mistook what Chief Michael Markle called a "pistol grip lighter" for a weapon. When asked about the shooting, Markle explained that his officers were "at a heightened state of awareness, a heightened state of alert." The city eventually settled for nearly three million dollars and both officers returned to duty.[18]

The infinite applicability of this logic is clearest, however, when officers justify their violence through a reframing of mundane objects as lethal weapons. In Boulder, Colorado, for example, Zayd Atkinson, a Black twenty-six-year-old college student, was using a bucket and thin clamper tool to pick up garbage outside the apartment building where he lived and worked. John Smyly, a white officer with the Boulder Police Department, approached Atkinson and demanded to know if he lived on the property. Even after Atkinson said that he did and gave the officer his name with a matching school ID, Smyly pressed on and asked for Atkinson's date of birth. Atkinson refused, picked up the bucket and grabber tool that were resting on the ground, and walked away from the officer. Smyly followed him around the side of the building, continually commanding him to sit down, and to put down the "weapon" he was carrying. The officer drew his Taser and threatened to use it. Then he drew his firearm. Atkinson, incredulous, asked him loudly, "You're gonna *shoot* me?" Smyly responded, "If you use that weapon against me, then yes, that is a consideration."

Again and again, Atkinson told Smyly that he didn't have a weapon. Smyly, in turn, said the opposite, "That's a weapon."

"This is a bucket!"

Pointing at the clamper, Smyly corrected him, "No, that's a weapon, right there,"

"This is a clamper for picking up garbage," responded Atkinson, clicking the clamper open and closed and even picking up some mulch from the ground for emphasis.

"Put it down. I'm telling you I'm threatened by it."

"It's not a weapon. You're not threatened. I'm threatened. You have a fucking gun that kills people." Holding up the clamper, he yelled, "How am I supposed to kill someone with this?" Eventually, eight other officers and a sergeant arrived on scene and encircle Atkinson. More than twenty minutes after Smyly first approached Atkinson, and only after another resident of the building told police Atkinson also lived there, did police leave.[19] In response to public outrage following the incident, Smyly resigned from the Boulder Police Department and Atkinson was offered a $125,000 settlement.[20]

Such cases evidence officers' familiarity with and willingness to deploy logic rooted in the assumption of infinite threat to justify and explain their violence. This logic is rooted in a shared reality of intense and boundless danger, reflected in myriad danger signals amplified by the danger imperative's unceasing emphasis on violence and potential death. Even though Officer Smyly did not shoot Atkinson, his repeated claims of feeling threatened by Atkinson's trash clamper, his decision to draw his firearm in anticipation of an attack, and his stated willingness to shoot Atkinson—an innocent man doing cleanup outside his home—are all outcomes encouraged by the danger signals produced, shared, and amplified within policing. The practically limitless supply of danger signals detailing weapons is designed to sensitize officer perception to the peril of policing. A comb or phone case could be just that; it could also be a deadly weapon. Even if it doesn't transform into a firearm or conceal a blade, any object can be weaponized. When this binary becomes axiomatic, divested from the infinitesimally low probability of encountering a knife coin or being beaten to death with trash clampers, officers cannot afford to assume that any object—or any person—is less than potentially lethal.

HOT SHEETS AND THE ROUTINIZATION OF VIOLENCE

Alongside signals that detail weapons and the assailants who wield them, the ritual of lineup amplifies information about cases of violence that occurred during prior shifts. The description of violent crime during lineup routinizes and normalizes the danger imperative's preoccupation with violence and officer safety. That police are rarely the targets of the violence discussed at lineup is less important than the implication that each incident is definitive proof of the violence and its perpetrators that could, at any moment, injure or kill an officer.

Although violent crimes are much rarer than the nonemergency calls that consume the overwhelming majority of police resources, lineup discussion of prior shifts focuses overwhelmingly on robberies, shootings, and homicides.[21] Violence is recounted dispassionately, as a matter of course, before the ranking officer running lineup seamlessly transitions into routine work issues. In contrast to the breathless coverage of an evening newscast or a dramatic newspaper headline that emphasizes the surprising or irrational nature of violence, lineup shows officers that violence is a persistent and unavoidable feature of their work.

At one Elmont lineup, the sergeant at the front of the room informed officers of two robberies in Freemont, a largely Latino and low-income area of the city. Without missing a beat, he then reminded officers that overtime slips needed to include documentation of who approved the overtime. During another lineup, a homicide was described in detached detail by one of the EPD's rare female commanders. She began by telling officers that the victim, who was eighteen or nineteen years old, was shot eleven times. She also made it a point to clarify that this initial count might be incorrect. "You have in, you have out, folds of your stomach," she explained. "So we won't know for sure until after the autopsy." This starkly unemotional description of a brutal murder was immediately followed by a request for a volunteer to guard a prisoner at a local hospital.

Such matter-of-fact discussion neither minimizes nor trivializes the severity of the violence that occurs outside the walls of the police department. On the contrary, the routine and aseptic discussion of even the most gruesome incidents transforms tragedy into an assumption of the police milieu, baking violence into the department's daily operations. Just as disease is discussed during patient rounds on a hospital floor, violence is a regularly occurring challenge presented to police officers. Though robbery and murder are certainly not as quotidian as the procedure for submitting overtime hours, they nevertheless become permanent fixtures of departmental life. Before every shift, lineup reminds officers that violence is their lot and professional responsibility. Being a police officer requires knowing and appreciating the violence that transpires on the street.

The taken-for-granted nature of violence and its routine amplification during lineup are aided by documents that compile and summarize violent incidents across a department's jurisdiction. In West River, this summary takes the form of a "hot sheet," a daily printout of crimes from prior shifts. In addition to the police radio code for a given crime, each summary includes key information about the incident: time, location, description of suspects, presence of weapons, stolen property, vehicle description and license plate, and suspects' direction of flight from the scene. For example, the summary of a 315 (armed robbery) read:

315ARMED OCCD AT THE BUSN 4932 FREMONT AVE (FREMONT CLEANERS) AT 1755HRS—S1 MB, 30–40, 6'0 200 GOATEE, GLASSES, GRY KNIT CAP, BLK HOODED JKT, BLK PANTS ARMED W/UNKNOWN BLACK HANDGUN— LOSS: $200—INC REC150608000238

On their face, hot sheets are designed to help officers identify and apprehend the perpetrators of such crimes. A description of the suspect, weapons, vehicles, and stolen property can all be used by an officer on the street to articulate reasonable suspicion for a stop or the probable cause necessary for a lawful arrest.[22] Assistant Chief Valdez, an officer who worked his way from patrol into the top echelons of the department over more than twenty years, explained to me that hot sheets help detectives enlist the eyes and ears of line-level officers who might encounter a suspect or learn relevant information about a case on patrol. Despite the supposed utility of these descriptions for ongoing investigations, however, most of these crimes are never solved. Nationally, less than 46 percent of violent crimes were cleared by police in 2019; the clearance rate for robberies is just over

THE THREAT NETWORK 133

30 percent.[23] In West River, the 2018 robbery clearance rate was scarcely more than 15 percent.[24]

More salient than the investigatory value of hot sheets is their utility as concrete, daily reminders of the violence with which officers must contend. Though each hot sheet usually covers only five or six incidents, most of these incidents describe robberies or other violent crimes that involve firearms. This curated set of violent crimes represents about one quarter of 1 percent of the WPD's two thousand daily calls for service, a tiny sliver of the incidents to which WPD officers respond. But each one of them is proof that dangerous suspects, many armed with lethal weapons, are still walking the streets.

The purpose of hot sheets as a mechanism to inform officers of threats to their safety is clearly stated in some summaries, especially when a firearm was used. Such was the case in this description of an armed robbery denoted as "FOR OFCR SAFETY":

ATTN UNITS FOR OFCR SAFETY A315/365A OCC'D AT 1835HRS ON 5200 BLOCK EASTERN AV SUSP/MB LIGHT COMPLX 21–23 6 200 LSW WHI ABERCROMBIE T-SHT BLU JEANS ARMED W/BLK SEMI AUTOMATIC HAND-GUN—DOF ON FOOT SB ON EASTERN WB on 50th REC1506130000333[25]

Though this summary appears replete with information—the robbery's time, location, and a description of the suspect as a Black man between 21 and 23 years old wearing a white t-shirt and blue jeans—it is unlikely that these details would allow a patrol officer to reliably identify and apprehend a robbery suspect. In fact, I never observed an officer use hot sheet information to effect an arrest. Far more important than the investigatory value of this information is its utility as evidence of the firearms and endless violence which pose threats to officer safety.

Hot sheet summaries need not explicitly reference officer safety to be squarely aimed at enhancing it. One hot sheet described an armed robbery (315A) and assault with a deadly weapon (365) during which two armed suspects held a local business and its customers at gunpoint. The suspects fled the scene on foot, making off with the business's safe, victims' cell phones, and their wallets.

315(A)/365 PW OCD 0645HRS 10JUL15 @ 1200 12TH ST—S1/MB 28 YRS 5'10 SKINNY DRK CLOTHING S2/M0 (SAMOAN) 30'S 6'2 220 GRY HOODIE LONG DENIM JEAN SHORTS BOTH ARMED WITH BL SEMI AUTO PISTOLS—LOSS: SAFE FROM BUSN, CP'S AND WALLETS FROM MULTIPLE VICTS—SUSP FLED ON FOOT EB ON RALEIGH WY

The letters PW at the beginning of the incident summary are vital. PW is shorthand for "pistol whip," wherein a firearm is used as a blunt object to strike someone. Instead of relying solely on the mention of black semiautomatic pistols later in the summary, putting PW at the front of the summary allows officers to immediately intuit that this 365 involved firearms. As one officer explained, "Officers need to know the suspect was armed with a gun. If it didn't have that code, officers would think it was a stick or other weapon." Such an assumption could prove fatal.

Hot sheet summaries that focus on officer safety extend beyond robberies and other violent crimes involving firearms. One such summary described a domestic battery (342D) by a man in his late fifties. In addition to the battery, the summary noted, he had made 902s (suicide threats), as well as threats of what is colloquially known as "suicide by cop."[26]

OFCR SAFETY-342D SUSP MULLINS, CLARENCE DOB 03011957 MB 5'9 185 DK COMPLEX SHORT ALMOST SHAVED HEAD, POSS DRIVING 1994 ACURA RSX 2D BLU LIC/123ABC

SUSP HAS MADE 902'S AND INDICATED 902 BY COP.
REC150613000091

A domestic battery without weapons is unlikely to appear on a hot sheet; this was the only such incident I saw listed on a hot sheet while in West River. Not coincidentally, it was also the only case that mentioned a suspect who had indicated they may try to precipitate their own death by engaging in threatening behavior that police might respond to with lethal violence.

Lineup after lineup, officers receive these organizationally tailored signals detailing the violence for which officers must prepare. The purpose of hot sheets—enhancing officer safety—is not their only consequence. Crucially, the violence detailed in hot sheets for which officers must be on guard is disconnected from the structural forces that generate it. This is to be expected: hot sheets are a simple, low-cost means of transmitting danger signals to officers, not an avenue for detailing how centuries of structural disadvantage drive the concentration of contemporary violence across time and space. Be it suicide by cop or armed gunmen, hot sheet summaries provide clear and present evidence of threats to officer safety. The root causes of violence are far less important to police than its existence and implications for their survival.

But the routine use of hot sheets does more than remind officers of violence on the street. The daily distribution of hot sheets and the ritual enumeration of recent violence normalizes the significant attention dedicated to cataloging and discussing comparatively rare incidents of violence. As a ritual built into the daily functioning of the police department, the routine compilation and description of violence re-creates the skewed assumption that police work is primarily concerned with violence. In turn, it also perpetuates the collective understanding of policing as a profoundly dangerous affair. Further, hot sheets that aseptically detail information about violent incidents routinely reinforce common stereotypes of race, place, and violence.

This is not to say that the violence being described is not real, nor is it untrue that violence is disproportionately concentrated in disadvantaged Black and Latino communities.[27] But when violence is flattened into its barest facts—race, gender, age, location, time, weapons—its concentration in disadvantaged communities and among minority men is decoupled from the social forces that drive it, leaving a highly distilled record limited by the existing data infrastructure of the police department.[28] At best, this ritual enumeration of violence does two things: it obfuscate the structural roots of violence over which police have little (if any) control, and it perpetuates the assumption that violence is and should be officers' core concern. At worst, it provides endless, ostensibly empirical fodder for the consolidation of racialized assumptions concerning which people and places are synonymous with threats to officers' lives.

OFFICER SAFETY BULLETINS AND CROWDSOURCED DANGER

Another mechanism for the amplification of danger in policing is the use of officer safety bulletins. These announcements precisely detail a variety of threats to officers' lives and are openly displayed and discussed by police. Flatscreen TVs in multiple Sunshine lineup rooms loop through these bulletins, some headed "Officer Safety" in bold, red letters. These bulletins, which are also printed in hard copy and kept in "the book" in each substation's lineup room, were passed around from officer to officer at lineups across the city to provide them with descriptions of individuals of whom they should be especially wary on patrol.

Below two mug shots of a white man in his early twenties, one officer safety bulletin detailed the man's history of suicidal ideation and a prior altercation in which he attempted to grab a Sunshine officer's firearm. The bulletin also detailed the SPD's most recent contact with the young man: he threatened to throw himself in front of a train and told officers he'd force them to shoot him if they approached. At the bottom, the dangers he posed to anyone who might encounter him were enumerated: "Anti-police, Suicidal, SMI [severe mental illness], Violent, will fight, kick, and spit." Another officer safety bulletin, this one about a Black, nineteen-year-old male, detailed the man's prior fight with police and noted that "he did not like 'white officers.'" It advised: "Confrontational during contact with Law Enforcement. *Has fought with officers, causing injury.*"

Even bulletins that were not specifically labeled as related to officer safety included information on threats to officers' lives. So-called 10–81s and 10–82s described people whom officers should "stop and question" or "stop and arrest" if they were encountered on patrol. Whereas officer safety bulletins cited specific incidents of violence or the presence of weapons, 10–81s and 10–82s focused on individuals who were neither violent nor had directly victimized any officers. These bulletins focused overwhelmingly on nonviolent offenses, including failure to return a rented U-Haul truck, indecent exposure, theft of cigarettes from a gas station, and pawning a stolen bicycle.

Nonetheless, the need to ensure officer safety when dealing with *any* suspect was clearly stated. Even with no mention of weapons or violence, other details were provided to insinuate that suspects were volatile and potentially violent: mental illness, drug use, or association with known drug users were all listed on bulletins as factors relevant to officer safety. Even if there were no clear and present threats to officers, the section of each bulletin dedicated to officer safety still suggested that officers take "usual precautions." No matter the underlying crime that might bring police into contact with a suspect, these bulletins reiterate to officers the need to keep their safety front and center. Officers cannot afford to treat anyone or any interaction as less than potentially deadly.

Crucially, officer safety bulletins are not restricted to local threats. Other danger signals are created and transmitted to police

departments from across the United States through a diffuse information-sharing network. The crowdsourcing and transmission of
these extralocal signals is made possible by a diffuse web of state-level
"fusion centers." According to the Department of Homeland Security (DHS), fusion centers are "state-owned and operated centers that
serve as focal points in states and major urban areas for the receipt,
analysis, gathering and sharing of threat-related information between
State, Local, Tribal and Territorial (SLTT), federal and private sector
partners."[29]

As discussed by sociologist Sarah Brayne, fusion centers were
initially formed after the 9/11 attacks to gather and disseminate
terrorism-related intelligence. Over the past two decades, however, the mandate of these fusion centers has morphed into something else entirely. Rather than maintaining a concentrated focus
on terrorism, today's fusion centers, sprinkled across all fifty states,
Guam, and Puerto Rico, curate and circulate information on a
never-ending stream of potential threats drawn from local, state,
and federal agencies.[30]

While fusion centers came into being at the start of the twenty-
first century, they make use of an institutional infrastructure that dates
to the 1970s and the genesis of the war on drugs. From 1973 to 1981,
six regional intelligence or information centers were formed across
the United States. Together, these centers make up the Regional
Information Sharing System (RISS) Program. Today, RISS allows
fusion centers and more than 9,400 law enforcement agencies and
50,000 users to connect to some eighty intelligence databases through
the RISS Secure Cloud (RISSNET).[31] It also provides access to the
Homeland Security Intelligence Network (HSIN), a joint initiative
with the Department of Defense.[32] The RISS Officer Safety Website
is a "one stop shop" for law enforcement agencies to share "officer-
safety related information" with one another, including resources on
armed and dangerous subjects, narcotics, gangs, domestic terrorism,
border security, line-of-duty deaths, and officer safety-related videos.[33]

Altogether, RISS makes more than 62.1 million records available to police across the United States and also provides data access to England, New Zealand, and Canada.[34] This vast collection of danger signals, drawn from law enforcement agencies across the United States, generates and disseminates more evidence of the unyielding danger of officers' work than would be possible for any one law enforcement agency, continually expanding range of possible threats far beyond the limits of an officer's home department.

State-level fusion centers are key to the creation and distribution of danger signals, connecting the local-level threats of individual law enforcement agencies to the danger imperative's occupational-level preoccupation with violence and officer safety. Some officer safety bulletins distributed by state fusion centers facilitate the transfer of danger signals between proximate departments: one bulletin in the SPD provided details about a suspect from Govalle, a small city of fewer than 60,000 residents about an hour from Sunshine. The bulletin, headed "Use Caution—Officer Safety—Use Caution," warned officers that the pictured suspect, a Latino man in his early fifties, was due to be released from the county jail that summer. His initial arrest three years earlier was for aggravated assault on a police officer, during which the man pulled a large knife. The bulletin also stated that the man was "schizophrenic" and had reportedly called the FBI prior to his earlier arrest and said that he wanted to kill a police officer. Given that the man had family living in the same county in which Sunshine officers patrolled, SPD officers were warned to "**Use Caution If Contacted**." Though the man in question had served his sentence, the officer safety bulletin made clear that his alleged mental illness and prior history of assault on police constituted an ongoing threat to police in Sunshine.

Other danger signals transmitted by and through fusion centers speak to threats that are tied to distant agencies spread across the country, often thousands of miles from the local departments where they are used to warn officers. Like danger signals that focus on a boundless array of hidden or concealed weapons, bulletins show discrete cases of such weapons being recovered by police in far-off places.[35] An officer safety bulletin in Sunshine described the seizure of two improvised firearms by the Montgomery County Police during a traffic stop of a wanted suspect in rural Maryland. These slap guns, constructed out of a simple steel pipe and other inexpensive household materials, cost only a few dollars to manufacture and can be used to fire a bullet or shotgun shell at close range.

The bulletin warned, "Slap guns are a growing trend and do not take professional skills or machinery to duplicate," though neither the bulletin itself nor any publicly available source I reviewed supported the claim of such a trend. Regardless, the underlying lesson of the bulletin—that anyone might be carrying an improvised lethal weapon made of household items—remained unchanged, echoing other danger signals emphasizing that officers must treat even seemingly mundane objects as potentially lethal weapons.

Other bulletins disseminated through fusion centers are Frankenstein-esque amalgamations of intelligence drawn from law enforcement agencies across the country. One such bulletin, produced by the Baltimore Police Department's Criminal Intelligence Section in 2009, was pinned to the wall in West River and showed a brightly colored Super-Soaker water gun retrofitted to conceal a Mossberg 12-gauge shotgun. The recovery of the customized water gun, however, had been carried out by the Hillsborough County Sheriff's Office in Florida, and the initial report of the recovery cited in the Baltimore bulletin was produced by the Miami Gardens Police Department.

In practice, the origin of danger signals transmitted by fusion centers is incidental. It is far more important that such weapons have *ever* been recovered by *any* police department. Even a threat detected years ago and thousands of miles away must be guarded against by every officer, everywhere.

To make matters worse, some danger signals transmitted by way of fusion centers do little more than amplify misinformation and

BALTIMORE POLICE DEPARTMENT
CRIMINAL INTELLIGENCE SECTION

INTELLIGENCE BULLETIN

Phone: 410-396-2640   Fax: 410-685-9028

February 26, 2009   Number: 19

OFFICER SAFETY
Shotgun Concealed in Toy

On 22 February 2009 a
patrol unit from the
Hillsborough County Sheriffs
Office recovered
a Mossberg 12-gauge
shotgun concealed within
a Super-Soaker (water gun).

The water gun was taken
apart and altered allowing
the shotgun to be encased
within the water gun, and to
remain fully functional.

*Source: Miami Gardens Police TB-09-003,
24 February 2009*

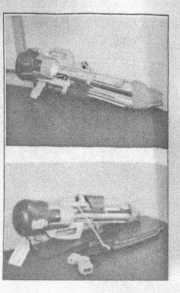

FIGURE 3.2 Baltimore Police Department intelligence bulletin, seen in
West River, originated in Florida. This bulletin warns officers, regardless of
where they patrol, to be on guard for the possibility of firearms hidden inside
children's toy water guns.

stigmatize vulnerable people. This was especially clear in bulletins warning officers of the danger posed by fentanyl, a powerful opioid. One bulletin from the Homeland Security Division of a nearby metro area's police department warned officers that fentanyl had been detected in a seized supply of synthetic marijuana, known more commonly as "spice."[36] After perpetuating the common myth of fatal skin-to-fentanyl contact, the bulletin implored officers to prepare themselves for dangers they may not even be able to perceive: "Above all, be careful when dealing with all threats, known and unknown."

Similar bulletins were transmitted by fusion centers to the SPD from far-off states. An "Officer Awareness" bulletin from the West Virginia Intelligence Exchange warned officers about the so-called Lazarus game, whereby groups of heroin users intentionally overdose and then use naloxone (commonly known by the brand name Narcan) to counteract the overdose. Like claims of fatal respiratory or skin exposure to fentanyl, the Lazarus game is little more than an urban legend.[37] Though justified as necessary to ensure officer safety, these bulletins focus on nonexistent threats and reproduce misinformation that contributes to the stigmatizing views of drug use and drug users held by police also goes beyond stigma & can lead to hesitancy to intervene in the event of an overdose—so direct harm.[38] Worse, this misinformation can directly harm the public by encouraging officers to hesitate in providing aid to someone experiencing an overdose.

Because fusion centers are designed to link law enforcement intelligence at every level of government, federal agencies also produce officer safety bulletins that amplify the possibility of violence for local police. After the murder of NYPD officers Liu and Ramos, for example, the FBI released a "National Situational Information Report" to warn officers across the United States of potential copycat attacks, drawing on intelligence from disparate agencies. The report, posted publicly by the Chicago chapter of the Fraternal Order of Police, included "uncorroborated" information from the Baltimore FBI office of threats against "white cops" by the Black Guerilla Family (BGF) prison gang.

WVIX

WEST VIRGINIA INTELLIGENCE EXCHANGE

TELEPHONE 304-746-2807

FAX: 304-746-2808

2016-0609-2

*********OFFICER AWARENESS*********

"THE LAZARUS GAME"

(U//LES) The West Virginia Intelligence Exchange W.V.I.X. has received recent reports from the Fayette County area in reference to subjects participating in what is known as the "Lazarus Game". It was reported there were eight overdoses in two days over the weekend of June 3rd and 4th.

(U//LES) This is a new trend that was first noted in Ohio and involves overdosing on drugs, such as heroin, and then using the NARCAN antidote drug to revive the overdosed individual. This action has been deemed the "Lazarus game" and those participating attempt to see how many times they can die and come back. (1)

(U) Naloxone, also known as Narcan, is an antidote used to revive someone who overdoses on drugs containing opioids. It has been used for decades by hospitals and ambulances to reverse overdoses, is legal, and has been approved by the Food and Drug Administration (FDA) recently, this drug can now be purchased over the counter in some pharmacy's. It neutralizes the opioids in a person's system and helps them to breathe again; however, it only works if a person has opioids in their system. (2)

(U//FOUO) If this is seen in your area or you know of any incidents regarding Naxolone and the "Lazarus Game," please forward the information to W.V.I.X at 304-746-2807 or wvix@wvsp.gov.

1(U)Report from Ohio Strategic Analysis and Information Center (SAIC).Officer/First Responder Awareness: Narcan-"Lazarus Game" 21 March 2016

2 (U) Community Care of North Carolina. "What is Naloxone?" Project Lazarus. http://projectlazarus.org/patients-families/what-naloxone. (Accessed 18 March 2016).

LAW ENFORCEMENT SENSITIVE

FIGURE 3.3 This officer awareness bulletin, seen in Sunshine but originating in West Virginia, details the myth of the "Lazarus game," wherein heroin users intentionally overdose to be resuscitated with naloxone.

Similar threats from an Ohio-based prison gang, the Heartless Felons Gang, were cited, as were online threats against police made in California, Colorado, and Tennessee. The shooting of two civilian vehicles, both of which had Maryland Fraternal Order of Police license plates, was also detailed, though the Washington, DC, Metro police had no evidence that the suspects believed the drivers were law enforcement officers. "The above information," the report stated, "is provided as a reminder to law enforcement partners to remain vigilant both on and off duty. Be mindful of displaying any type of identifiers related to law enforcement such as bumper or window stickers."

In comparison to direct threats made against law enforcement officers, other bulletins disseminated by fusion centers are far afield from the safety concerns of the average patrol officer. An "Awareness Bulletin" found in the Sunshine Police Department, for example, was not produced by a single agency; the bulletin came from the Correctional Intelligence Task Force (CITF), a partnership among the FBI, the California Department of Corrections and Rehabilitation, and the Federal Bureau of Prisons. It described the threat posed by the national prison strike, a prisoner-led movement spurred by economic exploitation and inhumane living conditions. In the summer of 2016, nonviolent strikes occurred in prisons located in nearly a dozen states. The bulletin, however, took special care to cast doubt on claims that the strike was a largely nonviolent movement by highlighting a riot at William C. Holman Correctional Facility in Atmore, Alabama, during which inmates set several fires and stabbed both a guard and the prison's warden.[39] The bulletin concluded with a request to any correctional or law enforcement officers to contact the CITF with any "recent intelligence" on the strike.

Other bulletins amplified within policing originate from the U.S. military. One Naval Criminal Investigative Service (NCIS) bulletin detailed "suspicious" phone calls made to several Navy and Marine recruitment centers by someone claiming to be from the American Chamber of Commerce. The caller would ask for general information, such as the recruitment center's hours of operation and address. These calls are examples of a well-known scam used to gather business details to craft more believable, targeted "spear phishing" attacks.[40] The report acknowledged the existence of this scam but still found ample reason to consider such calls suspicious, including the varying accents of callers and a *lack* of questions about financial topics or personal identifiable information. In effect, it was suspicious that callers did not ask more obviously sensitive questions that could be used in a scam. Despite no "specific, credible and imminent threat" to recruiting stations, recruiters were instructed to contact local police about "suspicious activity." The report also closed with a dire warning to officers that, even though there was no clearly identifiable threat at that time, local police should stay prepared for the "ongoing threat posed by lone actors and homegrown violent extremists." No matter an officer safety bulletin's source or accuracy, or the proximity of the threat described, nowhere at any time can be considered truly safe.

LINEUP TRAINING

While hot sheets, officer safety bulletins, and other danger signals help to maintain the danger imperative through the ritual enumeration of potential threats, it is the actual injury or death of police that most dramatically validates the danger imperative's emphasis on violence and officer safety. Regardless of their statistical rarity and whether they occur within an officer's department or far away, information about such attacks is proof of police work's mortal stakes. Every attack on an officer is an undeniable illustration of just how dangerous police work is.

In addition to written descriptions of weapons, crime, and violence, vivid videos of police being injured or killed are also shown during lineup. These videos are commonly hosted online and are easily accessed through a variety of outlets. These include police-centered websites like Police1, Officer, and Law Enforcement Today, social media accounts on Facebook and Instagram like Wolf Hunters International: LE United, Extreme Cop Videos (IG: @copclips), and Police Posts (IG: @policeposts), and YouTube channels that include PoliceActivity, Law&Crime Network, Active Self Protection, and those run by local news outlets.

Lineup videos, though very similar to those shown to recruits in the police academy, differ in two ways. First, unlike videos such as the Dinkheller traffic stop that are shown year after year to every class of recruits, lineup videos tend to draw on recent events. If Dinkheller's murder in 1998 proves that officers must be prepared to defend their lives during every interaction, videos of modern-day attacks prove that police work remains a decidedly dangerous affair. Online platforms ensure access to an ever-expanding corpus of videos that focus on rare but harrowing attacks on police from across the country.

Second, these videos are not restricted to academy recruits. Instead, they are presented to every officer, be they newly minted rookies or longtime veterans on the verge of retirement. No matter their time on the job, all officers get recurring reminders of just how quickly any given call can devolve into chaos and violence. These videos, shown to a multigenerational police audience, highlight that officers' socialization into the danger imperative is not restricted to the academy. Instead, violent videos are shown to police long after they graduate the academy to maintain the danger imperative and reinvigorate officers' adherence to the collective project of ensuring officer safety.

Officer Matthews, a Black officer who had been with the EPD for seven years, told me about one video of a traffic stop that he and other EPD officers were shown at lineup. The video began with an officer approaching the open driver-side door of a stopped vehicle. The car was still running. The officer, Matthew recalled, instructed the driver, a young Black man, "For my safety, please put the car in park and turn off the ignition." Instead of turning the car off, however, the driver began to stall, telling the officer that he was going to call his brother first. "For me, right there, that first sign of 'No,' I'm going to take you out of the car," Matthews said. "But this guy starts getting in a discussion with the driver, asking him again and again, and all the while the guy is just testing him more." Eventually, the officer reached into the car to go "hands on" and remove the driver, but the driver threw the car into drive and gunned the engine. "Officer gets dragged for 100 feet!" Matthews exclaimed.[41]

The lesson from the video was clear in Matthews's mind. "Sometimes you just have to act. You can't talk your way out of everything." Unlike the officer in the video, Matthew explained, he would have reacted immediately to the slightest resistance and removed the driver from the car. To do otherwise was to court disaster. "As soon you get a "No," he said, "that's a signal to me that things are starting to go wrong, or they could go wrong soon. You have to act right then, otherwise they're just going to keep pushing it and pushing it." These videos, Matthew said, were shown to him and his fellow officers because they so clearly encapsulated the necessity of always ensuring officer safety. "They want to reinforce officer safety. Officer safety, officer safety, officer safety. The number one rule is 'always go home at night.' The video reminds you to always be aware of your surroundings, to use your tactics, be safe."

I saw a different training video during a Monday morning lineup in West River. After informing officers of a series of robberies over the weekend, Lieutenant Aguillar directed officers' attention to a TV at the front of the room. She informed them that they were going to watch a video of a fatal officer-involved shooting in Cottonwood, Arizona, in which one suspect was wounded, one was killed, and one officer was nonfatally shot. Before dimming the lights, she prompted them, "Pay attention to issues of officer safety. What can we learn from it? Pay attention to everyone involved."

The dashcam video, which had been released about a month before, began with two Cottonwood police cruisers pulling into the parking lot of a Walmart. Unbeknownst to the WPD officers watching the video, the 911 call that prompted Cottonwood police to respond was a report of an assault on a Walmart employee. The two officers made their way to a white family of eight gathered at the back of an early-nineties Chevrolet Suburban—four men, two women, a fifteen-year-old boy, and an eleven-year-old girl. Two other officers, also white, were already on the scene, talking to the family. As the two newly arrived officers approached the group, one of the officers already engaged with the family said, "We need to separate these people to talk to them." One of the men being contacted responded, "There's no way you're going to separate me from my family."

Without warning, the fight was on. An officer took one of the men to the ground while others began fighting with the fifteen-year-old and his older sibling. Two other officers tackled or dragged family members to the ground, including one who tumbled to the asphalt over an overturned shopping cart. Without warning, a family member who had been standing out of view of the dashcam entered the fray and punched a third officer in the face. A Walmart employee, dressed in a gray T-shirt, was also part of the fight, swinging wildly at several of the family members to try and assist the officers.

The fight continued in a haze of grunts and shouts. One officer fired a Taser at the back of the fifteen-year-old who, after scuffling with that officer, had jumped on the back of an officer who was wrestling one of the boy's family members on the ground. Another officer fired their Taser at the back of the family's father, who was on top of another officer who had gone to ground. The Taser's barbs were stopped from penetrating the man's skin by his heavy coat. A third Taser was deployed, and one of the men toppled to the ground, muscles contracted by 50,000 volts. As soon as the electricity shut off, however, he was back on his feet to continue fighting with officers.

One officer drew his telescoping baton, or ASP, and began striking the family members still fighting, including the fifteen-year-old son. The boy's father screamed at officers, "Sir, you're hitting children! You're being a Nazi! You're being a Nazi!"

Near the edge of the camera's field of view, Sgt. Jeremy Daniels rolled on the ground with another male family member. Though it couldn't be made out in the moment, Cottonwood police report that this is when the struggle for Daniels's firearm began. The same report stated that at this point Daniels called out that someone had taken his gun, but he could not be heard over the cries and screams of the family and his fellow officers.[42]

Though the chaos of the fight obscured when OC spray was deployed by officers, one of the men peeled off from the group wiping at his eyes and face. Officers yelled out, "Get down! Get down!" but the family continued fighting. One of the officers then drew his firearm and shot one of the male family members in the abdomen. He then shot one of the two men struggling with Daniels in the head, killing him. Another officer, pistol drawn, kicked the remaining attacker in the head twice, dazing him. At some point during the frantic struggle over Daniels's firearm, the weapon discharged and shot Daniels in the leg.

Eventually, officers were able to pull Daniels's remaining attacker off. Weapons drawn, they yelled, "Everybody down!" at the rest of the family. Seconds later, the sound of approaching sirens pierced the melee, signaling the arrival of officers who came into frame moments later to lend aid. Daniels lay on his back while another officer applied a tourniquet to his wounded leg. After another few minutes of yelling, wrestling, baton strikes, Taser deployments, and pointing of firearms, the family was handcuffed and taken into custody.

In the moment, however, these details were largely lost amid shadows, screams, and chaos of the knock-down, drag-out brawl. One officer seated in front of me turned to his coworker, "I'm lost, bro." The other officer responded, "It's chaos! How're you supposed to remember everything you saw and did in a situation like that?" Though some events were obvious—a man spasming as a Taser sent electricity coursing through his body drew laughs from some of the WPD officers—it was impossible to clearly see what had occurred during the melee. My own notes from the lineup read, "By the end, I couldn't even see if someone had been shot, much less who did the shooting. . . .Utter mayhem."

The lights came back on and Aguillar summarized several training points. First, she said, the video showed how important it was to "stage medical," or have an ambulance on standby nearby, in the event of a serious injury. That she provided no reason for why officers should have anticipated an all-out melee that left one suspect dead, another wounded, and an officer shot in the leg was evidence of the underlying point: consummate officers should *always* expect the worst. Second, she emphasized how the officers in the video failed to appropriately control the interaction with the family in the Walmart parking lot. "Control the situation, keep people separated. These officers didn't and look what happened," she said. "A brawl."

Some might consider Aguillar's analysis overly critical. As shown in the video, an officer did articulate to their fellow officers that they needed to separate the family and talk to them. Before backup officers arrived, the officers on scene were outnumbered more than three to one. As the subsequent fight showed all too clearly, even doubling the number of officers on scene was no guarantee of compliance. Within the constraints of the danger imperative, however, Aguillar's critique is sound and predictable. The specifics of the video notwithstanding, the inability or unwillingness of officers to control the potential assailants with whom they were interacting was a necessary precondition for the situation to escalate into a deadly fight.

When considering the fight itself, Aguillar was more sympathetic. Referencing the video, she imitated one of the women who had yelled at police, "You're killing my babies!" Though Aguillar faulted the Cottonwood officers for allowing the situation to turn violent, their use of violence was understandable and acceptable once the fight with multiple individuals was in full swing. This was especially true, Aguillar said, because of the size of the men police were fighting. "They might be your babies, but they were big dudes!" she remarked, though the video showed the responding officers were as big or bigger than the entire family. That the individuals police were striking, tasing, spraying with OC, and eventually shooting were the woman's sons was irrelevant. "That might be your baby," she said, "But that's my suspect right now." Per the danger imperative and its unyielding demand for officer safety, officers are expected to do whatever necessary to survive. As Aguillar made clear, this expectation held even if the situation at hand was of the officers' own making.

WHEN VIOLENCE STRIKES

There is perhaps no more powerful contributor to the danger imperative within a police department than an instance of violence against one of its own officers. When such an attack occurs, the specifics of the incident are often relayed to officers at lineup. Such was the case during one lineup in West River, when officers were informed that Officer Romano, a female officer patrolling on the east side of the city, had been struck in the face by a bottle over the weekend. Unlike at most lineups, a captain was present to give the news, testament to the gravity of Romano's injuries.

Captain DeLeon explained to officers that Officer Romano was responding to an activation of the WPD's ShotSpotter system, a gunshot-detection technology that uses microphones to approximate the location of gunfire so officers can respond more efficiently. Unknown to Romano and another responding officer, the ShotSpotter activation had been generated when a crowd gathered for illegal street racing. When Romano arrived at the scene, her car was quickly surrounded by the crowd, and people began to throw rocks and other items at the patrol car.

Someone in the crowd also threw an empty tequila bottle that flew through Romano's open window and struck her in the face. "She was taken to the hospital and received about 100 stitches to close everything up," DeLeon told the officers. Another officer on scene was uninjured, though one of his patrol car's windows was shattered by a brick. Around the room, officers' faces were tight. A few shook their heads from side to side in a mixture of disbelief and disgust. One officer seated next to me whispered quietly, "Damn."

DeLeon told the lineup, "This kind of behavior is serious, and it's concerning to us and our safety." He assured the officers that the chief was looking into a plan to address the continued street-racing problem and suggested that the WPD would likely need the assistance of outside agencies to amass the manpower to address the large and unruly crowds. Whatever plan the WPD put into action, he assured the officers seated in front of him that that it would be "solid, safe, and effective."

Romano survived her injuries. But the attack on her and other officers was evidence of more than the danger posed by street-racing crowds; it also served as evidence of a broader antipolice sentiment police perceived in the years following Michael Brown's killing in Ferguson, Missouri.[43] "This just goes to show how the climate is right now," said DeLeon. "It's disturbing how violent and aggressive people are with officers." The reference to a pervasive and potent antipolice climate was the same one espoused by a sundry cast of police executives and political pundits throughout the mid-2010s. Just a few months before DeLeon told his officers of Romano's injuries, Ed Flynn, the chief of the Milwaukee Police Department, wrote about officers "depressed by the current environment," who felt "judged by the worst example anywhere in the country."[44] A few months later, Chuck Canterbury, the president of the Fraternal Order of Police, made it clear that the "vitriol, the hateful screeds and statements" critical of police were driving violence against officers:

It is not just talk; it is not just rhetoric. Those spewing this hatred and those calling for violence are having an impact. They have been given a platform by the media to convey the message that police officers are their enemy and it is time to attack that enemy from ambush, from hiding. Social media accounts are full of hatred and calls to target and kill police officers. There is a very real and very deliberate campaign to terrorize our nation's law enforcement officers.[45]

Fear of antipolice violence was especially pronounced among police after the murder of NYPD officers Wenjian Liu and Rafael Ramos in December 2014. At the time, Bill Bratton, then the NYPD commissioner for the second time, said the violence was reminiscent of the 1970s during which fifty-two NYPD officers were fatally shot. However, while Liu's and Ramos's murders were certainly comparable in terms of their tragic brutality, their deaths marked the first fatal shootings of NYPD officers in three years. Nine officers had been fatally shot over the previous decade, more than 138 percent fewer than the number of officers fatally shot in the 1970s.[46]

Nonetheless, the specter of a return to historic violence against police spurred precautionary measures. The NYPD tightened security out of fear that more attacks were on the horizon: the shifts of unarmed auxiliary officers were suspended, and officers on foot patrol were required to be in pairs.[47] Liu's and Ramos' deaths reverberated far outside New York City as well. In Washington DC, officers were warned to stay vigilant at all times, "while on duty on patrol, while stationary in a vehicle, and while in off-duty status." In Pittsburgh, one police official reported that officers' families were "nervous . . . fearful for the safety of their loved ones."[48]

The same fears reached Elmont. Like other officers, Officer Michaelson mentioned that the EPD leadership had mandated two-person cars for several weeks after Liu and Ramos were murdered. He recounted, "The chief came out and said that there was the potential for copycats" and that pairing officers up was a "precautionary measure." Fears were especially sharp given that the EPD had identified threats made against police via Twitter, Facebook, and Instagram. Someone had also spray-painted threats on a wall in The Wild, a housing project located near the EPD headquarters, that "called out" an officer by name.[49] Under the circumstances and mounting tensions across the country, Michaelson was grateful for the department's changes. "The two-man cars thing was comforting," he said, "because you never really know what's going to happen when you're out there. The chief also said it was as much for our safety as to give piece of mind to your families, our moms or wives. You know, so they didn't worry that their son or husband or brother is out by himself."

The threat of retaliatory violence was also discussed at lineup after line-of-duty shootings, including when no officer was harmed. This occurred during one lineup in West River following a fatal shooting that occurred after officers attempted to wake Dashawn Hamilton, a Black man in his thirties, who was sleeping in his car with a pistol on the passenger seat next to him.[50] After numerous attempts to wake him, WPD officers approached the car to smash a window and extricate the man. Upon the window being smashed by police, Hamilton stirred and, according to officers on scene, reached toward the passenger seat. One officer, who later claimed they feared for their life and that of other officers, shot the man twice, killing him.

While other lineups described the shooting itself and the tactics that officers employed, one graveyard-shift lineup focused on the possibility that cop-hating, gang-affiliated associates of the man killed by the WPD might look to exact vengeance on officers. According to police, Hamilton had been affiliated with Flo Block, a street gang whose roots could be traced back decades to Florence Street on the northwest side of West River. Sgt. Rachel explained to officers that, according to an anonymous informant, Flo Block members and affiliates were planning to ambush police in retribution for Hamilton's death.

The plan, she explained, was to lure WPD officers into a vehicle chase while two gunmen hid out of view in the back seat. The same informant alleged that Flo Block members were going to target officers driving Ford Explorers "because they roll over easier" than the smaller Ford Crown Victorias. As an aside, Sgt. Rachel mentioned that

THE THREAT NETWORK 155

there had been no corroboration of these threats by outside agencies. To allay any doubts that these threats should be taken seriously, she assured officers that members of Flo Block had assaulted WPD officers in the past.

She turned the floor over to Sgt. Grady, a veteran officer who had once patrolled the area around Florence Street and was familiar with Flo Block and members of Hamilton's family who used to live in the area. He warned officers:

> For those of you that haven't worked it, that is one gangster-ass neighborhood. The guy that got killed Saturday, his brother "Shiny" had like five kids when he was killed. He was only like nineteen or twenty. He hated us, hated the police. And these Flo Block guys, they've used this tactic before. One time I was working homicide surveillance and a unit goes to stop a car, there's a driver and a passenger. The driver bails to force a chase but the officers don't pursue. They do a felony car stop and the passenger throws a gun out of the window. We suspect he was waiting for us to chase, then get out and shoot us in the back.

Grady's warning was based on a worst-case hypothetical. Whereas he framed the flight of the driver as an attempt to lure officers into a foot chase and subsequent ambush, it was equally (if not far more) likely that the driver ran to escape potential arrest. By the same token, though it was possible that officers escaped being ambushed by the armed passenger who might have been waiting for them to chase the vehicle's driver, neither Grady nor any other officer had anything more than unsubstantiated suspicions to support such a theory.

This catastrophized hypothetical aside, Grady's warnings were also notable in their color-blindness. Without ever mentioning Shiny's race or the racial composition of Florence Street, he linked the threat of violent retribution to place, race, and gangs under the banner of antipolice hatred. Instead of only individuals hating police, these attitudes were representative of the entire "gangster-ass neighborhood" where dangerous Flo Block members lived. In describing Hamilton's already deceased brother, Shiny, he invoked racist tropes of irresponsible Black men who abandoned their children. Without ever mentioning race, Shiny's implied immorality was part and parcel of the antipolice hatred that should be expected of the Flo Block members who had attacked police and might do so again.[51]

Though a few lineups I observed ended with officers being encouraged to "Go forth and conquer" or wished "Happy hunting," most concluded with implorations to "Be safe." With the officers under her charge now freshly primed for the possibility of gangland ambushes, Sgt. Rachel concluded the lineup with similar exhortations. "When you're out there tonight," she began, "if the hairs on the back of your neck are rising up, pay attention to that. You're getting that feeling for a reason." She continued, "Do what you have to do to stay safe. I'm not saying to go out there and do anything crazy, but don't get over relaxed. I can't really tell you how to do your job but be careful." Though she did, in fact, wield operational authority over the officers under her command, Rachel understood that her authority would neither trump the discretion of her officers nor ensure their well-being. Ultimately, every officer is responsible for their own safety on patrol. If they hoped to return home after their shift, they must be prepared to do whatever was necessary to survive.

4

GOING HOME AT NIGHT

A short, rotund white man in his late forties, Officer Gagliano had a ready smile topped by a bushy mustache straight out of the 1970s. He had been an Elmont police officer for nearly twenty years and, by his own admission, was an "old school cop," distrustful of body-worn cameras and the now ubiquitous cell phones used to record officers on the street.

When Gagliano joined the EPD in 1995, long before everyone had a high-definition camera in their pocket, Elmont was just beginning to emerge from the despair and violence that spiked in many cities between the late 1980s and early 1990s.[1] That same year, John DiIulio, an Ivy League political scientist, penned the infamous "superpredator" thesis. DiIulio argued that, in the years to come, a new generation of Black and Latino children would mature into "hardened, remorseless juveniles" hellbent on murder and mayhem that would engulf the country.[2] The next year, Hillary Clinton—the first lady and future secretary of state—invoked the specter of the superpredator to praise the passage of the Violent Crime Control and Law Enforcement Act of 1994. Its provisions, including funding for one hundred thousand new police officers and nearly ten billion dollars for prisons, she proclaimed, were necessary to bring these superpredators "to heel."[3]

We know now that the bloody wave predicted by DiIulio never came to pass. In fact, violence had begun to decline years before DiIulio's dire prognostication; it would continue to plummet for the next twenty years.[4] Over the course of Gagliano's career, the Elmont homicide rate decline more than 60 percent from its zenith in the early 1990s. Still, the historical violence of those early years held sway over Gagliano's view of the streets he patrolled. On a cold night in January 2015, he drove us around Hollingwood, a predominately Black neighborhood in Elmont. He pointed to places and memories deeply marked by the violence of decades past. He showed me an area once home to open-air drug dealing called the Pit, after the muddy quagmire that would form when heavy rain waterlogged the earth of the once empty, wooded lot. Decades ago, Hollingwood and the Pit were notorious; both featured prominently in local and national news reporting about Elmont drug trafficking and gang violence. Hollingwood residents recounted the gunfire that could be heard at all hours. One resident compared their community to an active war zone: one night, he found a young man on his porch, shot. He was taken to a nearby hospital, where he died.

Today, the Pit is gone, replaced with a community garden and walking path that attract butterflies and songbirds. Hollingwood is now an area in transition, the creep of gentrification knocking at once impermeable borders. Near the neighborhood's edge, an abandoned factory that stood skeletal for thirty years had been converted into luxury apartments. The mix of foreclosed and still-occupied single-family homes that flanked the once shuttered factory were ripe, Gagliano told me, for being bought by the university to expand its already formidable foothold in Elmont. Deeper in the heart of Hollingwood, he pointed out new LED streetlights as proof of the change that marked the area.

But Gagliano did not fully see the butterflies or the neatly laid walking path of the new garden. He saw the infusion of capital and the light from the new LED bulbs dimly, as if through a haze.

While he could perceive the physical evolution of Hollingwood and Elmont, even point to its visible manifestations, he did not *feel* it. He still felt the Pit. Periodically, the job would claim another officer in some other department, proving beyond a doubt that no one wearing a badge is safe and reminding Gagliano that the specter of a violent death remained every police officer's lot.

As he drove to Starbucks near Elmont's downtown, a few miles south of his Hollingwood beat, he told me that the EPD had taken special steps following the line-of-duty murder of Wenjian Liu and Rafael Ramos, the two NYPD officers ambushed in their patrol car near the end of 2014. Whereas EPD officers were normally assigned to individual cars (in part to allow for more efficient clearance of calls for service), department leadership had mandated two-person cars. This was, Gagliano told me, "In case people get it in their heads that it's open season on cops, that they can just start killing cops."

From where we sat at a red light, he assured me that the daylight murder of two officers was something that could happen to any officer, be it in Brooklyn or Elmont. "You gotta understand," Gagliano explained, "it was just two officers sitting in their car, not doing anything. And they're murdered in cold bold. It could happen to anyone." Looking through his windshield, he spotted a middle-aged Black man standing on the sidewalk across the street. He was outside a dentist's office, its windows dark. Down the block, a high-rise apartment complex and the expensive grocery store that catered to its tenants stabbed into the sky above the surrounding bars and restaurants. The man was alone, huddling against the cold of the deepening night. "That guy right there," Gagliano warned, motioning to the man, "could open up on us with a little machine gun right now and there's nothing you or I could do about it. Nothing."

For twenty years, Gagliano had a firsthand view of Elmont's change as he patrolled its streets. He saw the open-air drug markets disappear. Street violence and crime had declined across the country for a generation.[5] Officer fatalities had also fallen, continuing a decline that began in the 1970s.[6] But now, in the twilight of his career, Gagliano continued to see his work through violence-tinted glasses. Long after the academy, he told me, it was vital for officers to continue preparing for a life-or-death fight. "You should be training," he told me. "Pretend you got shot three times in your right arm, practice unclipping [your seat belt], unholstering, turning [your gun] around, and shooting with your less-lethal [nondominant] hand." He went on, "Some people come on and don't think they'll ever have to shoot their weapon, defend themselves. You gotta decide if you're going to be a sheep or a wolf. Are you gonna be herded up and killed? Or you gonna make sure you go home?"

Gagliano's fixation on violence and the struggle to ensure that he returned home alive from his shift was neither aberrant nor undesirable. It was a common and intentionally fostered perspective within a working environment that constantly emphasizes violence, death, and the primacy of officer safety. The danger imperative constrains officers' view of the world around them to prepare them for violence that may strike at any moment. Beyond their individual perception, the danger imperative also shapes officer behavior tailored to maximize their safety at every turn. These behaviors—how officers dress, stand, drive, interact with the public, and use violence—are viewed as necessary to ensure officer survival.

Unfortunately, these survival strategies come with unintended and damaging consequences for the public and police alike. In their efforts to ensure their safety from violence, officers increase the likelihood of their own injury and death from nonviolent threats not emphasized by the danger imperative, such as high-speed car crashes that also injure and kill members of the public. Even when officers' actions don't result in grave injury or death, the danger imperative increases the likelihood that officers will behave in ways that damage their relationship with the public, force innocents to bear the costs of their mistakes, and subject vulnerable people to coercion instead of aid.

Crucially, these behaviors do not rely on the bias or racial animus of individual officers. To be clear, policing is far from immune to racism and bigotry: racist jokes, discrimination against minority officers, and officers who are members of white supremacist groups are all undeniable features of contemporary policing.[7] But the danger imperative, unlike explicit appeals to the inferiority or inherent criminality of racial minorities, provides a consistent and color-blind logic for officers to motivate and justify their behavior on the street. By the same token, it allows them to make sense of other officers' violence, even in cases that result in the deaths of innocents.

While the aseptic language of "threat," "tactics," and "officer safety" that aligns with the danger imperative pointedly avoids mention of race, officers operating within this frame are part of an institution that disproportionately funnels them into minority communities. In turn, residents of these communities are the ones who bear the brunt of police stops, searches, arrests, and violence shaped by the danger imperative.[8] For this reason, even if one were to make the implausible assumption of perfectly unbiased officers, it is these communities that continue to disproportionately bear the costs of survival-centric policing.

THE TACTICAL IMAGINATION

A uniform and a gun do not a police officer make. Beyond the physical trappings of police work, officers must *think* like police. While the danger imperative exists at the insitutional level, continually cultivated across departments and uniting officers in a shared preoccupation with violence, officers also reify the danger imperative through the conscious perception of their work through this violence-centric frame. The cognitive manifestation of the danger imperative in officers' understanding of their environment is captured in their use of the "tactical imagination," a cognitive strategy shaped by the danger imperative that officers use to imagine and rehearse their response to life-threatening confrontations on patrol. As individual officers use their tactical imagination to envision life-or-death encounters, they re-create the danger imperative and collective assumptions of violent police work.

The tactical imagination is closely tied to hypervigilance, a state of heightened awareness that is common among police.[9] Echoing the description of other officers in the EPD, WPD, and SPD, Lt. Pinelli explained police hypervigilance while periodically glancing down at her department-issued laptop to stay abreast of the calls to which her officers were responding: "Your head's always on a swivel." True to form, her eyes ceaselessly flitted from her laptop, to me, to over my shoulder, constantly trying to monitor everything at once. In contrast to the public, police are expected to be prepared for rare but potentially lethal violence, including unprovoked ambushes while they eat, complete paperwork, or pump gas. Nowhere is truly safe, and officers cannot afford to let their guard down. "There's just a lot of things that I think normal people don't think about that we do," she said. "It almost becomes subconscious, if you will."

Though she did not use the term, Pinelli described how she and other SPD officers were explicitly encouraged by their field training officers (FTOs) to use their tactical imagination while on patrol to visualize a range of dangerous scenarios and how they would respond. As a former field training officer, Pinelli had firsthand experience with practicing and teaching the tactical imagination to new officers. To do so, she had them play what she called "the 'what-if' game." This game, she explained, required officers to make up and play out a variety of unlikely but potentially deadly situations.

She recalled how she would have rookie officers explain their hypothetical tactics across a wide range of imagined scenarios. "As we're just driving around doing routine patrol," she said, "I'm trying to get my rookie to talk out loud. Tell me what you're gonna do." As trainees described what they saw happening around them, she told me, she would provide a wide range of prompts to force them into the

sort of decision-making process they would need to re-create at lighting speed when violence struck. "You have them talking out loud, and
you're helping them along, too," she said. She re-created the sort of
conversation she would have with a trainee, effortlessly listing potential reactions that an officer must consider at any given moment:

> Okay, we're stopped at a red light. What happens if the driver of the car
> in front of you jumps out and points a gun and starts firing rounds off
> at you? What are you gonna do? Can you back up? Is there a car behind
> you? Have you left enough distance between the car in front of you
> to get out of the way? Are you gonna throw it in reverse and just high
> speed back? Are you gonna throw it in reverse and do a J-turn? Are you
> gonna get on the radio and call for help? Are you gonna pull your gun
> and shoot?

Repeated use of the tactical imagination is intended to hone officers' ability to recognize and respond to threats that may emerge at any
moment. Without mental rehearsal of their reaction to a deadly threat,
officers might freeze instead of defending themselves or innocents.
"In this profession, you do have to make those split-second decisions
sometimes. If you vapor lock, it's literally a matter of life and death," she
said.[10] "But if you play those scenarios out in your head . . . you practice
like you play. If you have a plan because you've trained for it, even if it's
just mentally, then when it happens, that's what you're gonna do."
  The tactical imagination is a cognitive adaptation to two structural features of police work that officers experience through the
danger imperative: uncertainty and firearms. Uncertainty is not a
wholly negative aspect of policing. Along with the freedom of not
being stuck behind a desk, officers spoke positively about the strange,
surprising, or exciting experiences that broke up the rigamarole of
mediating disputes or writing boilerplate reports. Talking to people,
solving problems, and making their own decisions were all described
by police officers as benefits stemming from the uncertainty of patrol.

But the uncertainty of police work also has a decidedly sharp edge in a country replete with firearms. Though the range of threats that police considered while on patrol was practically limitless—an aggressive dog, a bomb threat, a knife-wielding suspect—firearms overshadowed all other safety concerns. The supply of civilian firearms in the United States exceeds 393 million weapons, and the United States has the highest rate of gun homicide of all Western democratic nations.[11] Firearms are used in more than 90 percent of felonious officer killings, and firearms are largely responsible for why U.S. police are killed at a rate twenty-five times greater than their counterparts in England and Wales, and forty times greater than German police.[12] And though officers I spoke with knew that a gunfight was unlikely in the grand scheme of their work—most police will never fire their pistol in the line of duty—unlikely does not mean impossible.[13] This probabilistic truism imbues the uncertainty of police work with especially lethal significance and justifies the tactical imagination as a necessary cognitive strategy to prime officers for emergent threats.

For Officer Cisneros, the Elmont academy instructor with a penchant for the Punisher and all things tactical, the interplay of police work's uncertainty and the omnipresent threat of firearms provided the raw scaffolding onto which he could project infinite potential threats and the necessary actions to safeguard his life. During a conversation in one of the classrooms at the EPD academy, he explained that policing was a profession in which every split second was vital. No interaction could be treated as mundane. During a vehicle stop, he said, even a moment's delay gave a tactical advantage to an officer's hypothetical killer. "That tenth of a second is that guy prepping. The more time I give them to think, right, they're always thinking, 'What do I do?'" He went on, "When you get that guy that's on the fence: Do I do it? Do I not do it? Do I run? Do I not run? Do I shoot the cop? Do I not shoot at the cop? That pressure of you being on top of them more quickly, right—again, that tenth of a second makes a difference."

Though he recognized that, "statistically, a lot of calls are the same," and that he'd "been to the same house, [at] the same time" with no violence to speak of, prior calls or the statistical rarity of violence was no guarantee that any one call couldn't turn deadly. "How do you know that the [call] you go to right here, right now, today is not the one where the guy tries to shoot you in the face as you come around the corner?" he asked. "You don't know that. And in a world of uncertainty, you have to prepare for the unexpected. You have to expect it because if you don't, you're behind the eight ball." Being "behind the eight ball," being unprepared for violence, was an unacceptable risk.

Officer Jasper, a white, sandy-haired officer who'd been with the WPD for just over a year, echoed Cisneros's view that that officers could not afford to treat any interaction as mundane. Rather than claim, as some officers did, that they intuited threat from a tingle on the back of their neck, a "sixth sense," or simply a "feeling," Jasper told me that officer safety depended on entering every interaction cognitively prepared for violence. "So there's, like, a saying," he said. "'Treat everyone with respect and have a plan to kill them.'"[14] When I asked him if he thought that police officers were prone to focusing on worst-case scenarios, he responded that they were, and that this orientation was necessary to stay alive. "I think officers expect the worst. I think that's the only way that officers can stay safe," he said. "The day I show up to a scene and I just expect everything to be OK, is the day that somebody may be calling my wife and telling her that I messed up and I'm not coming home, or I'm hurt."

The threat of firearms and the uncertainty of the street were so prominent in officers' minds that they went so far as to recruit me to aid in their efforts to stay alive. Like others, Officer Nolte, a four-year SPD veteran in his early thirties, was keenly aware that his job might thrust him into a firefight. Following one lineup, we made our way to the parking lot to find his patrol vehicle. Before we got into the car, he called me over to the trunk and showed me a small black bag with several metal carabiners hanging from it. "In case I get shot," he advised me, the bag contained emergency medical equipment, including QuikClot, a hemostatic powder designed for soldiers during the Iraq War. When poured into a wound, the powder causes immediate coagulation and can save the life of someone who might otherwise bleed to death.[15] I asked him if he would want me to use his tourniquet—a CAT, or Combat Application Tourniquet—in the event he was shot. "Depends, I guess," he responded. Patting the bag he said, "But just know it's back here."

Whereas Nolte's instructions to me were focused on how to render medical aid if he were shot, Officer Burns, whom I met just over a year after he began to patrol West River, wanted to ensure that I would be able to defend myself from violence as well. In case "shit hits the fan," Burns told me, I needed to know how to draw and shoot his pistol, a 9mm Glock 17. He showed me how to disengage the retention mechanisms on his duty holster that were designed to secure his weapon and prevent it from being stolen by a suspect or dislodged during a fight. Once the weapon was drawn, he told me, it was ready to fire. "There's no safety," he said. "Pull it, point, and shoot," showing me once again how to flip the retention hood forward and depress the automatic holster lock with his thumb in a single, fluid motion. "Hopefully you won't ever need that, but just in case," he added.

Officers who contend with uncertainty and the possibility of firearms while perceiving their work through the danger imperative are encouraged to use their tactical imagination and enter interactions primed for violence. The logic of any call, vehicle stop, or interaction being potentially lethal is all but impossible to refute, in large part because it is technically true: any interaction *could* result in lethal violence, even if that possibility is perishingly small. What's more, every time an officer enters an interaction with the possibility of violence at the forefront of their mind and leaves it unscathed, their survival proves the utility of this violence-centric mindset.

TACTICAL COLOR-BLINDNESS

Along with how officers imagine potential violence that might harm or kill them, the danger imperative constrains how they understand violence used by police. In particular, officers deploy color-blind logics that align with and reinforce the danger imperative. Rather than interrogate how race was implicated in racially inequitable policing, officers' explanations for police violence centered on tactical considerations, such as training and threat perception. Along with appeals to individual responsibility that put the onus for police violence on those hurt or killed by police, this race-blind discourse further distanced police violence from race and re-created the color-blind frame of the danger imperative.[16]

In Elmont, one of the first officers I interviewed was Officer Paduch, a white man who'd been with the EPD for seven years. At the time, Paduch was working in a specialized unit focused on firearms and gangs. Like special forces soldiers who grew beards as a marker of their elite status among the rank and file, he had taken advantage of his specialized unit's looser grooming standards and grown a thick beard to complement his plainclothes dress.[17] A firearms enthusiast even by police standards, Paduch supplemented his income by providing firearms training to police and the public at a private facility a short drive from Elmont.

Paduch's explanations for police violence, like that of other officers I spoke to, elided mention of race. This was true even in the context of high-profile cases clearly tied to ongoing debates of racial bias in policing. Immediately after telling me that he would unfriend people on Facebook for "bashing cops"—"Fuck you. Don't even put that shit on my page. I don't want to see it," he said—Paduch brought up the fatal shooting of Oscar Grant, a twenty-two-year-old Black man, by Johannes Mehserle, a white Bay Area Rapid Transit (BART) officer.

During the incident on January 1, 2009, Grant was detained by BART officers in Oakland, California, who believed he was involved in a fight on a BART train. BART officer Tony Pirone, who is also white, punched and kneed Grant before kneeling on his neck. Mehserle then attempted to place Grant in handcuffs. According to his later testimony, Mehserle claimed that Grant did not present his hands and reached for his pocket. Fearing that Grant was reaching for a firearm, Mehserle drew his department-issue SIG Sauer P226 pistol and shot Grant in the back at point-blank range. Mehserle claimed that he had not intended to shoot Grant and had meant to draw his less-lethal Taser. Grant, who was unarmed, died.[18]

Cell-phone footage of Grant's killing, which was one of the earliest incidents of a viral police-shooting video, spurred public outcry over racial inequalities in police violence. In response, Mehserle's attorneys explicitly refuted the notion that race had anything to do Grant's death, arguing instead that Mehserle had meant to use his Taser. Despite their best efforts, Mehserle was found guilty of involuntary manslaughter, and Bay Area Rapid Transit paid $2.8 million to Grant's daughter and mother.[19] Grant's death sparked protests and riots in Oakland, a city with a long history of police brutality against its Black and Latino communities.[20] The racial dynamics of the shooting—an unarmed Black man fatally shot in the back by a white police officer—were clear, reflected in protests and public discourse years before Black Lives Matter rose to political prominence.[21]

Like Mehserle's attorneys, however, Paduch provided a race-blind explanation for Grant's death: "training issues." What's more, he believed that such training issues were to blame for most instances of excessive force. He explained, "In use of force incidents where people think that the use of force was either unjust or too much, I'm gonna take a [guess], but a majority are on training errors." He elaborated on the specifics of Grant's killing: "So, what happened is in this case, you hear him, in the video, he says, 'Taser, Taser!' Boom. And he's like, 'Oh, shit.' He went to go for the Taser—" he paused, motioning to the right side of his body, "because he usually had the Taser here. It wasn't there. He went for the gun first and ended up shooting the kid." He concluded, "Training issues."

Setting aside multiple factual inaccuracies in his recounting of the circumstances surrounding Grant's killing, Paduch's understanding of the incident fit neatly into the color-blind frame of the danger imperative.[22] Within a frame focused on violence and officer safety, broader considerations like race or well-documented racial inequalities in police violence were immaterial. This is not to say that training is not a relevant topic in consideration of police violence, fatal or otherwise. Paduch's explanation, however, was not intended to establish the salience of training to Grant's killing alone. This case was illustrative, he argued, of what drove the "majority" of "unjust" or excessive police violence. In practice, Paduch used police training to decouple police violence from any context beyond officers' insufficient training and tactical expertise, wholly avoiding consideration of either racial bias or the broader social conditions that shape police interactions with racial minorities.

Tamir Rice, a twelve-year-old Black child, was killed by Cleveland police during my fieldwork and was discussed by multiple officers across the EPD, WPD, and SPD. On November 22, 2014, Cleveland received reports of a "guy with a gun" outside a local recreation center. The caller specified that the person in question was "probably a juvenile" and that the gun was "probably fake," but this information was not relayed to the two Cleveland officers dispatched to the recreation center.

The two responding officers, both white men, were Frank Garmback, a six-year veteran, and Timothy Loehmann, who'd been an officer in Cleveland for less than a year. Garmback, who was Lohemann's training officer, drove their police vehicle over a curb to speed toward a gazebo where it was reported Rice was sitting.[23] Garmback hit the brakes and slid to a halt within a few feet of Rice. Rice stood up from the picnic table at which he was seated and slowly approached the police car as Loehmann exited the passenger side. Loehmann claimed that Rice reached for his waistband to grab the pellet gun he'd been reportedly pointing. Loehmann believed the pellet gun to be a real firearm. Loehmann, who claimed that he was in fear for his life, opened fire and killed Rice. The entire interaction lasted less than two seconds.[24]

Garmback was suspended for using improper tactics and required to participate in additional tactical training. Lohemann was fired, but not for the shooting; he was terminated for failing to disclose on his application to the Cleveland Police Department that he had resigned from another Ohio police agency after being found to be emotionally unstable and unfit to serve as a police officer.[25] Neither officer faced criminal charges. The City of Cleveland paid six million dollars to Rice's family.[26] Rice's killing, which occurred just months after Eric Garner was fatally choked by police in Staten Island, New York, and Michael Brown was fatally shot by police in Ferguson, Misssouri, further spurred nationwide protests against racial bias and brutality in policing.[27]

Like Paduch's color-blind assessment of the underlying cause of unjust or excessive force, Lt. Miles's perspective on Rice's killing relied exclusively on tactical considerations and omitted any mention of race. Miles, a white man in his early forties, was a short, muscular man who carried himself like he was ten feet tall. As a combat veteran and decorated officer who had been on the SWAT team and other specialized units since joining the WPD in the early 1990s, Miles was respected and admired by officers under his command.

When I told him that other WPD officers I'd spent time with viewed the incident as a "clean shoot"—shorthand for a legal and policy-compliant shooting—Miles invoked race-blind, tactical considerations to explain Rice's killing. Specifically, he noted that two Cleveland police officers had been killed near the same park where Rice was killed. One officer was killed in 1998, the other in 2006.[28] I told him that I had never heard that particular detail. He responded, "Right. No one has. But it changes how you think about things." This context, he explained, was crucial to understanding the officers' assumptions of

GOING HOME AT NIGHT 171

threat and their subsequent actions when they approached what they believed was an armed suspect in a park where other Cleveland police had been killed:

> Do you think that's the first-time police have been sent to that park? You have to think about the history of that particular park, what it means to officers in that department. You know that park is not in the best neighborhood, that officers have gone there for shootings before. All of that goes through an officer's head when they get sent to a call of a suspect with a gun.

Rather than consider how race and place were intertwined in the chain of events leading to Cleveland police killing Rice, Miles's assessment omitted race altogether and included only factors aligned with the danger imperative's preoccupation with violence. Place was only relevant to the shooting insofar as the park in which Rice was killed was part of the Cleveland Police Department's collective memory of violence and death.[29] The park's community center, swing set, and playground where children were likely to spend time were immaterial and unmentioned. What mattered was that the park was "not in the best neighborhood" and was associated with violence to which police had responded or fallen victim. In turn, the question of how race and place intersected to shape officers' perception of Rice and their ultimately lethal decisions went unasked and unanswered.[30]

Sergeant Kershaw, who'd been with the Sunshine Police Department for more than twenty years when I met him, also deployed tactical color-blindness in his explanation for Rice's killing. Like other officers I spoke to, Kershaw critiqued some of the tactics used by the two Cleveland officers. Though he recognized that the officers made decisions that created exigent circumstances—the officers removed space and time within which to respond to a threat—he ultimately concluded that these mistakes did not mean the shooting was unjustified:

When they show up, their tactics were not the smartest of tactics: they let themselves get way too close to things. But it just kind of popped out of nowhere when they came into the park there, and then Tamir starts pulling the gun out of his waistband. . . . So, the cops reacted to what they saw was a guy that had previously threatened citizens and now he's threatening them and [they thought] 'this is going to go sideways if I don't do something right now to save my life.' And so they shot him dead. It's a tragedy that it went that way but it was a legitimate perception of danger that they were reacting to.

Kershaw went further and wove color-blind ideals of individual responsibility into his tactical justifications for Rice's death. He told me frankly, "Tamir was a tragedy, but it was completely justifiable. The kid was a moron." He went on:

It's sad that he got killed because he was a moron. I mean that. But it was still a reasonable tragedy, by which I mean with what the officers knew and when they knew it and what they reacted to, they were in legitimate fear of their lives and took actions to protect themselves. . . . It was just an utterly stupid move on his part . . . an ignorant move, that's probably a more accurate statement because he was young and ignorant and maybe didn't know that pulling a gun on a cop after cops have been called about a man with a gun wasn't the thing to do.

In one breath, Kershaw described the officers who killed Rice as having agency, able to make choices and even mistakes on patrol. In the next, he described them as purely reactive, acting rationally and solely in response to the threatening behaviors of an "ignorant" twelve-year-old child. That it would have been impossible for Rice to know that police had been called about a man with a gun did not seem to occur to Kershaw. Instead, the color-blind discourse of tactics and individual responsibility allowed him to distance other officers from culpability and blame an innocent child for his own death.

Tactical color-blindness was not restricted to white officers. Officers of color also made sense of Rice's killing with discourse that emphasized tactics and individual responsibility while assiduously ignoring race. At around 3:00 A.M. in West River, Officer Lopez stopped the vehicle of a man he suspected was soliciting sex. While Lopez ran the man's driver's license through his in-car computer to check for warrants, I walked over to speak with Officer Kirkland, another WPD officer who had arrived with a trainee officer to provide backup for Lopez. I spoke to Kirkland, who remained in his patrol car, through the driver-side window while his trainee stood near the stopped vehicle to keep a watchful eye on the driver.[31]

I had met Kirkland, a Black man with a bald head and glasses, just a few days into ride-alongs in West River. Whereas some officers were wholly skeptical of my presence, he had approached me after one lineup to tell me, "I'm glad there's someone who is going to take the time and be objective about the work that we do in West River." When I saw him again almost two months later, he greeted me warmly and asked how my time on patrol had been. Standing outside his patrol-car door, I told him that I'd learned a great deal and was continually surprised by how much of police work went largely unseen by the public. He nodded along approvingly until I told him I had been surprised by officers who'd told me they believed the shooting of Tamir Rice was justified. The tone of our conversation, previously relaxed and friendly, suddenly tensed.

"You don't think it was a clean shoot?" Kirkland asked pointedly. I replied that it was hard for me to justify the killing of a child when the officers pulled up directly next to him and shot within a few seconds. I asked Kirkland whether he believed it was justified. He prefaced his response by stipulating, "I wasn't there and I don't know what the officer saw," a common refrain for police reticent to be a "Monday morning quarterback" who critiques other officers' decisions after the fact.[32] Like Sergeant Kershaw in Sunshine, Kirkland's explanation for Rice's death focused heavily on tactical considerations.

"Even if it's a toy gun," he said, "it looked like a real one. It didn't have the orange tip or anything. You don't have time to think about it if that black, gun-looking thing is a real gun or a toy one."

I pushed back, "But the kid was alone, in the middle of the day, in a park. He was twelve." Kirkland shrugged and seamlessly transitioned his explanation to one that simultaneously defined children as potentially lethal threats and blamed Rice for his own death.

"You don't think a twelve-year-old can kill you? Way I see it, that young man got himself killed. He was playing with what looked like a real gun in a public park." I pointed out to Kirkland that none of those things were illegal. His position remained unchanged. "Maybe not," he responded. "But the officers got a call, and when that happens, they're going in there and they're looking for a potentially lethal threat. That young man put himself in that position. If he hadn't been there, there would've been no call."

In contrast to Kirkland and others, some officers did consider how race influenced inequalities in police violence. Officer Voss, a thirty-four-year-old Black officer who grew up in Elmont, remembered having a less than positive impression of police as a child: "I fucking hated them, dude. Fuck." In addition to "seeing cops beat people up" and being stopped by police while riding his bike to be searched for guns, he vividly remembered police brutalizing his uncle. "I remember them choking my uncle out," he recalled. "They choked my uncle out until his face turned blue. My whole family was fighting them. I mean, my uncle was breaking the law but, you know, when you run into someone's house without a warrant, the cops are now breaking the law."

Whereas other officers omitted any discussion of race in the context of police killings like that of Rice or other Black people, Voss clearly interrogated whether Rice's race was a factor in police killing him. "They fucking shot him and left him there," he said, then proposed the racial counterfactual unuttered by other officers: "Make

Tamir Rice a white kid in the suburbs. They're gonna roll by him and fucking gun him down and leave? No. It's an ongoing debate. Does the area change the outcome of the crime? Does the area change the way police approach it? It shouldn't."

I responded, "Well, yeah, it shouldn't." Voss replied unequivocally, "It does."

However, neither Voss's racial identity, negative experiences with police, nor views on racial bias in policing obviated the danger imperative's preoccupation with violence. To the contrary, Voss was still acutely aware of the potential for being attacked on patrol. And like other officers, even those who omitted or minimized the role of race in policing, he practiced his work in ways that aided in his survival. Keeping suspects' hands out of their pockets and ensuring hands were always visible was vital, he explained, because "Hands kill people." When responding to calls for service, he said, it was important to "always go with other officers. Approach with numbers" to enhance officer safety.

Though Voss had a critical view of policing vis-à-vis race, these beliefs easily existed within the broader color-blind frame of the danger imperative. In practice, racialized police violence was a separate matter from officer safety. Individual officers' beliefs about or experiences with racism were superseded by the more fundamental matter of survival. Whether an officer believed that police violence was tied to race or not, the danger imperative's preoccupation with violence and officer safety remained. Even officers like Voss, a Black man who clearly articulated that police violence was shaped by race, could also believe, as he told me, "As a cop, anything bad can happen anywhere, especially when you have a car and a uniform. They see us from a mile away." As a result, Voss's preoccupation with officer safety, despite his own belief that race mattered in the context of police violence, re-created the color-blind frame of the danger imperative.

PREVENTIVE MEASURES

The danger imperative, through its influence on how officers perceive and understand their working environment, is also embodied in the practice of police work. Every shift, officers engage in behaviors designed to protect them from violence. And though individual officers engage in these behaviors, they do not do so in isolation; officers' actions are observed and mirrored by other officers socialized into the danger imperative. As a group operating with a shared appreciation for the possibility of violence and death, police officers, through their safety-enhancing actions, socially re-create the danger imperative as a cultural construct that is necessary to survive patrol.

Many of these safety-enhancing behaviors are discrete and do not depend on weapons, violence, or the overt exercise of police authority. Nor do they require that an officer be responding to an immediate or identifiable threat. Many safety-enhancing behaviors are intended to put officers in an advantageous position or minimize the possibility of attack even when they are not directly interacting with another person. When sitting down for a meal, for example, officers with whom I ate sat with their backs against a wall and with a clear line of sight to the restaurant's entrance. A wall at their back made sure no one could sneak up behind them, and a view of the door made sure they could easily see who was coming into the restaurant. To avoid being shot when responding to a call for service, officers avoided standing in front of windows or directly in front of a door.

Concern with being attacked at any moment extended to the patrol cars that—between driving to and from calls, transporting arrestees, eating, checking license plates and driver's licenses, and doing paperwork—were where officers often spent most of their shift. This included their choice of where and how to park their patrol cars, on which there was wide disagreement. Some officers preferred to park in the middle of an empty parking lot to allow them to see an attacker approach from any direction. Others parked with the rear end of the vehicle against a fence or wall to ensure that no one could sneak up on them from behind while they wrote reports or ate their lunch. Still others religiously reversed into parking spots instead of driving in headfirst; should they come under fire, they would be able to more quickly "get off the X" and take evasive action than if they first had to reverse out of a parking spot.[33] Despite disagreement on the optimal parking strategy to prevent an ambush—the rarity of ambushes allowing officers to reasonably claim that their preferred strategy was effective—the concern with being randomly attacked while in their patrol car was common.

Other behaviors encouraged by the danger imperative are used during interactions with members of the public, which officers assume always have a potential for violence. When interacting with someone on the street, for example, officers used a specific "POI," or position of interrogation, to be ready for violence. Rather than leaving their hands at their sides, officers assumed something like a relaxed boxing stance in which their hands were kept up near their chest. This stance was designed to help them block an incoming strike, push an assailant away, or throw their own punch more quickly. Officers' feet were also positioned in anticipation of violence, shoulder width apart and "bladed," with one foot slightly in front of the other. This positioning, besides giving officers greater mobility and balance should a fight break out, allowed officers to keep their gun-side hip further away from someone who might try and grab their firearm. It also allowed officers, should they draw their firearm, to quickly transition into a shooting stance that gave them better control of their firearm and minimized their body's profile (i.e., the area of their body exposed to gunfire).

Officers' safety-enhancing behaviors are clearest in the context of interactions that officers consider especially dangerous: vehicle or traffic stops. Though recent research shows that, conservatively, an officer is killed once in every 6.5 million traffic stops, the understanding of these stops as extremely dangerous remains an article of faith within policing.[34] This was the case across Elmont, West River, and Sunshine, where officers frequently emphasized that any vehicle they stopped might be driven by someone with a firearm. To make matters worse, they told me, officers engage in traffic stops with incomplete information about who they are stopping. Those in the vehicle might be fleeing from the scene of a crime, be on their way to commit a crime, have outstanding warrants, or simply hate police. Any of these possibilities could motivate an attack on an officer. A Sunshine officer explained this logic simply: "You never know whose car that [is] you're stopping on a traffic stop. And you can do everything you can do to be as safe as you can. But, I mean, there's always a chance that someone's got something planned for you, that you won't see coming kind of thing. And that's scary."

Unsurprisingly, officers' performance of traffic stops was deeply marked by the danger imperative's preoccupation with violence and officer safety. Officer Lewis, a tall, dark-skinned WPD rookie of Trinidadian descent, assiduously practiced a range of safety-enhancing tactics during traffic stops. Around 6:30 P.M., about midway through his shift, I watched him initiate a stop of a silver sedan with tinted driver's-side and front passenger windows—a violation of state law. Before approaching the driver's-side window, he called out over his police car's loudspeaker for the driver to roll down the windows. The stopped vehicles windows were lowered, and the stop proceeded uneventfully. Lewis got the licenses of the driver and passenger— both Black men around the same age as Lewis—while standing at the back edge of the driver's door, or the "B pillar." This position provides several advantages to officers: it forces a driver to crane their neck to see an officer while allowing the officer to easily observe the vehicle's front occupants. Most importantly, the B pillar shields an officer from the driver and forces a would-be gunman to awkwardly turn around and shoot at an officer from an extreme angle.[35]

After checking the driver and passenger for outstanding warrants via his in-car computer and finding none, Lewis returned their licenses and let them leave with a warning about the car's tints. Once the car left, Lewis pulled into a parking spot in front of a mechanic's shop to write the stop report: the reason for the stop, vehicle information, whom he contacted, and what action he took. While he typed, he described the safety considerations officers must keep in mind while undertaking every car stop. "If you're doing a car stop," he explained, "your spotlight is on. Do you know where you are? Did you put the spotlight at the right place? Do you have a cover unit? Who's in the car?" Officers should also park at a slight angle to the stopped vehicle. Officers never know when they might be shot at by someone; by parking at an angle, Lewis explained, they place more of their car's engine between them and potential bullets.

Another safety-enhancing behavior used by officers was touching the trunk or rear taillight of vehicles they stopped before proceeding to the driver's window.[36] After seeing multiple officers touch the trunk of the cars they stopped, I asked Officer Menendez, a twenty-three-year-old Mexican American and former Marine who'd been on the street less than a year, why he and other officers did so.

"It's to make sure the trunk is closed," he replied, as if the rationale was obvious. Confused, I asked him why the trunk being closed was important. He responded, "In case there's someone in the trunk that's going to shoot you." I inquired if he had ever heard of someone being attacked by a gunman hiding in the trunk of a car that had been stopped. He said that he had not. Still, he said, "I'm sure it's happened."

I pressed the point and asked him if he could admit that the probability of a gunman lying in wait inside a car's truck to spring out and kill an approaching officer was exceedingly low. His response made clear that the low probability of a gunman waiting in the trunk did not supersede the danger imperative and its emphasis on the unwavering possibility of violence: "It's low but that's how we're trained. We train for the worst-case scenario; we don't train to stop granny. We train to expect someone to have a gun, to try and hurt us. It doesn't happen often but it does happen. People do fight you."

Officer Richardson, a Black officer who left the Marine Corps and earned his bachelor's degree in sociology before joining the EPD, also touched the trunks of cars he stopped to guard against a hidden gunman. This behavior and its rationale, he recalled, were explicitly taught in the police academy. If a recruit failed to check the trunk during a traffic stop exercise, he recalled with a laugh, "You know [academy instructor] Stockton is going to be in the trunk with a gun!" Richardson considered this behavior part and parcel of maintaining constant vigilance in the face of rare but unpredictable threats to ensure his safety. He told me, "Officer safety; that's why they train you the way they do. It's the unknowns. Realistically, how often are you going to find someone in the trunk? But by training you that way, now you're looking for people in other places that you might not expect to find someone. It expands your mind, being vigilant makes you look for the unexpected."

Richardson also gave me another reason that he and other officers touched the trunk: to leave his fingerprint on the car. This was important, he said, in case an officer is killed during a traffic stop and the suspect flees. In conjunction with a clear and accurate description of the vehicle that officers should relay to dispatch before approaching a vehicle on foot, an officer's fingerprint on the rear of a vehicle can serve as evidence to tie that vehicle and its occupants to the murder of a police officer. "Say that person shoots and kills you and drives away," he explained. "My fingerprint is on the car now. And I've given a description of the car, so if they find the car they'll have my print on that car." Touching the trunk of stopped vehicles, then, is understood by officers as a means to ensure their safety through prevention of an ambush, as well as a means to aid in the capture and prosecution of anyone who succeeds in harming them during a traffic stop.

Through the daily practice of these varied safety-enhancing behaviors, officers accomplish two things. First, officers' repeated deployment of these safety-enhancing strategies re-creates the danger imperative's preoccupation with violence and officer safety. Officers engage in these behaviors because police work is dangerous. So long as officers touch the trunk of cars they've stopped and insist on sitting with their backs to the wall, the assumption of constant danger and the necessity of preparing for it remain. Second, these behaviors reify the utility of the danger imperative for understanding and navigating this dangerous working environment. Though parking a patrol car in an empty lot or using one's spotlight during a traffic stop is difficult to prove as the definitive reason an officer survived a given shift, every time an officer returns home alive serves as proof that their efforts to stay alive have served their purpose. As evidenced by their continued survival, assiduous adherence to the danger imperative and their repertoire of safety-enhancing behaviors is effective and necessary.

BLIND SPOTS, SPEED, AND SEAT BELTS

Some of officers' safety-enhancing behaviors, such as how they stand or where they sit for lunch, incur little if any cost to officers or the public. Others expose them to grave danger. This unfortunate irony is a direct consequence of the danger imperative. Like firefighters who hone their bodies and axes to confront roaring flames and billowing smoke, or electricians who insulate themselves from deadly electrical currents with their own specialized tools and training, the contextual challenges of police work constrain which threats officers attend to and their shared understanding of the proper responses to those threats.[37]

The danger imperative, as a cultural frame that filters officers' experience on patrol, is the perceptual mechanism that continually and specifically highlights the threat of violence. In practice, this filter and the pressures of police work encourage officers to focus on violence in lieu of other threats, creating a cultural blind spot among officers socialized to privilege the threat of violence above all else. To make matters worse, efforts to ensure officer survival, though appropriate and justifiable within the frame of the danger imperative, can place police and the public in harm's way.

The consequences of such blind spots are especially clear in the context of on-duty car crashes. According to the National Law Enforcement Officers Memorial Fund (NLEOMF), vehicle crashes between 2011 and 2020 accounted for approximately fifty line-of-duty deaths a year, or 21 percent of all line-of-duty deaths (excluding COVID-19 in 2020).[38] This says nothing, of course, about officers nonfatally injured in crashes. To make matters worse, police-related vehicle crashes also injure and kill thousands of citizens. Looking only at vehicle pursuits in which police are chasing a suspect in a car—a small subset of high-speed police driving—370 officers were killed during such pursuits between 1980 and 2014. Over approximately the same period, police pursuits led to the deaths of at least 6,300 suspects, some of whom were being pursued for offenses like shoplifting or minor traffic violations; bystanders and passengers in pursued vehicles accounted for more than five thousand deaths. Tens of thousands more were injured.[39]

Police are not ignorant of the danger posed by high-speed crashes. To mitigate the risk of high-speed driving, departments implement policies that restrict when officers can engage in high-speed driving with lights and sirens, commonly referred to as driving "code 3." These policies commonly restrict the number of police vehicles that can respond to a given call for service or engage in a vehicle pursuit. But, as explained to me by Officer Morales, a bald-headed, Latino officer who had rotated back into patrol after spending three years in the Sunshine gang unit, SPD officers commonly ignored policy restricting code 3 driving. According to the SPD's general orders, he said, "You cannot go code 3 to anything if there's already two units going code 3; it's only max two units code 3 to a scene. Same thing in a vehicle pursuit: you've got a lead car, back car, and that's it, going code 3, lights and sirens. Does that happen?" He laughed knowingly and answered his own question, "No."

Officers ignore these departmental policies in the name of officer safety. Officer Vance, a Black officer who grew up in Elmont and who had been on the street for four years, explained this logic to me as he drove Officer Roland, another Black officer, to his walking beat north of Elmont's downtown. Vance told me that he ignored the EPD's code 3 policy to ensure that he responded as quickly as possible to "priority 1" calls that denote emergency situations in which there is reason to believe there is an imminent threat to life.

Having read the EPD policy, I asked him if he got approval for driving code 3 before turning on his lights and sirens and driving at high speeds. He admitted, "You're supposed to [get approval] but I don't." Instead, his behavior was guided by informal "rules" about which calls merited a high-speed response, regardless of EPD policy. "There's different rules for it. If it's a serious call, a priority 1, I'll go code 3," he explained.

From the backseat, Officer Roland added his perspective on the matter. "I go [code] three to all priority 1 [calls]. I never ask for approval. I might get jammed up if I get in a 22 [traffic accident] but that's on me." I asked Roland why he knowingly broke departmental policy if it meant he would potentially be disciplined for getting involved in a crash while engaging in unauthorized high-speed driving. "Seconds matter if it's a hot call," he responded. "Getting there fast can keep someone alive and you'd want your buddies to come back you up if it were you, right?" For Roland, the risk of departmental discipline or a traffic accident while driving code 3 without authorization was outweighed by the need to provide speedy backup for fellow officers who he expected would also rush to his aid.

Officers also engaged in what they referred to as "code 2½" driving to conceal their unauthorized high-speed driving while racing to back one another up on patrol. Unlike the standard "code 2" driving which required officers to obey all traffic laws (included posted speed limits) and proper code 3 driving which mandated the use of lights and sirens to alert other motorists, code 2½ was an informal middle ground in which officers drove at high speeds without consistent use of their emergency lights and siren.

I was with Officer Mizel in West River when he gunned the engine to speed toward where another officer was responding to a report of an assault on a homeless man. Though he was driving faster than the posted speed limit on active roadways, he did so without leaving his lights and sirens on. Instead, he used this emergency equipment selectively, just long enough to make other vehicles move out of his lane or to "break" an intersection if he encountered a red light. Once his way was clear or he'd passed through an intersection, he deactivated his lights and sirens.

I asked Mizel, a White WPD rookie and son of a longtime WPD veteran, why he chose to not leave his lights and sirens activated if he was going to drive at high speeds. He looked at me through thick-framed glasses and explained that, though he was forbidden by WPD policy from engaging in unauthorized code 3 driving, the normative expectation among officers of providing speedy backup superseded formal departmental rules. "I can't go full lights and sirens," he told me, "but you'll drive a little more aggressively, go a little faster. You don't want to leave your teammates out there by themselves."

Mizel's and other officers' code 2½ driving was an attempt to abide by at least some of their department's driving policy while still racing to their fellow officers' aid. Though they did not describe it as such, it was also a means of concealing their out-of-policy driving from supervisors who might discipline them for breaking policy. This deviance, though understood through the danger imperative as necessary to fulfill the collective demand for officer safety, increased officers' and the public's risk of injury and death from high-speed crashes.

To make matters worse, officers' willingness to flout departmental policy in the name of officer safety also extended to their eschewing of seat belts. Whereas unauthorized code 3 and code 2½ driving were justified on the grounds of protecting their compatriots, officers commonly chose to not wear their seat belt to ensure they were able to address a violent threat more quickly.

Officer Estacio, the same EPD officer with a young daughter who told me about his fear of being ambushed on patrol, was one of several officers who left their seat belt off to enhance his safety. On the night that I met him, we listened to the police radio as two other EPD officers reported that a vehicle they had attempted to stop for a traffic violation had fled. "Let's see if we can get in the mix," Estacio said, and sped off toward his fellow officers. Estacio pushed the rough-ridden Ford Interceptor to upwards of sixty miles per hour. Parked cars zipped by on either side of the patrol car as he sped past a hospital, park, and school without his lights or sirens activated.

Before too long, a sergeant came over the radio and asked for what the vehicle was wanted. When officers reported that their justification for the stop was nothing more than a traffic violation, the sergeant shut down the would-be pursuit. Estacio reduced his speed, grumbling about not being allowed to chase vehicles. I took the lull in activity as an opportunity to ask Estacio why he and other officers didn't wear their seat belts, even when driving at high speeds.

The main reason, Estacio explained, was that seat belts obstructed his and other officers' access to their firearms. "I'd say 90 percent of us don't wear our seat belts," he said. "It's just too much for us. Tactically, some places the cops wear the vests or the carriers that have all their gear in the front or on their chest, then it's easier to wear the [seat] belt. But here . . ." He looked down at his waist and he pointed at his holstered pistol, nestled up against the seat belt buckle. "It's too much. I'd say only 10 percent actually wear [a seat belt]." This justification for eschewing a seat belt is an outgrowth of officers' belief, encouraged by the danger imperative, that they must always be ready to use their firearms and defend their lives on patrol. Any impediment to doing so is an unacceptable safety risk.

Similarly, officers chose to leave off their seat belts because they feared it might hinder them from speedily exiting their patrol car to address a threat. Officer Doyle, a Black twenty-five-year-old who'd joined the WPD after getting his bachelor's degree in criminal justice, was one such officer. "There's times where I'll be driving and the next thing you know I'll be like, "Oh shit, that dude's got a fucking gun!" he said. "I'll stop," he began, then mimicked the screech of a car's tires when it braked harshly. "Try to get out—fuck. Stuck on the seat belt. . . . I'd rather just be able to jump out on people, you know. If I have to, be able to jump out of this deathtrap of a car."

Doyle readily admitted that he relished the rush of car chases. He also recognized their inherent risk and asserted that he did his best to put on his seat belt when engaged in code 3 driving. Contrary to his claim, however, he left it off later that shift while swerving through traffic, driving in oncoming traffic lanes, and reaching speeds of nearly a hundred miles per hour to try and support a developing chase. Despite his best efforts and the danger in which he placed himself and innocent motorists, he never caught sight of the fleeing vehicle and WPD officers did not apprehend the suspect.

These dangerous behaviors, justified in the name of officer safety, persisted despite clear evidence of their unintended but inevitable consequences. Multiple Elmont officers recalled the high-speed crash that killed a veteran officer some years prior. Assistant Chief Altidore, who'd known the officer for nearly two decades, solemnly told me, "Had he been wearing his seat belt, he would have survived that crash." Another officer involved in that crash survived but was left in a vegetative state. This officer's picture, edited to show their face and an EPD patrol car floating among bright clouds, hung in the EPD lineup room.

One night in West River, Officer Jenkins, a rookie officer in his early twenties responded at high speed to a report of a suspicious person, without his lights and sirens, and without his seat belt. While en route, he collided with another vehicle, lost control of his patrol car, and smashed headlong into a parked semitruck trailer. Jenkins's injuries were devastating—to this day, he remains in a 24/7 medical care facility, unable to speak, eat, or move on his own. Nonetheless, these high-speed tragedies did not alter the danger imperative nor officers' narrow preoccupation with violence.

COMMAND PRESENCE AND UNINTENDED CONSEQUENCES

Along with the blind spots created by the danger imperative's preoccupation with violence, the danger imperative privileges officers' immediate safety over the long-term consequences of their safety-enhancing behavior. As a cultural frame that mediates individuals' perception as they move through their environment, the danger imperative constrains action in ways that are always, as described by sociologist Anthony Giddens, "located in one context of time and space."[40] People, including police, respond to the exigencies of the present without full apprehension of their decisions' downstream consequences. Officers parsing their environment through the danger imperative behave in ways designed to protect them from violence *in the moment*.

But like a stone cast into a still pond, officers' behavioral choices have ramifications that ripple outward beyond the bounds of a given call, interaction, or threat. These consequences, even if they affect their working environment in ways that damage police legitimacy, erode trust, and increase the likelihood of antagonistic interactions in the future, are overridden by the danger imperative's preoccupation with violence and officer safety in the present.

Officer violence, ranging from high-profile police killings to more common uses of physical coercion that include grabbing, punching, handcuffing, or using various less lethal weapons, is the most obvious officer behavior that can damage legitimacy and public well-being.[41] But physical violence is not necessary to create these negative downstream consequences. Before officers go "hands on" with a suspect or reach for their firearm, their very appearance and demeanor are understood and used as a preemptive safeguard against attack and a means to retain control of every interaction. This interactional style is commonly referred to as "command presence."

In the simplest sense, command presence is a combination of demeanor and appearance that exudes authority. In contrast to the intangible, moral underpinnings of legal legitimacy that influence public cooperation and compliance with the state, command presence speaks to the observable performance of officers' physical authority.[42] Part of this authoritative performance is an aesthetic holdover from policing's military roots: boots shined to gleaming, a pressed uniform, and sharp grooming are not only encouraged but often required by department policy. Such regimented dress is a hallmark of what some officers referred to as being "squared away," military slang for someone who shows consistency and competence in their duties.

Officer Lewis, the same officer who assiduously deployed safety-enhancing tactics during traffic stops, was a paragon of being squared away. Though in his early thirties, his crisp fade and clean shave would let him pass for someone in their early or mid-twenties. A military veteran, Lewis was familiar with maintaining himself and his environment in pristine order. The first thing he did on his shift the day I was with him was get his police car detailed at a local carwash that has a contract with the WPD. Before heading out to take calls, he purchased a small paper air freshener, tore it into pieces, and stuck them in the car's air-conditioning vents to freshen the cabin's scent. Being squared away, Lewis told me, was key to the successful performance of command presence.

"They taught us that in the academy," he recalled. "When you get out of the car and you're neat and clean: your uniform is pressed, you're clean shaven. Your command presence is what they call it." As soon as an officer is within eyesight, long before a punch is thrown or a gun is drawn, a well-fitted uniform, shined boots, and regimented grooming can help stave off violence. "Suspects, bad guys, people who are willing to do shit to hurt you are a little bit—maybe not always—but they're a little bit more willing to think twice before they do something or say something," Lewis told me as we drove back toward his beat.

Like Lewis, Officer Matthews, a Black EPD officer who had been on the street for seven years, also believed that exuding command presence could prevent an attack. He recalled a story that he and other officers had been told by Captain Wozniak, a twenty-year EPD veteran known for her dedication to community policing and outreach work with local youth, that proved the necessity of command presence. According to Wozniak, he said, "There was this guy who wanted to kill a cop." He continued, "This guy would sit at a Dunkin' Donuts every day and keep track of which officers came in, when, all that. One day, he just gets up, goes up to an officer, and kills him. When they're interviewing this guy, they ask him, 'Why this officer?' He responds, 'He looked sloppy. Overweight. I didn't think he'd put up much of a fight.'" Matthews was unable to recall where this unprovoked murder occurred but assured me, "Wozniak told us, though."[43]

Though I was unable to independently verify that such an incident occurred, claims of officers' command presence preventing attacks and enhancing officer safety are widely echoed by police consultants, law enforcement researchers, and prominent policing organizations like the International Association of Chiefs of Police.[44] These claims are, like Matthews's, often based on unverifiable anecdote. One article penned by a police lieutenant and training expert, for example, referenced two uncorroborated "stories" of officers being killed because they gave off "signals of struggling prey" rather than "a professional aura or air of authority."[45] No information about the officers, their agency, or even the city or state in which these incidents allegedly occurred could be found.

It is impossible, of course, to know conclusively whether an attack was caused by an officer's lack of command presence. But for police, it's more important that it's equally impossible to claim that command presence was *not* the reason an attack *didn't* occur. Given that command presence is assumed to have a practically infinite life-saving upside, its resonance with the danger imperative's preoccupation with violence ensures that it remains understood as a valuable part of officers' daily practice.

Command presence's safety-enhancing value is tied to officers' belief that it can prevent a loss of control that opens the door for an interaction to violently escalate. Matthews explained this justification for command presence to me while recounting an instance in which he had yelled and cursed at a drunk bar patron who had drawn close to where Matthews was responding to a call about a cab passenger who refused to pay her fare.

While Matthews talked to the cab driver and passenger, he told me, the drunken man got near him and demanded to know what was going on, claiming that he had a right as a citizen to know what police were doing. Matthews recounted his forceful and disrespectful response: "Actually, you *don't* have the right to know what's going on with a police investigation. Get the fuck out of here!" When the man persisted, Matthews grew angry. "I probably shouldn't have done this but I was pissed," he explained to me. "I said, 'If you don't get the fuck out of here I'm going to lock you up! You're taking my attention away from what I'm doing and you're intoxicated. Get out of here!'"

When I asked Matthews why he'd cursed at the drunken man, his initial response was one of chagrin, admitting, "I probably shouldn't have done that." In the next breath, he justified his actions as part of command presence that is necessary to prevent a situation from spiraling out of control. "You have to keep control of the situation," he told me. "You have to keep authority. This guy was drunk, he was taking my attention off what I was doing. You have to keep authority because when the citizen gets the authority that's when things go bad." He concluded, "It's all about command presence."

Later that shift, Matthews confirmed that command presence, though justified by him and other officers as necessary for ensuring their safety, can and does morph into disrespect and aggression that provokes fear, anger, and resentment.[46] Near the end of what had been a slow shift, Matthews received a call from an off-duty EPD officer who had found a wallet while working security at a local grocery store. After being texted a photo of an ID found in the wallet, Matthews set off to the listed address to try and notify the wallet's owner that it had been found.

After a short drive, Matthews parked outside a two-story house situated across the street from a local park. I followed him up the steps to the front porch; the two mailboxes next to the front door indicated that the home was divided into multiple units. Matthews rapped on the door and was greeted by a young, heavyset white woman with shoulder-length brown hair. She stayed just inside the house's threshold, the door concealing half her body but still wide enough for her to easily speak with Matthews.

"Hi . . . can I help you?" she asked, her eyes flitting from Matthews to me with the typical mix of confusion and apprehension caused by a police officer arriving at one's door for seemingly no reason.

"Hello. Are you . . ." Matthews began, pausing to look down at his phone for the name listed on the picture of the ID he'd been sent, "Laurie Roberts?" The woman said she was not, and Matthews asked if Roberts lived there.

"She's on the second floor," the woman answered, then asked, "What is this about?"

Matthews ignored her question and continued with more of his own. "Is she home?"

When the woman said she didn't know, Matthews forged ahead without any explanation. Rather than tell the woman at the door that he was there to notify Roberts that her wallet had been found, he declared, "Alright, I'm just going to go up and knock on her door."

The woman, visibly uncomfortable at this point, timidly asked, "Um . . . do you have a warrant or something?"

Matthews' tone, blunt but amicable up to that point, immediately shifted to confrontation and dominance. His jaw and face tightened, and he stepped forward to put his hand on the door.

"I don't need a warrant," he said with steel in his voice. "I'm coming inside."

The woman retorted, "No, you're not!" and tried to shut the door. Matthews, just shy of six feet tall and weighing at least two hundred pounds, towered over the woman as he raised his voice sharply, "Yes,

I am! Move!" He surged forward, easily overpowering the woman's attempt to shut the door with a powerful shove that forced the woman to step back into the first-floor landing.

He turned angrily on the woman who was now standing on a well-worn rug next to a small table covered in unopened mail. "What do you think you're doing? Do you live here?" The woman, wide-eyed in surprise and fear, began shrinking toward a door behind her. She pointed to it and replied meekly, "I live here."

Matthews pressed her, firing new questions at her in the same, heated tone. "What's your name? Who are you?" The woman was silent and looking down at the floor. Matthews raised his voice to just shy of a shout, "Who are you?!" Thoroughly cowed, the woman retreated toward her unit and closed the door behind her without another word.

Matthews turned to me with a look of disbelief on his face, "Are you serious?! So stupid!" He turned toward the stairs and switched on his flashlight to illuminate the darkened staircase, proclaiming loud enough for anyone in the house to hear, "Some people are just so fucking stupid!" He continued to complain heatedly as we climbed the stairs. "I don't need a warrant; it's a common living area. I'm not trying to get into her apartment. I'm not looking for her. It's none of her business." Even after knocking on the door and finding no one home, he complained all the way down the stairs, muttering furiously, "What an idiot!"

Once we were back in his patrol car, I asked him why he chose to interact so forcibly with the woman instead of explaining why he was there. His response was indignant. "Why should I have to explain anything to her? I'm legally allowed to do what I did, and I have no reason to be explaining myself to that woman. Why is she so concerned with what I'm doing? I'm not looking for her. I'm not going to go into her apartment. It's none of her business."

I suggested that, from the woman's perspective, it might have been scary to have two large men—one a uniformed officer and the other a stranger in plainclothes likely assumed to also be police—arrive at her door unannounced before being barraged with questions. Matthews was unswayed by the suggestion. "That may be true," he began, "But it's not her place to question what I can and cannot do. I was acting within the law. Why is she assuming that I'm doing something illegal? What have I done to suggest that I'm not acting lawfully? I'm just trying to do my job."

I offered that the confrontation might have been avoided if, instead of barging through the door, he had answered her questions about why he was there and explained he was trying to help get a lost wallet back to her neighbor. Matthews remained unmoved. "I see what you're saying, but you don't always have time to explain things to people," he explained. "Most people don't even want to hear your explanation. They're convinced they're right and that's it. Usually, I have that conversation with someone after the arrest has happened, once things are secure. I don't have time to explain things calmly if I'm trying to effect an arrest."

Matthews's justification for his behavior was rooted in the danger imperative. After indignant frustration at having his authority questioned, he invoked the necessity of ensuring officer safety as the reason for not answering the woman's very reasonable questions. Unlike a situation in which it is plausible to argue that questions are best left until after an officer has "secured" a suspect and the scene, Matthews had been doing nothing of the sort when he pushed his way through the woman's front door and verbally berated her. Ironically, this acutely aggressive and disrespectful interaction took place during what could have been a model case of an officer engaging in the nonpunitive, non-enforcement interactions that can enhance police legitimacy and build trust with the public.[47] Instead, Matthews's performance of the command presence that is encouraged by the danger imperative was little more than a retaliation for a citizen questioning his authority.

As Matthews's behavior makes clear, the performance of command presence, justified as necessary to retain control and ensure officer safety, can manifest as needless and punitive aggression known to damage police legitimacy and undermine public trust. And though this instance of hostility was directed at a White woman during a nonenforcement contact, aggressive police contact concentrates in poor communities and disproportionately targets minority men.[48] Rudeness and hostility masquerading as command presence can turn interactions into status competitions that result in reciprocal disrespect, a dynamic only exacerbated by long-standing distrust in minority communities born of a history of police mistreatment.[49]

When aggressive command presence begets disrespect that turns to noncompliance or resistance, the probability of violent confrontation increases. Though command presence is justified as a means to prevent interactions from escalating to violence, its propensity to become naked aggression is likely to undermine police legitimacy, officer safety, and public well-being alike. And so long as police officers operating according to the danger imperative's preoccupation with violence continue to concentrate on minority communities, it is the residents of these communities who will disproportionately bear the costs of police aggression and subsequent violence.

WHEN HELPING HURTS

Police are expected to respond to a wide and ever-expanding range of problems—what sociologist Egon Bittner described as situations involving "something-that-ought-not- to-be-happening-and-about-which-somebody-had-better-do-something-now!"[50] The police are called upon to wrestle with this seemingly boundless array of issues, in large part because they are empowered to demand or coerce compliance in varied and uncertain situations.[51] The smallest share of these situations, though disproportionately emphasized by police attached to their role as crime fighters, are related to serious crime or violence.[52] Police are called far more often to address nonviolent property crime, traffic accidents, "suspicious" persons, cars, noises, and disorder or "quality of life" issues that include vagrancy, noise complaints, graffiti, abandoned vehicles, and much more.[53] Police encounter murderers, robbers, and rapists far less often than they do people who, in ways large and small, need help.

The danger imperative, however, operates across the vast array of problems that police are summoned to solve. To be sure, some calls for service are more likely to engender clear and concerted efforts by police to prepare for violence and ensure their safety. Reports of an active shooter or an armed robbery in progress receive a very different baseline response than a run-of-the-mill noise complaint. But the danger imperative, its preoccupation with violence, and its encouragement of safety-enhancing behaviors are not restricted to situations in which there is a clear and present threat to life and limb. As police so often emphasize, all calls have a nonzero chance of becoming an officer's last. Unfortunately, while the danger imperative centers violence and officer safety, it does not do so while prioritizing public well-being. Predictably, officers dispatched to resolve myriad situations while mitigating the risk of their own violent victimization will, at times, harm people who need care, not coercion.

One such case occurred in Elmont a few weeks before Thanksgiving. After several slow and uneventful hours on patrol, I accompanied Officer Semenov as she responded to a report of an attempted arson at a residence. The reporting person was the suspect's mother, who informed dispatchers that her son, Alex, was twenty-eight years old and had been diagnosed with schizophrenia and bipolar disorder. The call text on Semenov's in-car computer screen was updated as she made her way to the listed address, including a report of the suspect's punching walls at some prior date. Officers commonly key in on indicators of prior violence, especially if it involved weapons or was directed at police.

Shortly after arriving at the two-story home, Semenov, a six-year EPD veteran with pale skin and platinum blonde hair pulled back in a bun, was joined by Officer Duncan, a large, heavyset white man who wore plain glasses. Together, they entered the home around 11:45 P.M. and found Alex quietly seated on the couch, sockless, dressed in black thermal underwear, a loose-fitting white T-shirt, and a green beanie. A space heater was blowing nearby, doing little to stave off the frigid cold. There was no sign of an attempted arson: no smell of smoke or accelerant, no scorch marks on the walls, floor, or furniture.

The officers began to gather information from Alex's mother. As was all too common on patrol, the call type selected by the 911 call taker and transmitted to officers by a dispatcher was markedly different from the reality of the situation at hand. As Alex's mother explained, she had come home and smelled smoke. The smell was emanating from a blanket that Alex had thrown over a lamp because, he told officers, the lamp was too bright. While Alex remained seated on the couch, his mother told officers that she thought he'd been off his medication for a few days. When questioned by officers, Alex confirmed that he'd run out of his medication but wasn't sure when.

While Duncan went to talk to Alex's older sister, who was standing nearby on the staircase, Semenov asked Alex for his full name and an ID. Alex didn't have his ID on him but gave his full name, which Semenov jotted down in a small notepad. Duncan rejoined Semenov and they continued talking to Alex, trying to piece together what had occurred before their arrival. At one point, Duncan mentioned the report that Alex had been hitting walls, prompting an angry outburst from Alex, "Who the fuck told you I was hitting, walls?! I'm not doing that shit!"

Duncan responded that he'd just spoken to his sister, who he said had confirmed that he'd been hitting walls. Before Alex could respond, Duncan asked whether Alex was calling his sister a liar. The insinuation only agitated Alex, who shouted, "This is bullshit!" and rose from the couch to move toward a darkened room adjacent to the living room. Duncan immediately stepped in his way and put out his arm to stop Alex from leaving. Just as officers are wary of hidden hands that might be holding a weapon, moving to a new area introduces the unacceptable possibility of a someone retrieving a weapon.

Instead of stopping, Alex tried to push Duncan's arm out of his way. The situation immediately escalated. Duncan went "hands on" with Alex, grabbing him with both hands and commanding loudly, "Alright, man, hands behind your back!"

Alex yelled back, "Get off me!" and pulled away from Duncan. With that, the situation erupted into a physical struggle. Seeing her fellow officer grappling with Alex, Semenov immediately jumped into the fray.

Alex's mother pleaded with her son, "Alex, please calm down!" One of Alex's younger sisters, who looked to be in her late teens, had come down from the second floor when she heard the commotion. She screamed at the officers, "This is bullshit! He's sick! Why are you treating him like that? He's sick!"

Semenov, Duncan, and Alex struggled in a lurching maul toward the front door. As they were trained to do, the officers forcefully took Alex to the ground to better control him. Both continued to command Alex to put his hands behind his back while he shouted and cursed at them, "Get off me!"

Duncan, using a half-squat, half-kneel position that allowed him to pin Alex to the ground with his knee, threatened, "Get your arms behind your back or I'm going to spray you!"

Facedown, Alex yelled back that he couldn't because the officers were on top of him. With that, Duncan unsheathed the small canister of OC spray from his duty belt and, with a quiet hiss, sprayed a stream of the chemical irritant directly into Alex's eyes, nose, and mouth.

The effect was instantaneous. Alex's face contorted and his eyes squeezed tight against the caustic OC spray. Between grunts, moans, and violent coughs, he screamed that his eyes were burning; tears streamed down his cheeks, mixing with the mucus pouring from his nose and the oily, orange spray coating his face. Though he continued to yell in pain, his body relaxed, and the officers were able to get his hands behind his back and into handcuffs. Alex's sister yelled at the officers from the stairs, "Fucking pigs!"

The officers quickly moved Alex toward the front door and away from the confines of the living room—in poorly ventilated areas, aerosolized OC can hang in the air and affect the breathing of officers and bystanders. Once outside, Alex continued to moan and grunt in pain. His mother brought a bowl of water to try and clean the OC spray out of her son's eyes, with little effect. Semenov and Duncan, seeing that Alex was sockless and wearing a T-shirt in near-freezing temperatures, decided to move him to the back of Duncan's patrol car. His family brought over slippers and a coat for Alex, who continued to yell and roll around in the back of the police car in anger and agony, "Why y'all motherfuckers do that?! This is bullshit!"

While the officers waited for an ambulance to arrive and transport Alex to the hospital, I talked quietly with another of Alex's sisters, this one older. I walked over to where she was standing quietly by the steps of the house and, after telling her I was a graduate student, asked her if this was the first time police had been to their home. She shook her head, telling me that this was the third time officers had been at the home in the past few months. When I asked her how she felt when the police arrive at her home, her response was numb, "Honestly? Nothing anymore. It's just routine now." A short while later, an ambulance arrived, and Alex was handcuffed to a stretcher for transport to the hospital where he'd likely be released after a few days of involuntary observation.

The initial call to which Semenov and Duncan responded was seemingly for an in-progress arson by an aggressive and mentally ill man. Upon arrival, it became clear that the situation was less dire. Rather than a violent crime, EPD officers found a man and his family grappling with the toll of mental illness. During officers' fact-finding, however, these symptoms collided with the danger imperative: irritability, hostility, and noncompliance are all understood as markers of potential violence. When Alex began to leave the room without

Duncan's permission, Duncan saw that his total control of the situation was faltering, increasing the perceived likelihood of violence. After all, Alex might have been moving to assault a family member or grab a weapon from somewhere else in the house. To preempt any number of potential catastrophes, Duncan grabbed Alex and commanded him to turn around so he could be handcuffed. When Alex pulled away, the interaction—as viewed through the danger imperative— reached a point of no return.

In some sense, the situation was resolved. Medical treatment was arguably an ideal outcome for Alex, who had run out of the medication used to treat his mental illness. But the path for Alex to receive care was paved with violence, including being grabbed, wrestled to the ground, OC sprayed, and handcuffed. Semenov and Duncan, despite the training EPD officers receive on de-escalation, mental illness, and substance abuse, were woefully ill equipped to address the actual issue—Alex's mental illness—which had contributed to his mother's dialing 911 in the first place. Even if there had been no violent struggle, it is wholly unlikely that they would have found a long-term solution to Alex's mental illness. Though it's certainly the case that specialized training can avert some violent altercations, such training does not guarantee that officers operating within the danger imperative will not default to behaviors—including violence—in the name of their own safety.

The danger imperative can also encourage officers to respond violently in situations where there is no active physical resistance. Such was the case during a late-night shift in West River. That night, I accompanied Officer Ryo, one of the few Asian officers I rode with. He was a short, barrel-chested man of twenty-nine who, in a holdover from his time in the Army, kept a wad of dipping tobacco stuck in his bottom lip throughout his shift. Before joining the WPD, he had aspired to be a doctor and completed two years of premed coursework. But, he recalled, "books got really, really expensive," so he dropped out and joined the Army. Over the course of two tours, he fell in love with the "Army mentality," the teamwork and patriotism that bind soldiers to one another. His tattoos paid homage to his love of country and the militaristic culture in which it was forged: along with the stars and stripes of the American flag, a pile of skulls was topped with a "battle cross," a symbolic arrangement of a rifle stuck into the ground muzzle down with a helmet balanced on its stock. The words, "NO MERCY," were also inked into his skin.

Around 3:40 A.M., a call of "threats" came over the radio. Though this call disposition was usually reserved for someone making threats against another person, the call text on Ryo's in-car computer explained that a man had called 911, said he was going to kill himself, and asked for help. Once Ryo reached the area from where the call came, he searched the night with his car's spotlight. He soon spotted a lone figure moving in the dark by some park benches. We exited the patrol car and moved toward the man, traversing a short downhill. As we drew closer, he came into better view: a white man, beard unkempt, dressed in camouflage pants and a dirty, cheetah-print jacket.

Ryo called out to the man to ask if he had called the police but received no answer. The man continued to walk away, shuffling slowly toward a bench on which a black plastic bag rested. When he spoke, his words were slurred, and I was close enough to catch the smell of alcohol on his breath. Ryo attempted to confirm if the man had called the police and if he wanted to kill himself, but the man told him only that he had been hit by a truck on some prior date. Ryo managed to get the man's ID just before his backup, Officer Bravo, a thin, young-faced man with hair buzzed short, arrived. Soon after, two paramedics—a white woman with long hair and a white man with a dark mustache and a receding hairline—joined us.

While Ryo was gone, Bravo and the female paramedic talked with the inebriated man, telling him that they were there to help and that they could take him to the ambulance to be checked out. The man shook his head and said he didn't want to go into any ambulance without his beer and his bag. The female paramedic told him that he wouldn't be allowed to take any beer to the hospital, but he could of course take his bag. Growing frustrated, the man raised his voice, "But what about my stuff?!" She attempted to soothe him and promised that he'd be allowed to bring his things into the ambulance, but the man demurred and continued to amble in place around the bench and his bag.

Ryo rejoined us, having confirmed that the man was the 911 caller and finding no open warrants. He moved close to Bravo and quietly told him that they were going to "green sheet" the man, a slang term for an involuntarily commitment to a hospital when someone cannot care for themself or poses a threat to themself or another person. He sent Bravo to get the required paperwork and turned his attention back to the man who had called 911, speaking quietly and trying to convince the man to come with him and the paramedics to the ambulance. The man ignored Ryo and moved toward his bag of belongings on the nearby bench.

As he drew closer and extended his arms toward the bag and its unknown contents, Ryo's demeanor shifted with lightning speed. "Get your hands out of there!" The man continued to ignore him and began to rummage in the black plastic bag.

Ryo commanded again, "Hey! Get your hands out of there!" Without further pause, Ryo sprang into action and grabbed the man with rough efficiency, shoving him away from the bag and into the wooden bench. The man hollered in surprise, "Aaauugghh! What the fuck?!" Ryo replied sternly, "It's time to listen!" and kept the man pinned to the bench beneath them. The paramedics moved in to help restrain the man and Ryo yelled to his backup officer, "Bravo!" Hearing Ryo's call, Bravo came jogging down to the bench and helped Ryo put the man in handcuffs.

With the man's hands secured, the two officers stood him up and searched him. No weapons were found on his person. With that, the two officers led him to the ambulance. One of the paramedics grabbed the man's bag and, once we reached the ambulance, set it on the curb. Before the man was placed on a gurney, Ryo searched him again. Repeated searches are common when preparing to transport someone who is under arrest; officers are trained never to trust the search of another officer who might have, because of laziness, incompetence, or honest error, failed to find a concealed weapon.

When the second search yielded no weapon, Ryo turned his attention to the man's bag. As he opened the bag, Ryo asked the man if the bag contained anything sharp that might poke him, knives, or any other weapons. The man, thoroughly enraged, shot back, "If I had anything I would've shot you!" Ryo ignored him and searched the bag, finding no weapons. He then helped the EMTs move the man onto a bright yellow gurney and secure him with thick, nylon straps. Once the officers gathered the necessary information from EMTs for their report, the ambulance doors were closed, and the man was transported to a nearby hospital.

Unlike Alex's angry outbursts and physical resistance in Elmont, the drunken man who'd called 911 in mental distress did not initially behave in ways that, when interpreted through the danger imperative, were signs of potential violence. Nor did he present signs that officers commonly mentioned as clues of someone concealing a weapon: a firearm "imprinting" through clothing, frequently touching one's pocket or waist to check that a weapon is secure, or a jacket sagging on one side because of a weapon's weight. As Ryo discovered after multiple searches, the man had no weapons on his person or in his bag. Throughout the interaction, there was never a sign of impending violence, much less an actual attack on officers or the EMTs.

Yet Ryo's interaction with a drunken man in mental distress transpired exactly as his training, departmental policy, and the law would predict. Ryo and other officers socialized into the danger imperative cannot afford to give anyone full benefit of the doubt, even someone who has called the police in crisis. Until someone's person and possessions are searched, they must be assumed to be armed. Whereas those uninitiated into the danger imperative might see only a drunken, suicidal man reaching for his belongings, officers are expected to anticipate such a movement as the first link in a chain of events that ends in their untimely death. To do otherwise is an unacceptable and potentially lethal mistake.

The behavior of Semenov, Duncan, Ryo, and Bravo showcase how the danger imperative structures the modal case of police violence. In contrast to rare occurences such as an officer firing their weapon, it is the grabbing, pushing, and handcuffing used by these officers that represent the most common subset of police violence. Overall, less than 1 percent of more than sixty-one million yearly police-public interactions involve officers using any physical violence. When violence does occur, it is overwhelmingly nonfatal: in contrast to the 990 people fatally shot by police in 2018, for example, some 430,00 people reported being grabbed, pushed, or struck by an officer.[54] The violence used by these officers is indicative of broader patterns in police behavior that is overwhelmingly aggressive in nature. In contrast to widely held assumptions that police violence is a defensive response to physical threat, most police violence is used to preemptively assert control over interactions or in response to passive, nonviolent resistance.[55]

As much as officers emphasize the possibility that they could become victims of violence on any given call, the arrival of police responding to a call for service introduces the possibility that officers will themselves use violence. When the public calls 911—when "residents have, at some level, lost control"—the officers who arrive do so with a limited set of tools.[56] The weapons on their duty belts, the bulk of their training, and the danger imperative that structures their perception and behavior are all attuned to violence, not care. This is true whether someone calls the police to report a suspicious noise, to report a family member in crisis, to ask for help, or simply because they don't know who else to call. Regardless of a citizen's intent or the ideal resolution of the situation, officers who respond to calls for service do so through the lens of the danger imperative.

FIGURE 4.1 An EPD officer's duty belt, including multiple pairs of handcuffs, a firearm, a flashlight, and a radio. Officers also carry extra magazines of ammunition, an expandable baton, OC spray, a Taser, and a tourniquet.

MISTAKES AND THE BURDEN OF ERROR

Policing is practiced by imperfect people. Perhaps more importantly, imperfect officers experiencing their work through the danger imperative also operate with incomplete and incorrect information. This information winds its way to officers via a multistep process: a caller dials 911, their report is triaged by a 911 call taker who discretionarily distills the content of the call, and then a dispatcher transmits this curated information to officers in the field.[57] This dispatch information is the raw material with which officers prepare themselves to enter situations that, per the danger imperative's preoccupation with violence and officer safety, must always be treated with the utmost caution. The confluence of human officers contending with limited information can result in mistakes that push the costs of policing errors—including physical violence—onto innocents.

One of these mistakes occurred while I was with officers in West River. Near the end of the twelve-hour shift, I sat in the passenger seat of a patrol car with Officer Willis, a Black woman and eight-year WPD veteran who had also worked in federal law enforcement. While she completed backlogged paperwork, I monitored the dispatch information coming into her in-car computer. A battery reported earlier in the day was updated to reflect that two officers were being dispatched to an address that, per the victim, was where the battery had occurred. With no further information, Willis continued writing and I rolled down my window and opened the car door to catch a breeze.

Suddenly, the radio burst to life with the voice of Officer Gomez, a young, Latino rookie I'd met earlier that shift, who was panting and calling out a foot pursuit and his location. Willis immediately dropped what she was doing and curtly instructed me, "Close that door. Roll up your window." She threw the car into gear, activated her lights and sirens, and sped off to her fellow officer's aid. Within a few minutes, instructions came over the radio to shut down code 3 driving. Shortly after, the call text was updated to reflect that there had been two Taser deployments and that the person in custody was the suspect from the earlier battery.

Willis and I arrived at the scene shortly before 6 P.M. An ambulance was already there, idling with its overhead lights flashing. A sergeant who was posted near the ambulance updated Willis on what had occurred: Gomez had chased a fleeing suspect, deployed his Taser twice, and then tackled the suspect onto the street before taking him into custody. I turned and saw the suspect in question, a young Black man, quietly strapped onto a gurney that had been loaded into the ambulance. Willis was instructed by the sergeant to begin canvassing on the left side of the street, where the chase took place.

I followed Willis, who made her way toward a one-story house with two WPD vehicles parked in front. As we entered the driveway, a middle-aged Black woman approached Willis and exclaimed, "You got Damarcus, not Daniel! You have my patient!" The woman showed Willis inside the house, explaining that it was an assisted living facility for men with serious mental illness. Another one of her patients was seated quietly inside. Daniel, the man named in the call as the suspect in the earlier battery, was another employee of the care home, she explained. He was not there when the WPD arrived. The man whom police had chased, tased, and handcuffed was Damarcus, a patient she said was diagnosed with autism and schizophrenia. Referring to Damarcus, she told Willis, "He probably just got nervous when he saw the police. He thought they were taking him to the mental hospital. They don't like it there. They get tied down when they go there. That's why he ran!"[58]

I turned from the woman and went to speak with Officer Bancroft, a white man in his forties who was Gomez's backup officer on the call. When I asked him what happened, he told me, "I saw Gomez go so I backed him up. For me it's reasonable officer standard. Fleeing felon, you know?" In this short explanation, Bancroft invoked the expectation of mutual aid encouraged by the danger imperative and legal precedent from two Supreme Court cases: *Graham v. Connor*, which established the "objective reasonableness" standard for judging police violence, and *Tennessee v. Garner*, which established the legal bounds of police violence (including lethal violence) against a fleeing felony suspect. In combination, the need to protect Gomez from harm and officers' legal authority to pursue and subdue a suspect were, in Bancroft's view, ample justification for his actions.

This assessment was unchanged after he learned that the man he'd helped take into custody was innocent. When Willis informed him that the young man in the back of the ambulance was not the suspect wanted for the battery, he remarked with a laugh, "The radio traffic must've sounded awful! At least he wasn't handcuffed *then* tased!" Rather than reconsider the propriety of his violence or his decision to back up Gomez without hesitation, Bancroft joked about the optics of his and Gomez's mistake. Instead of showing remorse or embarrassment, he rationalized his and Gomez's violence against an innocent, mentally ill man by comparing it to the tasing of a handcuffed suspect, an example of police violence that, unlike his own, would constitute unreasonable and excessive violence according to WPD policy and, potentially, the law.[59]

I left Bancroft to look for Gomez. I found him near the ambulance with a crime scene technician who was photographing a tear in Gomez's pants for later reports. I asked Gomez what happened. Pointing up the street, he said that he and Bancroft had come to the address the battery victim had given police earlier in the day. He continued:

> There's a guy in the front yard matching the description. I roll down the window and I go, 'Daniel!' The kid looks up and goes, 'What's up?' So, he responds to the name and I get out. As soon as I get out and start going towards him, he starts backing up. Now I'm thinking, 'This is about to go all kinds of bad.' I go to grab his wrist and the takes off on me and I go after him.

I asked him if he knew that the man who he'd chased and tackled was a mentally ill patient at the care home where the chase began. His responded bluntly, "How could anyone know that? He responded to the suspect's name and then he ran."

Gomez's recounting of his foot chase and subsequent violence was, like Bancroft's, informed by the objective reasonableness standard established in *Graham v. Connor*. Per the Court, the constitutionality of officers' violence must be judged based on what a reasonable officer on the scene would have known at the time, not with "the 20/20 vision of hindsight."[60] From Gomez's perspective, his actions were reasonable (i.e., legal) given that he didn't know that Damarcus was not the person for whom he was looking at the time.

Crucially, Gomez's objective reasonableness was constrained by the danger imperative. When the suspect began to move away from him, Gomez perceived that the interaction was, in his words, about "to go all kinds of bad." Gomez did not know that the man's retreat was, as explained by his caretaker, born of his past experiences with WPD officers that preceded traumatic stays in a mental hospital. All Gomez could see was a suspect and an interaction about to spin out of his control—an unacceptable and unsafe development when viewed through the frame of the danger imperative. In response, Gomez chose to preemptively escalate the situation. This decision, informed by perception shaped by the preoccupation with violence, set off a chain of events that resulted in an innocent, mentally ill man being chased, tased, tackled, and handcuffed by WPD officers.

Even when police mistakes do not result in physical harm, the circumstances they create in the name of officer safety place the burden of an interaction's potential costs on the public. One such mistake occurred during a graveyard shift in Sunshine. Around 10:30 P.M., I was closing in on two hours standing in a darkened parking lot while officers secured the scene of an armed robbery that had taken place at a large apartment complex. The suspect had fled, and detectives were beginning the hours-long process of gathering statements from victims and witnesses. While I waited with officers, Lt. Burt, a watch commander liked by patrol officers for his willingness to be out on the street with them instead of only monitoring their activity from the substation, asked if I would like to join him as he responded to a burglary in progress. I agreed, and we left the parking lot.

As we drove toward the scene, the call text was updated with new information, including that the male suspect might be armed and was in a blue BMW heading southbound on Chicon Street, just a few blocks from where Burt and I currently were. As we neared Chicon, Burt and I saw another SPD vehicle—a Chevrolet Tahoe—and, in front of it a blue BMW sedan. The voice of the officer driving the SPD Tahoe came over the radio and reported that they were following a blue BMW on Chicon and called in the license plate for a warrant check. Burt followed the other SPD vehicle and came to a stop a few car lengths behind the BMW at a red traffic light. The call text was updated to show there were no open warrants for the person to whom the car was registered. When the light turned green, the SPD Tahoe's emergency lights ignited; Burt followed suit and followed the other officer as they initiated a traffic stop.

The BMW did not immediately stop. It took one turn, drove slowly for another block, then turned again. The increasingly concerned voice of the officer in front of us came over the radio, updating dispatch and other officers that the car was not stopping; a driver who doesn't immediately pull over may be preparing to evade or attack police. Burt, recognizing the potential for the situation to escalate, keyed his car's radio handset and requested the support of an additional unit. After another hundred yards, the driver activated their turn signal and slowly came to a full stop on the side of the road. The SPD Tahoe stopped about two car lengths behind, and Burt angled his vehicle to stop on the right side of the Tahoe.

Without hesitation, Burt and the other SPD officer began what is known as a "high-risk stop." Unlike a standard traffic stop, high-risk stops involve special safety-enhancing tactics tailored for when officers believe they are stopping a suspect who poses a particularly acute threat. Before exiting their vehicles, Burt and the other officer—a white, middle-aged man named Thompson—pointed their patrol car's spotlights at the suspect vehicle's mirrors; this tactic is used to blind the occupants' view of officers' positions. In a blur, Burt exited his vehicle, drew his pistol, and circled around the back of his patrol car before taking aim at the vehicle. Thompson took a position at the left rear side of his Tahoe and pointed his firearm at the BMW.

As the officer who initiated the stop, Thompson took the lead on the high-risk stop. He called out to the car loudly, "Let me see your hands!" Immediately, three sets of hands went up inside the BMW: one in the driver's seat, one in the passenger's seat, and one in the back

FIGURE 4.2 High-risk stop of a stolen vehicle in West River. Though there was no indication that the suspect was armed, training and policy required that officers engage in the stop expecting lethal violence. During this stop, officers readied pistols, rifles, and Tasers in case the suspect attacked them.

seat. Thompson commanded them to keep their hands in the air and then turned his attention to the driver, specifically, telling them to turn off the car and step out of the vehicle.

The BMW's taillights winked out as the car's ignition was turned off, and a young, petite Latina woman in T-shirt and sweatpants exited the driver's side with her hands in the air, eyes squinted against the harsh spotlight beam she'd stepped into. Thompson continued issuing commands, "Turn, turn, turn!" until the woman was facing away from him. He then had her walk backward toward him until she was about fifteen feet away. He stopped her and instructed her to pull up her shirt by the back of its collar so he could visually inspect her waistband for weapons. She complied, exposing her midriff and lower back. No weapons were visible.

With that, he commanded her to keep her hands where they were, holstered his pistol, and handcuffed her. Burt kept his pistol drawn to provide "lethal cover" for Thompson—if the woman or someone in the car attacked them, he was ready to shoot. As Thompson put the handcuffed driver in the backseat of his Tahoe, two more SPD vehicles arrived on scene. Both officers exited their vehicles, unholstered their pistols, and took cover before also aiming their weapons at the stopped vehicle.

After speaking briefly with the handcuffed driver secured in his car, Thompson quietly spoke with Lt. Burt, "I think it's code 4," using police slang for "all clear" or "no further assistance needed." "She says she didn't know we were pulling her over," he continued. "It's her sister, sister's boyfriend, and two kids. Do we keep going with the high-risk or bring it down?" Burt told Thompson that they could ratchet the stop down from the high-risk procedures they'd been employing, prompting all the officers on scene to holster their firearms.

Lt. Burt now took over the stop and I followed him as he and other officers approached the vehicle. The driver's sister, a young Latina woman with glasses and braces, was in the front seat. In the back, a young man with acne and sparse facial hair sat next to two car seats.

In one car seat, a baby boy slept soundly. The other baby, a young girl, was wide awake and waved at Burt and me with a smile. After gathering the adults' IDs and handing them off to other officers to be checked for warrants, Burt turned back to the passengers. In a warm but firm tone, like that of a father describing an unpleasant truth to a child, he explained why they had been pulled over and held at gunpoint.

"Just so you're all aware of why we stopped you, there was a burglary in progress over in the trailer park, and the report was that the burglar left in a blue BMW, traveling south on Chicon." He paused, looking around knowingly at the blue BMW in front of him, before going on. "So, we saw this car, a blue BMW on Chicon, and thought it might've been him. When the officer tried to pull you over to check, the car didn't stop right away. So, we were thinking someone might be about to run. But it's all good now, everyone is OK. I just wanted you to know why things went down the way they did."

The young woman in the front seat nodded quietly, and the young man in the back replied quietly, "Yeah, yeah. I get it, I get it." With that, Burt told them to have a good night and said that officers would try to get them on their way soon. He waved goodbye to the little girl and we both returned to his patrol car.

From one perspective, this incorrectly targeted high-risk stop went about as well as could be hoped. No officers were hurt. Neither the adults nor children in the car mistakenly identified as the suspect vehicle were injured or killed. The stop was, per SPD policy and the reasonableness standard which informs it, readily justifiable based on information provided to officers about the suspect's vehicle and the possibility the suspect was armed. Upon seeing the driver was a woman and gathering new information about the passengers of the vehicle, SPD officers attenuated their tactics and holstered their weapons. Burt, unlike other officers I observed who were reticent to explain their decisions to the public, clarified the circumstances that led to the high-risk stop and provided evidence that the SPD's actions were based on observable facts, not biased opinion.[61]

Nonetheless, officers' misidentification of a car that they believed was tied to a burglary was the first in a series of developments, all filtered through the danger imperative, that resulted in five innocents, including two children, being held at gunpoint. This is not to say that officers behaved irrationally or predatorily. Officers received dispatcher information that indicated, above and beyond their usual preoccupation with firearms, that the suspect for which they were searching was potentially armed. Soon after, a vehicle matching the description and last known location of the suspect's was found. The perceived likelihood of the situation escalating into a pursuit or shootout only increased when the young woman driving the car did not immediately stop. Their tactics, deployed in the interest of officer safety, were in accordance with their training, SPD policy, and the law.

But this series of events makes clear that the danger imperative's preoccupation with violence does not—indeed, cannot—reliably parse suspects from innocents under conditions of uncertainty and imperfect information. The danger imperative highlights the possibility of violence and encourages officers to take steps necessary to ensure their own survival, even if their assumptions of threat are incorrect. These mistakes do not require malice or incompetence. Nor are they doomed to injure or kill innocents. Nonetheless, officers' safety-enhancing behavior, demanded by the danger imperative, will inevitably coincide with officer error in ways that increase the likelihood that innocents will be subjected to the threat or realization of police violence.

While police errors do not necessitate bias on the part of individual officers, there is ample evidence that police contact—including stops, searches, arrests, and violence—is structured by the confluence of race, place, and structural disadvantage.[62] Even with the strong assumption that police are equally likely to make honest mistakes across communities, the marked concentration of police contact and enforcement activity in some areas over others would correspondingly increase the number of mistakes in the most heavily policed areas. So long as policing concentrates in minority communities—a status quo that is itself a product of structural inequalities and racialized schemas of violent, immoral places—it is members of these communities who will disproportionately bear the cost of these mistakes. When officer-level racial bias is added to the equation, it is all the more likely that inequalities in policing, from stops and searches to injury and death, will be shouldered by the same communities.

DANGER AND THE CORRUPTION OF REASONABLENESS

In theory, the behavior of officers operating within the danger imperative should be constrained such that officers' actions are "reasonable" according to law and the departmental regulations that it informs.[63] Unreasonable behaviors that violate the law or needlessly endanger the public should not be understood by officers as viable options for meeting the danger imperative's demand for safety. However, the assumed power of law to constrain such behavior elides that the concept of reasonableness defers to officer perception shaped by the danger imperative.[64] Because their "subjective objectivity" is preoccupied with violence, officers have ample fodder with which to understand their actions as reasonable, even if there is scant evidence of criminal activity or impending violence.[65] The danger imperative can thus corrupt reasonableness, encouraging perception and behavior that, without articulable facts, is understood as reasonable so long as it is believed to enhance officer safety.

This corruption was evident during a shift in Elmont that I spent with Officer Errani, a twenty-nine-year-old who had joined the EPD six years earlier. He was outgoing, a former athlete who proudly told me he was "100 percent Italian." He'd completed all but a few classes of his undergraduate degree at a nearby university before dropping out to become a police officer, a point of contention between him and his fiancée who was an emergency room nurse at a local hospital.

FIGURE 4.3 Three men handcuffed by WPD officers while officers search a vehicle for drugs and guns. Nothing was found. Handcuffing people during vehicle searches is commonly justified as necessary for officer safety, even if a person is compliant and unarmed.

On the night I met Errani, the EPD was on high alert because of a planned protest of the presidential inauguration of Donald Trump. During lineup, Lt. Sherman, a burly Black man with splashes of gray in his short-cut hair, told the assembled officers that, because of an incendiary device that had exploded in Boston and "problems" in Washington, DC, officers needed to be wary of the protest spinning out of control. He warned officers that protestors were armed, though not with weapons. "They've armed themselves, so be ready," he said. "They may know what to say legally. They know what they can do legally, what we can do legally." Officers needed to prepare in kind. "Make sure you've armed yourself. Know what tactics they will be using, what their tactics are. Hopefully it doesn't get crazy."

That night, Errani was assigned to the Heights, an area of Elmont that was nearly 90 percent Black or Latino. The neighborhood abutted the southern side of EPD headquarters and extended southwest to the Elmont city limits and northwest to the edge of Elmont's downtown. Whereas most of the Heights was home to the working poor, its northwestern area was dominated by a large university medical center.

The streets of the Heights were quiet and still, a stark contrast to the discussion during lineup about potential chaos that night. In summer or springtime, the Heights was full of life—children on well-worn playground equipment and adults walking on the sidewalk or sitting on front porches—but the early sunset of deep winter had chilled the activity of the neighborhood. Usually, Friday nights brought a bump in call load; that night, 911 calls had also been slowed by the cold. As other officers did during slow shifts, Errani made use of the depressed call volume to engage in proactive enforcement.

His first stop was of a small sedan, a Toyota Camry, that made an illegal U-turn near the medical center at the edge of the Heights. He told me to hang back while he contacted the driver. Standing by the open passenger-side door of his patrol car, I watched Errani touch the Camry's trunk with an ungloved hand. After speaking with the driver for a moment, he waved me over.

The driver was a young Asian woman. Though her license was valid, and she had current insurance, Errani's check of her license plate via his in-car computer showed the vehicle's registration was expired. Per Elmont ordinance, unregistered vehicles were to be towed. Errani, however, was reluctant to do so. While seated in his patrol car and reviewing the information on his computer screen, he said, "Man, I don't want to give her a ticket . . . maybe DMV [Department of Motor Vehicles] is down." I asked him why he didn't want to ticket her. He explained:

She's respectable. She didn't give me an attitude and she said she didn't know the U-turn was illegal. And, you know, she has current insurance, she has a license. So, it's not like she's out here putting people in danger or anything by not having insurance. Maybe she forgot to make a payment for the registration, or maybe the system is just down and it didn't update our records.

I noted that it was possible she was simply lying to him. Errani shrugged, "Maybe. I don't have a reason to believe she's lying." Ultimately, he showed the driver mercy and let her leave with a warning instead of ticketing her for the traffic violation or impounding her unregistered vehicle.

A short while later, he employed his discretion again, to very different effect. Around 6pm, while driving down a darkened street in the heart of the Heights, Errani drove past a group of six Latino boys walking together on the sidewalk. He made it most of the way down the block with his eyes glued to his side-view mirror, then stopped in the middle of the street.

Still looking into the side-view mirror, he muttered aloud, "Look at these little shitheads." I asked him if he knew the boys. "No, I don't, actually" he responded, "I should, though. Let's talk to 'em."

He put his patrol car into reverse and backed up down the one-way street toward where the boys were still walking. Without taking his eyes from their reflection in his side-view mirror, he silently unholstered his pistol with his right hand and held it in his lap. His palm wrapped tightly around the pistol's grip and his index finger pressed firmly alongside the weapon's frame, parallel to the barrel.

He rolled down his window as he neared the group of boys. Noticing Errani's approach, they stopped walking and turned toward the patrol car. They were in their early to mid-teens, no older than high school sophomores. Errani finished pulling up alongside them and greeted them in a friendly tone. He kept his firearm out of sight and trained on the boys through the panel of his patrol car's door.

"What's up, guys?" he asked. The boys responded in a jumbled chorus of "Hey," and "What's up?"

"You guys out of school?"

The boys, again, responded altogether with a tangle of "Yes" and "Yeah."

Errani continued his questioning. "You staying out of trouble? Doing good in school?" One of the boys, partially hidden by his friends, chirped up and joked sarcastically, "Yeah, making straight A's!" The others laughed, one adding, "I definitely got some D's though, for real."

Errani did not acknowledge the boys' laughter or jokes. He only told them, "Alright, you guys stay out of trouble. Have a good night." Without waiting for a response, he drove away, leaving the boys standing in the night. Less than a minute had passed since Errani first spoke to them.

As he drove past the darkened windows of multifamily homes and weathered brick apartment buildings, he reholstered his firearm. Unprompted, he turned to me and explained why he had drawn his weapon, hidden it in his lap, and kept it pointed toward the group of boys walking along a sidewalk on a Friday evening: "I always do that when I'm just talking to someone out the window like that. You never know—they would've been able to shoot at us in a split second if they wanted. That's why I keep it down here, relaxed, finger off the trigger. But you have to be ready for that. Always have a plan of attack."

This interaction, as short as it was, shows how the danger imperative can corrupt reasonableness. This corruptive capacity is not dependent on wholesale disregard for the law. The lack of evidence that the boys were involved in any lawbreaking might lead some to assume that Errani's decision to contact the boys was, in and of itself, unconstitutional. After all, Errani did not suspect the boys of being involved in any illegal activity. There was no report of a crime in the area or suspect description that might justify an investigatory stop. By his own admission, Errani did not know who the boys were.

Police, however, are granted immense leeway to engage in "consensual encounters." Unlike investigatory stops, which require that police have "reasonable suspicion" predicated on articulable evidence of an ongoing, impending, or past crime, consensual encounters require no observable justification so long as an officer does not overtly use their authority, threats, or physical coercion to prevent someone leaving.[66] Recognizing that reams of legal scholarship argue "the average person will not feel free to leave a police official who has approached and addressed questions to him," it is still likely that Errani's decision to pull up to the boys and engage them in conversation would be considered a constitutional one.[67]

Rather than his decision to contact the boys, it was how Errani engaged in the interaction and then justified his actions that most clearly show reasonableness corrupted by the preoccupation with violence and officer safety. The danger imperative encourages officers like Errani to assume that they may be attacked at any moment. Despite no articulable evidence that the boys represented such a threat, the infinitesimally small probability that a group of teenagers might try and kill him allowed Errani to believe he was enhancing his safety by preemptively drawing his firearm and hiding it in his lap. Perhaps more importantly, this hypothetical threat—the one emphasized by the danger imperative—provided the means for him to understand and justify his behavior as compliant with law.

Despite these justifications, it is apparent that the danger imperative encouraged Errani to understand and perform his work in a manner that was wholly unreasonable. His decision to draw his weapon and hide it in his lap while pointing it toward the group of boys turned what would have been a questionable but nonetheless legal encounter into an unreasonable one out of step with EPD training and policy. This was confirmed by Lt. Costanza, the EPD's director of training. During a phone interview in which I described Errani's tactics, he stated unequivocally that they were out of step with those taught at the EPD academy. What's more, he stipulated, if an officer did believe a group of boys posed a potentially lethal threat, reversing down a street and speaking to them from the confines of his car was simply bad tactics.

"It's tactically unsound," he said. "You're setting yourself up, really. Because if they are *dangerous* and they pose a threat to you, sitting with a gun in your lap, in a car, you just reversed, you're at a tactical disadvantage." More fundamentally, Constanza viewed actions like Errani's as patently unjustifiable within the law and the EPD policy that it informs: "It was a use of force. Taking your gun out of your holster, using it, displaying it, pointing it, those are all considered uses of force. You have to justify using force. How does a group of kids standing on a corner—that I go up and talk to—justify using force?"

Errani's actions also reveal how the danger imperative, beyond its corrosive influence on what officers deem to be reasonable police practice, is implicated in the reproduction of racial inequalities in policing. When compared to the lenience with which Errani treated the Asian woman who committed a traffic violation in an unregistered vehicle, drawing his firearm to talk with a group of Latino boys walking on the sidewalk smacks of racist and capricious enforcement. He described the woman as "respectful"; he labeled the young Latino boys "shitheads" before even speaking to them. Of course, the danger imperative was also operating in his interaction with the woman whom he pulled over: as did other officers across the EPD, WPD, and SPD, Errani assiduously touched the trunk of the stopped vehicle to forestall being ambushed by a hidden assailant. The obvious difference between the two interactions was the intensity of Errani's supposedly safety-enhancing behavior: when talking with a group of Latino teens who provided no evidence of being armed or violent, Errani preemptively drew his firearm in preparation for a life-or-death fight.

Observations of a single shift with Errani do not provide for definitive diagnosis of racial animus or a more general pattern of racially biased policing. Even administrative data on the full range of

Errani's or the entire EPD's activity would not necessarily speak to the underlying motivations—unconscious or predatory—that generated stops, searches, arrests, or violence. But while it is impossible to know what was in Errani's heart when he chose to draw his weapon and force an interaction with a group of innocent boys, the confluence of the danger imperative with social categories of race, place, and gender are clear. Errani never claimed that the boys were more likely to pose a threat because they were male, Latino, or walking in a minority neighborhood. Nonetheless, it was precisely this combination of race, geography, and perceived threat—what sociologist Elijah Anderson terms the "iconic ghetto"—that predicated his behavior.[68] Regardless of his stated or real motivations, it was a group of Latino boys in a poor, minority neighborhood whom Errani chose to speak to with a gun in his lap.

Errani did not shoot any of the boys. Indeed, the boys likely had no idea that Errani had a pistol pointed in their direction while asking them about their grades in school. The interaction took less than a minute. With no body-worn camera on Errani's chest and no 911 call or incident report to record the encounter, only Errani and I knew the full extent of what occurred on that night in the Heights. But the lack of bloodshed does not alter that Errani, by drawing his firearm, needlessly increased the likelihood of lethal violence in the name of protecting his own life. If, instead of answering Errani's unwarranted questions, the boys had exercised their right not to interact with him, it is entirely plausible that Errani might have escalated the encounter beyond words and a hidden handgun. A shadow, a "furtive movement," a bulge in a pocket, or one of the boys fleeing out of fear could very well have tipped the interaction into deadly calamity.

Because the danger imperative can pervert the foundational concept of reasonableness, its corruptive effects are implicated across the full range of officers' coercive action, from stops to shootings. This does not mean that all police violence is destined to be immoral or illegal. But it does mean that officers' efforts to ensure officer safety can actively perpetuate unconstitutional policing. The gravity of this injustice is only exacerbated by existing schemas of minority criminality and violence that are filtered through the danger imperative to inform how officers practice their work.[69] So long as police continue to concentrate in minority communities like the Heights, it's these communities that will be subjected to harmful police action predicated on reasonableness corrupted by the danger imperative.

By extension, these communities will also continue to bear the negative downstream consequences of police contact and involvement in the criminal legal system. Beyond the physical injury and death caused by officers' violence,[70] these consequences include damaged mental health,[71] reduced educational attainment,[72] employment discrimination,[73] economic precarity,[74] estrangement from the legal system,[75] withdrawal from the democratic process,[76] and alienation from schools, hospitals, and banks.[77] Police do not bear sole blame for this vast array of deleterious effects. Employers, hospitals, banks, schools, and any number of institutions are rife with their own injustices. But as the legal agents whose actions precede every other step in the criminal legal pipeline, police are inextricably tied to the reproduction of inequalities across social life. These inequalities, regardless of officers' intent, are the price exacted by the danger imperative and policing's enduring preoccupation with violence.

CONCLUSION

THE SOUL OF POLICING

Across Elmont, West River, and Sunshine, officers' words and behaviors show how deeply danger permeates the lived experience of police work. Simultaneously, the re-creation of the danger imperative through officers' routine practice, pervasive symbols and signals of profound danger, and the rote procedure of departmental life transcends individual officers and their respective departments. Across time and space, the consistent preoccupation with violence is a core feature of the police institution. Whether in the heat of a southwest summer in Sunshine or on a frigid winter night in Elmont, officers' shared culture and the practice of police work continue to be powerfully oriented by the omnipresent possibility of a violent death.

The construction of the danger imperative begins in the police academy, where recruits are first introduced to the life-or-death stakes of the work that awaits them upon graduation. From their first days in the police academy, officers-in-training are taught that their number one priority is to ensure their safety at all costs. Under the tutelage of instructors already socialized into the danger imperative's preoccupation with violence and officer safety, recruits are taught to value their own violence as a righteous instrument they must master to defend the innocent, vanquish evil, and ensure their own survival.

Gruesome videos of officers being murdered on patrol highlight the deadly stakes of recruits' chosen profession. Hand-to-hand combat and weapons training test their willingness and ability to fight for their lives. Virtual and reality-based scenario training not only requires officers to practice the use of violence but also teaches them how to justify it in ways that resonate with the danger imperative's constant emphasis on officer safety.

Once they graduate the academy and have their badge pinned on their chest, the danger imperative is reinforced at every turn. The names and faces of fallen officers are enshrined throughout the police department. These commemorations, wrought in memory of those killed on streets near and far, in recent memory and in distant decades, coalesce into a shared understanding of policing's enduring danger. For the living who still stand on the thin blue line between order and chaos, the honored dead are constant reminders of the sacrifice they may be called to make in defense of law, order, and the nation itself. For any inclined to discount the exacting price paid by their fellow officers and the fate that awaits those who do not embrace the danger imperative, they need only look to the fallen, their deaths etched into the skin of their fellow officers and carved into the walls of the department.

Along with commemorations of on-duty deaths as powerful exemplars of the rarest, most extreme consequences of the violence emphasized by the danger imperative, the routine operation of the police department repeatedly amplifies the salience of deadly threat. During daily lineup meetings, sergeants and lieutenants focus on recent incidents of violent crime in their jurisdiction to enhance officer safety. Beyond local violence, a vast information network transmits danger signals between local and state police, federal law enforcement, and the military. These signals describe threats near and far, enumerating the enemies and the vast array of weaponry that police must prepare to confront on any given shift. YouTube, social media, and police-focused websites provide even easier access to videos and other signals that highlight the life-or-death stakes of police work. A threat to police anywhere, regardless of its rarity or relevance, is a threat to police everywhere.

The danger imperative is, most importantly, reproduced in the minds and through the actions of police officers set on returning home from their shift alive. Against a backdrop of police work's inherent uncertainty and the uniquely U.S. problem of ubiquitous, easily accessible firearms, officers use their tactical imagination to mentally rehearse their response to violence that may strike at any moment. This tactical imagination is conspicuously colorblind, assiduously omitting or discounting race as a factor in officers' use of violence. Officers also use a wide array of behaviors tailored to enhance their safety. Some, such as where they park their patrol cars or where they sit in a restaurant, are not focused on a readily identifiable threat but rather the infinitesimally small (but nonzero) probability of a random ambush attack. Others, like their bladed interview stance or their positioning during a traffic stop, are used to maximize their tactical advantage and the probability of surviving an attack when interacting with the public.

While some of these safety-enhancing behaviors incur relatively little cost, others erode police legitimacy and endanger life in the name of officer safety. To ensure that they maintain control of interactions and prevent violent escalation, officers use "command presence" that can quickly turn into aggressive dominance that damages police legitimacy and undermines public cooperation. Officers flout departmental policies restricting high-speed driving to ensure that they provide speedy backup to one another, and they refuse to wear their seat belts on the grounds that it prevents them from reaching their firearm to defend themselves from violence. These behaviors contribute to the injury and death of community members and police alike.

Even when operating within the bounds of policy and law, imperfect officers interpreting incomplete information through the danger imperative inevitably make mistakes, such as identifying the wrong suspect or vehicle, that can anger, injure, or kill innocents. More commonly, officers preoccupied with violence and operating with limited tools engage in behaviors that, while legal, harm public well-being in the name of officer safety. Most disturbingly, the danger imperative can encourage officers to engage in unconstitutional policing that violates the rights and threatens the lives of those they are sworn to serve.

None of the behaviors encouraged by the danger imperative depend on racial animus. Nor does the perpetuation of the danger imperative through academy training, the department's routine operation, and officer practice require overtly racist language or logic. All officers, whether their behavior is motivated by racial animus or not, are socialized to expect violence and prioritize their safety. Even in a hypothetical scenario in which policing achieved hiring and training processes that perfectly excised all racist officers and racial bias from their ranks, the wider arrangement of social inequalities in housing, education, and employment would remain.

Accordingly, crime and violence tied to the intergenerational transmission of this structural disadvantage would, barring alternatives to the existing police apparatus, ensure the continued concentration of police resources in poor, minority communities long overpoliced and underprotected.[1] There, the danger imperative's preoccupation with violence would continue to shape officer perception and practice as it did in Elmont, West River, and Sunshine. The negative effects of police behavior structured by the danger imperative would, in turn continue to concentrate in the same places they have for generations regardless of officers' intent.

A more credible consideration of the danger imperative recognizes that even officers with no overtly racist attitudes or intent would still be subject to the racialized schemas of criminality and violence that pervade U.S. society.[2] The danger imperative does nothing to temper or minimize the effect of these schemas on officer perception and behavior; it only refracts them through its overarching concern with violence and officer safety. So long as police are deployed as part of governance strategies designed to reify divisions of race, class, and power, it is all but guaranteed that racial minorities—especially Black men—implicitly associated with aggression and criminality will continue to be disproportionately contacted by officers preoccupied with their own survival.[3] Under these conditions, there is little reason to doubt that inequalities in police violence will persist.[4]

There are officers who, despite whatever effort departments make to identify, retrain, or discipline them, harbor explicitly racist attitudes. Though officers that I observed did not use racial epithets or express views of racial minorities as inferior or inherently violent, examples of explicit police racism abound in departments across the country.[5] More commonly, as was the case with officers I spent time with, police use color-blind logics that elide mention of race, pointing to "culture" or "parenting" to explain crime and violence, thereby denying the salience of race in racial inequality.[6] Others minimize the scale and severity of racial bias in policing by blaming immoral (and isolated) "bad apples" unrepresentative of policing writ large.[7]

It is not currently known what proportion of U.S. police express overtly racist attitudes or color-blind ideology, though survey research indicates that both Black and white police officers exhibit more implicitly and explicitly racist attitudes than the general public.[8] But regardless of an officer's intent or motivations, the end result for a citizen who is stopped, searched, or shot is the same. More importantly, whether an officer espouses overt racism or color-blind ideology, the danger imperative provides the means for them to justify their actions in ways that accord with policy and law.

The danger imperative is an institutional cultural frame that transcends any one department or officer. This frame is reconstructed through the routine operations of distinct departments and the lived experiences of individual officers preoccupied with staying safe. As diverse as the demands made of police are, none supersedes the necessity of survival. In short, the danger imperative is policing's soul.

"Soul" does not refer to an a priori or immutable essence of the policing institution. Policing, like all institutions, is a product of human action embedded within a complex web of social, economic, and political context. The meaning, purpose, and performance of policing are contested, albeit on a field that remains strongly tilted in favor of police, the state, and the status quo. By describing the "style or ethos of action" that underlies the routine and often unseen operations of policing, "soul" speaks to how policing is iteratively, intentionally *reconstructed* with danger, violence, and death at its cultural core.[9] The soul of policing describes not only what policing is, but how and why it persists in ways that recreate longstanding inequalities in police violence.

THE INERTIA OF POLICING

Articulation of policing's soul allows us to better understand the function of the institution and its consequences. Without a coherent account of the institutional structures that re-create the danger imperative and its emphasis on violence, it is all too easy to assume that inequities in policing are born of happenstance or "bad apples." Because the danger imperative links the wider policing milieu to the perception and behavior of officers preoccupied with survival, it reveals how perpetuation of these inequities is neither accidental nor dependent on immorality. It is policing working as intended. There is little reason to bet against this damaging equilibrium persisting for the foreseeable future.

The persistence of the danger imperative and its consequences is all the more likely when one considers the organizational actors outside individual police departments that also contribute to policing's political, operational, and cultural inertia. At the local level, police unions amplify the danger imperative through bellicose messaging about antipolice violence and the ever-mounting threat posed by a hateful public. In the summer of 2019, for example, incidents of water being thrown at New York City police officers went viral on social media. Alongside a video of children using buckets and brightly colored water guns to drench several officers, the NYPD Sergeant's Benevolent Association (SBA) catastrophized the incident in life-or-death terms, urging officers: "DEFEND YOURSELF before YOU get seriously injured or KILLED. These buckets can contain ACID, BLEACH or other CHEMICALS."[10]

Other messages perpetuate blatant falsehoods. The Detectives Endowment Association, the union representing NYPD detectives, tweeted out an internal memo that claimed three NYPD officers had been poisoned by restaurant workers. The Police Benevolent Association (PBA), which represents approximately 24,000 NYPD patrol officers, tweeted about the alleged poisoning: "We cannot afford to let our guard down for even a moment." Subsequent reporting found no evidence that the alleged poisoning ever occurred.[11]

Union appeals to officer safety, in addition to reinforcing the danger imperative, are powerful tools to fight police accountability. Like individual officers, police unions across the country defend line-of-duty killings on the grounds that officers killed in defense of their own lives.[12] One such case occurred after Chicago officer Jason Van Dyke killed seventeen-year old Laquan McDonald by shooting him sixteen times. Patrick Camden, the spokesman for the Fraternal Order of Police Lodge #7, told reporters that McDonald had "a 100-yard stare" and "lunged" at Van Dyke with a knife, forcing Van Dyke to open fire.

Video footage and the subsequent trial of Van Dyke revealed that Camden's claims were a fabrication: McDonald was walking away from Van Dyke when he was fatally shot.[13] While unions' defense of even egregious misuse of violence like Van Dyke's are commonplace, his subsequent prosecution for the killing and his conviction for second-degree murder and aggravated battery are decided outliers.[14] Thanks, in part, to the legal protections afforded to officers who claim they perceived a threat to their lives (even in cases where there is no evidence of aggression or weapons), criminal charges against police involved in on-duty killings remain exceedingly rare. Convictions are rarer still.[15]

Unions also invoke officer safety to fight reforms that would make police disciplinary records public.[16] In New York, for example, multiple unions repeatedly sued to prevent the release of records on the grounds that revealing officers' names would lead to violence against them.[17] During these efforts in 2019, Patrick Lynch, the president of the PBA in New York City, claimed that the release of disciplinary records "ignored both the serious risks to police officer safety and the reputational harm of publishing false allegation" and was "designed to once again demonize police officers."[18]

Similar arguments were used by the Peace Officers Research Association of California (PORAC), a state-level union that represents 75,000 officers, to fight against "sunshine laws" that would allow for the public disclosure of police disciplinary records.[19] Only after years of union obstruction and costly legal battles did New York and California reform their police record laws. At present, thirty-one states and the District of Columbia still have closed or restricted police records laws that hide police misconduct from the public.[20]

At the national level, the Fraternal Order of Police, which has 330,000 members across 2,220 local lodges, also perpetuates the danger imperative and leverages officer safety to its political ends. The FOP's vice president, Joe Gamaldi, uses frequent appearances on Fox News to attack progressive politicians and prosecutors for their "disgusting" efforts at criminal legal reform.[21] In one appearance, he raged, "Thanks to rogue prosecutors and bail reform and the continued demonization of law enforcement, crime is through the roof in our cities. . . . Our cities are war zones. Our country is in turmoil and police officers are being hunted in the street."

The FOP's Twitter account, which frequently posts about the "war" on police and the "anarchy" against which only police stand, at times veers into barely veiled threats. One post on the FOP's official Twitter account included a video of a Chicago police vehicle being pelted with debris and struck with street signs by a crowd of people; one of the vehicles repeatedly attempted to ram into members of the crowd. The FOP's caption read: "They aren't coming for the police, they are coming for you and we are the only thing standing in the way of this insanity. This cannot stand."[22]

Less overtly, the FOP also funds lobbying efforts on Capitol Hill. These efforts to influence legislation include urging expansion of the Law Enforcement Officers Safety Reform Act. This act exempts active and retired officers from local and state prohibitions on the carrying of concealed firearms on the grounds that "law enforcement officers are targets—in uniform and out, on-duty and off."[23] The FOP also supports several pieces of legislation, including the Protect and Serve Act, the Back the Blue Act, and the Thin Blue Line Act, that seek to impose stiffer penalties for assaults on police and to make it easier to secure the death penalty for those convicted of killing a police officer.[24]

FOP politicking also includes endorsement of political candidates. Most recently, the FOP endorsed presidential candidate Donald J. Trump, a self-proclaimed "law and order candidate" whom the FOP praised for his "real commitment to law enforcement."[25] The FOP's endorsement spurred significant increases in political activism among police, and counties that were home to more FOP lodges showed a significant increase in Republican votes during the 2016 election.[26]

Finally, the danger imperative is reinforced by the federal government. Though policing is a largely local function without direct federal oversight, federal agencies actively contribute to the re-creation of policing's preoccupation with violence and officer safety. The FBI's "LEOKA Officer Safety Awareness Training," for example, is billed to police departments as training for the prevention of officers' being "killed feloniously, accidentally, and assaulted." Of the eight-hour course, thirty minutes are dedicated to the dangers of high-speed driving and car crashes. The remaining seven and a half hours are filled with topics that include "Street Combat Veterans," "Facing Drawn Gun," and "Will to Win/Will to Survive."

In addition to dozens of videos of "the offenders and victim law enforcement personnel," the training is augmented with concerted study of three FBI-produced studies focused on select cases of violence against police: "Killed in the Line of Duty," "Violent Encounters" and "In the Line of Fire."[27] None of these studies, the most recent of which was published in 2006, mentions the decades-long decrease in violence against police.

The Bureau of Justice Assistance (BJA), under the auspices of the Department of Justice, created the VALOR Initiative (Preventing Violence Against Law Enforcement and Ensuring Officer Resilience and Survivability). Unveiled in 2010 with an initial investment of $800,000 to "train officers in techniques for approaching violence [sic] encounters," its "Survive and Thrive" training course is designed to "build skills that contribute to going home safely at the end of every shift."[28] At the conclusion of this training, instructors pose the "Not Today" challenge that requires officers to "remain alert, aware, and prepared" and "to never allow any person to gain the advantage."[29] By 2019, BJA grant funding for VALOR programming ballooned to $7.2 million, reaching more than 54,000 officers across 6,000 law enforcement agencies.[30]

THE CONTROL OF POLICING

Given a policing institution that will persist for the foreseeable future, reforms aimed at blunting the sharpest edges of the danger imperative are needed. To formulate viable policy interventions, it is necessary to recognize that the danger of policing's preoccupation with violence and officer safety lies not in its existence but in its intensity and unquestioned utility. As reiterated throughout this book, police *do* confront violence. The claim that that any interaction *could* erupt into violence is a mathematically accurate one, even if the observable probability of violence is exceedingly low.

Further, policing's focus on rare but potentially catastrophic outcomes is not uniquely irrational. Bias in assessing probability under conditions of uncertainty is a pervasive human phenomenon, as is "probability neglect" that leads people to take drastic steps to guard against highly unlikely—but infinitely costly—outcomes.[31] The same underlying phenomenon is why some people fear nuclear power more than handguns, smoking, and alcohol, or why others increase the likelihood of their own death by choosing to drive cross-country instead of fly.[32]

It is also true that as weighty as the consequences of the danger imperative are, and as damaging as the misuse of police violence is, officers can and do also use violence in ways that prevent harm. Sometimes that violence is lethal, such as when officers kill a gunman intent on shooting as many people as possible in a mall, church, or school. Far more often, the violence is nonlethal, such as when officers fight with and arrest a domestic abuser, or wrestle a drunk and aggressive bar patron to the ground. Though it is not possible to estimate exactly how many injuries or deaths have been avoided because of the danger imperative's effect on police behavior, there is no doubt that it has contributed to police protecting themselves and the public from harm.

But while the danger imperative is tied to commonplace risk heuristics and police violence can be used morally, neither of these facts absolves policing of its pathologies. It is true that police at times confront violence that merits violence in turn. It is equally true that the danger imperative encourages behaviors that infringe on individual liberty and harm the public.

Recognizing that the danger imperative and its role in policing are not wholly destructive, it is abundantly clear that the cost of ensuring officer safety is often borne by the public. While miscalculations related to probability and rare, catastrophic events are not unique to police, police are unique in that behavior shaped by the

(mis)perception of risk can have life-altering or life-ending consequences for those the state is supposed to protect and serve. Unfortunately, contemporary policing rarely considers the steep public price
of the danger imperative, choosing instead to emphasize its necessity
for preserving the lives of officers.

There is a clear, bright line between police using judicious violence
in defense of life and interacting with the public under the assumption of constant peril. As outlined in chapter 1, the mode and content
of academy training that melds fear and violence into officers' earliest socialization blurs this line to an unacceptable degree. The teachings of Lt. Col. Dave Grossman, the founder of "killology," glorify
violence, dehumanize the public, and perpetuate an "us versus them"
mentality among police. This violent vision continues to find its way
into policing through officers' attendance at Grossman seminars and
academy curricula that draw on Grossman's teachings. This sort of
training has no place in an institution that so loudly proclaims its
commitment to service, cooperation, and the protection of public
well-being.

Grossman's seminars are but one of an ever-growing number of
for-profit training options that preserve and intensify the danger
imperative among police. The internet and social media have only
expanded the avenues for this training to reach police. Street Cop
Training, for example, has amassed more than 250,000 social media
followers, produces a podcast that has more than three hundred thousand subscribers and five million yearly downloads, and employs forty
instructors who teach seminars across the country. Its annual Street
Cop Conference includes special forces soldiers as keynote speak-
ers, as well as popular right-wing pundits like Tomi Lahren, a leading proponent of the "war on cops" narrative.[33] The description of its
"Street Academy: Survival Tactics for Police Officers" seminar reads:
"We have forgotten that you will be killed when you treat this profession like it won't happen. We're going to remind you. We're going to
provide you with the knowledge you must have to stay alive."[34]

In addition to in-person seminars, training providers are increasingly operating online. Grossman and Street Cop Training both provide online training. Police1, though perhaps best known for its popular articles and videos focused on officer safety and survival, is also a leading provider of online police training. This for-profit company, which in 2019 merged with Lexipol, a company that produces written policy for police departments, sells access to a massive library of training courses via its Police1 Academy platform.[35] This state-approved training covers forty-three states and touches on topics that include Defensive Tactics, Officer Survival, Officer Safety, Officer Tactical Training, and Ambush Awareness and Preparation.[36] Some states, including Arizona, Arkansas, Colorado, Indiana, Florida, Minnesota, Nebraska, Maryland, New Hampshire, Oklahoma, Oregon, South Carolina, South Dakota, Texas, and Utah, allow officers to complete 100 percent of their yearly, state-mandated training hours via Police1 Academy.

This rapidly expanding and increasingly opaque training ecosystem is in dire need of transparency and oversight. At the local level, city governments and departments should audit police training curricula and remove material like the "killology" teachings of Lt. Col. Dave Grossman and others who valorize violence in the name of officer survival. With the possible exception of training that delineates specific tactics used by police in rare situations such as hostage rescue or other dynamic tactical operations, all course outlines and training materials should be made readily available to the public, policy makers, and researchers. Recognizing that seminars like Grossman's are hosted outside the purview of police academies, police executives could also restrict members of their agencies from attending these seminars. Even if police leaders were unable to effectively ban attendance—officers would likely still be able to attend whatever training they wanted while off-duty—they have the power not to approve the use of taxpayer dollars to fund officers' participation in violence-centric, fear-based training.

Local-level intervention is a first step. More effective policy change would operate at the state level. To curtail the use and spread of this training, state-level Peace Officer Standards and Training (POST) bodies should prioritize the transparent and rigorous review of curricula created by police departments and third-party training companies before approving them as training courses that count toward state-mandated training hours. Existing state-approved curricula and all proposed training, whether in-person or online, should be systematically audited. Proposed training that centers fear, glorifies violence, and dehumanizes the public should be denied state approval. Current training that contains such material should have its approval rescinded until it is appropriately edited. These changes would not only mean that unapproved courses no longer counted toward state-mandated training hours but also that public funds could not be used for such training in states where funding is restricted to POST-approved training.

These efforts will be resisted by some officers and the unions that represent them, on the grounds that it will be detrimental to officer safety. Such was the case in Minneapolis when, after the police killing of Philando Castile by an officer who had attended a "Bulletproof Warrior" seminar, the mayor of Minneapolis banned officers from attending such "warrior" training, even in their off-duty hours. In response, the Police Officers Federation of Minneapolis partnered with Law Officer, a popular policing website that has provided training to police agencies across the country, to defy the mayor's ban and "provide the heroes of the Minneapolis Police Department daily training that can ensure they will return home each day to their family regardless of the dangers that they may face and the ignorance of some politicians."[37]

This politicized resistance, now de rigueur in U.S. policing, must not be allowed to impede commonsense reforms. These changes are exceedingly low-hanging fruit for police administrators and policy makers to implement. State-level reforms will certainly require that resources be expended to support the expansion of state-level POST and similar regulatory bodies. The scale of these expenditures is at present unclear, but it is undoubtedly a cheaper and less logistically fraught scenario to support fifty regulatory offices than thousands of individual departments operating with relative autonomy. This says nothing of the multimillion-dollar lawsuits, injuries, and deaths that might be avoided with less extreme, survival-centric training.

If history is any guide, the implementation of such reforms will be a long and hard-fought process. And it bears emphasizing that none of these proposed changes provides wholesale solutions for the many problems endemic to policing. Without interventions that address the structural-level forces that have shaped policing into its current state, fundamental change in the policing institution will remain elusive. But as argued by Thomas Abt in the context of firearm violence, the need for long-term solutions to structural inequalities in housing, education, and employment cannot supplant targeted efforts to reduce harm in the present.[38]

The problem of policing is of a kind. Though the proposed reforms to training content and oversight will not revamp policing as we know it, these changes would increase transparency, enable greater oversight of police training, and provide the infrastructure for ensuring that police training accords with evidence-based practice that reduces risk to officers and the public.[39] If nothing else, they would help excise training material that actively intensifies the danger imperative, runs counter to policing's stated goals of forming cooperative police-public relationships, and encourages aggression and violence. These training-focused reforms, while necessarily incomplete, are morally necessary to reduce harm and protect the public today.

THE FUTURE OF POLICING

Though reform is vital to mitigate the ongoing harms born of policing and the danger imperative, history provides ample fodder for skepticism about the long-term viability of police reform. As described by sociologist Peter Manning, creating change in policing is akin to a dance, with the set of practices and procedures informed by the organizational pressures of the department—the music—setting the bounds for change. He notes that while policing might incorporate various new steps in its performance—community policing, implicit bias training, procedural justice, COMPSTAT, body-worn cameras, Tasers, and many more—the "music" of policing is inevitably "shadowed by the past," perpetually beholden to policing's cultural and operational exigencies. Manning concludes that, despite decades-long reform efforts to shift policing's managerial, technological, and cultural bedrock, "the dance of police has little changed."[40]

Rather than persist in halting reforms that continually run up against policing's institutional inertia, there are those who begin from the assumption that policing is unable and unwilling to achieve fundamental change. Abolitionists and proponents of "defunding" the police eschew the premise of incremental reform. Instead of piecemeal policy changes, abolitionists seek to sharply constrain the scope and power of policing en route to its ultimate dissolution. Pointing to a long line of incomplete and ineffective reforms, including enhanced diversity, procedural justice training, and civilian review boards, abolitionist sociologist Alex Vitale writes that reducing the harms of policing requires that we "replace police with empowered communities working to solve their own problems."[41]

For those committed to police abolition, the danger imperative and the diversity of mechanisms by which it is perpetuated likely serve as further evidence of policing's unreformability. Rather than try to mute the intensity of the danger imperative and its negative consequences, an abolitionist approach to reducing harm rests on divesting policing of power and resources that total more than $115 billion per year.[42] This funding, abolitionists argue, would be better used on local efforts that directly and nonpunitively address community needs, including violence interrupters, mental health professionals, restorative justice, and harm reduction.[43] Instead of defaulting to police as frontline responders to homelessness, mental illness, and substance abuse, abolitionists envision a society in which communities can care for themselves. With enough investment in communities, writes the abolitionist organizer and educator Mariame Kaba, "there would be less need for the police in the first place."[44]

Many are quick to dismiss the goal of police abolition as unrealistic, unreasonable, or even dangerous.[45] Without police, who would address the brutal reality of violence which disproportionately harms disadvantaged communities of color? But even violence, so often treated as policing's unique charge, can be mitigated with interventions that do not hinge on state coercion.

For example, the addition of 10 non-profits focused on reducing violence and building stronger communities reduces a city's violent crime rate by 6 percent and its murder rate by 9 percent.[46] Providing summer jobs to youth can also reduce violence.[47] Simply improving the physical structure of a city—improving public lighting, clearing vacant lots, and rehabilitating the facades of dilapidated buildings—can reduce violence without deploying police and at a fraction of the cost.[48]

What's more, our overreliance on punitive solutions to public safety leave police starkly isolated in their efforts to address violence. Instead of approaching violence as a collective challenge best addressed with more than handguns and handcuffs, our society has continually embraced punishment over empowerment.[49] Policing has followed suit, continually expanding its power and resources by claiming professional dominion over the control of violence.

As a result, the responsibility of ensuring officer safety is largely shouldered by officers equipped with only the coarsest means to do so. Firearms allow officers to respond to deadly threats; they also enable lethal mistakes and miscarriages of justice. Ballistic vests and emergency tourniquets can be the difference between an officer being fatally or non-fatally shot; they do nothing to stop a shooting from occurring in the first place. These technologies, like the danger imperative, reflect a society which has largely relegated the control of violence to its police. The injury and death of officers, in turn, are assumed to be tragic but necessary sacrifices in the fight against violence that no other institution can hope to properly control.

Policing need not relegate itself to the impossible task of single handedly solving violence. Officer safety and public safety are not mutually exclusive. Along with fewer incidents of violence to which police would respond, non-police interventions can reduce violence directed at police. At the county level, the addition of four behavioral health centers significantly reduces on-duty assaults of police.[50] At an even broader scale, federal and state firearm regulation that minimizes the ease with which firearms can be acquired would save the lives of citizens *and* police.[51] Safe storage laws would not only help reduce firearm suicides and accidents but also firearm thefts that swell the black market for firearms used in violent crime.[52] All of these methods to reduce violence would ultimately decrease the probability of officers' being injured and killed in the line of duty. Though a change in the measurable risk of officer victimization may not directly translate to less *perceived* risk of violence, wholesale eradication of the danger imperative is not necessary to protect police or the public they serve.

To be sure, realizing these policy changes and community-level interventions will be a politically fraught task. And all interventions are limited. Neither safe storage laws nor mental health clinics alter the reality of some 400 million firearms in private hands, much less the systemic inequalities in housing, education, and employment intertwined with policing.[53] But the perfect cannot be the enemy of the good. The elimination of inequality and racism is not a precondition for implementation of policies that reduce harm and disproportionately benefit communities of color. Nor should non-police interventions be expected to manifest immediate and transformative change. Just as reformers have been afforded decades and billions of dollars to realize halting change in police culture and operations, the same allowance should be given to those invested in providing for public wellbeing without policing and its attendant harms.

Minimizing our reliance on police and increasing direct investment in community institutions is neither a harbinger of anarchy nor an inherent indictment of policing. It is a recognition that police will never be able to provide for the full array of the public's needs. If nothing else, the vision of a future in which communities are so well resourced, healthy, and safe that police are no longer required provides space to interrogate a policing apparatus that has become the de rigueur solution for a host of social problems that police are neither well equipped nor especially rewarded for addressing.[54]

Policing is, was, and will remain an institution centered around violence. Without their weaponry and their authority to use violence on behalf of the state, police would cease to be the police. Violence is the defining feature of policing, not a bug. There is a place for armed agents of the state in a functioning democratic society. But the current equilibrium in which police act as a violent stop gap for ineffective and inequitable governance is unjust and unacceptable. Police administrators and elected officials must do more than tinker with training and departmental policies that can only dampen the most egregious harms of the danger imperative. They must empower the public, and resist uncritical reliance on police in the name of "safety."

METHODOLOGICAL APPENDIX AND REFLECTION

FINDING A QUESTION

Reading through a published article or book, it's easy to assume the author always knew their destination. That a reader might come away from a text with this assumption is not exactly accidental. Among researchers, there is an informal pressure to perform a sort of assured competence, to exude in demeanor and diction a sense that one's research is the distillation of the most rigorously laid and assiduously followed plans. We convince ourselves—perhaps because we hope that others might believe it of our own work—that such carefully crafted arguments must surely be the product of the researcher's clear and unflagging intent.

For my part, though I hope that readers are convinced of my argument's merit, this book was very far from my mind when I sat down in the front seat of a police car for the first time. At the outset, an ethnography is a decidedly uncertain affair. And though it gradually grows into something more surefooted as the researcher uncovers the contours of the social world they seek to understand, it does not ever rest on fully settled ground.

My study of police did not begin with the intention of exploring how danger is understood and embodied by officers. I did not even set out to study police officers when I began my graduate studies in sociology at Yale University. Initially, I had my sights set on study-ing street gangs and how honor culture might vary across gangs of different races and ethnicities. By chance, the summer I arrived in New Haven, Connecticut, coincided with the early stages of Proj-ect Longevity, a focused-deterrence program designed to reduce gun violence in the city. The program, pioneered by David Kennedy and his collaborators in Boston during the bloodshed of the early 1990s, was slated for implementation in two other Connecticut cit-ies, Bridgeport and Hartford; New Haven was to be the pilot site.[1] Two Yale faculty members—Tracey Meares and Andrew Papachris-tos, who would both be part of my dissertation committee—were involved in the early stages of Longevity and brought me on as a research assistant.

This, I thought, might be a way to meet the young men at the heart of community gun violence. As part of the project, I was tasked with spearheading "group audits," a focus group–style meeting aimed at collecting information from officers about street groups actively involved in gun violence.[2] These audit data allow a collaborative of police, community members, and social services to focus on the per-ishingly small number of individuals at highest risk of pulling a trig-ger or being shot themselves. Rather than flood entire communities with police after a shooting has occurred, focused deterrence looks to intervene only with those who are most likely to be perpetrators and victims of gun violence.

The audits were also the first time I spoke at any length with a police officer who wasn't stopping me or writing me a citation. In some ways, officers were special by the nature of their work. I was struck by the matter-of-factness with which officers spoke about vio-lence and their ability to recall the dates and locations of shootings, the names of those shot, and those suspected of shooting them. They were, in their way, experts on violence. Their positionality and presen-tation of self were also a reflection of their occupation. Like policing writ large, the officers at the audits were overwhelmingly white and male. Many were walking, talking stereotypes of primetime police dramas: they cursed like sailors, their heads were shaved bald, and more than a few had heavily tattooed arms straining their sleeves.

But in other ways they were shockingly mundane. Though there was an evident penchant for bulky, rubberized Casio G-Shock watches and Oakley sunglasses popularized in the military, their off-duty or plainclothes dress was indistinguishable from the homogenized, logo-laden style of many middle- and working-class men. Under Armor and Nike hoodies, baseball caps, and sneakers abounded. During lulls in the audit, their conversations, too, were ordinary: they recalled recent vacations, complained about their work schedule, and updated each other on their children.

I noted this combination of odd and unremarkable but did little more, even as I continued my gun violence research in New Haven and supported similar work carried out by the National Network for Safe Communities in departments across the United States. At the start of the fall semester in 2014, my research focus was still on violence prevention. I thought my dissertation could build on my work with Project Longevity, perhaps through a qualitative study of the program's various stakeholders and the young men on whom the intervention focused. I had a field site and access.

That was the plan.

Then Michael Brown was fatally shot by a police officer in Ferguson, Missouri.

Along with the rest of the world, I watched the violent, militarized police response unfold in Ferguson. When the tear gas and smoke gave way to punditry, explanations for Brown's death at the hands of officer Darren Wilson were endless: inadequate emphasis on de-escalation, "warrior" police training, "legal cynicism" in the Black community, qualified immunity, for-profit enforcement, and many more. Adjudicating these potential explanations, I learned, was all but impossible given the lack of high-quality data on police training, policies, personnel, and operations. What data existed were fragmented—available one city at a time with little consistency—plagued by reporting bias, or woefully incomplete. It would be years before journalists and activists crowdsourced data to answer fundamental questions like "How many people are fatally shot by the police every year in the United States?" To this day, we don't know how many people are nonfatally shot by police.

Though I did not yet have a fully formed research question about police, I decided that trying to wring blood from the quantitative stone was ill suited to answering the questions roiling around me. The more I read, the more I became convinced that the surest way to generate new insights was to follow in the footsteps of prior scholars who had tried to document police practice and culture from the ground up. As in the seminal work of Westley, Banton, Van Maanen, Skolnick, and Manning, I set out to understand the social world of police one shift and one conversation at a time.

During early ride-alongs in my first field site, Elmont, my observations and questions focused on how officers understood and practiced community policing. Officers were generally supportive of the theory of community policing: they believed that positive interactions could foster cooperation and enhance public safety. Even skeptics who thought community policing was an empty term believed that building trust with the community was vital to doing "good police work" and apprehending lawbreakers.

But before long, it became clear that officers' stated support of community policing meant little for how their work unfolded. In spite of the EPD's and officers' claims of commitment to community policing, the strictures of limited resources and day-or-night calls for service pushed community policing into the background. More importantly, when I began to ask officers why they took particular actions—why they didn't park directly outside the address listed on their in-car computer, why they didn't wear a seat belt, why they touched the trunk of a stopped vehicle, why they stood to the side of a door when knocking—their responses had nothing to do with community policing, procedural justice, legitimacy, or any other fashionable concept in contemporary policing debates.

Repeatedly, the answer to my question was met with two words: officer safety.

Officers parked a few houses down so as not to alert a potential assailant that they had arrived. They didn't wear their seat belts because it might prevent them from quickly exiting their car to engage in a gunfight. They touched the trunk of stopped vehicles to ensure that a hidden gunman didn't jump out and murder them. They moved to the side when knocking at a listed address to avoid being shot by someone who assumed they were standing in front of the door. Seemingly, there was nothing that could not be tied in some way back to officers' concern with their survival.

Officers' preoccupation with the danger of their work has, of course, been detailed by scholars for decades.[3] What was notable was that this perception and the bourgeoning narrative of a "war on cops" were so stark at a time of historically low violence against police. This observation was a finding in search of a question.[4] The puzzle was not whether police were preoccupied with their safety but how this preoccupation was perpetuated and, more importantly, how it shaped inequalities in policing. With time, those questions became the focus of my inquiry and my hours on patrol.

ACCESS, IDENTIFICATION, AND ABSTRACTION

Access to police departments can be surprisingly straightforward under certain circumstances. In professionalized, urban departments like those I observed, there is often a ride-along program that allows for a member of the public to observe police work upclose. Though not explicitly described as such, ride-alongs are also a useful recruitment tool to introduce those interested in becoming a police officer to the reality of the job. Even after I told officers that I was a graduate student working on a research project, some officers asked if I was interested in becoming an officer or "getting on." Some departments also incorporate ride-alongs as part of Explorer programs that serve the dual function of youth outreach and early-stage recruitment. More broadly, a ride-along program offers a modicum of transparency, allowing the public to observe police activity from much closer than officers would let them if they were simply to walk up to where officers were working.

In practice, however, there are multiple bureaucratic ways to prevent someone from going on a ride-along. Those with a criminal record, for example, are explicitly forbidden from ride-alongs in my second and third field sites: West River and Sunshine. All the departments I observed require background checks of potential riders. WPD policy goes so far as to allow the unilateral denial of a ride-along by any supervisor or the officer assigned to the front desk of a WPD facility. Other amorphous criteria can affect departmental administrators' approval decisions, such as EPD paperwork that requires would-be riders to explain why they want to go on a ride-along. Presumably, answers to this question are incorporated into ride-along approval decisions, including denials.

Though I was fortunate not to have a criminal record that would disqualify me from doing ride-alongs with police, there were other hurdles to gaining access. As part of having my research protocol approved by my university's Institutional Review Board, I would need the explicit approval of police executives to ride with, observe, and speak to their officers across all days of the week, all parts of the city, and during all shifts. More pointedly, I would need approval to do so at a time when police departments across the country were under intense media, public, and political scrutiny.

This political context shaped my consideration of whether and how to identify my field sites. On the one hand, ethnographic tradition encourages the obfuscation of field sites in the name of protecting research participants. On the other, social scientists have critiqued anonymization on methodological and practical grounds. Not only do anonymous field sites prevent other researchers from repeat observations of the same field site, but the reality of the internet and powerful search engines make anonymity all but impossible to guarantee.[5]

Ultimately, I chose to anonymize my field sites and use pseudonyms for the officers I observed. The decision was strategic: I believed that I would increase the probability of gaining access if police administrators had written assurance on university letterhead that I would not name their department or any of their officers. Additionally, I reasoned that it would be easier to build rapport with officers if I could promise that neither they nor their place of employment would be named in my research. In addition to giving pseudonyms to officers and field sites, I altered small details of phenomena that are so rare as to be identifying if described with complete accuracy. The clearest example of this is description of the circumstances in which officers were killed or the total number of officers a department has lost in its history. I also changed the names of places, streets, buildings, and other identifying characteristics to "un-Google" easily searchable terms and frustrate identification of my field sites.[6]

Besides its utility for allaying anxiety and building trust, anonymization also helped push me to consider the structural and cultural commonalities across departments. This orientation stands in contrast to an infatuation with variation curiously common to social scientists and police. The former are keen to ask to how social phenomena differ across departments according to city demographics, crime trends, state training requirements, departmental policies, level of civilian oversight, and many other variables. At the individual level, they are quick to point out that culture is not monolithic and ask whether white officers, female officers, gay officers, rookie officers, old officers, officers with military experience, second-generation police officers, etc. differ in their attachment to and performance of police culture. Officers themselves are wont to say that *they* police differently (and better) than other officers or that *their* department is different from others. This is especially clear when discussing a department that is the site of yet another high-profile police killing or scandal or when claiming that they have not directly observed clear evidence of racial bias in their own department.

To be sure, my field sites were a product of the complex interplay of macro- and meso-level context across time—each department was ensconced in a wider web of local institutions and history. I selected these three departments, in part, because they differed from one another. They were on opposite sides of the country, operated under different state and local laws, had their own police academies, and did not have any overt connections to one another. But these three departments, like permutations of any other institution, are not infinitely unique. At their most basic, they are part of the same occupation. Their bureaucracies are very similar. And much as they may differ from one another (and certainly from smaller or nonurban departments) on other axes, the patrol officers of the EPD, WPD, and SPD contend with the same combination of uncertainty and rigamarole when answering calls for service.

Without anonymization, it would have been especially tempting to interpret my observations in each department as products of unique circumstance: a past chief, a past scandal, a new policy, a new mayor, a particular academy instructor, or a particular line-of-duty death. To keep my promise to officers that I would not identify them or their department, I eschewed an emphasis on potentially identifying idiosyncrasy. In its place, I focused on description of the common assumptions, processes, rituals, symbols, and practices that perpetuate policing's long-standing preoccupation with violence. While this inevitably frustrates the most nuanced possible account of how danger shapes culture and work in a specific department, it aids theoretical abstraction from empirical data that can be readily applied (and tested) across any number of cases.[7]

Nor were the officers in my field sites infinitely differentiable based on their demographic characteristics. Unsurprisingly, the experiences of Black, Latino, or female officers were, in some ways, different from those of the white men who continue to dominate policing. Some nonwhite officers spoke of negative experiences with police while growing up or even after becoming police officers themselves. Some women recounted the commonplace sexism and misogyny espoused by their counterparts. But however much ink has been spilled drawing distinctions among officer "types" or policing "styles," the concern with physical danger was a stable and pervasive feature of the police institution.[8]

There were certainly officers who could have been more cleanly categorized into one of the myriad types that describe an aggressive, violent, hypermasculine police officer: the "warrior," the "hard charger," the "enforcer," or the "New Centurion."[9] But all officers, regardless of their identity, privileged the possibility of violence in their understanding and practice of police work. What's more, my time on patrol revealed that an emphasis on particular officer types did not capture the mundane and pervasive ways that danger anchored officers' behavior and departmental operations. It was not only those most aligned with the "warrior" who constantly scanned their surroundings, sat with their back to the wall, or touched the trunk of vehicles they stopped. Not just "hard chargers" received reminders of policing's danger at daily lineup. Nor were typological distinctions drawn among the fallen officers immortalized on memorial walls.

My decision to describe officers' shared experiences, assumptions, logics, and behaviors was motivated by my chosen unit of analysis: the police institution. Whereas prior scholarship has provided useful insight into how officers of different races and genders navigate police work, my goal was to better understand a core assumption of the institution that structures the lived experienced of all officers. There is undeniable variation in how strongly officers aligned with the danger imperative. Not all officers were like Cisneros, the jujitsu-training, gun-loving, EPD academy instructor infatuated with special forces soldiers and the Punisher comic-book character. In my view, however, too much attention to typologizing officers or even placing them at discrete points on a cultural spectrum runs the risk of reifying "bad apples" explanations for policing's harmful effects. More important than the intensity of Cisneros's militancy is that he was part of a social institution in which it was acceptable—even desirable—to have him serve as an academy instructor. A focus on individuals, be it Cisneros or high-complaint officers or officers responsible for the deaths of innocents, will likely elide the organizational and occupational structure within which they and the most model officers both operate.

Future research might very well find a department or departments where the danger imperative is not re-created through a range of processes, symbols, rituals, and behaviors. Or it might document officers (or some type of officer) impervious or highly resistant to the corrosive effects of the preoccupation with violence and officer safety that I documented in the EPD, WPD, and SPD. It is my view, however, that the measurement of what quantitative inquiry might describe as "significant" variation across departments or officers' demographic categories is distinct from an empirical account of the danger imperative and its real-world consequences. It is the latter that I have endeavored to provide in this book.

RAPPORT, CULTURAL CAPITAL, AND EMPATHY

As fraught as gaining access to a police department can be, it is far more daunting to build some modicum of trust with officers. I was usually introduced to a shift of officers at the beginning of lineup by a sergeant or lieutenant who had been briefed by their superior officers on my project. If they chose to wait until later in lineup to introduce me, curious, steely glances from gathered officers were the norm. Some introductions by a supervising officer played on the distrust that police have toward outsiders. One WPD sergeant joked that I was a reporter with a local independent newspaper known among officers for its scathing critique of their department and profession. Before another shift, Lt. McWilliams told his officers, "He's doing a paper for his class at Milton," a local community college. Amid the laughter from officers, some of whom I'd already met, he clarified for those I hadn't, "No, he's at Yale, working on his doctorate." Though I was never explicitly labeled as hostile or untrustworthy, I was clearly and explicitly marked as an outsider and, perhaps most importantly, *not* a police officer.

Still, I was often given the opportunity to introduce myself and my project to assembled officers, and I eventually began proactively asking whoever was running lineup if I could do so. After giving my name and informing them I was a doctoral student in sociology, I explained to officers how the police killing of Michael Brown had shifted my focus from gun violence prevention to policing. I explained, "After Michael Brown was killed, I heard from lots of people: police chiefs, activists, lawyers, academics. But I never heard from a patrol officer." I was committed, I told them, to seeing for myself what policing looked like; I needed their valuable perspective and expertise to better understand their work. I told them that my role as a researcher was to remain as objective as possible and let the data speak for itself. I also assured them that whatever they said to me was confidential, that I would not share any notes or interview recordings with their agency or supervisors, and that neither they nor their department would be named in my research.

Unsurprisingly, my promises did not sway officers wholesale. Outside of EPD headquarters, for example, two young officers pulled up in their cruiser to talk to the officer I was riding with that day. After I introduced myself, they remarked that I might actually be an undercover "fed" or someone planted by Internal Affairs to surveil them.

It was unclear to what extent the comment was a joke or sincere suspicion. During one interview with another Elmont officer, I assured
him that I hadn't "burned" any officers by divulging their views to
journalists or their supervisors. He looked me in the eye, arms folded,
and replied with one word, "Yet."

Then there were officers who simply did not believe that I, an
outsider, could possibly understand their world or work. After lineup
during one of my first days in West River, a tall, white officer in his
early forties stopped me in the hall. He told me in no uncertain terms
that, as well-intentioned as I might be, I would never be able to fully
apprehend what it was like to be a police officer.

"I think it's great that you're coming out here to talk to officers.
I do," he began. "But you're never going to really understand what
we deal with unless you actually do this job." He paused briefly, then
asked, "You ever been shot at?"

"I have not, no," I responded.

He shrugged slightly and cocked his head knowingly, suspicion
confirmed. "Most people haven't. And they'll never know what it's
like to brush that close with their mortality. It changes you."

More often, though, officers were eager to talk to someone about
their work and give their opinions, particularly at a time when the
news and social media were suffused with criticism of police. My
choice to put my body in the field with officers, rather than rely on
only interviews or impersonal surveys, was particularly meaningful. Some officers spoke approvingly of what they described as me
"forming my own opinion" on policing by coming to see their work
for myself, rather than opine on a profession (and people) with which
I had no direct experience. As put by WPD sergeant Caldwell just
before a ride-along with some of his officers, he appreciated my decision to study police up close and expose myself to some of the challenges that police confront. If someone were to write about police
without talking to and spending time with them on the street, he told
me, "You['d] have no credibility with me."

These differing perspectives cut to the heart of a delicate balancing act I encountered in the field. On the one hand, no amount of time in the front seat of a patrol car would change that I was a researcher, not a police officer. As many calls and interactions as I might observe, I could not claim to have *done* the job or wrestled with its stakes as officers did. To pretend otherwise would have been, at best, a pretentious gambit liable to be ridiculed among officers once I was out of earshot. At worst, it would be offensive to officers who had experienced things that I and most others could scarcely imagine.

But while I was not a police officer, my time with officers provided ways for me to signal that I was not wholly ignorant of their social world. Along with the accumulation of cultural capital such as familiarity with radio codes or the geography of each city, learning mundane but vital features of officers' work provided openings to build familiarity and trust. I quickly learned, for example, that the pace of an officer's shift was usually defined by the call load. When I sat down in the front seat of a patrol car and asked an officer, "How's the board look?" I signaled familiarity not only with insider slang but also with the centrality of call volume. Similarly, I quickly learned that police work is delineated by shift schedules far afield from the standard Monday to Friday nine-to-five. Asking an officer at the start of a ride-along, "What day of the week is it for you?" concisely signaled that I was familiar with a concrete, quotidian, but vital part of officers' lives: their work schedule. Rather than jump straight into pointed queries about them, their work, or the state of U.S. policing, low-stakes and contextually informed questions like these helped open up conversation with officers.

The most surefire way to build rapport was to be useful. Being English-Spanish bilingual was particularly handy when officers needed to communicate with a Spanish-speaker. In West River, I helped officers locate shell casings after a nighttime shooting for crime-scene technicians to photograph. Other times, I peered into trash cans and sifted through waist-high grass alongside officers looking for weapons or evidence tied to a crime they were investigating. In Sunshine, rather than shelter in an air-conditioned car, I helped officers unload a car full of abandoned property to be transported to the SPD's evidence storage facility. Once it was transported, I helped them sort, bag, and tag a mountain of miscellanea unlikely to ever be claimed or used in a court proceeding. By being part of the solution to problems they encountered, even in small or bureaucratic ways, I was able to create circumstances for police to see me as helpful. In turn, I provided concrete evidence that I was not wholly and irredeemably "anticop."

There were, however, limits to how much I cooperated with police. I never aided officers in their use of violence against a member of the public, be it grabbing, pushing, handcuffing, or any other use of coercive force. Despite multiple officers showing me how to access their weapons if we came under fire or telling me that I should feel free to jump into a fight if they were being physically bested, such a situation never came to pass. This wasn't because there were no struggles or incidents of violence: I observed officers grab, push, and attempt to forcefully control someone multiple times. But I never perceived that officers' lives were in imminent danger, and no call for service ended with serious injury or death to officers or members of the public. Similarly, while I watched officers use violence, I did not observe them engage in violence that I believed rose to the level of brutality or excessive force.

Ethnographic hindsight is always a decidedly murky affair, but perhaps especially so when considering weighty issues like violence. That no interactions I observed on patrol ended in bloodshed is largely a matter of probability and design: serious violence is rare, and officers have a range of weapons, the benefit of armed collaborators, and radios to summon aid if needed. The odds are skewed against an ethnographer's confronting the immediate possibility that, without their intervention, they or someone else might be hurt or killed. But across enough shifts, it is possible that I might have watched an officer be overpowered, disarmed, or worse. With enough hours on patrol, I might also have witnessed officers violently abuse members of the public. In either case, I would have found myself in a position where my decision to intervene (or not) could prove profoundly consequential. In my view, any ethnographer who claims they *know* what they would have done in such a situation—whether it be throw themselves into a fight, run, call for help, or freeze—is pretending to incredible foresight. Now, years removed from the field, I am grateful that I did not have to make the decision to intervene based on my ad hoc assessment of whether an officer or a member of the public was in imminent physical danger. Any researcher who chooses to spend time with or around police runs a nonzero risk of confronting this decision.

There were also experiences on patrol that allowed me to empathize with officers who felt threatened—ideologically and physically—from all sides. Because I rode in the front seat of a patrol car with a uniformed officer, passersby were likely to assume that I was also a police officer. Multiple times, a passerby would make eye contact with me and then spit on the ground before locking eyes again. Another time, someone gave a silent middle finger. Someone else called out as we drove past, "What the fuck are you looking at?"

Though I was not a police officer, it is not an unreasonable logical leap to assume that someone in the front seat of a patrol car is also an officer. At a time when the "war on cops" narrative was gaining traction and officers bemoaned biased media coverage, these brushes with resentment and disrespect allowed me to empathize with officers' experiences with a hostile public. Even if I knew that data on officer injury and death provided scant evidence of a "war," my own experiences with moments of acute public hostility enabled a more credible commiseration with officers who frequently mentioned being the targets of public prejudice, distrust, and antipathy.

In West River and Sunshine, my decision to wear a ballistic vest on patrol also helped build a connection with officers.[10] My initial choice to wear a vest was driven largely by my family's concern for my safety while with police. To their credit, though the risk of being shot on patrol was exceedingly low, it was certainly higher than in my day-to-day life. Additionally, I thought that wearing a vest would aid in understanding a unique feature of officers' work and their experience of patrol.

In one sense, wearing a vest did give me a window into officers' daily preparation for the challenges of patrol. Donning a vest became part of my routine ride-along preparation and tangibly signaled my (re)entry into officers' occupational world. My vest, lent to me by veteran officers in the WPD and SPD, was only one piece of my preparation for ride-alongs, of course. In addition to my phone and audio recorder, I kept a small reporter-style notepad and waterproof pen. Because officers also used notepads when jotting information about complainants, victims, or suspects, my notepad did not stand out as much as might be expected. A waterproof pen helped with notetaking when rain or sweat dampened my notepad's pages. I carried a small flashlight to illuminate street signs and addresses, light up dark hallways, or help officers look for shell casings lost in shadow. Disposable gloves were helpful for sifting through garbage or abandoned property, and thick leather boots with slip-proof soles were preferable for walking through water, mud, or prickly underbrush.[11] This says nothing of blood, vomit, excrement, and other bodily fluids, all of which I encountered while with officers.

Unlike my flashlight or boots, however, the vest I wore was a poignant reflection of the violence with which officers were so preoccupied. Along with the heft of a firearm, ammunition, Taser, and other equipment, a ballistic vest allowed for the possibility of violence to be *felt*. The snug pressure of the vest was constant; no other piece of equipment is worn as close to an officer's heart. When seated, the bottom of a vest would dig uncomfortably into my midriff if I slouched. In the summer, my vest trapped sweat around my chest like a hot, soggy towel. I quickly learned that officers grabbed and pulled down on the neckline of their vests not only to keep their arms from banging against their gear-laden belt but also to circulate fresh air against their body and allow excess heat to escape. All this discomfort was a physical reminder of the danger that necessitated officers' wearing a vest in the first place.

Empathy with officers' physical discomfort when wearing a vest and whatever rapport that common experience built were secondary benefits. The more meaningful effect was my vest's signal to officers that I took seriously the possibility of being injured or killed while with them. Officers commented multiple times that my proximity to them (and the likely assumption of the public that I was an officer too) put me in physical danger. During one of my first rides in Sunshine, Lt. Pinelli asked a room full of officers if anyone had a spare vest to let me borrow during my time on patrol. She commented, "He's going to be wearing a vest during the hottest time of the year, but that's part of the experience." One of the officers in the audience commented gravely, "You got to. You got to," underscoring the absolute necessity of anyone in a patrol car taking preventive measures to stay alive.

My choice to wear a ballistic vest was certainly not a sweeping solution to the issue of officer distrust. Still, that I would choose to suffer the sweat, stink, and discomfort of a vest that officers are required to wear meant that I recognized the possibility of being shot. This was true, even though I knew the probability of being shot was perishingly low. Even if we agreed on little else, the imprint of a vest through my shirt suggested I recognized that officers can and do confront deadly violence.

REFLEXIVITY, POSITIONALITY, AND INFERENCE

Rather than wholly excise the role of researcher in the hope of insinuating enhanced empiricism, ethnographic inquiry increasingly emphasizes "reflexivity" and the need for researchers to consider how they—their presence, actions, and identities—influenced their research.[12] In this book, I sought to balance transparency about what *I* saw, said, felt, and did with a focus on how officers themselves understood and moved through their social world. Unlike ethnographers whose role in the field required them to navigate comparable challenges and make similar choices as their research subjects, I was an outsider who had never been through police training and did not bear the legal or professional responsibility that officers did.[13] Though I denote my presence and questions to show where I most obviously prompted or influenced officers' words and behaviors, too strongly centering the "I" in my analysis would risk equating my lived experience to that of the officers I sought to understand. At the same time, wholly excising myself from my analysis or masking my role in the field with generalities or pseudonyms would also misrepresent the provenance of some data.

Different facets of my identity also influenced my time in the field. My identity as a straight man in his early to mid-twenties was undeniably useful for navigating the overwhelmingly heterosexual, male environment of policing. Though such activities are not inherently male, my experience with hobbies in which officers commonly engaged—weightlifting, CrossFit, competitive sports, martial arts, and shooting—aligned with the normative performance of masculinity within policing that valued strength and physical competence vis-à-vis the danger imperative. More instrumentally, my familiarity with these activities allowed me to engage in informal conversations with officers about their interests and extracurricular lives with relative ease.

Other parts of my identity were leveraged strategically: when officers commented on how much education I had relative to them or how much it must have cost, I would reference that I went to Texas public schools before pursuing a PhD that was fully funded. If they made self-deprecating remarks about their lack of advanced education, I would take the opportunity to assure them that, even though I had many more years of schooling, they were still experts from whom I could learn a great deal. When asked about myself, I would frequently mention that I was the child of immigrants, that my mother had served in the U.S. Army, and that my grandfather had served as a police officer in Colombia. Though none of these things necessarily indicated my political views, I invoked specific parts of my upbringing and identity to find common ground with officers to whom I was more similar than they might have anticipated.

In the context of an institution with a torrid history of overt and violent racism, it's reasonable to ask whether my race—I am a phenotypically brown Latino—influenced my time in the field. Some may wonder whether I was mistreated by officers because of my race. Officers' interactions with me were not marked by racialized disrespect, such as making assumptions about my immigration status, criminal history, or involvement with street gangs. Then there is the question of whether I observed police mistreat the public because of racial animus. Thankfully, I did not observe officers engage in overtly racist denigration or brutalization of the minority citizens with whom they interacted on patrol.

That I did not directly experience or observe such interactions is not altogether surprising. Officers were alerted to me and my research at lineups prior to ride-alongs, and I saw multiple messages between officers on their in-car computers telling them to expect my presence at calls. And as much as being a straight man with a similar class background and shared interests mitigated some of the social distance between officers and me, I was not a police officer. Between my presence, the ubiquity of citizen cell phones, and officers' own body-worn cameras, there were multiple, visible deterrents to unabashed bigotry.

That said, while I did not directly observe racist expletives or brutality, I did document officers' use of color-blind rhetoric to re-create racialized schemas of Black criminality and avoid discussion of racism or racial bias in policing. As described in chapter 3, race was never mentioned during lineups when officers were warned about the potential for retaliatory ambushes after the WPD killed a Black man found sleeping in his car with a firearm in the passenger seat. Instead, this threat to officer safety was linked to the inherent violence and antipolice "hatred" of an entire "gangster-ass neighborhood." And, as described in chapter 4, officers' explanations for fatal shootings of Black people assiduously omitted any mention of race. Instead, officers interpreted cases of lethal police violence through the danger imperative: they emphasized tactical considerations that centered threats to officer safety and wholly avoided discussion of race, structural racism, or racial bias in policing.

Then there was the interaction between Officer Erikson and a group of Latino boys on a dark Elmont Street. Erikson never mentioned the boys' race—he referred to them as "shitheads"—and the encounter did not result in arrest or bloody violence. But the interaction still boiled down to a police officer drawing and hiding his firearm in his lap to talk to a group of innocent boys. Without any observable indication of criminal activity, much less physical threat, Erikson justified his preparation to use lethal violence on the grounds that even a group of boys might try to murder him at any moment. Though it is impossible to know conclusively the full content of Erikson's motivations and biases, it is clear that the danger imperative encourages and provides color-blind, safety-centric logic that officers can readily deploy to justify actions that re-create racial inequalities in policing and police violence. "Color-blindness," after all, is shorthand for "color-blind racism."[14]

No ethnographer can conclusively know the world as it is when they are not present. But absence of evidence is not evidence of absence. Though I did not observe it directly, a cursory internet search reveals that explicit racial animus continues to exist within U.S. policing.[15] The lack of such animus in my data from three departments, all of them large urban departments that are more professionalized and diverse than the modal U.S. police department, should not be heralded as indicating that racism and racial bias do not exist in these departments or others.

It bears considering, however, how my efforts to justify why I did not observe overtly racist police acts or attitudes risk reifying two problematic assumptions. First, focus on the lack of evidence documenting patently racist policing can create the perception that a lack of such evidence is indicative of an inadequate or limited analysis. Multiple, detailed examples of unwarranted violence or unconstitutional stops of racial minorities might be necessary for some readers to conclude that I or another ethnographer successful captured the true nature of policing. Should an empirical account of policing not provide such data points, these same readers are liable to conclude that the ethnographer's analysis is, at best, invalid, and at worst, deceitful.

Unsurprisingly, I disagree with such assumptions and assessments of ethnographic inquiry, whether of policing or another institution. For one, the lack of such interactions during my time in the field, rather than undermining my argument, supports my claims that the danger imperative and officers' attunement to violence exists without a reliance on naked bigotry. What's more, if I had observed a racist tirade or wanton brutality on patrol, these data would not invalidate my argument. The danger imperative does not preclude the existence of racism or racialized organizations. But neither do the continued existence of these phenomena preclude the existence of the danger imperative, the color-blind organizational processes that maintain it, or the color-blind logics and practices to which it contributes. Rather than mention (much less mitigate) the reality of racially biased policing, the danger imperative and its emphasis on officer safety provide the color-blind impetus for police behavior that continually produces racial inequalities in stops, searches,

264 METHODOLOGICAL APPENDIX AND REFLECTION

arrests, and violence. These inequalities, in turn, contribute to inequitable outcomes that span employment, health, education, and civic life.[16] In short, the danger imperative and its safety-centric logic is a mechanism for the re-creation of structural racism within and beyond policing.

Second, justifying what some might assume to be "missing" data on race and racism places an unequal burden of proof on ethnographers of color whose research focuses on predominately white institutions. In these contexts, minority scholars are unlikely to be afforded the assumption that white police officers (or prosecutors or bankers or real-estate agents or doctors or teachers) are predisposed to share their true beliefs about race. Whether that assumption is premised on the belief that white participants view white ethnographers as sympathetic to their racial attitudes or that such ethnographers are more adept at building rapport, the result is the same: ethnographers of color must argue the merit of their research from an implicit deficit of credibility and/or ability.

This is not to say that scholars of color, women, or those with another minoritized identity should be wholly excused from reflexive discussion of their positionality. Consideration of how one's presence and identity were embraced, rejected, contested, or ignored can shed light on the powerful but often unstated assumptions of a group, neighborhood, occupation, or organization. So, too, can discussion of a researcher's identity contextualize the conditions under which ethnographic data emerged. The interrogation of identity, interaction, and inference can and should be practiced by ethnographers who are committed to reconciling—or at least recognizing—the limitation and promise of their chosen method.

But scholars must not allow the consideration of identity to become a decontextualized litmus test for the quality or validity of ethnographic research. This caution is especially true given that, at present, the task of interrogating one's positionality is overwhelmingly shouldered by women and racial minorities.[17] Should this pattern persist, discussion of researcher positionality would inevitably reify racial and gender hierarchies that presume the need for women and people of color to justify themselves as a deviation from whiteness and maleness. This risks turning attention too strongly from research to researcher themselves, obscuring the theoretical and empirical value of their work. The burden of considering and valuing the "I" in research should be borne by all.

NOTES

PREFACE

1. President's Commission on Law Enforcement and Administration of Justice, "The Challenge of Crime in a Free Society" (Washington, DC, 1967), 100–101, https://www.ncjrs.gov/pdffiles1/nij/42.pdf.
2. President's Task Force on Twenty-First Century Policing, "Final Report of the President's Task Force on Twenty-First Century Policing" (Washington, DC: Office of Community Oriented Policing Services, 2015), 41.
3. I confirmed this in 2022 with the WPD's records division.
4. Bianca Padró Ocasio, "Police Group Director: Obama Caused a 'War on Cops,'" Politico, July 8, 2016, https://www.politico.com/story/2016/07/obama-war-on-cops-police-advocacy-group-225291; Heather Mac Donald, "The Big Lie of the Anti-Cop Left Turns Lethal," *City Journal*, December 22, 2014, https://www.city-journal.org/html/big-lie-anti-cop-left-turns-lethal-11479.html; Aaron C. Davis, "'YouTube Effect' Has Left Police Officers Under Siege, Law Enforcement Leaders Say," *Washington Post*, October 8, 2015, https://www.washingtonpost.com/news/post-nation/wp/2015/10/08/youtube-effect-has-left-police-officers-under-siege-law-enforcement-leaders-say/; Thomas Sowell, "The Demagogues' War on Cops," National Review (blog), July 11, 2016, https://www.nationalreview.com/2016/07/war-cops-black-lives-matter-racial-tension-heightened/.
5. Ron Martinelli, "America's Turning Point—The War on Police," *Police Magazine*, September 1, 2015, https://www.policemag.com/374505/americas-turning-point-the-war-on-police.

6. Perry Bacon Jr., "Trump and Other Conservatives Embrace 'Blue Lives Matter' Movement," *NBC News*, July 23, 2016, https://www.nbcnews.com /politics/2016-election/trump-other-conservatives-embrace-blue-lives-matter -movement-n615156; Dara Lind, "How 'Blue Lives Matter' Went from a Reactive Slogan to White House Policy," Vox, February 9, 2017, https://www .vox.com/policy-and-politics/2017/2/9/14562560/trump-police-black-lives.

7. Meghan Keneally, "Donald Trump's Praise of 'Stop and Frisk' at Odds with Court Ruling," *ABC News*, September 22, 2016, https://abcnews.go.com/Politics /donald-trumps-praise-stop-frisk-odds-court-ruling/story?id=42276382; Joseph Goldstein, "Judge Rejects New York's Stop-and-Frisk Policy," *New York Times*, August 12, 2013, https://www.nytimes.com/2013/08/13/nyregion/stop-and -frisk-practice-violated-rights-judge-rules.html.

8. Julián Aguilar, "Border Patrol Union Endorses Trump for President," *Texas Tribune*, March 30, 2016, https://www.texastribune.org/2016/03/30/border-patrol -union-endorses-trump-president/; Louis Nelson, "Trump Wins Endorsement from Fraternal Order of Police," Politico, September 16, 2016, https://www .politico.com/story/2016/09/trump-fraternal-order-of-police-endorsement -228296; Michael Tanenbaum, "Philadelphia Police Union Endorses Donald Trump for President," *PhillyVoice*, September 18, 2016, https://www.phillyvoice .com/philadelphia-police-union-endorses-donald-trump-president/; DNAinfo Staff, "Chicago Police for Trump? FOP Sticks with National Union's Endorsement," DNAinfo, October 14, 2016, https://www.dnainfo.com/chicago/20161014 /downtown/police-union-endorses-donald-trump-for-president; Evan Mac-Donald, "Cleveland Police Union Votes to Endorse Trump," cleveland.com, October 1, 2016, https://www.cleveland.com/metro/2016/10/cleveland_police _union_overwhe.html; Michael Zoorob, "Blue Endorsements Matter: How the Fraternal Order of Police Contributed to Donald Trump's Victory," *PS: Political Science & Politics* 52, no. 2 (April 2019): 243–50, https://doi.org/10.1017 /S1049096518001841.

9. Anthony Brooks, "On Campaign Trail, Trump Makes No Apologies for Call to Temporarily Bar Muslims," wbur.org, December 11, 2015, https://www.wbur .org/news/2015/12/11/campaign-trail-trump.

10. Bacon, "Trump and Other Conservatives Embrace 'Blue Lives Matter' Movement."

11. Zoorob, "Blue Endorsements Matter"; Ed Pilkington, "Trump's Scrapping of Obama-Era Reforms Hinders Police Reform," *Guardian*, June 7, 2020, https:// www.theguardian.com/us-news/2020/jun/07/police-consent-decrees-trump -administration-oversight; German Lopez, "Under Trump and Sessions,

Federal Prosecutors Are Ramping Up the War on Drugs," Vox, October 24, 2017, https://www.vox.com/policy-and-politics/2017/10/24/16534812/trump-sessions-war-on-drugs.

12. Elizabeth Hinton, *America on Fire: The Untold History of Police Violence and Black Rebellion Since the 1960s* (New York: Liveright, 2021), 16.

13. Mike Baker et al., "Three Words. 70 Cases. The Tragic History of 'I Can't Breathe.,'" *New York Times*, June 28, 2020, https://www.nytimes.com/interactive/2020/06/28/us/i-cant-breathe-police-arrest.html.

14. Amy Forliti, "Officer to Floyd: 'It Takes . . . a Lot of Oxygen to Talk,'" *AP News*, April 20, 2021, https://apnews.com/article/thomas-lane-ap-top-news-racial-injustice-mn-state-wire-us-news-24f07a3f4c803166a4292c774f451f25.

15. Larry Buchanan, Quoctrung Bui, and Jugal K. Patel, "Black Lives Matter May Be the Largest Movement in U.S. History," *New York Times*, July 3, 2020, sec. U.S., https://www.nytimes.com/interactive/2020/07/03/us/george-floyd-protests-crowd-size.html.

16. Marc Tracy and Rachel Abrams, "Police Target Journalists as Trump Blames 'Lamestream Media' for Protests," *New York Times*, June 1, 2020, https://www.nytimes.com/2020/06/01/business/media/reporters-protests-george-floyd.html.

17. Kristofor A. Olson et al., "Penetrating Injuries from 'Less Lethal' Beanbag Munitions," *New England Journal of Medicine* 383, no. 11 (September 10, 2020): 1081–83, https://doi.org/10.1056/NEJMc2025923.

18. Meryl Kornfield, "Two Buffalo Police Officers Charged with Assault for Allegedly Shoving 75-Year-Old Protester," *Washington Post*, June 6, 2020, https://www.washingtonpost.com/nation/2020/06/06/buffalo-officers-charged/.

19. Hannah Knowles, "Buffalo Police Officers Who Shoved 75-Year-Old Protester in Viral Video Will Not Face Charges," *Washington Post*, February 11, 2021, https://www.washingtonpost.com/nation/2021/02/11/buffalo-police-shove-grand-jury/.

20. Mark Berman, "As Derek Chauvin's Former Bosses Line Up to Condemn Him, 'Policing in America Is on Trial,'" *Washington Post*, April 11, 2021, https://www.washingtonpost.com/nation/2021/04/11/derek-chauvin-trial-thin-blue-line/.

21. Bocar A. Ba, "How Far Are You Willing to Go Against the Police? Evaluating the Effects of Citizen Affidavits in Chicago," *SSRN Electronic Journal*, 2016, https://doi.org/10.2139/ssrn.2897063; Shaila Dewan and Serge F. Kovaleski, "Thousands of Complaints Do Little to Change Police Ways," *New York Times*, May 30, 2020, https://www.nytimes.com/2020/05/30/us/derek-chauvin-george-floyd.html; John Kelly and Mark Nichols, "We Found 85,000 Cops Who've Been Investigated for Misconduct. Now You Can Read Their Records.," *USA Today*, June 11, 2020, https://www.usatoday.com

/in-depth/news/investigations/2019/04/24/usa-today-revealing-misconduct
-records-police-cops/3223984002/; Curt Devine et al., "Minneapolis Police
Are Rarely Disciplined for Complaints, Records Show," *CNN*, June 12, 2020,
https://www.cnn.com/2020/06/11/us/minneapolis-police-discipline-invs
/index.html; Evan Allen, Matt Rocheleau, and Andrew Ryan, "Within the
Boston Police Department, Complaints Against Officers Are Rarely Confirmed or Result in Punishment," *Boston Globe*, July 18, 2020, https://www
.bostonglobe.com/2020/07/18/metro/within-boston-police-department
-complaints-against-officers-are-rarely-confirmed-or-result-punishment/.

22. Amelia Thomson-DeVeaux, Nathaniel Rakich, and Likhitha Butchireddygari,
"Why It's So Rare for Police Officers to Face Legal Consequences," FiveThirty
Eight, June 4, 2020, https://fivethirtyeight.com/features/why-its-still-so-rare
-for-police-officers-to-face-legal-consequences-for-misconduct/; Kate Levine,
"How We Prosecute the Police," *Georgetown Law Journal* 104 (2016): 745; German Lopez, "Police Officers Are Prosecuted for Murder in Less than 2 Percent
of Fatal Shootings," Vox, December 14, 2020, https://www.vox.com/21497089
/derek-chauvin-george-floyd-trial-police-prosecutions-black-lives-matter.

23. Jamiles Lartey and Abbie VanSickle, "The People Derek Chauvin Choked
Before George Floyd," *MPR News*, February 5, 2021, https://www.mprnews
.org/story/2021/02/05/that-could-have-been-me-the-people-derek-chauvin
-choked-before-george-floyd; Jon Skolnik, "Derek Chauvin Charged with
Violating the Civil Rights of a Black Child in 2017," *Salon*, May 7, 2021,
https://www.salon.com/2021/05/07/derek-chauvin-charged-with-violating
-the-civil-rights-of-a-black-child-in-2017/.

24. Stephanie Pagones, "Police Defunded: Major Cities Feeling the Loss of Police
Funding as Murders, Other Crimes Soar," *Fox News*, April 1, 2021, https://
www.foxnews.com/us/police-defunded-cities-murders-crime-budget.

25. Zusha Ellison, Dan Frosch, and Joshua Jamerson, "Cities Reverse Defunding
the Police Amid Rising Crime," *Wall Street Journal*, May 26, 2021, https://
www.wsj.com/articles/cities-reverse-defunding-the-police-amid-rising
-crime-11622066307; Sarah Holder, Fola Akinnibi, and Christopher Cannon,
"America's Big Cities Aren't Defunding the Police," Bloomberg CityLab,
September 22, 2020, https://www.bloomberg.com/graphics/2020-city-budget
-police-defunding/.

26. White House, "President Biden's Safer America Plan," White House, August
1, 2022, https://www.whitehouse.gov/briefing-room/statements-releases/2022
/08/01/fact-sheet-president-bidens-safer-america-plan-2/.

INTRODUCTION

1. William J. Bratton, "Two NYPD Police Officers Killed in the Line of Duty," *NYPD News*, December 20, 2014, http://nypdnews.com/2014/12/two-nypd-police-officers-killed-in-the-line-of-duty/.

2. Hudson Hongo, "Cop Killer's Instagram: 'I'm Putting Wings on Pigs Today,'" *Gawker*, December 21, 2014, http://gawker.com/cop-killers-instagram-im-putting-wings-on-pigs-today-1673793374.

3. Janon Fisher and Danielle Tcholakian, "Man Who Killed NYPD Officers Told Bystanders: 'Watch What I'm Going to Do,'" DNAinfo, December 21, 2014, https://www.dnainfo.com/new-york/20141221/bed-stuy/man-who-killed-nypd-officers-told-bystanders-watch-what-im-going-do.

4. Benjamin Mueller and Al Baker, "Two N.Y.P.D. Officers Killed in Brooklyn Ambush; Suspect Commits Suicide," *New York Times*, December 20, 2014, https://www.nytimes.com/2014/12/21/nyregion/two-police-officers-shot-in-their-patrol-car-in-brooklyn.html.

5. "NYPD Murders: 'There Is Blood on Many Hands', Says Police Union President—Video," *Guardian*, December 21, 2014, https://www.theguardian.com/us-news/video/2014/dec/21/nypd-murders-blood-on-many-hands-police-union-video.

6. Steven W. Thrasher, "Two NYPD Cops Get Killed and 'Wartime' Police Blame the Protesters. Have We Learned Nothing?," *Guardian*, December 21, 2014, https://www.theguardian.com/commentisfree/2014/dec/21/two-nypd-cops-killed-wartime-police-protesters.

7. Heather Mac Donald, *The War on Cops: How the New Attack on Law and Order Makes Everyone Less Safe* (New York: Encounter, 2016).

8. Howard Safir, "War on Police Is Causing Violence to Increase," *Time*, May 13, 2015, http://time.com/3857023/national-police-week-war-on-police/.

9. "Sheriff: 'War Has Been Declared' on Police," *CNN*, 2015, https://www.youtube.com/watch?v=gpOZ2KvwzQM.

10. "Testimony Before the President's Task Force on Twenty-First Century Policing" (Washington, DC, February 2015), 5, https://fop.net/CmsDocument/Doc/tst_20150223.pdf.

11. FBI, "Table 80: Law Enforcement Officers Assaulted: Region and Geographic Division, 2018," https://ucr.fbi.gov/leoka/2018/tables/table-80.xls; David M. Bierie, "Assault of Police," *Crime & Delinquency* 63, no. 8 (July 2017): 899–925, https://doi.org/10.1177/0011128715574977.

12. U.S. Bureau of Labor Statistics, "Fact Sheet | Police Officers 2018," April 17, 2020, https://www.bls.gov/iif/oshwc/cfoi/police-2018.htm.

13. Michael D. White, Lisa M. Dario, and John A. Shjarback, "Assessing Dangerousness in Policing: An Analysis of Officer Deaths in the United States, 1970–2016," *Criminology & Public Policy* 18, no. 1 (February 2019): 11–35, https://doi.org/10.1111/1745-9133.12408; John A. Shjarback and Edward R. Maguire, "Extending Research on the 'War on Cops': The Effects of Ferguson on Nonfatal Assaults Against U.S. Police Officers," *Crime & Delinquency*, November 26, 2019, https://doi.org/10.1177/0011128719890266; Michael Sierra-Arévalo and Justin Nix, "Gun Victimization in the Line of Duty: Fatal and Nonfatal Firearm Assaults on Police Officers in the United States, 2014–2019," *Criminology & Public Policy* 19, no. 3 (August 2020): 1041–66, https://doi.org/10.1111/1745-9133.12507.

14. Ted Chiricos, Kathy Padgett, and Marc Gertz, "Fear, TV News, and the Reality of Crime," *Criminology* 38, no. 3 (2000): 755–86, https://doi.org/10.1111/j.1745-9125.2000.tb00905.x; Andrew J. Baranauskas and Kevin M. Drakulich, "Media Construction of Crime Revisited: Media Types, Consumer Contexts, and Frames of Crime and Justice," *Criminology* 56, no. 4 (2018): 679–714, https://doi.org/10.1111/1745-9125.12189; Lincoln Quillian and Devah Pager, "Estimating Risk: Stereotype Amplification and the Perceived Risk of Criminal Victimization," *Social Psychology Quarterly* 73, no. 1 (March 2010): 79–104, https://doi.org/10.1177/0190272509360763.

15. Richard K. Moule, "Under Siege?: Assessing Public Perceptions of the 'War on Police,'" *Journal of Criminal Justice* 66 (January 2020): 4–5, https://doi.org/10.1016/j.jcrimjus.2019.101631.

16. Rich Morin et al., "Police Views, Public Views," Pew Research Center, February 8, 2017, 80, 64, http://www.pewsocialtrends.org/2017/01/11/police-views-public-views/.

17. Justin Nix, Scott E. Wolfe, and Bradley A. Campbell, "Command-Level Police Officers' Perceptions of the 'War on Cops' and De-Policing," *Justice Quarterly* 35, no. 1 (January 2018): 33–54, https://doi.org/10.1080/07418825.2017.1338743.

18. Cynthia Lum, Christopher S. Koper, and Xiaoyun Wu, "Can We Really Defund the Police? A Nine-Agency Study of Police Response to Calls for Service," *Police Quarterly*, July 22, 2021, https://doi.org/10.1177/10986111211035002; Jerry H. Ratcliffe, "Policing and Public Health Calls for Service in Philadelphia," *Crime Science* 10, no. 1 (2021): 5, https://doi.org/10.1186/s40163-021-00141-0; John A. Webster, "Police Task and Time Study," in *Policing: A View from the*

Street, ed. Peter K. Manning and John Van Maanen (New York: Random House, 1978), 105–28; Albert J. Reiss, *The Police and the Public* (New Haven, CT: Yale University Press, 1975), 72–77; Barry Friedman, "Disaggregating the Policing Function," *University of Pennsylvania Law Review* 169, no. 4 (2021): 925–99.

19. Michael Bauman, "Police Productivity: A State of Mind, An Approach to the Job," *Police Magazine*, December 31, 1999, https://www.policemag.com/338713/police-productivity-a-state-of-mind-an-approach-to-the-job.

20. Peter Moskos, *Cop in the Hood: My Year Policing Baltimore's Eastern District* (Princeton, NJ: Princeton University Press, 2009), 22.

21. L. J. Krivo, R. D. Peterson, and D. C. Kuhl, "Segregation, Racial Structure, and Neighborhood Violent Crime," *American Journal of Sociology* 114, no. 6 (2009): 1765–1802, https://doi.org/10.1086/597285; R. J. Sampson, "Racial Stratification and the Durable Tangle of Neighborhood Inequality," *Annals of the American Academy of Political and Social Science* 621, no. 1 (2009): 260–280, https://doi.org/10.1177/0002716208324803

22. A. A. Braga, R. K. Brunson, and K. M. Drakulich, "Race, Place, and Effective Policing," *Annual Review of Sociology* 45, no. 1 (2019), https://doi.org/10.1146/annurev-soc-073018-022541

23. Monica C. Bell, "Police Reform and the Dismantling of Legal Estrangement," *Yale Law Journal* 126 (2017): 2054–2151.

24. Elijah Anderson, *Code of the Street: Decency, Violence, and the Moral Life of the Inner City* (New York: Norton, 1999); David S. Kirk and Andrew V. Papachristos, "Cultural Mechanisms and the Persistence of Neighborhood Violence," *American Journal of Sociology* 116, no. 4 (2011): 1190–1233, https://doi.org/10.1086/655754.

25. Frank Edwards, Hedwig Lee, and Michael Esposito, "Risk of Being Killed by Police Use of Force in the United States by Age, Race–Ethnicity, and Sex," *Proceedings of the National Academy of Sciences* 116, no. 34 (August 20, 2019): 16793–98, https://doi.org/10.1073/pnas.1821204116; Rory Kramer and Brianna Remster, "Stop, Frisk, and Assault? Racial Disparities in Police Use of Force During Investigatory Stops," *Law & Society Review* 52, no. 4 (2018): 960–93, https://doi.org/10.1111/lasr.12366; Brianna Remster, Chris M. Smith, and Rory Kramer, "Race, Gender, and Police Violence in the Shadow of Controlling Images," *Social Problems*, April 5, 2022, spac018, https://doi.org/10.1093/socpro/spac018; William Terrill and Stephen D. Mastrofski, "Situational and Officer-Based Determinations of Police Coercion," *Justice Quarterly* 19 (2002): 215–48; Justin Nix et al., "A Bird's Eye View of Civilians Killed by

Police in 2015," *Criminology & Public Policy* 16, no. 1 (2017): 309–40, https://doi.org/10.1111/1745-9133.12269; Eric L. Piza and Victoria A. Sytsma, "The Impact of Suspect Resistance, Informational Justice, and Interpersonal Justice on Time Until Police Use of Physical Force: A Survival Analysis," *Crime & Delinquency*, June 25, 2022, 1–26, https://doi.org/10.1177/00111287221106947; Marisa Omori, Rachel Lautenschlager, and Justin Stoler, "Organizational Practice and Neighborhood Context of Racial Inequality in Police Use-of-Force," *Social Problems*, May 27, 2022, spac031, https://doi.org/10.1093/socpro/spac031; Marie Ouellet et al., "Network Exposure and Excessive Use of Force," *Criminology & Public Policy* 18, no. 3 (2019): 675–704, https://doi.org/10.1111/1745-9133.12459.

26. Eugene A. Paoline, "Taking Stock: Toward a Richer Understanding of Police Culture," *Journal of Criminal Justice* 31 (2003): 199–214.

27. Jason R. Ingram, Eugene A. Paoline, and William Terrill, "A Multilevel Framework for Understanding Police Culture: The Role of the Workgroup," *Criminology* 51, no. 2 (May 2013): 365–97, https://doi.org/10.1111/1745-9125.12009; Jason R. Ingram, William Terrill, and Eugene A. Paoline, "Police Culture and Officer Behavior: Application of a Multilevel Framework," *Criminology* 56, no. 4 (November 2018): 780–811, https://doi.org/10.1111/1745-9125.12192; Paoline, "Taking Stock"; Eugene A. Paoline, "Shedding Light on Police Culture: An Examination of Officers' Occupational Attitudes," *Police Quarterly* 7, no. 2 (June 1, 2004): 205–36, https://doi.org/10.1177/1098611103257074; Eugene A. Paoline and Jacinta M. Gau, "Police Occupational Culture: Testing the Monolithic Model," *Justice Quarterly* 35, no. 4 (June 7, 2018): 670–98, https://doi.org/10.1080/07418825.2017.1335764; William Terrill, Eugene A. Paoline, and Peter K. Manning, "Police Culture and Coercion," *Criminology* 41, no. 4 (November 2003): 1003–34, https://doi.org/10.1111/j.1745-9125.2003.tb01012.x.

28. Bethan Loftus, "Police Occupational Culture: Classic Themes, Altered Times," *Policing and Society* 20, no. 1 (March 2010): 1–20, https://doi.org/10.1080/10439460903281547; William A. Westley, *Violence and the Police: A Sociological Study of Law, Custom, and Morality* (Cambridge, MA: MIT Press, 1970); Michael Banton, *The Policeman in the Community* (New York: Basic Books, 1964); John Van Maanen, "Observations on the Making of a Policeman," in *Policing: A View from the Street*, ed. Peter K. Manning and John Van Maanen (New York: Random House, 1978), 292–308; Jerome H. Skolnick, *Justice Without Trial: Law Enforcement in Democratic Society* (New York: Wiley, 1966).

29. Egon Bittner, *The Functions of the Police in Modern Society: A Review of Background Factors, Current Practices, and Possible Role Models* (Chevy Chase, MD:

National Institute of Mental Health, Center for Studies of Crime and Delinquency, 1970), 46; J. H. Skolnick, *Justice Without Trial: Law Enforcement in Democratic Society*, 4th ed. (New Orleans, LA: Quid Pro Quo Books, 2011).

30. Samuel Walker, *Taming the System: The Control of Discretion in Criminal Justice, 1950–1990* (New York: Oxford University Press, 1993); Peter K. Manning, *Police Work: The Social Organization of Policing* (Cambridge, MA: MIT Press, 1977); Robert Reiner, *The Politics of the Police*, 4th ed. (Oxford: Oxford University Press, 2010).

31. Ann Swidler, "Culture in Action: Symbols and Strategies," *American Sociological Review* 51, no. 2 (April 1986): 276.

32. Steve Herbert, "'Hard Charger' or 'Station Queen'? Policing and the Masculinist State," *Gender, Place & Culture* 8, no. 1 (March 2001): 55–71, https://doi.org/10.1080/09663690120026325.

33. William K. Muir, *Police: Street Corner Politicians* (Chicago: University of Chicago Press, 1977).

34. Seth W. Stoughton, "Principled Policing: Warrior Cops and Guardian Officers," *Wake Forest Law Review* 51 (2016): 611–76.

35. Peter B. Kraska and Victor E. Kappeler, "Militarizing American Police: The Rise and Normalization of Paramilitary Units," *Social Problems* 44 (1997): 1–18; Radley Balko, *Rise of the Warrior Cop: The Militarization of America's Police Forces* (New York: PublicAffairs, 2013).

36. Seth Stoughton, "Law Enforcement's Warrior Problem," *Harvard Law Review Forum* 128, no. 6 (April 2015): 225–34 (227).

37. Samantha J. Simon, "Training for War: Academy Socialization and Warrior Policing," *Social Problems*, September 12, 2021, https://doi.org/10.1093/socpro/spab057; Beck M. Strah, Jocelyn M. Pollock, and Laurie T. Becker, "Shifting from Warriors to Guardians: Officer Reflections on Law Enforcement Training in Washington State," *Crime & Delinquency* 69, no. 2 (February 2023): 439–63, https://doi.org/10.1177/00111287221117488; Sue Rahr and Stephen K. Rice, "From Warriors to Guardians: Recommitting American Police Culture to Democratic Ideals," *New Perspectives in Policing Bulletin* (Washington, DC: U.S. Department of Justice, National Institute of Justice, 2015), https://www.ncjrs.gov/pdffiles1/nij/248654.pdf; Stoughton, "Law Enforcement's Warrior Problem."

38. Jeffrey Guhin, Jessica McCrory Calarco, and Cynthia Miller-Idriss, "Whatever Happened to Socialization?," *Annual Review of Sociology* 47, no. 1 (2021): 109–29 (110), https://doi.org/10.1146/annurev-soc-090320-103012.

39. Talcott Parsons, *The Social System* (New York: Free Press, 1951), 211.

40. Stoughton, "Principled Policing," 615.

41. Michael Sierra-Arévalo, "The Commemoration of Death, Organizational Memory, and Police Culture," *Criminology* 57, no. 4 (November 2019): 632–58, https://doi.org/10.1111/1745-9125.12224.

42. Emily D. Buehler, "State and Local Law Enforcement Training Academies, 2018—Statistical Tables," U.S. Department of Justice, Office of Justice Programs, July 2021, https://www.ojp.gov/library/publications/state-and-local-law-enforcement-training-academies-2018-statistical-tables.

43. Janet Chan, "Changing Police Culture," *British Journal of Criminology* 36, no. 1 (Winter 1996): 109–34 (110), https://doi.org/10.1093/oxfordjournals.bjc.a014061.

44. For a more general discussion of how organizations structure the perception and action of organizational members in response to organizationally defined problems, see Paul J. DiMaggio and Walter W. Powell, "The Iron Cage Revisited: Institutional Isomorphism and Collective Rationality in Organizational Fields," *American Sociological Review* 48, no. 2 (1983): 147–60, https://doi.org/10.2307/2095101.

45. Michèle Lamont and Mario Small, "How Culture Matters: Enriching Our Understanding of Poverty," in *The Colors of Poverty: Why Racial and Ethnic Disparities Persist*, ed. Ann Lin Harris and David Harris (New York: Russell Sage Foundation, 2008), 76–102.

46. Robert Brame et al., "Demographic Patterns of Cumulative Arrest Prevalence by Ages 18 and 23," *Crime & Delinquency* 60, no. 3 (April 2014): 471–86, https://doi.org/10.1177/0011128713514801; Charles R. Epp, Steven Maynard-Moody, and Donald P. Haider-Markel, *Pulled Over: How Police Stops Define Race and Citizenship* (Chicago: University of Chicago Press, 2014); Edwards, Lee, and Esposito, "Risk of Being Killed by Police Use of Force"; Shytierra Gaston, "Producing Race Disparities: A Study of Drug Arrests Across Place and Race," *Criminology*, 2019, https://doi.org/10.1111/1745-9125.12207; Nix et al., "A Bird's Eye View of Civilians Killed by Police in 2015"; Joscha Legewie, "Racial Profiling and Use of Force in Police Stops: How Local Events Trigger Periods of Increased Discrimination," *American Journal of Sociology* 122, no. 2 (2016): 379–424, https://doi.org/10.1086/687518; Kramer and Remster, "Stop, Frisk, and Assault?"; Andrew Gelman, Jeffrey Fagan, and Alex Kiss, "An Analysis of the New York City Police Department's 'Stop-and-Frisk' Policy in the Context of Claims of Racial Bias," *Journal of the American Statistical Association* 102, no. 479 (September 2007): 813–23, https://doi.org/10.1198/016214506000001040; Shytierra Gaston and Rod K. Brunson, "Reasonable Suspicion in the Eye of

the Beholder: Routine Policing in Racially Different Disadvantaged Neighborhoods," *Urban Affairs Review* 56, no. 1 (January 2020): 188–227, https://doi.org/10.1177/1078087418774641; Victor M. Rios, Greg Prieto, and Jonathan M. Ibarra, "Mano Suave–Mano Dura: Legitimacy Policing and Latino Stop-and-Frisk," *American Sociological Review* 85, no. 1 (February 2020): 58–75, https://doi.org/10.1177/0003122419897348; Bocar A. Ba et al., "The Role of Officer Race and Gender in Police-Civilian Interactions in Chicago," *Science* 371, no. 6530 (February 12, 2021): 696–702, https://doi.org/10.1126/science.abd8694.

47. Stoughton, "Law Enforcement's Warrior Problem"; Ingram, Paoline, and Terrill, "A Multilevel Framework for Understanding Police Culture"; Ingram, Terrill, and Paoline, "Police Culture and Officer Behavior"; Sierra-Arévalo, "The Commemoration of Death, Organizational Memory, and Police Culture"; Paoline, "Taking Stock"; Paoline and Gau, "Police Occupational Culture"; Loftus, "Police Occupational Culture."

48. Nicole Gonzalez Van Cleve and Lauren Mayes, "Criminal Justice Through 'Colorblind' Lenses: A Call to Examine the Mutual Constitution of Race and Criminal Justice," *Law & Social Inquiry* 40, no. 2 (2015): 406–32, https://doi.org/10.1111/lsi.12113.

49. Allan Silver, "The Demand for Order in a Civil Society," in *The Police: Six Sociological Essays*, ed. David J. Bordua (New York: Wiley, 1967), 1–24.

50. Sally Hadden, "Police and Slave Patrols: A History of State-Sponsored White-on-Black Violence," in *The Ethics of Policing: New Perspectives on Law Enforcement*, ed. Ben Jones and Eduardo Mendieta (New York: New York University Press, 2021), 205–21; Philip L. Reichel, "Southern Slave Patrols as a Transitional Police Type," *American Journal of Police* 7, no. 2 (1988): 51–77.

51. Michelle Alexander, *The New Jim Crow: Mass Incarceration in the Age of Colorblindness* (New York: New Press, 2012); Brandon T. Jett, *Race, Crime, and Policing in the Jim Crow South: African Americans and Law Enforcement in Birmingham, Memphis, and New Orleans, 1920–1945* (Baton Rouge: Louisiana State University Press, 2021).

52. Simon Balto, *Occupied Territory: Policing Black Chicago from Red Summer to Black Power* (Chapel Hill: University of North Carolina Press, 2019); Max Felker-Kantor, *Policing Los Angeles: Race, Resistance, and the Rise of the LAPD* (Chapel Hill: University of North Carolina Press, 2018); Balto, *Occupied Territory*; Kristian Williams, *Our Enemies in Blue: Police and Power in America*, rev. ed. (Oakland, CA: AK Press, 2015); Sidney L. Harring, *Policing a Class Society: The Experience of American Cities, 1865–1915*, 2nd ed. (Chicago: Haymarket, 2017).

53. Khalil Gibran Muhammad, *The Condemnation of Blackness: Race, Crime, and the Making of Modern Urban America* (Cambridge, MA: Harvard University Press, 2010).

54. FBI, "About the UCR Program," September 2018, https://www.fbi.gov/file-repository/ucr/about-the-ucr-program.pdf/view; Muhammad, *The Condemnation of Blackness*, 266n155,156.

55. Elijah Anderson, "The Iconic Ghetto," *Annals of the American Academy of Political and Social Science* 642, no. 1 (July 2012): 8–24, https://doi.org/10.1177/0002716212446299.

56. Kimberly Barsamian Kahn and Paul G. Davies, "Differentially Dangerous? Phenotypic Racial Stereotypicality Increases Implicit Bias Among Ingroup and Outgroup Members," *Group Processes & Intergroup Relations* 14, no. 4 (July 2011): 569–80, https://doi.org/10.1177/1368430210374609; Justin D. Levinson and Danielle Young, "Different Shades of Bias: Skin Tone, Implicit Racial Bias, and Judgments of Ambiguous Evidence," *West Virginia Law Review* 112 (2010): 307–50; Jennifer L. Eberhardt et al., "Seeing Black: Race, Crime, and Visual Processing," *Journal of Personality and Social Psychology* 87, no. 6 (2004): 876–93, https://doi.org/10.1037/0022-3514.87.6.876; Katherine B. Spencer, Amanda K. Charbonneau, and Jack Glaser, "Implicit Bias and Policing," *Social and Personality Psychology Compass* 10, no. 1 (January 2016): 50–63 (54–55), https://doi.org/10.1111/spc3.12210; Kimberly Barsamian Kahn et al., "Protecting Whiteness: White Phenotypic Racial Stereotypicality Reduces Police Use of Force," *Social Psychological and Personality Science* 7, no. 5 (July 2016): 403–11, https://doi.org/10.1177/1948550616633505; Lorie A. Fridell, "The Science of Implicit Bias and Implications for Policing," in *Producing Bias-Free Policing: A Science-Based Approach*, ed. Lorie A. Fridell (Cham, Switzerland: Springer, 2017), 10–15, https://doi.org/10.1007/978-3-319-33175-1_2.

57. Jerome H. Skolnick, *The Politics of Protest: Task Force on Violent Aspects of Protest and Confrontation of the National Commission on the Causes and Prevention of Violence* (New York: NYU Press, 2010), https://www.jstor.org/stable/j.ctv12pnp6w; Gerald Horne, *Black Liberation/Red Scare: Ben Davis and the Communist Party* (Newark: University of Delaware Press, 1994); Edward J. Escobar, "The Dialectics of Repression: The Los Angeles Police Department and the Chicano Movement, 1968–1971," *Journal of American History* 79, no. 4 (1993): 1483–1514, https://doi.org/10.2307/2080213.

58. Stuart Schrader, Badges Without Borders (Oakland: University of California Press, 2019).

59. Elizabeth Hinton, "'A War Within Our Own Boundaries': Lyndon Johnson's Great Society and the Rise of the Carceral State," *Journal of American History* 102, no. 1 (June 2015): 100–12 (110), https://doi.org/10.1093/jahist/jav328.

60. Balko, *Rise of the Warrior Cop*.

61. James Forman, *Locking Up Our Own: Crime and Punishment in Black America* (New York: Farrar, Straus and Giroux, 2017).

62. James Forman Jr., "Exporting Harshness: How the War on Crime Helped Make the War on Terror Possible," *New York University Review of Law & Social Change* 33 (2009): 331–74; Bruce L. Benson, David W. Rasmussen, and David L. Sollars, "Police Bureaucracies, Their Incentives, and the War on Drugs," *Public Choice* 83, no. 1–2 (April 1995): 21–45, https://doi.org/10.1007/BF01047681.

63. Peter K. Manning, "The Police: Mandate, Strategies, and Appearances," in *Policing: A View from the Street*, ed. Peter K. Manning and John Van Maanen (New York: Random House, 1978), 7–31; William A. Westley, "Violence and the Police," *American Journal of Sociology 59*, no. 1 (July 1953): 34–41 (35).

64. Ryan J. Foley, "Police Guide That Calls BLM a Terrorist Group Draws Outrage," AP News, December 2, 2020, https://apnews.com/article/police-guide-calls-blm-terrorist-group-8dcoafce2ce6b6odbaaod1d9c53ce1e3.

65. Brame et al., "Demographic Patterns of Cumulative Arrest Prevalence by Ages 18 and 23"; Epp, Maynard-Moody, and Haider-Markel, *Pulled Over*; Edwards, Lee, and Esposito, "Risk of Being Killed by Police Use of Force"; Gaston, "Producing Race Disparities"; Nix et al., "A Bird's Eye View of Civilians Killed by Police in 2015"; Legewie, "Racial Profiling and Use of Force in Police Stops"; Kramer and Remster, "Stop, Frisk, and Assault?"; Gelman, Fagan, and Kiss, "An Analysis of the New York City Police Department's 'Stop-and-Frisk' Policy"; Gaston and Brunson, "Reasonable Suspicion in the Eye of the Beholder"; Rios, Prieto, and Ibarra, "Mano Suave–Mano Dura"; Ba et al., "The Role of Officer Race and Gender in Police-Civilian Interactions in Chicago."

66. August Vollmer, "Wickersham Report on Police," *American Journal of Police Science* 2, no. 4 (1931): 337–48, https://doi.org/10.2307/1147362; Christopher Commission, "Report of the Independent Commission on the Los Angeles Police Department," 1991, https://archive.org/details/ChristopherCommissionLAPD; Kerner Commission, "Report of the National Advisory Commission on Civil Disorders," 1968; President's Commission on Law Enforcement and Administration of Justice, "The Challenge of Crime in a Free Society," 1967; Skolnick, *The Politics of Protest*; President's Task Force on Twenty-First Century

Policing, "Final Report of the President's Task Force on Twenty-First Century Policing," 2015; St. Clair Commission, "Report of the Boston Police Department Management Review Committee" (Boston, January 14, 1992), http://vault.blackstonian.org/wp-content/uploads/2016/10/St.-Clair-Commission-Report.pdf; U.S. Commission on Civil Rights, "Police Practices and Civil Rights in New York City" (Washington, DC, August 2000), https://www.hsdl.org/?view&did=726672; U.S. Commission on Civil Rights, "Police Use of Force: An Examination of Modern Policing Practices" (Washington, DC, November 2018), https://www.usccr.gov/pubs/2018/11-15-Police-Force.pdf; Commission on Police Integrity, "Report of the Commission on Police Integrity" (Chicago, November 1997), https://static1.squarespace.com/static/5385f942e4b0f52de5677500/t/54bb16e9e4b06e38ad65905f/1421547241585/police-integrity-report-1997.pdf; Christopher Commission, "Report of the Independent Commission on the Los Angeles Police Department"; National Commission on Law Observance and Enforcement, "Report on the Enforcement of the Prohibition Laws of the United States" (Washington, DC, January 7, 1931), https://www.ncjrs.gov/pdffiles1/Digitization/44540NCJRS.pdf.

67. Dean Knox, Will Lowe, and Jonathan Mummolo, "Administrative Records Mask Racially Biased Policing," *American Political Science Review* 114, no. 3 (August 2020): 619–37, https://doi.org/10.1017/S0003055420000039; GBD 2019 Police Violence US Subnational Collaborators, "Fatal Police Violence by Race and State in the USA, 1980–2019: A Network Meta-Regression," *Lancet* 398, no. 10307 (October 2, 2021): 1239–55, https://doi.org/10.1016/S0140-6736(21)01609-3.

68. Abigail A. Sewell and Kevin A. Jefferson, "Collateral Damage: The Health Effects of Invasive Police Encounters in New York City," *Journal of Urban Health* 93, no. 1 (April 2016): 42–67, https://doi.org/10.1007/s11524-015-0016-7; Naomi F. Sugie and Kristin Turney, "Beyond Incarceration: Criminal Justice Contact and Mental Health," *American Sociological Review* 82, no. 4 (August 2017): 719–43, https://doi.org/10.1177/0003122417713188; Joscha Legewie and Jeffrey Fagan, "Aggressive Policing and the Educational Performance of Minority Youth," *American Sociological Review* 84, no. 2 (April 2019): 220–47, https://doi.org/10.1177/0003122419826020; Sarah Brayne, "Surveillance and System Avoidance: Criminal Justice Contact and Institutional Attachment," *American Sociological Review* 79, no. 3 (June 2014): 367–91, https://doi.org/10.1177/0003122414530398; Joe Soss and Vesla Weaver, "Police Are Our Government: Politics, Political Science, and the Policing of Race–Class Subjugated Communities," *Annual Review of Political Science* 20, no. 1 (2017): 565–91,

https://doi.org/10.1146/annurev-polisci-060415-093825; Bell, "Police Reform and the Dismantling of Legal Estrangement."

69. Alice Speri, "Unredacted FBI Document Sheds New Light on White Supremacist Infiltration of Law Enforcement," The Intercept (blog), September 29, 2020, https://theintercept.com/2020/09/29/police-white-supremacist-infiltration-fbi/.

70. Speri, "Unredacted FBI Document."

71. Michael German, "Hidden in Plain Sight: Racism, White Supremacy, and Far-Right Militancy in Law Enforcement," Brennan Center for Justice, August 27, 2020, https://www.brennancenter.org/our-work/research-reports/hidden-plain-sight-racism-white-supremacy-and-far-right-militancy-law.

72. Will Carless and Michael Corey, "Inside Hate Groups on Facebook, Police Officers Trade Racist Memes, Conspiracy Theories and Islamophobia," *Reveal News*, June 14, 2019, http://revealnews.org/article/inside-hate-groups-on-facebook-police-officers-trade-racist-memes-conspiracy-theories-and-islamophobia/; Jesselyn Cook and Nick Robins-Early, "Inside the Dangerous Online Fever Swamps of American Police," *HuffPost*, June 17, 2020, https://www.huffpost.com/entry/police-protests-floyd-law-enforcement-today-rant_n_5ee3ef5fc5b699cea53196b4; Emily Hoerner and Rick Tulsky, "Cops Across the US Have Been Exposed Posting Racist and Violent Things on Facebook. Here's the Proof.," *BuzzFeedNews* July 23, 2019, https://www.buzzfeednews.com/article/emilyhoerner/police-facebook-racist-violent-posts-comments-philadelphia.

73. Ryan Jerome LeCount, "More Black than Blue? Comparing the Racial Attitudes of Police to Citizens," *Sociological Forum* 32, no. S1 (2017): 1051–72, https://doi.org/10.1111/socf.12367; Jomills H. Braddock et al., "How Many Bad Apples? Investigating Implicit and Explicit Bias Among Police Officers and the General Public," *Contexts*, October 27, 2020, https://contexts.org/articles/how-many-bad-apples-investigating-implicit-and-explicit-bias-among-police-officers-and-the-general-public/.

74. Eduardo Bonilla-Silva, *Racism Without Racists: Color-Blind Racism and the Persistence of Racial Inequality in the United States* (Rowman & Littlefield, 2006); Megan Welsh, Joshua Chanin, and Stuart Henry, "Complex Color-blindness in Police Processes and Practices," *Social Problems* 68, no. 2 (May 2021): 374–92, https://doi.org/10.1093/socpro/spaa008; Jennifer C. Mueller, "Producing Colorblindness: Everyday Mechanisms of White Ignorance," *Social Problems* 64, no. 2 (May 2017): 219–38; Simon, "Training for War"; Daanika Gordon, "The Bureaucratic Dissociation of Race in Policing: From State Racial Projects to Colorblind Ideologies," *Social Problems*, March 30, 2022,

spaco19, https://doi.org/10.1093/socpro/spaco19; Nikki Jones et al., "'Other than the Projects, You Stay Professional': 'Colorblind' Cops and the Enactment of Spatial Racism in Routine Policing," *City & Community* 22, no. 1 (March 2023): 3–21, https://doi.org/10.1177/15356841221123820.

75. Victor Ray, "A Theory of Racialized Organizations," *American Sociological Review* 84, no. 1 (2019): 26–53, https://doi.org/10.1177/0003122418822335.

In Elmont, traffic-stop data show that minority drivers are about twice as likely to be stopped as white drivers. Black drivers are almost three times as likely to be stopped and are significantly more likely to be ticketed for speeding than white drivers. Sunshine Police Department data show that Black people are arrested at nearly three times the rate for whites, and police use force on Black people at a rate four times higher than for whites based on their share of the local population. Controlling for officer and neighborhood characteristics, West River data show marked racial disparities in who is stopped, searched, handcuffed, and arrested. Another independent analysis found that Black men were eight times more likely to be stopped than white men. Use-of-force data show that Blacks account for a share of arrests and police killings about 2.5 times greater than their share of the West River population.

76. Van Cleve and Mayes, "Criminal Justice Through 'Colorblind' Lenses"; Amada Armenta, "Racializing Crimmigration: Structural Racism, Colorblindness, and the Institutional Production of Immigrant Criminality," *Sociology of Race and Ethnicity* 3, no. 1 (January 2017): 82–95, https://doi.org/10.1177/2332649216648714.

77. Devah Pager, "The Mark of a Criminal Record," *American Journal of Sociology* 108, no. 5 (March 2003): 937–75, https://doi.org/10.1086/374403; Elizabeth Korver-Glenn, "Compounding Inequalities: How Racial Stereotypes and Discrimination Accumulate Across the Stages of Housing Exchange," *American Sociological Review* 83, no. 4 (August 2018): 627–56, https://doi.org/10.1177/0003122418781774; Armando Lara-Millán, "Public Emergency Room Overcrowding in the Era of Mass Imprisonment," *American Sociological Review* 79, no. 5 (October 2014): 866–87, https://doi.org/10.1177/0003122414549552; Mario L. Small et al., "Banks, Alternative Institutions and the Spatial–Temporal Ecology of Racial Inequality in US Cities," *Nature Human Behaviour* 5, no. 12 (December 2021): 1622–28, https://doi.org/10.1038/s41562-021-01153-1; Matthew Desmond, *Evicted: Poverty and Profit in the American City* (New York: Crown, 2016); Jo C. Phelan and Bruce G. Link, "Is Racism a Fundamental Cause of Inequalities in Health?," *Annual Review of Sociology* 41, no. 1 (2015): 311–30,

https://doi.org/10.1146/annurev-soc-073014-112305; Devah Pager, Bart Boni-kowski, and Bruce Western, "Discrimination in a Low-Wage Labor Market: A Field Experiment," *American Sociological Review* 74, no. 5 (October 2009): 777–99, https://doi.org/10.1177/000312240907400505; Small et al., "Banks, Alternative Institutions and the Spatial–Temporal Ecology of Racial Inequality in US Cities"; Keeanga-Yamahtta Taylor, *Race for Profit: How Banks and the Real Estate Industry Undermined Black Homeownership* (Chapel Hill: University of North Carolina Press, 2019).

78. Victor Ray, "A Theory of Racialized Organizations," *American Sociological Review* 84, no. 1 (February 2019): 26–53, https://doi.org/10.1177/0003122418822335.

79. Sarah Brayne, "Big Data Surveillance: The Case of Policing," *American Sociological Review* 82, no. 5 (October 2017): 997–1008 (997), https://doi.org/10.1177/0003122417725865.

80. Patrick Sharkey, *Stuck in Place: Urban Neighborhoods and the End of Progress Toward Racial Equality* (Chicago: University of Chicago Press, 2013); Ruth D. Peterson and Lauren Joy Krivo, *Divergent Social Worlds: Neighborhood Crime and the Racial-Spatial Divide* (New York: Russell Sage Foundation, 2010); Balto, Occupied Territory, 1; Forman, *Locking Up Our Own*; Ba et al., "The Role of Officer Race and Gender in Police-Civilian Interactions in Chicago."

81. Westley, "Violence and the Police"; Jonathan Rubinstein, *City Police* (New York: Farrar, Straus and Giroux, 1973); Skolnick, *Justice Without Trial*; Manning, *Police Work*; Van Maanen, "Observations on the Making of a Police-man"; John Van Maanen, "The Asshole," in *Policing: A View from the Street*, ed. Peter K. Manning and John Van Maanen (New York: Random House, 1978), 221–37; Muir, *Police*; Arthur Niederhoffer, *Behind the Shield: The Police in Urban Society* (Garden City, NY: Doubleday, 1967); Michael K. Brown, *Working the Street: Police Discretion and the Dilemmas of Reform* (Russell Sage Foundation, 1988); Westley, *Violence and the Police*.

82. David M. Hureau and Anthony A. Braga, "The Trade in Tools: The Market for Illicit Guns in High-Risk Networks," *Criminology* 56, no. 3 (August 2018): 510–45 (520), https://doi.org/10.1111/1745-9125.12187; James P. Spradley, *The Ethnographic Interview* (New York: Holt, Rinehart and Winston, 1979).

83. Officers, following the FBI definition, are "individuals who ordinarily carry a firearm and a badge, have full arrest powers, and are paid from governmental funds set aside specifically for sworn law enforcement." This excludes what are commonly referred to as civilian or nonsworn employees who work as records keepers, administrative assistants, crime scene technicians, mechanics, and in other nonenforcement roles. FBI, "Police Employee Data," 2019,

https://ucr.fbi.gov/crime-in-the-u.s/2018/crime-in-the-u.s.-2018/topic-pages/police-employee-data.

84. Shelley Hyland, "Full-Time Employees in Law Enforcement Agencies, 1997–2016" (Washington, DC: U.S Department of Justice, Office of Justice Programs, Bureau of Justice Statistics, 2018), https://www.bjs.gov/content/pub/pdf/ftelea9716.pdf.

85. Dan Keating and Kevin Uhrmacher, "Police Are Consistently Whiter than the Communities They Work In, Particularly in Urban Areas," *Washington Post*, June 4, 2020, https://www.washingtonpost.com/nation/2020/06/04/urban-areas-police-are-consistently-much-whiter-than-people-they-serve/.

86. Kenneth Bolton and Joe Feagin, *Black in Blue: African-American Police Officers and Racism* (New York: Routledge, 2004); Glenn E. Rice, Luke Nozicka, and Katie Moore, "Racism in the KCPD: There's No Thin Blue Line for Black Officers, Star Investigation Finds," *Kansas City Star*, March 27, 2022, https://www.kansascity.com/news/local/article259140453.html; Kenneth Bolton, "Shared Perceptions: Black Officers Discuss Continuing Barriers in Policing," *Policing: An International Journal of Police Strategies & Management* 26, no. 3 (January 2003): 386–99, https://doi.org/10.1108/13639510310489458; Roberto Gallardo, "'I Don't Think I Have, But I've Heard.': Examining Perceptions of Race Relations in the Los Angeles Police Department Among Male Mexican-American Police Officers," *Race and Justice*, October 19, 2020, https://doi.org/10.1177/2153368720967442; Kayla Preito-Hodge, "Behind the Badge and the Veil: Black Police Officers in the Era of Black Lives Matter," *Psychology of Violence* 13, no. 3 (2023): 171–82, https://doi.org/10.1037/vio0000462.

87. Preito-Hodge, "Behind the Badge and the Veil"; Vicky M. Wilkins and Brian N. Williams, "Representing Blue: Representative Bureaucracy and Racial Profiling in the Latino Community," *Administration & Society* 40, no. 8 (January 2009): 775–98, https://doi.org/10.1177/0095399708326332; Bolton and Feagin, *Black in Blue*; Gallardo, "'I Don't Think I Have, But I've Heard.'"

88. Ingram, Terrill, and Paoline, "Police Culture and Officer Behavior"; Eugene A. Paoline, William Terrill, and Logan J. Somers, "Police Officer Use of Force Mindset and Street-Level Behavior," *Police Quarterly* 24, no. 4 (December 2021): 547–77, https://doi.org/10.1177/1098611211025523.

89. Rianna P. Starheim, "Women in Policing: Breaking Barriers and Blazing a Path" (Washington, DC: National Institute of Justice, July 2019).

90. Joan Acker, "Hierarchies, Jobs, Bodies: A Theory of Gendered Organizations," *Gender & Society* 4, no. 2 (June 1990): 139–58, https://doi.org/10.1177/089124390004002002.

91. Susan Ehrlich Martin, "Police Force or Police Service? Gender and Emotional Labor," *Annals of the American Academy of Political and Social Science* 561, no. 1 (January 1999): 111–26 (115), https://doi.org/10.1177/000271629956100108.

92. Jennifer C. Hunt, "The Logic of Sexism Among Police," *Women & Criminal Justice* 1, no. 2 (April 1990): 3–30 (8), https://doi.org/10.1300/J012v01n02_02.

93. Jennifer Hunt, "Police Accounts of Normal Force," *Urban Life* 13, no. 4 (January 1985): 315–41, https://doi.org/10.1177/0098303985013004001.

94. Paoline and Gau, "Police Occupational Culture"; Paoline, "Taking Stock"; Ismail Cenk Demirkol and Mahesh K. Nalla, "Police Culture: An Empirical Appraisal of the Phenomenon," *Criminology & Criminal Justice* 20, no. 3 (July 2020): 319–38, https://doi.org/10.1177/1748895818823832.

95. Loftus, "Police Occupational Culture"; Westley, *Violence and the Police*; Banton, *The Policeman in the Community*; Van Maanen, "Observations on the Making of a Policeman"; Skolnick, *Justice Without Trial*; Moskos, *Cop in the Hood*; Simon, "Training for War"; P. A. J. Waddington, "Police (Canteen) Sub-Culture. An Appreciation," *British Journal of Criminology* 39, no. 2 (March 1999): 287–309, https://doi.org/10.1093/bjc/39.2.287.

96. William Terrill and Logan J. Somers, "Viewing Firearm Danger Through the Lens of Police Officers," *Homicide Studies* 27, no. 1 (February 2023): 55–76, https://doi.org/10.1177/10887679221108329.

97. Andrea M. Gardner and Kevin M. Scott, "Census of State and Local Law Enforcement Agencies, 2018—Statistical Tables" (Washington, DC: U.S. Department of Justice, Bureau of Justice Statistics, October 2022), https://bjs.ojp.gov/sites/g/files/xyckuh236/files/media/document/csllea18st.pdf.

1. SURVIVAL SCHOOL

1. These words and eight other "Peelian principles" are often attributed to Sir Robert Peel, the English statesman who spearheaded the formation of the London Metropolitan Police in 1829. It should be noted, however, that scholars cast serious doubt on Peel's having ever said or written these words. See Susan A. Lentz and Robert H. Chaires, "The Invention of Peel's Principles: A Study of Policing 'Textbook' History," *Journal of Criminal Justice* 35, no. 1 (January 2007): 69–79, https://doi.org/10.1016/j.jcrimjus.2006.11.016.

2. Nathan James, "Community Oriented Policing Services (COPS) Program," *In Focus* (Washington, DC: Congressional Research Service, updated February 17, 2023), https://fas.org/sgp/crs/misc/IF10922.pdf.

3. David Smith, "Entering 2011 in a 'Conspiracy of Safety,'" *Police1*, January 24, 2011, https://www.policeone.com/Officer-Safety/articles/3227758-Entering-2011-in-a-conspiracy-of-safety/.

4. Samantha J. Simon, "Training for War: Academy Socialization and Warrior Policing," *SocArXiv Papers*, June 30, 2021, https://doi.org/10.31235/osf.io/me4cv.

5. Robin S. Engel, Hannah D. McManus, and Tamara D. Herold, "Does De-Escalation Training Work?," *Criminology & Public Policy* 19, no. 3 (2020): 721–59, https://doi.org/10.1111/1745-9133.12467; Robin S. Engel et al., "Assessing the Impact of De-Escalation Training on Police Behavior: Reducing Police Use of Force in the Louisville, KY Metro Police Department," *Criminology & Public Policy* 21, no. 2 (2022): 199–233, https://doi.org/10.1111/1745-9133.12574; Li Sian Goh, "Did De-Escalation Successfully Reduce Serious Use of Force in Camden County, New Jersey? A Synthetic Control Analysis of Force Outcomes," *Criminology & Public Policy* 20, no. 2 (2021): 207–41, https://doi.org/10.1111/1745-9133.12536.

6. Brian A. Reaves, "State and Local Law Enforcement Training Academies, 2013" (Washington, DC: Bureau of Justice Statistics, 2016), 4–5, https://www.bjs.gov/content/pub/pdf/slleta13.pdf.

7. Other POST minimum standards are drawn from state records of law enforcement training standards. Data on academy training hours were provided by EPD, WPD, and SPD personnel. These hour totals are based on the hour breakdown provided by the department at one moment in time. Because state standards and departmental curricula change in response to legal and policy shifts, the state and departmental training hours presented here almost certainly differ from year to year.

8. For a more thorough discussion of variation in departmental body-worn camera policies, see Michael D. White and Aili Malm, *Cops, Cameras, and Crisis: The Potential and the Perils of Police Body-Worn Cameras* (New York: New York University Press, 2020).

9. Robin S. Engel, Hannah D. McManus, and Tamara D. Herold, "The Deafening Demand for De-Escalation Training: A Systematic Review and Call for Evidence in Police Use of Force Reform" (Cincinnati, OH: IACP/UC Center for Police Research Policy, 2019), https://www.theiacp.org/sites/default/files/IACP_UC_De-escalation%20Systematic%20Review.pdf; IACP, "Improving Police Response to Persons Affected by Mental Illness," Report from the March 2016 IACP Symposium (Alexandria, VA, 2016), https://www.theiacp.org/sites/default/files/2018-08/ImprovingPoliceResponsetoPersonswithMentalIllnessSymposiumReport.pdf.

10. John Van Maanen, "Observations on the Making of Policemen," *Human Organization* 32, no. 4 (December 1973): 407–18, https://doi.org/10.17730/humo .32.4.13h7x811 87mh8km8; P. A. J. Waddington, "Police (Canteen) Sub-Culture. An Appreciation," *British Journal of Criminology* 39, no. 2 (March 1999): 287– 309, https://doi.org/10.1093/bjc/39.2.287.

11. Police1, "Our Mission," 2022, https://www.police1.com/info/about/; Police1, "Police1 Member Registration," 2022, https://www.police1.com/registration/.

12. Law Officer, "The Kyle Dinkheller Murder Shows Us Why There Is More to the Tulsa Incident," *Law Officer*, September 20, 2016, https://www.lawofficer .com/the-kyle-dinkheller-murder-shows-us-why-there-is-more-to-the-tulsa -incident/

13. Supreme Court of Georgia, *Brannan v. The State*, No. S01P1789, March 25, 2002, https://caselaw.findlaw.com/ga-supreme-court/1197164.html.

14. Thomas Lake, "The Trigger and the Choice: Part 1, The Endless Death of Kyle Dinkheller," *CNN Politics*, August 2017, https://cnn.com/interactive /2017/politics/state/kyle-dinkheller-police-video/; Pate McMichael, "The Last Casualty: Part 1, 1998–2000," *Bitter Southerner*, June 14, 2016, https://bitter southerner.com/the-last-casualty-chapter-one.

15. Tom Laemlein, "The M1 Carbine in Vietnam," *American Rifleman*, June 13, 2018, https://www.americanrifleman.org/articles/2018/6/13/the-m1-carbine-in -vietnam/.

16. Lake, "The Trigger and the Choice"; Brian S. Kammer and L. Joseph Love-land, Petition for Writ of Certiorari in *Andrew Howard Brennan v. Carl Humphrey, Warden, Georgia Diagnostic & Classification State Prison* (Supreme Court of the United States, April 7, 2014).

17. Lake, "The Trigger and the Choice."

18. Dan Lamothe, "Vietnam Veteran Andrew Brannan Executed for Murder After PTSD Defense Fails," *Washington Post*, January 13, 2015, https://www .washingtonpost.com/news/checkpoint/wp/2015/01/13/vietnam-veteran -andrew-brannan-executed-for-murder-after-ptsd-defense-fails/.

19. Dinkheller's coworkers reported that Dinkheller was informally disciplined. Tim Dees, "'Dinkheller' Documentary Tells the Real Story," *Police1*, December 26, 2018, https://www.police1.com/officer-safety/articles/dinkheller-documentary -tells-the-real-story-V6FoGoQg47ySGVbp/; Lake, "The Trigger and the Choice."

20. Lake, "The Trigger and the Choice."

21. Jim McNeff, "'I'd Rather Be Judged by Twelve Than Carried by Six,' but Going to Prison Sucks," *Law Officer*, November 23, 2019, https://www.lawofficer.com /id-rather-be-judged-by-12-than-carried-by-6-but-going-to-prison-sucks/.

22. Kevin Michaelowski, "Judged by Twelve or Carried by Six? Learn to Avoid Both," USCCA, September 8, 2021, https://www.usconcealedcarry.com/blog/; Lupe Laguna, "To Be Judged by Twelve or Carried by Six? Quasi-Involuntariness and the Criminal Proescution of Service Members for the Use of Force in Combat—A Grunt's Perspective," *Journal of Criminal Law and Criminology* 105, no. 2 (2015): 431–61.

23. In his ethnography of crack markets in East Harlem, Bourgois recounts being stopped and questioned by police who assumed that an adult white male in the largely Black area of New York City must be a drug user. Philippe Bourgois, *In Search of Respect: Selling Crack in El Barrio* (Cambridge: Cambridge University Press, 1996).

24. Louise Marie Jupe and Vincent Denault, "Science or Pseudoscience? A Distinction That Matters for Police Officers, Lawyers and Judges," *Psychiatry, Psychology, and Law* 26, no. 5 (August 2019): 753–65, https://doi.org/10.1080/13218719.2019.1618755.

25. Calibre Press, "Ten Non-Verbal Signs All Officers Should Be Able to Recognize and Interpret," *Police1*, August 12, 2019, https://www.police1.com/officer-safety/articles/10-non-verbal-signs-all-officers-should-be-able-to-recognize-and-interpret-Xjobx7nVnoPRlDne/; Dave Young, "Pre-Attack Indicators," *Police Magazine*, February 8, 2018, https://www.policemag.com/342414/pre-attack-indicators.

26. Kimberly Barsamian Kahn, Jean M. McMahon, and Greg Stewart, "Misinterpreting Danger? Stereotype Threat, Pre-Attack Indicators, and Police-Citizen Interactions," *Journal of Police and Criminal Psychology* 33, no. 1 (March 2018): 45–54, https://doi.org/10.1007/s11896-017-9233-1.

27. Justin T. Pickett, Amanda Graham, and Francis T. Cullen, "The American Racial Divide in Fear of the Police," *Criminology* 60, no. 2 (2022): 291–320, https://doi.org/10.1111/1745-9125.12298; Cecilia Menjívar and Cynthia Bejarano, "Latino Immigrants' Perceptions of Crime and Police Authorities in the United States: A Case Study from the Phoenix Metropolitan Area," *Ethnic and Racial Studies* 27, no. 1 (2004): 120–48.

28. Police Posters, "Police Workout Motivation Poster (PWV1)," Police Posters, 2022, https://policeofficerposters.com/home/police-officer-workout-motivation-poster/.

29. Steve Herbert, "'Hard Charger' or 'Station Queen'? Policing and the Masculinist State," *Gender, Place & Culture* 8, no. 1 (March 2001): 55–71, https://doi.org/10.1080/09663690120026325.

30. Hitler's actual words were "He alone who owns the youth gains the future." Candan Iscan, "Hitler Youth: The Indoctrination of a Population," *Wiener*

Holocaust Library Blog, October 5, 2016, https://www.wienerlibrary.co.uk /Blog?item=200&returnoffset=40.

31. United States Holocaust Memorial Museum. (2020). The Role of the German Police. Holocaust Encyclopedia. https://encyclopedia.ushmm.org/content/en /article/the-role-of-the-police.

32. Isabel Wilkerson, *Caste: The Origins of Our Discontents* (New York: Random House, 2020), 72–82.

33. Seth W. Stoughton, "Principled Policing: Warrior Cops and Guardian Officers," *Wake Forest Law Review* 51 (2016): 611–76 (612).

34. Prior to his murder at the hands of a military veteran suffering from PTSD, Kyle made several unverifiable or false claims related to his military service and events following his discharge from the Navy. For example, he claimed to have received more medals than reported in Pentagon records and to have killed two men who attempted to steal his pickup truck outside a Texas gas station. According to Kyle, responding police officers let him go after speaking to the Pentagon. He also claimed to have been sent to New Orleans by the U.S. government after Hurricane Katrina. While there, he claimed to have killed thirty looters while perched atop the Superdome. Former governor of Minnesota, Jesse Ventura, was awarded $1.8 million after a judge found that Kyle's claims of having punched Ventura unconscious during a bar fight constituted defamation. J. Weston Phippen, "Correcting the Legend of 'American Sniper' Chris Kyle," *Atlantic*, July 11, 2016, https://www.theatlantic .com/news/archive/2016/07/chris-kyle-medals/490751/; Terrence McCoy, "The 'Unverifiable' Legacy of Chris Kyle, the Deadliest Sniper in American History," *Washington Post*, June 30, 2014, https://www.washingtonpost.com /news/morning-mix/wp/2014/07/30/the-complicated-but-unveriable-legacy -of-chris-kyle-the-deadliest-sniper-in-american-history/.

35. Chris Kyle, Scott McEwen, and Jim DeFelice, *American Sniper: The Autobiography of the Most Lethal Sniper in U.S. Military History*, Reprint edition (New York: HarperCollins, 2013).

36. Mike Avila, "It's Time for Marvel to Retire the Punisher's Skull Logo," *Syfy Wire*, January 8, 2021, https://www.syfy.com/syfy-wire/punisher-skull-logo -marvel-capitol-riots.

37. Brian Cronin, "A History of the Punisher Logo Being Used by Police, Military and Politicians," CBR, July 17, 2019, https://www.cbr.com/punisher -history-logo-used-police-military-politicians/.

38. On January 6, 2020, violent right wing extremists, including the Proud Boys and Oathkeepers, displayed Punisher skulls as they laid siege to the

U.S. capitol in attempts to overturn the 2020 presidential election. Kyle Sal-
lee, "Decoding Hate: Understanding the Far-Right Symbology of January
6," American University, July 1, 2021. https://www.american.edu/sis/centers
/security-technology/decoding-hate-understanding-far-right-symbology.cfm.

39. Whereas #thinblueline has several million users across social media platforms,
other hashtags have only several thousand. I omit other verbatim hashtags to
minimize the likelihood of participants and/or field sites being identified via
online searches.

40. Jocko Podcast, *A Good Man Is Dangerous—Jocko Willink and Jordan Peterson*,
2019, https://www.youtube.com/watch?v=xE0VM61OoXA.

41. Steve Herbert, "'Hard Charger' or 'Station Queen'? Policing and the Masculinist State," *Gender, Place & Culture* 8, no. 1 (March 2001): 55–71, https://doi
.org/10.1080/09663690120026325; Jennifer Carlson, "Police Warriors and Police
Guardians: Race, Masculinity, and the Construction of Gun Violence," *Social
Problems* 67, no. 3 (August 2020): 399–417, https://doi.org/10.1093/socpro/spz020.

42. In 2020, the population of Swift County was estimated at less than 10,000.
According to the FBI, between 1995, when Mattison joined the Swift County
Sheriff's Department (SCSD), and his retirement in 2010, there were never
more than six violent crimes reported in a single year across the entire county.
There has not been a homicide reported in Swift County since 1993. Caro-
lyn Lange, "Swift County Sheriff Plans to Retire Before End of Term," *West
Central Tribune*, April 7, 2010, https://www.wctrib.com/news/swift-county
-sheriff-plans-to-retire-before-end-of-term.

43. Stephen Lyng, "Edgework: A Social Psychological Analysis of Voluntary
Risk Taking," *American Journal of Sociology* 95, no. 4 (1990): 851–86 (860).

44. Killology Research Group, "Presentations," 2016, https://www.killology.com
/trained-to-kill.

45. Dave Grossman, "Book Excerpt: On Sheep, Wolves, and Sheepdogs," Police1,
July 3, 2008, https://www.policeone.com/police-products/training-products
/articles/book-excerpt-on-sheep-wolves-and-sheepdogs-UmiU5ujhwNg3douX/.

46. Dave Grossman and Loren W. Christensen, *On Combat: The Psychology and
Physiology of Deadly Conflict in War and Peace*, 3rd ed. (Millstadt, IL: Human
Factor Research Group, 2012), 177.

47. The most recently revised version of this lesson plan I was able to access
was published in June 2014. No SPD or state POST staff member I contacted was able to provide a more recent version of the lesson plan. Office
recalled an email he had received around 2015 or 2016 from the state POST
that instructed the training staff at academies throughout the state to ignore
lesson plan content that mentioned "predator." He was not able to recollect

exactly which points were to be ignored by academy staff or to provide the email sent by the state POST. When contacted, POST staff informed me that the defensive tactics lesson plans were in "re-write" as of February 2020.

48. Early scholarship refers to this drive for dominance in police-public interactions as a need to "maintain the edge." John Van Maanen, "Working the Street: A Developmental View of Police Behavior," in *The Potential for Reform of Criminal Justice*, ed. Herbert Jacob (Beverly Hills, CA: Sage, 1974), 83–130.

49. Doug Wylie, "How Strong Command Presence Can Quickly Resolve Dynamic Incidents," *Police1*, March 10, 2017, https://www.policeone.com/Officer-Safety/articles/299987006-How-strong-command-presence-can-quickly-resolve-dynamic-incidents/.

50. Jonathan Rubinstein, *City Police* (New York: Farrar, Straus and Giroux, 1973), 321.

51. David Klinger, "Police Responses to Officer-Involved Shootings" (Washington, DC: U.S. Department of Justice, 2001), https://www.ojp.gov/ncjrs/virtual-library/abstracts/police-responses-officer-involved-shootings;AlexisArtwohl, "Perceptual and Memory Distortion During Officer-Involved Shootings Research Forum," *FBI Law Enforcement Bulletin* 71, no. 10 (2002): 18–24, https://heinonline.org/HOL/P?h=hein.journals/fbileb71&i=334; Audrey L. Honig and Jocelyn E. Roland, "Shots Fired; Officer Involved," *Police Chief*, 1998, http://www.aele.org/law/2008FPAUG/shots-fired.pdf.

52. Mark Bonchek and Chris Fussell, "Decision Making, Top Gun Style," *Harvard Business Review*, September 12, 2013, https://hbr.org/2013/09/decision-making-top-gun-style.

53. Jeffrey Vagle, "Tightening the OODA Loop: Police Militarization, Race, and Algorithmic Surveillance," *Michigan Journal of Race and Law* 101 (2016): 102–37, https://doi.org/10.31228/osf.io/9z65d.

54. Reaves, "State and Local Law Enforcement Training Academies, 2013."

55. Description of recruit training is based on recorded video of this training produced by academy instructors or in cooperation with departmental academies, as well as the recollections of officers with whom I spoke. For example, videos of firearms training, driving training, defensive tactics, TASER training, etc. are made by academy staff as memento "highlight" videos to show at academy graduation ceremonies.

56. Jason Smith and Ian Greaves, "The Use of Chemical Incapacitant Sprays: A Review," *Journal of Trauma and Acute Care Surgery* 52, no. 3 (March 2002): 595–600; M. F. Yeung and William Y. M. Tang, "Clinicopathological Effects of Pepper (Oleoresin Capsicum) Spray," *Hong Kong Medical Journal* 21, no. 6 (December 2015): 542–52, https://doi.org/10.12809/hkmj154691.

57. Description of this exercise is based on a recording posted to Cisneros's social media.

58. Cubic Technologies, "PRISim Suite," Cubic Corporation, 2020, https://www .cubic.com/solutions/training/ranges/prisim-suite.

59. Rich Morin and Andrew Mercer, "Police Views, Public Views," Pew Research Center, February 8, 2017, http://www.pewsocialtrends.org/2017/01/11/police -views-public-views/; Michael Sierra-Arévalo and Justin Nix, "Gun Victimization in the Line of Duty: Fatal and Nonfatal Firearm Assaults on Police Officers in the United States, 2014–2019," *Criminology & Public Policy* 19, no. 3 (August 2020): 1041–66, https://doi.org/10.1111/1745-9133.12507.

60. The objective reasonableness approach established in *Graham v. Connor* is decidedly deferential to police officers' perception. *Graham* justifies this approach on the grounds that the situations officers face on patrol are "tense, uncertain, and rapidly evolving." While it is true that an officer's perception is not above questioning, Stoughton, Noble, and Alpert note that "There has been an unfortunate tendency to read *Graham* as forestalling post hoc review, especially within policing itself." See Seth W. Stoughton, Jeffrey J. Noble, and Geoffrey P. Alpert, *Evaluating Police Uses of Force* (New York: New York University Press, 2020), 22.

61. Roy Bedard, "Shooting Center Mass: Shooting to Kill or to Stop?," *Police1*, April 8, 2011, https://www.policeone.com/use-of-force/articles/shooting-center -mass-shooting-to-kill-or-to-stop-PQF7FCeGiwheykSX/.

62. The description of the 2016 EPD graduation ceremony is based on local news coverage and EPD-produced video, which was reviewed by the author. Similar videos, also reviewed by the author, are shown at WPD graduation ceremonies and used by the SPD as part of their recruitment program.

63. Michael Cummings and Eric Cummings, "The Surprising History of American Sniper's 'Wolves, Sheep, and Sheepdogs' Speech," *Slate*, January 21, 2015, https:// slate.com/culture/2015/01/american-snipers-wolves-sheep-and-sheepdogs -speech-has-a-surprising-history-with-conservatives-and-the-right-wing.html.

64. Nicole Loraux, "The Spartans' 'Beautiful Death,'" in *The Experiences of Tiresias*, ed. Nicoel Loraux and Paula Wissing (Princeton, NJ: Princeton University Press, 1997), 63–74, https://doi.org/10.1515/9781400864065.63.

2. GHOSTS OF THE FALLEN

1. Images of the Wake Forest Police Department memorial were provided by an employee of the WFPD. Town of Wake Forest, "Police Memorial," November 13, 2018, https://www.wakeforestnc.gov/police/about-us/police-memorial.

2. GHOSTS OF THE FALLEN 293

2. Chicago Park District, "Gold Star Family Memorial," 2021, https://www
   .chicagoparkdistrict.com/parks-facilities/gold-star-family-memorial.
3. Edgar H. Schein, *Organizational Culture and Leadership*, 4th ed. (San Fran-
   cisco: Jossey-Bass, 2010).
4. Steven M. Click, "The Brotherhood," *Police Magazine*, May 1, 2002, https://
   www.policemag.com/338886/the-brotherhood.
5. Brian A. Kinnaird, "Life After Law Enforcement," *Psychology Today*, July 15, 2015,
   https://www.psychologytoday.com/blog/the-hero-in-you/201507/life-after
   -law-enforcement.
6. U.S. Senate and U.S. House of Representatives, "Public Law 87–726," October 1,
   1962, https://www.govinfo.gov/content/pkg/STATUTE-76/pdf/STATUTE
   -76-Pg676.pdf.
7. National Law Enforcement Officers Memorial Fund, "Police Weekend 2021,"
   2021, https://nleomf.org/programs-events/national-police-week; National
   Police Week, "National Police Week 2021," 2021, https://www.policeweek.org
   /index.html.
8. Franklin E Zimring, *The Great American Crime Decline* (Oxford: Oxford University Press, 2006).
9. George H. W. Bush, "Remarks at the Dedication of the National Law
   Enforcement Officers Memorial," The American Presidency Project, October
   15, 1991, https://www.presidency.ucsb.edu/documents/remarks-the-dedication
   -the-national-law-enforcement-officers-memorial.
10. H. A. Shapiro, "The Iconography of Mourning in Athenian Art," *Ameri-
    can Journal of Archaeology* 95, no. 4 (1991): 629–56, https://doi.org/10.2307
    /505896.
11. Quotes are drawn from statements made at the time of Patterson's murder.
12. Concerns of Police Survivors, "Mission Statement: Rebuilding Shattered
    Lives of Survivors and Co-Workers Affected by Line-of-Duty Deaths,"
    2023, https://www.concernsofpolicesurvivors.org/aboutcops; Fund the First,
    "Browse Campaigns," 2023, https://fundthefirst.com/campaign/browse?grou
    p=1&state=&category=&sort=total-raised.
13. Maurice Chammah and Cary Aspinwall, "The Short, Fraught History of
    the 'Thin Blue Line' American Flag," *Politico*, June 9, 2020, https://www
    .politico.com/news/magazine/2020/06/09/the-short-fraught-history-of-the
    -thin-blue-line-american-flag-309767.
14. Timothy C. Brown, Julie M. Baldwin, Rick Dierenfeldt, and Steven McCain,
    "Playing the Game: A Qualitative Exploration of the Female Experience in
    a Hypermasculine Policing Environment," *Police Quarterly* 23, no. 2 (June

2020): 143–73, https://doi.org/10.1177/1098611119883423; Rianna P. Starheim, "Women in Policing: Breaking Barriers and Blazing a Path" (Washington, DC: National Institute of Justice, July 2019); FBI: UCR, "Crime in the United States 2019, Table 74: Full-Time Law Enforcement Employees, by Population Group," 2020, https://ucr.fbi.gov/crime-in-the-u.s/2019/crime-in -the-u.s.-2019/tables/table-74/table-74.xls.

15. Peter K. Manning, *Police Work: The Social Organization of Policing* (Cambridge, MA: MIT Press, 1977), 4.

16. Abigail Tracy, "Fatal Shooting of Three Black Men in Three Days Reignites Outrage Over Police Brutality," *Vanity Fair*, July 7, 2016, https://www .vanityfair.com/news/2016/07/fatal-police-shootings; Christopher Ingraham, "Officer Who Shot Philando Castile Said Smell of Marijuana Made Him Fear for His Life," *Washington Post*, June 21, 2017, https://www.washingtonpost .com/news/wonk/wp/2017/06/21/officer-who-shot-philando-castile-said -smell-of-marijuana-made-him-fear-for-his-life/; German Lopez, "Alton Sterling Police Shooting: No Charges Filed Against Baton Rouge Officers," *Vox*, July 6, 2016, https://www.vox.com/2016/7/6/12105380/alton-sterling-police-shooting -baton-rouge-louisiana.

17. William Arkin, Tracy Connor, and Jim Miklaszewski, "Dallas Shooter Micah Johnson Was Army Veteran and 'Loner,'" *NBC News*, July 9, 2016, https:// www.nbcnews.com/storyline/dallas-police-ambush/dallas-shooter-micah -xavier-johnson-was-army-veteran-n606101; WFAA Staff, "Timeline: Here's How the July 7 Police Ambush in Dallas Unfolded," WFAA ABC 8, July 7, 2021, https://www.wfaa.com/article/news/local/7-7/timeline-how-july-7-police -ambush-dallas-unfolded/287-63312e94-fa2a-4961-be3c-4ed1d19b753e; Matt Zapotosky, Adam Goldman, and Scott Higham, "Police in Dallas: 'He Wanted to Kill White People, Especially White Officers,'" *Washington Post*, July 8, 2016, https://www.washingtonpost.com/world/national-security/police-in-dallas -he-wanted-to-kill-white-people-especially-white-officers/2016/07/08/fe66fe52 -4553-11e6-88d0-6adee48be8bc_story.html; William Branigin and Adam Goldman, "Dallas Police Chief: Shooter Seemed Delusional, Scrawled Cryptic Messages in Blood," *Washington Post*, July 10, 2016, https://www.washingtonpost .com/politics/dallas-police-chief-shooter-seemed-delusional-scrawled-cryptic -messages-in-blood/2016/07/10/bd1cod96-46a9-11e6-bdb9-701687974517_story .html; Violence Policy Center, "Understanding the Saiga AK-74 Assault Rifle Used in the Dallas Police Shooting" (Washington, DC: Violence Policy Center, July 2016), https://vpc.org/studies/Saigabackgrounder.pdf.

18. Avi Selk, Hannah Wise, and Conor Shrine, "Eight Hours of Terror: How a Peaceful Protest Turned Into the Dallas Police's Deadliest Day," July 8, 2016, http://interactives.dallasnews.com/2016/dallas-police-ambush-timeline/.

19. Brian New, "Timeline of July 7 Dallas Police Ambush," CBS 11 DFW, July 7, 2017, https://dfw.cbslocal.com/2017/07/07/timeline-july-7-dallas-police-ambush/.

20. Ernest Scheyder and Marice Richter, "Charging Police, Dallas Gunman Shows Tactical Skill in Ambush," *Reuters*, July 8, 2016, https://www.reuters.com/article/us-usa-police-reconstruction-idUSKCN0ZO2KY; "Dallas Gunman Micah Johnson Honed Tactics at Local Combat School," *CBS News*, July 10, 2016, https://www.cbsnews.com/news/dallas-gunman-micah-johnson-honed-tactics-local-combat-school/.

21. Fiona Ortiz, "Newlywed, Iraq Veteran Among the Five Dallas Police Officers Killed," *Reuters*, July 8, 2016, https://www.reuters.com/article/uk-usa-police-victims-idUKKCN0ZO263; WFAA, "The Heroes' Perspective: Here's How the July 7 Police Ambush in Dallas Unfolded," 2021, https://www.youtube.com/watch?v=iLZexc_Srn4.

22. WFAA, "The Heroes' Perspective: Officers Pursue Dallas Ambush Gunman on July 7th, 2016," 2021, https://youtu.be/6C4n9cd5vyQ; The Dallas Morning News, *Dallas Police Shooting, July 7: Here's What Happened*, 2016, https://www.youtube.com/watch?v=6uCP3EfXvhc.

23. WFAA, "The Heroes' Perspective: Officers Pursue Dallas Ambush Gunman on July 7th, 2016."

24. WFAA; Sam Thielman, "Use of Police Robot to Kill Dallas Shooting Suspect Believed to Be First in US History," *Guardian*, July 8, 2016, https://www.theguardian.com/technology/2016/jul/08/police-bomb-robot-explosive-killed-suspect-dallas.

25. Natasha Bertrand, "Military Experts: Dallas Police Attacker Appeared 'Tactically Professional' and 'Focused,'" *Business Insider*, July 8, 2016, https://www.businessinsider.com/military-experts-on-dallas-police-shootings-2016-7.

26. Gregg Zoroya, "U.S. Police on High Alert in Wake of Dallas Shootings," *USA Today*, July 8, 2016, https://www.usatoday.com/story/news/nation/2016/07/08/police-safeguards-dallas-shootings/86847240/.

27. Geoff Pursinger, "After Dallas Shootings, Local Cops Feel the Love," *Beaverton Valley Times*, July 13, 2016, https://pamplinmedia.com/bvt/15-news/314843-193724-after-dallas-shootings-local-cops-feel-the-love-; Jennifer Johnson, "Park Ridge Police to Wear Bands of Mourning 'in Honor of the Lives Lost in Dallas,'" *Capital Gazette*, July 8, 2016, https://www.capitalgazette.com/ct-prh

-police-mourning-tl-0707-20160708-story.html; CBS News, "Dallas Gunman Micah Johnson Honed Tactics at Local Combat School."

28. Claire Z. Cardona and Hannah Wise, "Message of Hope Prevails at Vigil: 'We Are Dallas Strong. Go in Peace,'" *Dallas Morning News*, July 11, 2016, https://www.dallasnews.com/news/2016/07/11/message-of-hope-prevails-at -vigil-we-are-dallas-strong-go-in-peace/; Madeline Conway and John Reynolds, "The Brief: With Vigil and Memorial, Dallas Mourns," *Texas Tribune*, July 12, 2016, https://www.texastribune.org/2016/07/12/brief-july-12-2016/.

29. Jamie Stockwell, "Fallen, but Not Forgotten," *Washington Post*, June 30, 2005, https://www.washingtonpost.com/archive/local/2005/06/30/fallen-but-not -forgotten/28dd75ef-7f91-46d5-963f-8d535bcc3d0a/; Jamie Stockwell, "Oakton Man's Web Site Honors Police Who Died in Line of Duty," *Washington Post*, August 18, 2005, https://www.washingtonpost.com/archive/local/2005/08/18 /oakton-mans-web-site-honors-police-who-died-in-line-of-duty/4725237d -3fac-4169-99a9-8721bc4ed2dc/.

30. Michael D. White, Lisa M. Dario, and John A. Shjarback, "Assessing Dangerousness in Policing: An Analysis of Officer Deaths in the United States, 1970–2016," *Criminology & Public Policy* 18, no. 1 (February 2019): 11–35, https:// doi.org/10.1111/1745-9133.12408.

31. Officer Down Memorial Page, https://www.odmp.org/.

32. George W. Bush, "Selected Speeches of President George W. Bush, 2001–2008," White House Archive, 2008, https://georgewbush-whitehouse.archives.gov /infocus/bushrecord/documents/Selected_Speeches_George_W_Bush.pdf, 82, 117, 163, 176, 264.

33. NYPD, "9/11 Tribute," 2021, https://www1.nyc.gov/site/nypd/about/memorials /9-11-tribute.page.

34. Los Angeles Police Department, "Funeral Protocols," 2008, http://www.theiacp .org/Portals/0/pdfs/PreventingLESuicideCD/LAPD%20Funeral%20Protocol%20-%20Revised%207-10-08.pdf; Nicole Zedeck, "Huntsville Police Honor Guard Honors Sgt. Nick Risner with Rifle Salute," *WAAY News*, October 11, 2021, https://www.waaytv.com/content/news/HPDs-Honor-Guard-pays-respect -to-Sgt-Risner-with-a-rifle-salute-575491331.html; Honolulu Police Department, "Funeral Honors and Ceremonies for Police Personnel," 2021, https://www .honolulupd.org/policy/policy-funeral-honors-and-ceremonies-for-police -personnel/.

35. Assemblyman Perkins and Senator Raggio, "Assembly Concurrent Resolution No. 27," Nevada State Legislature, 2005, https://www.leg.state.nv.us/73rd /bills/ACR/ACR27_EN.pdf; Pittsburgh Murals and Public Art, "Law

Enforcement Officers Memorial of Allegheny County," April 10, 2016, http://
pghmurals.blogspot.com/2016/04/law-enforcement-officers-memorial-of
.html.

36. The image of the kneeling officer is a re-creation of a bronze statue produced
by Brodin Studio, Inc., a company founded by a Minneapolis police officer
and his brother in 1978. Today, the kneeling officer can be found in more
than two dozen police memorials across the country. Although unnoted in
the print, the poem is titled "The Monument" and was written by the late
LAPD detective sergeant George Hahn, Jr. "The Monument" is permanently
displayed as part of the California Peace Officers' Memorial. Brodin Studio,
"About," 2021, https://www.brodinstudios.com/about/; "George Henry Hahn,
1933–2007," *Bakersfield Californian*, September 12, 2007, https://www.legacy
.com/us/obituaries/bakersfield/name/george-hahn-obituary?id=24580572.

37. The 2016 award ceremony was the first in several years and covered a backlog
of awards from 2011 through 2015.

38. Michael Sierra-Arévalo, "Reward and 'Real' Police Work," in *The Ethics of
Policing: New Perspectives on Law Enforcement*, ed. Benjamin Jones and Eduardo Mendieta (New York: New York University Press, 2021), 66–92.

39. Officer Down Memorial Page; Blue H.E.L.P., "The Numbers," 2021, https://
bluehelp.org/the-numbers/.

40. Police Executive Research Forum, "An Occupational Risk: What Every
Police Agency Should Do to Prevent Suicide Among Its Officers," Critical Issues in Policing (Washington, DC: Police Executive Research Forum,
2019), 4.

41. IACP, EDC, and National Action Alliance for Suicide Prevention, "Preventing Suicide Among Law Enforcement Officers: An Issue Brief" (Alexandria, VA: National Consortium on Preventing Law Enforcement Suicide),
accessed December 2, 2021, https://www.theiacp.org/sites/default/files/2020
-02/_NOSI_Issue_Brief_FINAL.pdf, 10; John Violanti, "Police Suicide: The
Hidden Danger," in *Practical Considerations for Preventing Police Suicide: Stop
Officer Suicide*, ed. Olivia Johnson, Konstantinos Papazoglou, John Violanti,
and Joseph Pascarella (Cham, Switzerland: Springer, 2022), 55–69.

3. THE THREAT NETWORK

1. Michael Sierra-Arévalo, "Reward and 'Real' Police Work," in *The Ethics of
Policing: New Perspectives on Law Enforcement*, ed. Benjamin Jones and Eduardo Mendieta (New York: New York University Press, 2021), 66–92; Peter

Moskos, *Cop in the Hood: My Year Policing Baltimore's Eastern District* (Princeton, NJ: Princeton University Press, 2009), 137.

2. National Law Enforcement Officers Memorial Fund, "Preliminary 2014 Law Enforcement Officer Fatalities Report," 2015, https://time.com/wp-content/uploads/2014/12/preliminary-2014-officer-fatalities-report.pdf; Bill Chappell, "Number of Police Officers Killed by Gunfire Fell 14 Percent in 2015, Study Says," NPR, December 29, 2015, https://www.npr.org/sections/thetwo-way/2015/12/29/461402091/number-of-police-officers-killed-by-gunfire-fell-14-percent-in-2015-study-says.

3. Roger E. Kasperson, Ortwin Renn, Paul Slovic, Halina S. Brown, Jacque Emel, Robert Goble, Jeanne X. Kasperson, and Samuel Ratick, "The Social Amplification of Risk: A Conceptual Framework," *Risk Analysis* 8, no. 2 (June 1988): 177–87, https://doi.org/10.1111/j.1539-6924.1988.tb01168.x. The "download" model of culture is often attributed to Talcott Parsons and critiqued as overly deterministic. For a thorough discussion of Parsons and the utility of socialization as a concept in the study of culture, see Jeffrey Guhin, Jessica McCrory Calarco, and Cynthia Miller-Idriss, "Whatever Happened to Socialization?," August 29, 2020, https://doi.org/10.31235/osf.io/zp2wy.

4. Both of these monikers are pseudonyms for similarly named street groups in West River.

5. A similar list of gangs was displayed in a hallway inside the Elmont police department. This poster was produced by the state's department of corrections and detailed a dozen prison gangs, or "security threat groups," and the local street gangs with which they were affiliated. Like the poster in Sunshine, the gang information displayed in Elmont was quite dated, having been produced in 2008.

6. Julie Barrows and C. Ronald Huff, "Gangs and Public Policy: Constructing and Deconstructing Gang Databases," *Criminology & Public Policy* 8, no. 4 (2009): 675–703, https://doi.org/10.1111/j.1745-9133.2009.00585.x.

7. Patrick Sharkey, *Stuck in Place: Urban Neighborhoods and the End of Progress Toward Racial Equality* (Chicago: University of Chicago Press, 2013); Ruth D. Peterson and Lauren Joy Krivo, *Divergent Social Worlds: Neighborhood Crime and the Racial-Spatial Divide* (New York: Russell Sage Foundation, 2010); Robert J. Sampson, "Racial Stratification and the Durable Tangle of Neighborhood Inequality," *Annals of the American Academy of Political and Social Science* 621, no. 1 (January 2009): 260–80, https://doi.org/10.1177/0002716208324803; Robert J. Sampson, "Urban Black Violence: The Effect of Male Joblessness and Family Disruption," *American Journal of Sociology* 93 (1987): 348–83.

8. Heather Mac Donald, "The Danger of the 'Black Lives Matter' Movement," *Imprimis* 45, no. 4 (April 2016), https://imprimis.hillsdale.edu/the-danger-of-the-black-lives-matter-movement/.

9. Timothy Williams, "Police Leaders Join Call to Cut Prison Rosters," *New York Times*, October 21, 2015, https://www.nytimes.com/2015/10/21/us/police-leaders-join-call-to-cut-prison-rosters.html.

10. Joe Barrett, "Some Police Push Back on Bail Reform, Citing Wave of Killings," *Wall Street Journal*, July 16, 2021, https://www.wsj.com/articles/some-police-push-back-on-bail-reform-citing-wave-of-killings-11626441851; Holmes Lybrand and Tara Subramaniam, "Fact-Checking Claims Bail Reform Is Driving Increase in Violent Crime," CNN, July 7, 2021, https://www.cnn.com/2021/07/07/politics/bail-reform-violent-crime-fact-check/index.html.

11. Sierra-Arévalo, "Reward and 'Real' Police Work"; Moskos, *Cop in the Hood*, 137.

12. Franklin E. Zimring, *When Police Kill* (Cambridge, MA: Harvard University Press, 2017), 94–97.

13. Despite explicitly citing the pistol's ability to fire "armor-piercing" rounds, the report also includes a link to an online post titled "The 5.7x28mm 'Cop Killer' Cartridge Myth." Because the armor-piercing variants of the 5.7x28mm cartridge fired by the FN Five-seven are only purchasable by law enforcement and military personnel, the post deems the "cop killer" round no more than an "urban legend." Barr H. Soltis and Chuck Hawks, "5.7x28mm 'Cop Killer' Cartridge Myth," Chuckhawks.com, https://www.chuckhawks.com/5-7x28_cop_killer.htm.

14. John Williams, "Improvised Weapons and Other Officer Safety Concerns" (Los Angeles: Los Angeles County Sheriff's Office, 2009), https://info.publicintelligence.net/LA-DisguisedWeapons.pdf; Wendy Kierstead, "Law Enforcement Safety Handbook: Unusual Weapons, Concealment Methods for Contraband and Things That Make You Wonder Why You Ever Became a Cop," 5th ed. (Brunswick, ME: Brunswick Police Department, March 2006), https://ebin.pub/law-enforcement-safety-handbook-unusual-weapons-concealment-methods-for-contraband-amp-things-that-make-you-wonder-why-you-ever-became-a-cop-5thnbsped.html.

15. FBI, "Bulletin Highlights—Unusual Weapons," FBI: Law Enforcement Bulletins, 2016, https://leb.fbi.gov/bulletin-highlights/unusual-weapons; Officer.com, "Unusual and Disguised Weapons," Police Forums & Law Enforcement Forums@Officer.com, 2021, https://forum.officer.com/forum/officers-and-law

-enforcement-professionals-only/the-squad-room/officer-safety/138310
-unusual-and-disguised-weapons?view=stream.

16. David Smith, "This Is Not a Gun: The Objects Police Mistook for Weapons Before Shooting," *Guardian*, December 7, 2020, http://www.theguardian .com/artanddesign/2020/dec/07/this-is-not-a-gun-cara-levine-interview -objects-police-mistook-for-weapons; "Trigger Warning," *Harper's Magazine*, December 2016, https://harpers.org/archive/2016/12/trigger-warning/; Aaron Karp, "Estimating Global Civilian-Held Firearms Numbers," Briefing Paper (Geneva: Small Arms Survey, June 2018), 4, http://www.smallarmssurvey.org /fileadmin/docs/T-Briefing-Papers/SAS-BP-Civilian-Firearms-Numbers.pdf.

17. David Kempa, "Stephon Clark: Police Officers Who Shot Man Eight Times Will Not Be Charged," *Guardian*, March 3, 2019, sec. US news, https://www .theguardian.com/us-news/2019/mar/02/stephon-clark-police-officers-no -charges.

18. Alexandria Rodriguez, "Man Shot by Corpus Christi Police Will Get $2.9 Million from Settlement," *Caller-Times*, January 28, 2020, https://www.caller .com/story/news/local/2020/01/28/city-corpus-christi-comes-agreement -police-shooting-lawsuit/4598250002/; "Texas Police Officer Mistakes Lighter for Weapon, Shoots Man," AP News, March 27, 2019, https://apnews.com /article/e3a73743f74a49838efc7e80764316a7.

19. Colorado Public Radio, "Boulder Police Officer Resigns After Confronting Black Man Picking Up Trash," CPR News, May 17, 2019, https://www.cpr .org/2019/05/17/boulder-police-officer-resigns-after-confronting-black-man -picking-up-trash/.

20. Shay Castle, "Boulder Settles with Zayd Atkinson, Confronted by Armed Police Officers," Boulder Beat, March 13, 2020, https://boulderbeat.news/2020 /03/13/boulder-settles-with-zayd-atkinson/.

21. Jeff Asher and Ben Horwitz, "How Do the Police Actually Spend Their Time?," *New York Times*, June 19, 2020, https://www.nytimes.com/2020/06/19 /upshot/unrest-police-time-violent-crime.html; John A. Webster, "Police Task and Time Study," in *Policing: A View from the Street*, ed. Peter K. Manning and John Van Maanen (New York: Random House, 1978), 105–28.

22. Andrew E. Taslitz, "What Is Probable Cause, and Why Should We Care?: The Costs, Benefits, and Meaning of Individualized Suspicion," *Law and Contemporary Problems* 73, no. 3 (2010): 145–210.

23. FBI: UCR, "2019 Crime in the United States: Clearances," 2020, https://ucr.fbi .gov/crime-in-the-u.s/2019/crime-in-the-u.s.-2019/topic-pages/clearances. Limitations of UCR data make it likely that clearance rate calculations are

overestimates. Because the UCR records only arrests and crime incidents, its clearance rate calculations are a simple ratio of arrests/incidents. Given that a single incident can result in multiple arrests, some recorded arrests in the UCR likely correspond to common incidents. Were one able to address this issue, it would reduce the numerator in the arrests/incidents calculation, in turn shrinking the clearance rate.

24. My estimate of clearance rate is the number of robberies in 2018 that resulted in a charge divided by the total number of reported robberies. Crucially, a suspect can be charged with a crime without being arrested. The WPD calculates its clearance rate differently: instead of dividing the number of charged cases by the total number of robberies, it divides charged cases by the smaller number of robberies that are assigned to robbery unit investigators. This calculated clearance rate is higher: 25 percent.

25. To prevent agency identification, I have removed the specific radio codes used to denote criminal offenses. Such codes vary widely across state and individual agencies. I have also changed the license plate listed for vehicles, birth dates, addresses, and names.

26. Christina L. Patton and William J. Fremouw, "Examining 'Suicide by Cop': A Critical Review of the Literature," *Aggression and Violent Behavior* 27 (March–April 2016): 107–20, https://doi.org/10.1016/j.avb.2016.03.003.

27. Alma A. Hernandez, María B. Vélez, and Christopher J. Lyons, "The Racial Invariance Thesis and Neighborhood Crime: Beyond the Black–White Divide," *Race and Justice* 8, no. 3 (July 2018): 216–43, https://doi.org/10.1177/2153368716669986; Lauren J. Krivo, María B. Vélez, Christopher J. Lyons, Jason B. Phillips, and Elizabeth Sabbath, "Race, Crime, and the Changing Fortunes of Urban Neighborhoods, 1999–2013," *Du Bois Review: Social Science Research on Race* 15, no. 1 (2018): 47–68, https://doi.org/10.1017/S1742058X18000103.

28. Khalil Gibran Muhammad, *The Condemnation of Blackness: Race, Crime, and the Making of Modern Urban America* (Cambridge, MA: Harvard University Press, 2010).

29. U.S. Department of Homeland Security, "Fusion Centers," July 6, 2009, https://www.dhs.gov/fusion-centers.

30. Sarah Brayne, *Predict and Surveil: Data, Discretion, and the Future of Policing* (New York: Oxford University Press, 2020), 21–22.

31. U.S. Department of Homeland Security, "Fusion Centers and RISS Centers," May 9, 2014, https://www.dhs.gov/fusion-centers-and-riss-centers; Regional Information Sharing Systems (RISS), "RISSIntel Brochure," 2020,

302 3. THE THREAT NETWORK

https://www.riss.net/files/rissintel-brochure/; RISS, "About the RISS Program: A Proven Resource for Law Enforcement," 2022, https://www.riss.net/about-us/.

32. U.S. Department of Homeland Security, "DHS Announces New Information-Sharing Tool to Help Fusion Centers Combat Terrorism," September 14, 2009, https://www.dhs.gov/news/2009/09/14/new-information-sharing-tool-fusion-centers-announced.

33. RISS, "Officer Safety Website," January 2020, https://www.riss.net/files/officer-safety-brochure/; RISS.

34. RISS, "About the RISS Program."

35. It is possible that the compilation of weapons and other threats observed in Sunshine originally came via fusion center transmission. Unlike other danger signals, however, the report did not explicitly state which fusion center, if any, transmitted it to the SPD.

36. Jordan Trecki, Roy Gerona, and Michael Schwartz, "Synthetic Cannabinoid-Related Illnesses and Deaths," *New England Journal of Medicine* 373 (2015): 103–7, https://doi.org/10.1056/NEJMp1505328.

37. Alexis Crabtree and Jeffrey R. Masuda, "Naloxone Urban Legends and the Opioid Crisis: What Is the Role of Public Health?," *BMC Public Health* 19, no. 670 (May 2019), https://doi.org/10.1186/s12889-019-7033-5; Troy Farah, "The Latest Dangerous Drug Trend Doesn't Actually Exist," Outline, July 31, 2017, https://theoutline.com/post/1964/narcan-parties-heroin-overdoses.

38. Jennifer Murphy and Brenda Russell, "Police Officers' Views of Naloxone and Drug Treatment: Does Greater Overdose Response Lead to More Negativity?," *Journal of Drug Issues* 50, no. 4 (October 2020): 3, https://doi.org/10.1177/0022042620921363.

39. Beth Schwartzapfel, "A Primer on the Nationwide Prisoners' Strike," Marshall Project, September 28, 2016, https://www.themarshallproject.org/2016/09/27/a-primer-on-the-nationwide-prisoners-strike; Alice Speri, "The Largest Prison Strike in U.S. History Enters Its Second Week," Intercept, September 16, 2016, https://theintercept.com/2016/09/16/the-largest-prison-strike-in-u-s-history-enters-its-second-week/.

40. Stu Sjouwerman, "American Chamber of Commerce Scam Is Spear-Phishing Prep," KnowBe4, February 6, 2016, https://blog.knowbe4.com/american-chamber-of-commerce-scam-is-spear-phishing-prep; News Bulletin Contributor, "Chamber of Commerce Scam Targets Northwest Florida Businesses," Destin Log, February 9, 2016, https://www.thedestinlog.com/article/20160209

/NEWS/160209077; Elizabeth Garcia, "Chamber of Commerce Scam Targets Small Businesses," WHNT, February 8, 2016, https://whnt.com/taking-action/bbb-consumer-alerts/chamber-of-commerce-scam-targets-small-businesses/.

41. Kristen Lambertsen, "Shocking Video: Police Body Cam Records Officer Being Dragged by Suspect's Car in Savannah," WBTW News 13, May 14, 2015, https://www.wbtw.com/news/shocking-video-police-body-cam-records-officer-being-dragged-by-suspects-car-in-savannah/.

42. "Video: Ariz. Chief Breaks down Wal-Mart Brawl Video," Police1, April 13, 2015, https://www.police1.com/close-quarters-combat/videos/ariz-chief-breaks-down-wal-mart-brawl-video-9usYnQ3QKMh6V4Jp/.

43. Heather Mac Donald, *The War on Cops: How the New Attack on Law and Order Makes Everyone Less Safe* (New York: Encounter, 2016); Justin Nix, Scott E. Wolfe, and Bradley A. Campbell, "Command-Level Police Officers' Perceptions of the 'War on Cops' and De-Policing," *Justice Quarterly* 35, no. 1 (January 2018): 33–54, https://doi.org/10.1080/07418825.2017.1338743.

44. Ed Flynn, "Milwaukee Police Chief Ed Flynn: Officers Are Depressed by the Current Climate," *Time*, April 9, 2015, https://time.com/3814703/milwaukee-police-chief-ed-flynn-officers-are-depressed-by-the-current-climate/.

45. Chuck Canterbury, "Statement of FOP Chuck Canterbury on Recent Violence Targeting Law Enforcement," New Jersey Fraternal Order of Police, September 4, 2015, https://njfop.org/2015/09/statement-for-fop-chuck-canterbury-on-recent-violence-targeting-law-enforcement/.

46. Nolan Hicks, "Bratton Raises Specter of Return to 1970s," *New York Daily News*, December 22, 2014, https://www.nydailynews.com/new-york/nyc-crime/bratton-raises-specter-return-1970s-article-1.2054110; Officer Down Memorial Page, "New York City Police Department," 2021, https://www.odmp.org/agency/2758-new-york-city-police-department-new-york.

47. Per LIjas, "New York Mourns Slain Officers as Police Tighten Security," *Time*, December 22, 2014, https://time.com/3643543/new-york-police-nypd-wenjian-liu-rafael-ramos/.

48. "Nation's Police on Edge After New York Ambush," NBC News, December 22, 2014, https://www.nbcnews.com/news/us-news/nations-police-edge-after-new-york-ambush-n273381.

49. I could not independently verify these online or spray-painted threats.

50. Deshawn Hamilton is a pseudonym.

51. Flo Block, Florence Street, and Shiny are all pseudonyms.

4. GOING HOME AT NIGHT

1. Alfred Blumstein, "Youth Violence, Guns, and the Illicitz-Drug Industry," *The Journal of Criminal Law & Criminology* 86 (1995): 10–36; Jeffrey Fagan and Deanna L. Wilkinson, "Guns, Youth Violence, and Social Identity in Inner Cities," *Crime and Justice* 24 (1998): 105–88.

2. John DiIulio, "The Coming of the Super-Predators," *The Weekly Standard*, November 27, 1995, https://www.washingtonexaminer.com/weekly-standard /the-coming-of-the-super-predators.

3. *1996: Hillary Clinton on "Superpredators" (C-SPAN)*, 2016, https://www.youtube .com/watch?v=jouCrA7ePno.

4. Patrick Sharkey, *Uneasy Peace: The Great Crime Decline, the Renewal of City Life, and the Next War on Violence* (New York: Norton, 2018); Franklin E Zimring, *The Great American Crime Decline* (Oxford: Oxford University Press, 2006); John Gramlich, "What the Data Says (and Doesn't Say) about Crime in the United States," Pew Research Center, November 20, 2020, https:// www.pewresearch.org/fact-tank/2020/11/20/facts-about-crime-in-the-u-s/.

5. Zimring, *The Great American Crime Decline*; Sharkey, *Uneasy Peace*.

6. Michael D. White, Lisa M. Dario, and John A. Shjarback, "Assessing Dangerousness in Policing: An Analysis of Officer Deaths in the United States, 1970–2016," *Criminology & Public Policy* 18, no. 1 (February 2019): 11–35, https:// doi.org/10.1111/1745-9133.12408.

7. Michael German, "Hidden in Plain Sight: Racism, White Supremacy, and Far-Right Militancy in Law Enforcement," Brennan Center for Justice, August 27, 2020, https://www.brennancenter.org/our-work/research-reports /hidden-plain-sight-racism-white-supremacy-and-far-right-militancy -law; E. J. Dickson, "How a Right-Wing Troll Managed to Manipulate the Mainstream Media," *Rolling Stone*, September 3, 2019, https://www .rollingstone.com/culture/culture-features/andy-ngo-right-wing-troll -antifa-877914/; Kenneth Bolton and Joe Feagin, *Black in Blue: African-American Police Officers and Racism* (New York: Routledge, 2004); Will Carless and Michael Corey, "To Protect and Slur: Inside Hate Groups on Facebook, Police Officers Trade Racist Memes, Conspiracy Theories and Islamophobia," Reveal News, June 14, 2019, http://revealnews.org/article/inside-hate -groups-on-facebook-police-officers-trade-racist-memes-conspiracy-theories -and-islamophobia/; Raúl Pérez and Geoff Ward, "From Insult to Estrangement and Injury: The Violence of Racist Police Jokes," *American Behavioral Scientist* 63, no. 13 (November 2019): 1810–29, https://doi.org/10.1177/0002764219842617;

Adam Gabbatt, "'Good Day for a Chokehold': The Police Endorsing Racism and Violence on Facebook," *Guardian*, June 25, 2019, sec. US news, https://www.theguardian.com/us-news/2019/jun/24/police-facebook-posts-racism-violence-plain-view-project.

8. Robert Brame et al., "Demographic Patterns of Cumulative Arrest Prevalence by Ages 18 and 23," *Crime & Delinquency* 60, no. 3 (April 2014): 471–86, https://doi.org/10.1177/0011128713514801; Charles R. Epp, Steven Maynard-Moody, and Donald P. Haider-Markel, *Pulled Over: How Police Stops Define Race and Citizenship* (Chicago: University of Chicago Press, 2014); Frank Edwards, Hedwig Lee, and Michael Esposito, "Risk of Being Killed by Police Use of Force in the United States by Age, Race–Ethnicity, and Sex," *Proceedings of the National Academy of Sciences* 116, no. 34 (August 20, 2019): 16793–98, https://doi.org/10.1073/pnas.1821204116; Shytierra Gaston, "Producing Race Disparities: A Study of Drug Arrests Across Place and Race," *Criminology* 57, no. 3 (August 2019): 424–51, https://doi.org/10.1111/1745-9125.12207; Justin Nix, Bradley A. Campbell, Edward H. Byers, and Geoffrey P. Alpert, "A Bird's Eye View of Civilians Killed by Police in 2015," *Criminology & Public Policy* 16, no. 1 (February 2017): 309–40, https://doi.org/10.1111/1745-9133.12269; Joscha Legewie, "Racial Profiling and Use of Force in Police Stops: How Local Events Trigger Periods of Increased Discrimination," *American Journal of Sociology* 122, no. 2 (September 2016): 379–424, https://doi.org/10.1086/687518; Rory Kramer and Brianna Remster, "Stop, Frisk, and Assault? Racial Disparities in Police Use of Force During Investigatory Stops," *Law & Society Review* 52, no. 4 (December 2018): 960–93, https://doi.org/10.1111/lasr.12366; Andrew Gelman, Jeffrey Fagan, and Alex Kiss, "An Analysis of the New York City Police Department's 'Stop-and-Frisk' Policy in the Context of Claims of Racial Bias," *Journal of the American Statistical Association* 102, no. 479 (September 2007): 813–23, https://doi.org/10.1198/016214506000001040; Shytierra Gaston and Rod K. Brunson, "Reasonable Suspicion in the Eye of the Beholder: Routine Policing in Racially Different Disadvantaged Neighborhoods," *Urban Affairs Review* 56, no. 1 (January 2020): 188–227, https://doi.org/10.1177/1078087418774641; Victor M. Rios, Greg Prieto, and Jonathan M. Ibarra, "Mano Suave–Mano Dura: Legitimacy Policing and Latino Stop-and-Frisk," *American Sociological Review* 85, no. 1 (February 2020): 58–75, https://doi.org/10.1177/0003122419897348; Bocar A. Ba, Dean Knox, Jonathan Mummolo, and Roman Rivera, "The Role of Officer Race and Gender in Police-Civilian Interactions in Chicago," *Science* 371, no. 6530 (February 12, 2021): 696–702, https://doi.org/10.1126/science.abd8694.

9. John A. Wangler, JoAnne Brewster, and Lennis Echterling, "Hypervigilance and Cynicism in Police Officers," *Journal of Police and Criminal Psychology* 11, no. 1 (March 1996): 2–4, https://doi.org/10.1007/BF02803680; Kevin M. Gilmartin, "Hypervigilance: A Learned Perceptual Set and Its Consequences on Police Stress," in *Psychological Services for Law Enforcement*, ed. J. T. Reese and H. A. Goldstein (Washington, DC: U.S. Government Printing Office, 1986), 443–46, http://emotionalsurvival.com/hypervigilance.htm; John P. Crank, *Understanding Police Culture* (New York: Routledge, 2014), 158.

10. "Vapor lock" refers to the phenomenon of liquid fuel in an engine being vaporized, leading to a drop in fuel line pressure and subsequent loss of engine power.

11. Aaron Karp, "Estimating Global Civilian-Held Firearms Numbers," Briefing Paper (Geneva: Small Arms Survey, June 2018), http://www.smallarmssurvey .org/fileadmin/docs/T-Briefing-Papers/SAS-BP-Civilian-Firearms -Numbers.pdf; Champe Barton and Daniel Nass, "Exactly How High Are Gun Violence Rates in the U.S., Compared to Other Countries?," The Trace, October 5, 2021, https://www.thetrace.org/2021/10/why-more-shootings-in -america-gun-violence-data-research/.

12. Franklin E. Zimring, *When Police Kill* (Cambridge, MA: Harvard University Press, 2017), 94–97, 85–87.

13. Rich Morin and Andrew Mercer, "Police Officers Who Have Fired a Gun on Duty: A Closer Look," Pew Research Center, February 8, 2017, https://www .pewresearch.org/fact-tank/2017/02/08/a-closer-look-at-police-officers-who -have-fired-their-weapon-on-duty/.

14. This sentiment paraphrased the infamous words of Marine Corps General "Mad Dog" Mathis, a central figure in U.S. military operations in the Middle East. Mathis is credited with telling a group of Marines stationed in Iraq in 2003, "Be polite, be professional, but have a plan to kill everybody you meet." Derek Caney, "Friday Morning Briefing: 'Have a Plan to Kill Everyone You Meet,'" *Reuters*, December 2, 2016, https://www.reuters.com/article /us-newsnow-mattis-idUSKBN13R1E2.

15. Melissa Healy, "Lifesaving Product of the War," *Los Angeles Times*, June 23, 2003, https://www.latimes.com/archives/la-xpm-2003-jun-23-he-quickclot23 -story.html.

16. Eduardo Bonilla-Silva, *Racism Without Racists: Color-Blind Racism and the Persistence of Racial Inequality in the United States* (Lanham, MD: Rowman & Littlefield, 2006).

17. Adrian Bonenberger and Adam Weinstein, "The Sum of All Beards," *New Republic*, June 4, 2019, https://newrepublic.com/article/154033/american-beards -military-culture.

18. Sam Levin, "Officer Punched Oscar Grant and Lied About Facts in 2009 Killing, Records Show," *Guardian*, May 2, 2019, https://www.theguardian .com/us-news/2019/may/02/officer-punched-oscar-grant-and-lied-about -facts-in-2009-killing-records-show; Demian Bulwa, "Mehserle Weeps: 'I Didn't Think I Had My Gun,'" *SFGate*, June 26, 2010, https://www.sfgate.com /crime/article/Mehserle-weeps-I-didn-t-think-I-had-my-gun-3183875.php.

19. Donald Alva, "Mehserle Defense Seeks to Exclude Pirone's Use of a Racial Slur," California Beat, June 10, 2010, https://www.californiabeat.org/mehserle -defense-seeks-to-exclude-pirones-use-of-a-racial-slur/; Levin, "Officer Punched Oscar Grant"; Bay Area Rapid Transit, "BART Reaches $1.3M Settlement with Oscar Grant's Mother," June 28, 2011, https://www.bart.gov/news/articles /2011/news20110628b.

20. William T. Armaline, Claudio G. Vera Sanchez, and Mark Correia, "'The Biggest Gang in Oakland': Re-Thinking Police Legitimacy," *Contemporary Justice Review* 17, no. 3 (July 2014): 375–99, https://doi.org/10.1080/10282580.2 014.944795; Ali Winston and Darwin BondGraham, *The Riders Come Out at Night: Brutality, Corruption, and Cover-up in Oakland* (New York: Simon & Schuster, 2023).

21. Demian Bulwa, Charles Burress, Matthew B. Stannard, and Matthai Kuru-vila, "Protests Over BART Shooting Turn Violent," *SFGate*, January 8, 2009, https://www.sfgate.com/bayarea/article/Protests-over-BART-shooting-turn -violent-3255351.php#photo-2312844; Paul Harris, "Oakland Police: Controversial History Sets Tone for City's Discord," *Guardian*, October 26, 2011, https:// www.theguardian.com/world/blog/2011/oct/26/oakland-police-department -black-community.

22. First, there is no video in which one can hear anyone call out "Taser, Taser." Mehserle testified that he shouted, "I'm going to Tase him" twice. He also testified that these alleged shouts could not be heard on video of the shooting. Second, while Taser placement was a relevant factor in the case, the issue was not that the Taser was not placed in the usual spot on Mehserle's duty belt. Instead, Mehserle had positioned his Taser holster so that it required him to reach across his body with his dominant hand (the same one used to draw his pistol) if he wanted to draw his Taser. This was pointed to by the defense, along with inadequate Taser training, as proof that Mehserle

accidentally killed Grant because of "Taser confusion." Dan Brekke, "BART Cop Johannes Mehserle Recalls Details of Oscar Grant Shooting," KQED, June 13, 2014, https://www.kqed.org/news/138809/bart-cop-johannes-mehserle -testifying-in-oscar-grant-shooting-lawsuit; Demian Bulwa, "Position of Mehserle's Taser Holster May Be Key," *SFGate*, February 14, 2010, https:// www.sfgate.com/crime/article/position-of-mehserle-s-taser-holster-may-be -key-3200231.php; Demian Bulwa, "Trainer: Mehserle Was Warned of Taser Blunders," *SFGate*, June 24, 2010, https://www.sfgate.com/crime/article/trainer -mehserle-was-warned-of-taser-blunders-3260798.php.

23. Adam Ferrise, "Officer in Tamir Rice Shooting Has Suspension Cut in Half," *Police1*, July 25, 2018, https://www.police1.com/officer-misconduct-internal -affairs/articles/officer-in-tamir-rice-shooting-has-suspension-cut-in-half -c5bKnaRf405Ugffo/.

24. Eric Heisig, "Tamir Rice Shooting: A Breakdown of the Events That Led to the 12-Year-Old's Death," Cleveland.com, January 14, 2017, https://www.cleveland .com/court-justice/2017/01/tamir_rice_shooting_a_breakdow.html; Timothy Williams and Mitch Smith, "Cleveland Officer Will Not Face Charges in Tamir Rice Shooting Death," *New York Times*, December 28, 2015, https:// www.nytimes.com/2015/12/29/us/tamir-rice-police-shootiing-cleveland.html.

25. Colin Dwyer, "Officer Who Killed Tamir Rice Fired for Rule Violations on Job Application," *NPR*, May 30, 2017, https://www.npr.org/sections/thetwo -way/2017/05/30/530733542/officer-who-killed-tamir-rice-fired-for-rule -violations-on-job-application.

26. Ferrise, "Officer in Tamir Rice Shooting Has Suspension Cut in Half."

27. Lauren Gambino, Steven W. Thrasher, and Kayla Epstein, "Thousands March to Protest Against Police Brutality in Major US Cities," *Guardian*, December 14, 2014, sec. US news, https://www.theguardian.com/us-news/2014/dec/13 /marchers-protest-police-brutality-new-york-washington-boston.

28. Rachel Dissell, "Cleveland's Cudell Neighborhood Fights Madison Madhouse Gang Using Cameras, Tips to Police," Cleveland.com, June 7, 2009, https:// www.cleveland.com/metro/2009/06/clevelands_cudell_neighborhood .html.

29. See chapter 2.

30. Elijah Anderson, "The Iconic Ghetto," *Annals of the American Academy of Political and Social Science* 642, no. 1 (July 2012): 8–24, https://doi.org/10.1177 /0002716212446299; I. Bennett Capers, "Policing, Race, and Place," *Harvard Civil Rights–Civil Liberties Law Review* 44, no. 1 (2009): 43–78; Gaston, "Producing Race Disparities."

31. The trainee was in the final stage of field training, called the "shadow phase," in which trainees are expected to operate independently, with minimal assistance from their field training officers.

32. Ken Wallentine, "How Police Officers Can Avoid Claims of Excessive Force," *Police1*, September 5, 2007, https://www.police1.com/police-products /firearms/articles/how-police-officers-can-avoid-claims-of-excessive-force -FsvoCCj22dhIgjPZ/; David D. Kirkpatrick, "Split-Second Decisions: How a Supreme Court Case Shaped Modern Policing," *New York Times*, April 25, 2021https://www.nytimes.com/2021/04/25/us/police-use-of-force.html.

33. "Get off the X" is a popular adage in the world of gunfighting and tactical training that stresses the importance of movement and forcing an adversary to expend valuable time adjusting to one's changing position. Kevin Davis, "Get Off the X," Officer.com, December 31, 2008, https://www.officer.com /training-careers/article/10248338/get-off-the-x.

34. Jordan Blair Woods, "Policing, Danger Narratives, and Routine Traffic Stops," *Michigan Law Review* 117, no. 4 (2019): 635–712; see also Illya D Lichtenberg and Alisa Smith, "How Dangerous Are Routine Police–Citizen Traffic Stops? A Research Note," *Journal of Criminal Justice* 29, no. 5 (September 2001): 419–28, https://doi.org/10.1016/S0047-2352(01)00106-4; Dean Scoville, "The Hazards of Traffic Stops," *Police Magazine*, October 19, 2010, https://www .policemag.com/340410/the-hazards-of-traffic-stops; Doug Wylie, "Traffic Stops: New Ideas on Positioning, Movement, and Safety," *Police1*, May 13, 2013, https://www.police1.com/police-trainers/articles/traffic-stops-new-ideas -on-positioning-movement-and-safety-twYiLVPF9rvcxejY/; Jeff Moreland, "Traffic Stops Are 'One of the Most Dangerous Situations' for Police Officers," *Advocate-Messenger*, September 25, 2020, https://www.amnews.com/2020/09 /25/traffic-stops-are-one-of-the-most-dangerous-situations-for-police-officers/; Jeffrey A. Fagan and Alexis D. Campbell, "Race and Reasonableness in Police Killings," *Boston University Law Review* 100 (2020): 951–1015 (967n75).

35. Law Officer, "The Not-So-Basic Traffic Stop," *Law Officer* (blog), April 27, 2012, https://www.lawofficer.com/the-not-so-basic-traffic-stop/; Police1, "Using the 'B Pillar' during Traffic Stops," July 28, 2014, https://www.police1.com /officer-safety/articles/using-the-b-pillar-during-traffic-stops-j1VkfDb-k6KCoRnbR/.

36. Some officers consider the driver-side approach to be tactically unsound and prefer to approach the passenger side, both to improve their ability to see passengers and the vehicle interior and to maintain the element of surprise over drivers expecting them to appear at the driver-side window. Another benefit

of the passenger-side approach is that it keeps officers farther away from the roadway, reducing the likelihood of being struck by traffic.

37. Mary Douglas and Aaron Wildavsky, *Risk and Culture* (Berkeley: University of California Press, 1983); Paul J. DiMaggio and Walter W. Powell, "The Iron Cage Revisited: Institutional Isomorphism and Collective Rationality in Organizational Fields," *American Sociological Review* 48, no. 2 (1983): 147–60, https://doi.org/10.2307/2095101.

38. National Law Enforcement Officers Memorial Fund, "Causes of Law Enforcement Deaths," July 19, 2021, https://nleomf.org/memorial/facts-figures /officer-fatality-data/causes-of-law-enforcement-deaths/.

39. Estimates for nonofficer deaths are for 1979 through 2013. Officer death estimates are for 1980 through 2014. Thomas Frank, "FBI Vastly Understates Police Deaths in Chases," *USA Today*, October 26, 2015, http://www.usatoday.com /story/news/2015/10/26/fbi-police-deaths-vehicle-pursuits-chases/74349056/; Thomas Frank, "High-Speed Police Chases Have Killed Thousands of Innocent Bystanders," *USA Today*, July 30, 2015, http://www.usatoday.com/story /news/2015/07/30/police-pursuits-fatal-injuries/30187827/.

40. Anthony Giddens, *The Constitution of Society: Outline of the Theory of Structuration*, (Berkeley: University of California Press, 1986), 14.

41. Abigail A. Sewell and Kevin A. Jefferson, "Collateral Damage: The Health Effects of Invasive Police Encounters in New York City," *Journal of Urban Health* 93, no. 1 (April 2016): 42–67, https://doi.org/10.1007/s11524-015-0016-7; Tyler T. Reny and Benjamin J. Newman, "The Opinion-Mobilizing Effect of Social Protest Against Police Violence: Evidence from the 2020 George Floyd Protests," *American Political Science Review* 115, no. 4 (November 2021): 1499–1507, https://doi.org/10.1017/S0003055421000460; Jacinta M. Gau and Rod K. Brunson, "Procedural Justice and Order Maintenance Policing: A Study of Inner-City Young Men's Perceptions of Police Legitimacy," *Justice Quarterly* 27, no. 2 (April 2010): 255–79; Patrick J. Carr, Laura Napolitano, and Jessica Keating, "We Never Call the Cops and Here Is Why: A Qualitative Examination of Legal Cynicism in Three Philadelphia Neighborhoods," *Criminology* 45 (2007): 445–80; Matthew Desmond, Andrew V. Papachristos, and David S. Kirk, "Police Violence and Citizen Crime Reporting in the Black Community," *American Sociological Review* 81, no. 5 (October 2016): 857–76, https://doi .org/10.1177/0003122416663494; Victor M. Rios, *Punished: Policing the Lives of Black and Latino Boys* (New York: New York University Press, 2011).

42. Tom R. Tyler, *Why People Obey the Law* (New Haven, CT: Yale University Press, 1990); Tom R. Tyler and Jonathan Jackson, "Popular Legitimacy and

the Exercise of Legal Authority: Motivating Compliance, Cooperation, and Engagement.," *Psychology, Public Policy, and Law* 20, no. 1 (2014): 78–95, https://doi.org/10.1037/a0034514.

43. I was unable to independently corroborate Officer Matthews's story of a police officer being killed at a Dunkin' Donuts by a suspect who targeted that officer because of their sloppy dress. The most similar incidents I found were the 2015 killing of a police officer in a Dunkin' Donuts in Philadelphia while attempting to stop an armed robbery and the 2009 murder of four officers in a Lakewood, Washington, coffee shop. No coverage of these incidents mentioned that officers were targeted because of dress or demeanor that indicated vulnerability. Associated Press, "Philadelphia Police Officer Shot in Head at Dunkin' Donuts Dies," *Fox News*, March 25, 2015, https://www.foxnews.com/story/philadelphia-police-officer-shot-in-head-at-dunkin-donuts-dies; Seattle Times Staff, "Four Lakewood Officers Slain; Ex-Con Sought for Questioning," *Seattle Times*, December 2, 2009, https://web.archive.org/web/20091202064239/http://seattletimes.nwsource.com/html/localnews/2010382767_webfourdead29m.html.

44. Anthony J. Pinizzotto, Edward F. Davis, and Charles E. Miller, "The Deadly Mix: Officers, Offenders, and the Circumstances That Bring Them Together," *FBI Law Enforcement Bulletin*, January 2007, https://doi.org/10.1037/e591742007-001; Michael C. Harper and Matthew Wagner, "Enhancing Officer Safety & Survivability," *Police Chief Magazine*, May 19, 2021, https://www.policechiefmagazine.org/enhancing-officer-safety-survivability/; Lee Lofland, "Cops and Command Presence: What's Up with That Look?," Graveyard Shift, January 4, 2021, https://leelofland.com/cops-and-command-presence-whats-up-with-that-look/.

45. John Bennet, "How Command Presence Affects Your Survival," *Police1*, October 7, 2010, https://www.policeone.com/Officer-Safety/articles/2748139-How-command-presence-affects-your-survival/.

46. Mary Newman, "*Barnes v. City of Cincinnati*: Command Presence, Gender Bias, and Problems of Police Aggression," *Harvard Journal of Law & Gender* 29 (2006): 485–92.

47. Kyle Peyton, Michael Sierra-Arévalo, and David G. Rand, "A Field Experiment on Community Policing and Police Legitimacy," *Proceedings of the National Academy of Sciences* 116, no. 40 (October 2019): 19894–98, https://doi.org/10.1073/pnas.1910157116.

48. Gelman, Fagan, and Kiss, "An Analysis of the New York City Police Department's 'Stop-and-Frisk' Policy"; Rios, Prieto, and Ibarra, "Mano Suave–Mano Dura"; Jan Haldipur, *No Place on the Corner: The Costs of Aggressive Policing*

(New York: New York University Press, 2018); Gau and Brunson, "Procedural Justice and Order Maintenance Policing."

49. Frank Rudy Cooper, "'Who's the Man?': Masculinities Studies, Terry Stops, and Police Training," *Columbia Journal of Gender and Law* 18 (2009): 671–742; John Van Maanen, "The Asshole," in *Policing: A View from the Street*, ed. Peter K. Manning and John Van Maanen (New York: Random House, 1978), 221–37; Dennis P. Rosenbaum, Amie M. Schuck, Sandra K. Costello, Darnell F. Hawkins, and Marianne K. Ring, "Attitudes Toward the Police: The Effects of Direct and Vicarious Experience," *Police Quarterly* 8, no. 3 (September 2005): 343–65; Monica C. Bell, "Police Reform and the Dismantling of Legal Estrangement," *Yale Law Journal* 126 (2017): 2054–2151; John Hagan, Bill McCarthy, and Daniel Herda, "Race, Legal Cynicism, and the Machine Politics of Drug Law Enforcement in Chicago," *Du Bois Review: Social Science Research on Race* 15, no. 1 (2018): 129–51, https://doi.org/10.1017/S1742058X18000085; Bill McCarthy, John Hagan, and Daniel Herda, "Neighborhood Climates of Legal Cynicism and Complaints About Abuse of Police Power," *Criminology* 58, no. 3 (August 2020): 510–36, https://doi.org/10.1111/1745-9125.12246.

50. Egon Bittner, "Florence Nightingale in Pursuit of Willie Sutton: A Theory of the Police," in *The Potential for Reform of Criminal Justice*, ed. Herbert Jacob (Beverly Hills, CA: Sage, 1974), 3:30.

51. The unique capabilities and structure of policing—e.g., the 911 system, specialized equipment and training, legal protection and powers, and decentralized and motorized patrol units—also inform why the police are so often tapped as the state actors who will address some exigent social problem. Of course, why police were chosen as the public institution that would be continually funded and expanded to address a growing repertoire of responsibilities is tied to macro-level historical, political, and cultural developments that led to investment in punishment over care. See David Garland, *The Culture of Control: Crime and Social Order in Contemporary Society* (Chicago: University of Chicago Press, 2002); Elizabeth Hinton, *From the War on Poverty to the War on Crime: The Making of Mass Incarceration in America* (Cambridge, MA: Harvard University Press, 2016); Anne E. Parsons, *From Asylum to Prison: Deinstitutionalization and the Rise of Mass Incarceration After 1945* (Chapel Hill: University of North Carolina Press, 2018).

52. Barry Friedman, "Disaggregating the Policing Function," *University of Pennsylvania Law Review* 169, no. 4 (2021): 948–51; Steve Herbert, "'Hard Charger' or 'Station Queen'? Policing and the Masculinist State," *Gender, Place & Culture*

8, no. 1 (March 2001): 55–71, https://doi.org/10.1080/09663690120026325; Seth W. Stoughton, "Principled Policing: Warrior Cops and Guardian Officers," *Wake Forest Law Review* 51 (2016): 611–76; Michael Sierra-Arévalo, "Reward and 'Real' Police Work," in *The Ethics of Policing: New Perspectives on Law Enforcement*, ed. Benjamin Jones and Eduardo Mendieta (New York: New York University Press, 2021), 66–92; Michael Sierra-Arévalo, "The Commemoration of Death, Organizational Memory, and Police Culture," *Criminology* 57, no. 4 (2019): 632–58, https://doi.org/10.1111/1745-9125.12224.

53. Cynthia Lum, Christopher S. Koper, and Xiaoyun Wu, "Can We Really Defund the Police? A Nine-Agency Study of Police Response to Calls for Service," *Police Quarterly* 25, no. 3 (2021): 255–80, https://doi.org/10.1177/10986111211035002; Jerry H. Ratcliffe, "Policing and Public Health Calls for Service in Philadelphia," *Crime Science* 10, no. 5 (2021), https://doi.org/10.1186/s40163-021-00141-0; John A. Webster, "Police Task and Time Study," *Journal of Criminal Law and Criminology* 61, no. 1 (1970): 94–100; Jeff Asher and Ben Horwitz, "How Do the Police Actually Spend Their Time?," *New York Times*, June 19, 2020, https://www.nytimes.com/2020/06/19/upshot/unrest-police-time-violent-crime.html.

54. "Fatal Force: 2018 Police Shootings Database," *Washington Post*, June 1, 2020, https://www.washingtonpost.com/graphics/2018/national/police-shootings-2018/; Erika Harrell, "Contacts Between Police and the Public, 2018" (Washington, DC: Bureau of Justice Statistics, December 2020), https://bjs.ojp.gov/content/pub/pdf/cbpp18st.pdf.

55. Seth W. Stoughton, "Policing Facts," *Tulane Law Review* 88 (2014): 867–69.

56. Peter Moskos, *Cop in the Hood: My Year Policing Baltimore's Eastern District* (Princeton, NJ: Princeton University Press, 2009), 38.

57. Jessica W. Gillooly, "How 911 Callers and Call-Takers Impact Police Encounters with the Public: The Case of the Henry Louis Gates Jr. Arrest," *Criminology & Public Policy* 19, no. 3 (2020): 787–804, https://doi.org/10.1111/1745-9133.12508.

58. The name of the mental hospital that the woman used has been removed to prevent field site identification.

59. WPD policy on Taser use discourages the tasing of handcuffed suspects unless they are "actively resisting and their actions present an immediate threat to officers, third parties, or themselves." Though legal precedent has found some officers' use of Tasers on a handcuffed or compliant suspect, there is no bright line delineating when TASER use becomes patently unreasonable. Michael R. Smith, Matthew Petrocelli, and Charlie Scheer, "Excessive Force, Civil

Liability, and the Taser in the Nation's Courts: Implications for Law Enforcement Policy and Practice," *Policing: An International Journal of Police Strategies and Management* 30 (2007): 398–422.

60. Graham v. Connor, 490 U.S. 386, 396–97 (U.S. Supreme Court 1989).

61. This was an example of a procedurally just interaction, which is associated with improved public perceptions of police legitimacy. Jason Sunshine and Tom R. Tyler, "The Role of Procedural Justice and Legitimacy in Shaping Public Support for Policing," *Law & Society Review* 37, no. 3 (September 2003): 513–48.

62. Tammy Rinehart Kochel, David B. Wilson, and Stephen D. Mastrofski, "Effect of Suspect Race on Officers' Arrest Decisions," *Criminology* 49, no. 2 (May 2011): 473–512, https://doi.org/10.1111/j.1745-9125.2011.00230.x; Epp, Maynard-Moody, and Haider-Markel, *Pulled Over*; Jacinta M. Gau, Clayton Mosher, and Travis C. Pratt, "An Inquiry Into the Impact of Suspect Race on Police Use of Tasers," *Police Quarterly* 13, no. 1 (March 2010): 27–48, https://doi.org/10.1177/1098611109357332; Gaston, "Producing Race Disparities"; Kenneth J. Novak and Mitchell B. Chamlin, "Racial Threat, Suspicion, and Police Behavior: The Impact of Race and Place in Traffic Enforcement," *Crime & Delinquency* 58, no. 2 (2008): 275–300, https://doi.org/10.1177/0011128708322943; Eugene A. Paoline III, Jacinta M. Gau, and William Terrill, "Race and the Police Use of Force Encounter in the United States," *British Journal of Criminology* 58, no. 1 (January 2018): 54–74, https://doi.org/10.1093/bjc/azw089; Jeff Rojek, Richard Rosenfeld, and Scott Decker, "Policing Race: The Racial Stratification of Searches in Police Traffic Stops," *Criminology* 50, no. 4 (November 2012): 993–1024, https://doi.org/10.1111/j.1745-9125.2012.00285.x; Marisa Omori, Rachel Lautenschlager, and Justin Stoler, "Organizational Practice and Neighborhood Context of Racial Inequality in Police Use-of-Force," *Social Problems*, May 27, 2022, spaco31, https://doi.org/10.1093/socpro/spaco31; William Terrill and Michael D. Reisig, "Neighborhood Context and Police Use of Force," *Journal of Research in Crime and Delinquency* 40 (2003): 291–321; Daanika Gordon, "The Police as Place-Consolidators: The Organizational Amplification of Urban Inequality," *Law & Social Inquiry* 45, no. 1 (February 2020): 1–27, https://doi.org/10.1017/lsi.2019.31; Kramer and Remster, "Stop, Frisk, and Assault?"; Sharad Goel, Justin M. Rao, and Ravi Shroff, "Precinct or Prejudice? Understanding Racial Disparities in New York City's Stop-and-Frisk Policy," *Annals of Applied Statistics* 10, no. 1 (March 2016): 365–94, https://doi.org/10.1214/15-AOAS897; Emma Pierson,

Camelia Simoiu, Jan Overgoor, Sam Corbett-Davies, Daniel Jenson, Amy Shoemaker, Vignesh Ramachandran, Phoebe Barghouty, Cheryl Phillips, Ravi Shroff, and Sharad Goel, "A Large-Scale Analysis of Racial Disparities in Police Stops Across the United States," *Nature Human Behaviour* 4, no. 7 (July 2020): 736–45, https://doi.org/10.1038/s41562-020-0858-1; Gelman, Fagan, and Kiss, "An Analysis of the New York City Police Department's 'Stop-and-Frisk' Policy."

63. Rachel A. Harmon, "When Is Police Violence Justified?," *Northwestern University Law Review* 102 (2008): 1119–88.

64. John P. Gross, "Judge, Jury, and Executioner: The Excessive Use of Deadly Force by Police Officers," *Texas Journal on Civil Liberties & Civil Rights* 21, no. 2 (Spring 2016): 155–81 (161); Anna Lvovsky, "Rethinking Police Expertise," *Yale Law Journal* 131, no. 2 (2021): 475–572.

65. Geoffrey P. Alpert and William C. Smith, "How Reasonable Is the Reasonable Man? Police and Excessive Force," *Journal of Criminal Law and Criminology* 85, no. 2 (1994): 481–501 (486), https://doi.org/10.2307/1144107.

66. There is ample reason for skepticism of the judicial assumption that people are aware of their right not to interact with, or to leave an interaction with, a police officer when they are not formally detained. Daniel J. Steinbock, "The Wrong Line Between Freedom and Restraint: The Unreality, Obscurity, and Incivility of the Fourth Amendment Consensual Encounter Doctrine," *San Diego Law Review* 38, no. 2 (2001): 507–63 (519), https://heinonline.org/HOL/P?h=hein.journals/sanlr38&i=513.

67. Tracey Maclin, "Decline of the Right of Locomotion: The Fourth Amendment on the Streets," *Cornell Law Review* 75, no. 6 (1990): 1258–1337 (1301n205).

68. Elijah Anderson, "The Iconic Ghetto," *Annals of the American Academy of Political and Social Science* 642, no. 1 (2012): 8–24, https://doi.org/10.1177/0002716212446299.

69. Victor Ray, "A Theory of Racialized Organizations," *American Sociological Review* 84, no. 1 (February 2019): 26–53, https://doi.org/10.1177/0003122418822335; Brianna Remster, Chris M Smith, and Rory Kramer, "Race, Gender, and Police Violence in the Shadow of Controlling Images," *Social Problems*, April 5, 2022, spac018, https://doi.org/10.1093/socpro/spac018; Douglas A. Smith, "The Neighborhood Context of Police Behavior," *Crime and Justice* 8 (January 1986): 313–41.

70. Edwards, Lee, and Esposito, "Risk of Being Killed by Police Use of Force"; David Chang, Mallory Williams, Naveen F. Sangji, and L. D. Britt, "Pattern of Law Enforcement–Related Injuries in the United States," *Journal*

of Trauma and Acute Care Surgery 80, no. 6 (June 2016): 870–76, https://doi
.org/10.1097/TA.0000000000001000; Nix et al., "A Bird's Eye View of Civilians Killed by Police in 2015"; Kramer and Remster, "Stop, Frisk, and Assault?"

71. Sewell and Jefferson, "Collateral Damage"; Kristin Turney, "Depressive Symptoms
Among Adolescents Exposed to Personal and Vicarious Police Contact," *Society
and Mental Health* 11, no. 2 (July 2021): 113–33, https://doi.org/10.1177
/2156869320923095; Naomi F. Sugie and Kristin Turney, "Beyond Incarceration:
Criminal Justice Contact and Mental Health," *American Sociological Review*
82, no. 4 (August 2017): 719–43, https://doi.org/10.1177/0003122417713188;
Courtney E. Boen, "Criminal Justice Contacts and Psychophysiological
Functioning in Early Adulthood: Health Inequality in the Carceral State,"
Journal of Health and Social Behavior 61, no. 3 (September 2020): 290–306,
https://doi.org/10.1177/0022146520936208; Kristin Turney and Dylan B. Jackson, "Mothers' Health Following Youth Police Stops," *Preventive Medicine*
150 (September 1, 2021): 106693, https://doi.org/10.1016/j.ypmed.2021.106693.

72. Joscha Legewie and Jeffrey Fagan, "Aggressive Policing and the Educational
Performance of Minority Youth," *American Sociological Review* 84, no. 2
(April 2019): 220–247, https://doi.org/10.1177/0003122419826020; Aaron Gott-
lieb and Robert Wilson, "The Effect of Direct and Vicarious Police Contact
on the Educational Achievement of Urban Teens," *Children and Youth Services
Review* 103 (August 2019): 190–99, https://doi.org/10.1016/j.childyouth.2019
.06.009.

73. Devah Pager, "The Mark of a Criminal Record," *American Journal of Sociology*
108, no. 5 (March 2003): 937–75, https://doi.org/10.1086/374403; Devah Pager,
Bart Bonikowski, and Bruce Western, "Discrimination in a Low-Wage Labor
Market: A Field Experiment," *American Sociological Review* 74, no. 5 (October
2009): 777–99, https://doi.org/10.1177/000312240907400505.

74. Robert Apel and Kathleen Powell, "Level of Criminal Justice Contact and
Early Adult Wage Inequality," *RSF: The Russell Sage Foundation Journal of
the Social Sciences* 5, no. 1 (February 2019): 198–222, https://doi.org/10.7758
/RSF.2019.5.1.09; Alexes Harris, *A Pound of Flesh: Monetary Sanctions as
Punishment for the Poor* (New York: Russell Sage Foundation, 2016); Brittany Friedman and Mary Pattillo, "Statutory Inequality: The Logics of Monetary Sanctions in State Law," *RSF: The Russell Sage Foundation Journal of
the Social Sciences* 5, no. 1 (February 2019): 174–96, https://doi.org/10.7758/RSF
.2019.5.1.08.

75. Bell, "Police Reform and the Dismantling of Legal Estrangement"; David S.
Kirk and Andrew V. Papachristos, "Cultural Mechanisms and the Persistence

of Neighborhood Violence," *American Journal of Sociology* 116, no. 4 (January 2011): 1190–1233, https://doi.org/10.1086/655754.

76. Amy E. Lerman and Vesla M. Weaver, *Arresting Citizenship: The Democratic Consequences of American Crime Control* (Chicago: University of Chicago Press, 2014); Vesla M. Weaver and Amy E. Lerman, "Political Consequences of the Carceral State," *American Political Science Review* 104, no. 4 (November 2010): 817–33, https://doi.org/10.1017/S0003055410000456.

77. Sarah Brayne, "Surveillance and System Avoidance: Criminal Justice Contact and Institutional Attachment," *American Sociological Review* 79, no. 3 (June 2014): 367–91, https://doi.org/10.1177/0003122414530398.

CONCLUSION

1. Patrick Sharkey, *Stuck in Place: Urban Neighborhoods and the End of Progress Toward Racial Equality* (Chicago: University of Chicago Press, 2013); Ruth D. Peterson and Lauren Joy Krivo, *Divergent Social Worlds: Neighborhood Crime and the Racial-Spatial Divide* (New York: Russell Sage Foundation, 2010); Simon Balto, *Occupied Territory: Policing Black Chicago from Red Summer to Black Power* (Chapel Hill: University of North Carolina Press, 2019), 1; James Forman, *Locking Up Our Own: Crime and Punishment in Black America* (New York: Farrar, Straus and Giroux, 2017); Bocar A. Ba, Dean Knox, Jonathan Mummolo, and Roman Rivera, "The Role of Officer Race and Gender in Police-Civilian Interactions in Chicago," *Science* 371, no. 6530 (February 12, 2021): 696–702, https://doi.org/10.1126/science.abd8694.

2. Elijah Anderson, "The Iconic Ghetto," *Annals of the American Academy of Political and Social Science* 642, no. 1 (July 2012): 8–24, https://doi.org/10.1177/0002716212446299; I. Bennett Capers, "Policing, Race, and Place," *Harvard Civil Rights–Civil Liberties Law Review* 44, no. 1 (2009): 43–78; Katheryn Russell-Brown, *The Color of Crime: Racial Hoaxes, White Fear, Black Protectionism, Police Harassment, and Other Macroaggressions* (New York: New York University Press, 1997); Elizabeth Hinton and DeAnza Cook, "The Mass Criminalization of Black Americans: A Historical Overview," *Annual Review of Criminology* 4, no. 1 (2021): 261–86, https://doi.org/10.1146/annurev-criminol-060520-033306.

3. Daanika Gordon and Anthony Davis-Pait, "Police Redistricting Reforms and Urban Governance," *Law & Policy*, no. 4 (October 2022): 302–24, https://doi.org/10.1111/lapo.12196; Kimberly Barsamian Kahn and Paul G. Davies, "Differentially Dangerous? Phenotypic Racial Stereotypicality Increases Implicit

Bias Among Ingroup and Outgroup Members," *Group Processes & Intergroup Relations* 14, no. 4 (July 2011): 569–80, https://doi.org/10.1177/1368430210374609; Justin D. Levinson and Danielle Young, "Different Shades of Bias: Skin Tone, Implicit Racial Bias, and Judgments of Ambiguous Evidence," *West Virginia Law Review* 112 (2010): 307–50; Jennifer L. Eberhardt, Phillip Atiba Goff, Valerie J. Purdie, and Paul G. Davies, "Seeing Black: Race, Crime, and Visual Processing," *Journal of Personality and Social Psychology* 87, no. 6 (2004): 876–93, https://doi.org/10.1037/0022-3514.87.6.876; Katherine B. Spencer, Amanda K. Charbonneau, and Jack Glaser, "Implicit Bias and Policing," *Social and Personality Psychology Compass* 10, no. 1 (2016): 54–55, https://doi.org/10.1111 /spc3.12210; Kimberly Barsamian Kahn, Phillip Atiba Goff, J. Katherine Lee, and Diane Motamed, "Protecting Whiteness: White Phenotypic Racial Stereotypicality Reduces Police Use of Force," *Social Psychological and Personality Science* 7, no. 5 (July 2016): 403–11, https://doi.org/10.1177/1948550616633505; Lorie A. Fridell, "The Science of Implicit Bias and Implications for Policing," in *Producing Bias-Free Policing: A Science-Based Approach*, ed. Lorie A. Fridell (Cham, Switzerland: Springer, 2017), 10–15, https://doi.org/10.1007/978-3-319 -33175-1_2.

4. Robert Brame, Shawn D. Bushway, Ray Paternoster, and Michael G. Turner, "Demographic Patterns of Cumulative Arrest Prevalence by Ages 18 and 23," *Crime & Delinquency* 60, no. 3 (April 1, 2014): 471–86, https://doi.org/10.1177 /0011128713514801; Charles R. Epp, Steven Maynard-Moody, and Donald P. Haider-Markel, *Pulled Over: How Police Stops Define Race and Citizenship* (Chicago: University of Chicago Press, 2014); Frank Edwards, Hedwig Lee, and Michael Esposito, "Risk of Being Killed by Police Use of Force in the United States by Age, Race–Ethnicity, and Sex," *Proceedings of the National Academy of Sciences* 116, no. 34 (August 20, 2019): 16793–98, https:// doi.org/10.1073/pnas.1821204116; Shytierra Gaston, "Producing Race Disparities: A Study of Drug Arrests Across Place and Race," *Criminology* 57, no. 3 (August 2019): 424–51, https://doi.org/10.1111/1745-9125.12207; Justin Nix, Bradley A. Campbell, Edward H. Byers, and Geoffrey P. Alpert, "A Bird's Eye View of Civilians Killed by Police in 2015," *Criminology & Public Policy* 16, no. 1 (2017): 309–40, https://doi.org/10.1111/1745-9133.12269; Joscha Legewie, "Racial Profiling and Use of Force in Police Stops: How Local Events Trigger Periods of Increased Discrimination," *American Journal of Sociology* 122, no. 2 (2016): 379–424, https://doi.org/10.1086/687518; Rory Kramer and Brianna Remster, "Stop, Frisk, and Assault? Racial Disparities in Police Use of Force During Investigatory Stops," *Law & Society Review* 52, no. 4 (2018): 960–93,

https://doi.org/10.1111/lasr.12366; Andrew Gelman, Jeffrey Fagan, and Alex Kiss, "An Analysis of the New York City Police Department's 'Stop-and -Frisk' Policy in the Context of Claims of Racial Bias," *Journal of the American Statistical Association* 102, no. 479 (September 2007): 813–23, https://doi.org /10.1198/016214506000001040; Shytierra Gaston and Rod K. Brunson, "Reasonable Suspicion in the Eye of the Beholder: Routine Policing in Racially Different Disadvantaged Neighborhoods," *Urban Affairs Review* 56, no. 1 (January 2020): 188–227, https://doi.org/10.1177/1078087418774641; Victor M. Rios, Greg Prieto, and Jonathan M. Ibarra, "Mano Suave–Mano Dura: Legitimacy Policing and Latino Stop-and-Frisk," *American Sociological Review* 85, no. 1 (February 2020): 58–75, https://doi.org/10.1177/0003122419897348; Ba et al., "The Role of Officer Race and Gender in Police-Civilian Interactions in Chicago."

5. Shaila Dewan, "Minneapolis Officers Found to Engage in Racist Policing," *New York Times*, April 27, 2022, https://www.nytimes.com/2022/04/27/us /minneapolis-police-racism-human-rights.html; Will Carless and Michael Corey, "To Protect and Slur: Inside Hate Groups on Facebook, Police Officers Trade Racist Memes, Conspiracy Theories and Islamophobia," *Reveal*, June 14, 2019, http://revealnews.org/article/inside-hate-groups-on-facebook -police-officers-trade-racist-memes-conspiracy-theories-and-islamophobia/; Joshua Kaplan and Joaquin Sapien, "'No One Took Us Seriously': Black Cops Warned About Racist Capitol Police Officers for Years," *ProPublica*, January 1, 2021, https://www.propublica.org/article/no-one-took-us-seriously-black-cops -warned-about-racist-capitol-police-officers-for-years; "Cincinnati Police Officer's Racist Outburst Caught on Camera," NBC News, July 26, 2022, https:// www.nbcnews.com/video/cincinnati-police-officer-s-racist-outburst-caught-on -camera-144825413792; Emily Hoerner and Rick Tulsky, "Cops Across the US Have Been Exposed Posting Racist and Violent Things on Facebook. Here's the Proof.," *BuzzFeed News*, July 23, 2019, https://www.buzzfeednews.com/article /emilyhoerner/police-facebook-racist-violent-posts-comments-philadelphia; Michael German, "Hidden in Plain Sight: Racism, White Supremacy, and Far-Right Militancy in Law Enforcement," Brennan Center for Justice, August 27, 2020, https://www.brennancenter.org/our-work/research-reports /hidden-plain-sight-racism-white-supremacy-and-far-right-militancy-law.

6. Daanika Gordon, "The Bureaucratic Dissociation of Race in Policing: From State Racial Projects to Colorblind Ideologies," *Social Problems*, March 30, 2022, spac019, https://doi.org/10.1093/socpro/spac019; Amada Armenta, "Racializing Crimmigration: Structural Racism, Colorblindness, and the Institutional

Production of Immigrant Criminality," *Sociology of Race and Ethnicity* 3, no. 1 (January 2017): 82–95, https://doi.org/10.1177/2332649216648714; Megan Welsh, Joshua Chanin, and Stuart Henry, "Complex Colorblindness in Police Processes and Practices," *Social Problems* 68, no. 2 (May 2021): 374–92, https://doi .org/10.1093/socpro/spaa008; Eduardo Bonilla-Silva, *Racism Without Racists: Color-Blind Racism and the Persistence of Racial Inequality in the United States* (Rowman & Littlefield, 2006).

7. Michael Sierra-Arévalo and Andrew Papachristos, "Bad Apples and Incredible Certitude," *Criminology & Public Policy* 20, no. 2 (May 2021): 371–81, https:// doi.org/10.1111/1745-9133.12545.

8. Jomills H. Braddock II, Rachel E. Lautenschlager, Alex R. Piquero, and Nicole Leeper Piquero, "How Many Bad Apples? Investigating Implicit and Explicit Bias Among Police Officers and the General Public," *Contexts*, October 27, 2020, https://contexts.org/articles/how-many-bad-apples-investigating-implicit -and-explicit-bias-among-police-officers-and-the-general-public/.

9. Ann Swidler, "Culture in Action: Symbols and Strategies," *American Sociological Review* 51, no. 2 (April 1986): 273–286 (276).

10. Rachelle Hampton, "We Need to Cool Down About Police Officers Getting Doused with Water," *Slate*, August 23, 2019, https://slate.com/news-and -politics/2019/08/nypd-water-attacks-overreaction.html.

11. Madeleine Aggeler, "Wait, What Happened With the NYPD and Shake Shack?," *The Cut*, June 23, 2020, https://www.thecut.com/2020/06/wait-what -happened-with-the-nypd-and-shake-shack.html.

12. German Lopez, "Why Police Unions Protect the Worst Cops," Vox, December 18, 2014, https://www.vox.com/2014/12/18/7415135/police-unions; Jamelle Bouie, "The Cloak of 'Fear,'" *Slate*, June 23, 2017, https://slate.com/news-and -politics/2017/06/why-fear-was-a-viable-defense-for-killing-philando-castile .html; Martel A. Pipkins, "'I Feared for My Life': Law Enforcement's Appeal to Murderous Empathy," *Race and Justice* 9, no. 2 (April 2019): 180–96, https:// doi.org/10.1177/2153368717697103.

13. Yana Kunichoff and Sam Stecklow, "How Chicago's 'Fraternal Order of Propaganda' Shapes the Story of Fatal Police Shootings," *Chicago Reader*, February 3, 2016, http://chicagoreader.com/news-politics/how-chicagos-fraternal -order-of-propaganda-shapes-the-story-of-fatal-police-shootings/.

14. Catherine L. Fisk and L. Song Richardson, "Police Unions," *George Washington Law Review* 85 (2017): 747–49; Benjamin Levin, "What's Wrong with Police Unions?," *Columbia Law Review* 120, no. 5 (2020): 1348–52, https://doi.org /10.2139/ssrn.3469958; AP, "Van Dyke Ends Effort to Overturn McDonald

Murder Conviction," *AP News*, October 9, 2020, https://apnews.com/article
/laquan-mcdonald-jason-van-dyke-shootings-chicago-illinois-6a1b84c2560
fd4907bf06deceoce1dac.

15. Amelia Thomson-DeVeaux, Nathaniel Rakich, and Likhitha Butchireddygari, "Why It's So Rare for Police Officers to Face Legal Consequences,"
FiveThirtyEight, June 4, 2020, https://fivethirtyeight.com/features/why-its
-still-so-rare-for-police-officers-to-face-legal-consequences-for-misconduct/.

16. Katherine J. Bies, "Let the Sunshine In: Illuminating the Powerful Role
Police Unions Play in Shielding Officer Misconduct," *Stanford Law and Policy
Review* 28 (2017): 109–49 (140–41()).

17. Asher Stockler, "Lawmakers Made NY Police Discipline Records Public. But
Courts Will Have the Final Say.," *Journal News*, July 22, 2021, https://www
.lohud.com/story/news/2021/07/22/new-york-50-a-repeal-courts-have-final
-say-police-transparency/8028750002/.

18. Richard Khavkine, "PBA Rips City Council Bill to Reopen Police Disciplinary Records," *Chief*, February 11, 2019, https://thechiefleader.com/news/news
_of_the_week/pba-rips-city-council-bill-to-reopen-police-disciplinary-records
/article_47b34e82-2e43-11e9-90a2-3b85cbc5d068.html.

19. Bies, "Let the Sunshine In," 135–39.

20. Kallie Cox and William Freivogel, "Police Misconduct Records Secret, Difficult to Access," Pulitzer Center, January 24, 2022, https://pulitzercenter.org
/stories/police-misconduct-records-secret-difficult-access.

21. National Fraternal Order of Police (FOP) [@GLFOP], "We Implore the
Folks in the Media, Who've Been Dismissing the Dangerous Policies of
Rogue Prosecutors for Too Long, to Comprehend the Level of Public Out-
rage. The Growing Concern over #BailReform Is a Sign That You Can No
Longer Turn a Blind Eye—America Expects You to Cover It! Https://T
.Co/BxE4BbzSjF," Twitter, November 24, 2021, https://twitter.com/GLFOP
/status/1463569600092819456; National Fraternal Order of Police (FOP) [@
GLFOP], "🚨Antifa Terrorist Arrested 3 Times for Rioting & Assaulting a
Police Officer. She Received $0 Bond Each Time & Only Got 30 Hours of
Community Service. The Revolving Door for Criminals Is All Too Common,
Thanks to Woke Politicians Who Don't Give a Damn about Their Communi-
ties. Https://T.Co/OhLaw84qBb," Twitter, December 31, 2021, https://twitter
.com/GLFOP/status/1476749193918222338; "Joe Gamaldi: 'Liberal Policies
Have Led to This High Crime Rate,'" *America Reports* (Fox News, December
10, 2021), https://www.foxnews.com/video/6286173389001; "Soft-on-Crime
Criminal Justice Is 'Disgusting,' a 'Failed Social Experiment': Gamaldi,"

Faulkner Focus (Fox News, June 20, 2022), https://www.foxnews.com/video /6309771585112.

22. National Fraternal Order of Police (FOP) [@GLFOP], "The End Result of the Horrific Rhetoric Towards Law Enforcement and the Defund the Police Movement Had Embolden These Miscreants. They Aren't Coming for the Police, They Are Coming for You and We Are the Only Thing Standing in the Way of This Insanity. This Cannot Stand . . . https://T.Co /BXfKLobybH," Twitter, August 28, 2022, https://twitter.com/GLFOP/status /1563985198269841408.

23. Fraternal Order of Police, "FOP Priority Bill 'LEOSA Reform Act' Introduced in House," Fraternal Order of Police, February 24, 2021, https://fop.net /2021/02/fop-priority-bill-leosa-reform-act-introduced-in-house/.

24. GovTrack, "LEOSA Reform Act (H.R. 1156), 116th Congress," GovTrack.us, February 13, 2019, https://www.govtrack.us/congress/bills/116/hr1156; Gov-Track, "Thin Blue Line Act (H.R. 99), 116th Congress," GovTrack.us, January 3, 2019, https://www.govtrack.us/congress/bills/116/hr99; OpenSecrets, "National Fraternal Order of Police Profile: Lobbying," 2020, https://www .opensecrets.org/orgs/lobbying?id=D000027848.

25. Louis Nelson, "Trump Wins Endorsement from Fraternal Order of Police," *Politico*, September 16, 2016, https://www.politico.com/story/2016/09/trump -fraternal-order-of-police-endorsement-228296.

26. Michael Zoorob, "Blue Endorsements Matter: How the Fraternal Order of Police Contributed to Donald Trump's Victory," *PS: Political Science & Politics* 52, no. 2 (April 2019): 243–50, https://doi.org/10.1017/S1049096518001841.

27. FBI, "LEOKA Officer Safety Awareness Training," FBI: Law Enforcement Bulletin, 2022, https://leb.fbi.gov/file-repository/leoka-officer-safety-awareness -training.pdf/view; Anthony J. Pinizzotto, Edward F. Davis, and Charles E. Miller III, "In the Line of Fire: Violence Against Law Enforcement" (Washington, DC: Federal Bureau of Investigation, 1997), https://valorfiles.blob .core.windows.net/documents/Clearinghouse/FBI-In_the_Line_Of_Fire .pdf?sv=2017-04-17&sr=b&sig=jsIGdIJvkoUfsdYV29l2HqzbV3J%2BNutV4 eslTtkx7sA%3D&se=2022-09-23T20%3A28%3A42Z&sp=r; Anthony J. Pinizzotto, Edward F. Davis, and Charles E. Miller III, "Violent Encounters: A Study of Felonious Assaults on Our Nation's Law Enforcement Officers" (Washington, DC: U.S. Department of Justice, Federal Bureau of Investigation, National Institute of Justice, 2006), http://www.fairfaxcounty.gov/police commission/materials/band-readahead.pdf; Federal Bureau of Investigation, "Killed in the Line of Duty: A Study of Selected Felonioius Killings of Law

Enforcement Officers" (Washington, DC: Federal Bureau of Investigation, September 1992), https://www.ojp.gov/pdffiles1/Digitization/139198NCJRS .pdf.

28. James H. Burch II, "VALOR Initiative Strengthens Department's Commitment to Officer Safety," U.S. Department of Justice Archives, October 26, 2010, https://www.justice.gov/archives/opa/blog/valor-initiative-strengthens -department-s-commitment-officer-safety; VALOR, "Training Overview," VALOR Officer Safety and Wellness Program, 2019, https://www.valorforblue .org/VALOR-Training/Training-Descriptions.

29. VALOR, "Training Overview"; VALOR, "Not Today Challenge," VALOR Officer Safety and Wellness Program, 2019, https://www.valorforblue.org /ValorStory/NotTodayChallenge.

30. Bureau of Justice Assistance, "Preventing Violence Against Law Enforcement Officers and Ensuring Officer Resilience and Survivability (VALOR) Initiative FY 2019 Competitive Solicitation" (Washington, DC: U.S. Department of Justice, Office of Justice Programs, Bureau of Justice Assistance, May 21, 2019), https://www.bja.gov/funding/valor19.pdf; VALOR, "Home," VALOR Officer Safety and Wellness Program, 2019, https://www.valorforblue.org/Home.

31. Daniel Kahneman and Amos Tversky, "Prospect Theory: An Analysis of Decision Under Risk," *Econometrica* 47, no. 2 (1979): 263–91, https://doi.org /10.2307/1914185; Amos Tversky and Daniel Kahneman, "Judgment Under Uncertainty: Heuristics and Biases," *Science* 185, no. 4157 (September 27, 1974): 1124–31, https://doi.org/10.1126/science.185.4157.1124; Cass R. Sunstein, "Probability Neglect: Emotions, Worst Cases, and Law," *Yale Law Journal* 112 (2002): 61–107.

32. Paul Slovic, "Perceptions of Risk," *Science* 236, no. 4799 (April 17, 1987): 280–85, https://doi.org/10.1126/science.3563507.

33. Robert Klemko, "Much of America Wants Policing to Change. But These Self-Proclaimed Experts Tell Officers They're Doing Just Fine.," *Washington Post*, January 26, 2022, https://www.washingtonpost.com/national-security /2022/01/26/police-training-reform/; Tomi Lahren, "There Is a War on Cops," *Fox News*, 2021, https://www.youtube.com/watch?v=5LWtRYODKQw.

34. Street Cop Training, "Street Academy: Survival Tactics for Police Officers," 2022, https://www.streetcoptraining.com/training/courses/street-academy -survival-tactics-for-police-officers/.

35. Lexipol, "Lexipol and Praetorian Digital Merge, Creating Comprehensive Content, Training and Policy Platform for Public Safety," GlobeNewswire, February 8, 2019, https://www.globenewswire.com/news-release/2019/02/08

/1714214/14064/en/Lexipol-and-Praetorian-Digital-Merge-Creating-Comprehensive-Content-Training-and-Policy-Platform-for-Public-Safety.html.

36. PoliceOne Academy, "Certified, Accredited Law Enforcement Training," 2022, https://www.policeoneacademy.com/accreditation/.

37. Law Officer, "Law Officer Training," April 25, 2021, https://www.lawofficer .com/training; Law Officer, "Following the Banning of 'Warrior Training'— Minneapolis Police Are Provided Free Training by Law Officer," April 23, 2019, https://lawofficer.com/wp-content/uploads/2019/04/MinneapolisPressRelease1.pdf.

38. Thomas Abt, *Bleeding Out: The Devastating Consequences of Urban Violence— and a Bold New Plan for Peace in the Streets* (New York: Basic Books, 2019), 24–26.

39. Brandon Garrett and Seth Stoughton, "A Tactical Fourth Amendment," *Virginia Law Review* 103, no. 2 (2017): 211–308.

40. Peter K. Manning, *The Technology of Policing: Crime Mapping, Information Technology, and the Rationality of Crime Control* (New York: New York University Press, 2011), 22, 257.

41. Alex S. Vitale, *The End of Policing* (London: Verso, 2017), 30.

42. Vera, "What Policing Costs: A Look at Spending in America's Biggest Cities," Vera Institute of Justice, June 2020, https://www.vera.org/publications/what -policing-costs-in-americas-biggest-cities.

43. Philip V. McHarris and Thenjiwe McHarris, "No More Money for the Police," *New York Times*, May 30, 2020, https://www.nytimes.com/2020/05/30/opinion /george-floyd-police-funding.html.

44. Mariame Kaba, "Yes, We Mean Literally Abolish the Police," *New York Times*, June 12, 2020, https://www.nytimes.com/2020/06/12/opinion/sunday/floyd -abolish-defund-police.html.

45. Jeffrey C. Isaac, "Why 'Abolition of the Police' Is a Bad Idea," Public Seminar, June 18, 2020, https://publicseminar.org/essays/why-abolition-of-the-police-is -a-bad-idea/; Jacqueline B. Helfgott, "The Movement to Defund the Police Is Wrong, and Here's Why," *Seattle Times*, June 9, 2020, https://www.seattletimes .com/opinion/the-movement-to-defund-the-police-is-wrong-and-heres-why/.

46. Patrick Sharkey, Gerard Torrats-Espinosa, and Delaram Takyar, "Community and the Crime Decline: The Causal Effect of Local Nonprofits on Violent Crime," *American Sociological Review* 82, no. 6 (2017): 1214–40, https://doi.org /10.1177/0003122417736289.

47. Sara B. Heller, "Summer Jobs Reduce Violence among Disadvantaged Youth," *Science* 346, no. 6214 (December 5, 2014): 1219–23, https://doi.org/10.1126/science .1257809.

48. Aaron Chalfin, Benjamin Hansen, Jason Lerner, and Lucie Parker, "Reducing Crime Through Environmental Design: Evidence from a Randomized Experiment of Street Lighting in New York City," *Journal of Quantitative Criminology* 38, no. 1 (2022): 127–57, https://doi.org/10.1007/s10940-020-09490-6; Charles C. Branas, Michelle C. Kondo, Sean M. Murphy, Eugenia C. South, Daniel Polsky, and John M. MacDonald, "Urban Blight Remediation as a Cost-Beneficial Solution to Firearm Violence," *American Journal of Public Health* 106, no. 12 (December 2016): 2158–64, https://doi.org/10.2105/AJPH.2016.303434

49. Heather Schoenfeld, *Building the Prison State: Race and the Politics of Mass Incarceration* (Chicago: University of Chicago Press, 2018); David Garland, *The Culture of Control: Crime and Social Order in Contemporary Society* (Chicago: University Of Chicago Press, 2002); Elizabeth Hinton, *From the War on Poverty to the War on Crime: The Making of Mass Incarceration in America* (Cambridge, MA: Harvard University Press, 2016).

50. Monica Deza, Thanh Lu, Johanna Catherine Maclean, and Alberto Ortega, "Behavioral Health Treatment and Police Officer Safety," National Bureau of Economic Research, June 2023, https://doi.org/10.3386/w31391.

51. Daniel S. Nagin, "Firearm Availability and Fatal Police Shootings," *Annals of the American Academy of Political and Social Science* 687, no. 1 (January 2020): 49–57, https://doi.org/10.1177/0002716219896259; David Hemenway, Deborah Azrael, Andrew Conner, and Matthew Miller, "Variation in Rates of Fatal Police Shootings across US States: The Role of Firearm Availability," *Journal of Urban Health* 96, no. 1 (February 2019): 63–73, https://doi.org/10.1007/s11524-018-0313-z; David I. Swedler, Molly M Simmons, Francesca Dominici, and David Hemenway, "Firearm Prevalence and Homicides of Law Enforcement Officers in the United States," *American Journal of Public Health* 105, no. 10 (October 2015): 2042–48; Eric W. Fleegler, Lois K. Lee, Michael C. Monuteaux, David Hemenway, and Rebekah Mannix, "Firearm Legislation and Firearm-Related Fatalities in the United States," *JAMA Internal Medicine* 173, no. 9 (2013): 732–40, https://doi.org/10.1001/jamainternmed.2013.1286.

52. Aaron Karp, "Estimating Global Civilian-Held Firearms Numbers," Briefing Paper. Geneva, Switzerland: Small Arms Survey, June 2018, http://www.smallarmssurvey.org/fileadmin/docs/T-Briefing-Papers/SAS-BP-Civilian-Firearms-Numbers.pdf.

53. Emma C. Hamilton, Charles C. Miller III, Charles S. Cox Jr., Kevin P. Lally, and Mary T. Austin, "Variability of Child Access Prevention Laws and Pediatric Firearm Injuries," *Journal of Trauma and Acute Care Surgery* 84, no. 4 (April 2018): 613–19, https://doi.org/10.1097/TA.0000000000001786; David

C. Grossman, Beth A. Mueller, Christine Riedy, M. Denise Dowd, Andres Villaveces, Janice Prodzinski, Jon Nakagawara, John Howard, Norman Thiersch, and Richard Harruff, "Gun Storage Practices and Risk of Youth Suicide and Unintentional Firearm Injuries," *JAMA* 293, no. 6 (2005): 707–14, https://doi.org/10.1001/jama.293.6.707; David Hemenway, Deborah Azrael, and Matthew Miller, "Whose Guns Are Stolen? The Epidemiology of Gun Theft Victims," *Injury Epidemiology* 4, no. 1 (2017): 11, https://doi.org/10.1186/s40621-017-0109-8; Anthony A. Braga, Philip J. Cook, David M. Kennedy, and Mark H. Moore, "The Illegal Supply of Firearms," *Crime and Justice* 29 (2002): 319-352 (320), https://doi.org/10.2307/1147711.

54. Egon Bittner, "Florence Nightingale in Pursuit of Willie Sutton: A Theory of the Police," in *The Potential for Reform of Criminal Justice*, ed. Herbert Jacob (Beverly Hills, CA: Sage, 1974), 3:11–44; Steve Herbert, "'Hard Charger' or 'Station Queen'? Policing and the Masculinist State," *Gender, Place & Culture* 8, no. 1 (March 2001): 55–71, https://doi.org/10.1080/09663690120026325; Michael Sierra-Arévalo, "Reward and 'Real' Police Work," in *The Ethics of Policing: New Perspectives on Law Enforcement*, ed. Benjamin Jones and Eduardo Mendieta (New York: New York University Press, 2021), 66–92.

METHODOLOGICAL APPENDIX AND REFLECTION

1. David M. Kennedy, *Don't Shoot: One Man, a Street Fellowship, and the End of Violence in Inner-City America* (London: Bloomsbury, 2011).

2. Michael Sierra-Arévalo and Andrew V. Papachristos, "Applying Group Audits to Problem-Oriented Policing," in *Disrupting Criminal Networks: Network Analysis in Crime Prevention*, ed. Gisela Bichler and Aili Malm (Boulder, CO: Lynne Rienner, 2015), 27–46.

3. Jerome H. Skolnick, *Justice Without Trial: Law Enforcement in Democratic Society* (New York: Wiley, 1966); William A. Westley, "Violence and the Police," *American Journal of Sociology* 59, no. 1 (July 1953): 34–41, http://www.jstor.org/stable/2771674; John Van Maanen, "Observations on the Making of a Policeman," in *Policing: A View from the Street*, ed. Peter K. Manning and John Van Maanen (New York: Random House, 1978), 292–308.

4. Jessica Calarco, "Answering the 'So What?' Question," February 3, 2021, http://www.jessicacalarco.com/tips-tricks.

5. Colin Jerolmack and Alexandra K. Murphy, "The Ethical Dilemmas and Social Scientific Trade-Offs of Masking in Ethnography," *Sociological Methods & Research* 48, no. 4 (November 2019): 801–27, https://doi.org/10.1177/0049124117701483.

6. Jeffrey Lane, *The Digital Street*, Illustrated edition (New York: Oxford University Press, 2018), 184–86.

7. Kieran Healy, "Fuck Nuance," *Sociological Theory* 35, no. 2 (June 2017): 118–27, https://doi.org/10.1177/0735275117709046.

8. John J. Broderick, *Police in a Time of Change* (Morristown, NJ: General Learning, 1977); Michael K. Brown, *Working the Street: Police Discretion and the Dilemmas of Reform* (New York: Russell Sage Foundation, 1988); William K. Muir, *Police: Street Corner Politicians* (Chicago: University of Chicago Press, 1977); Robert Reiner, *The Blue-Coated Worker: A Sociological Study of Police Unionism* (Cambridge: Cambridge University Press, 1978); Susan O. White, "A Perspective on Police Professionalization," *Law & Society Review* 7, no. 1 (1972): 61–85, https://doi.org/10.2307/3052829.

9. Seth W. Stoughton, "Principled Policing: Warrior Cops and Guardian Officers," *Wake Forest Law Review* 51 (2016): 611–76; Steve Herbert, "'Hard Charger' or 'Station Queen'? Policing and the Masculinist State," *Gender, Place & Culture* 8, no. 1 (March 2001): 55–71, https://doi.org/10.1080/09663690120026325.

10. I was told multiple times that a vest could be found for me in Elmont but this never materialized.

11. Everett Cherrington Hughes, *Men and Their Work* (Westport, CT: Greenwood, 1958).

12. Forrest Stuart, "Introspection, Positionality, and the Self as Research Instrument—Toward a Model of Abductive Reflexivity," in *Approaches to Ethnography: Analysis and Representation in Participant Observation*, ed. Colin Jerolmack and Shamus Rahman Khan (Oxford: Oxford University Press, 2018), 211–37.

13. Shamus Rahman Khan, *Privilege: The Making of an Adolescent Elite at St. Paul's School* (Princeton, NJ: Princeton University Press, 2012); Peter Moskos, *Cop in the Hood: My Year Policing Baltimore's Eastern District* (Princeton, NJ: Princeton University Press, 2009); Ashley Mears, *Pricing Beauty: The Making of a Fashion Model* (Berkeley: University of California Press, 2011); Mitchell Duneier, *Sidewalk* (New York: Farrar, Straus and Giroux, 1999).

14. Eduardo Bonilla-Silva, *Racism Without Racists: Color-Blind Racism and the Persistence of Racial Inequality in the United States* (Rowman & Littlefield, 2006).

15. Michael German, "Hidden in Plain Sight: Racism, White Supremacy, and Far-Right Militancy in Law Enforcement," Brennan Center for Justice, August 27, 2020, https://www.brennancenter.org/our-work/research-reports /hidden-plain-sight-racism-white-supremacy-and-far-right-militancy-law;

Will Carless and Michael Corey, "To Protect and Slur: Inside Hate Groups on Facebook, Police Officers Trade Racist Memes, Conspiracy Theories and Islamophobia," *Reveal*, June 14, 2019, http://revealnews.org/article/inside-hate -groups-on-facebook-police-officers-trade-racist-memes-conspiracy-theories -and-islamophobia/; Jesselyn Cook and Nick Robins-Early, "Inside The Dangerous Online Fever Swamps Of American Police," *HuffPost*, June 17, 2020, https://www.huffpost.com/entry/police-protests-floyd-law-enforcement -today-rant_n_5ee3ef5fc5b699cea53196b4; Emily Hoerner and Rick Tulsky, "Cops Across the US Have Been Exposed Posting Racist and Violent Things on Facebook. Here's the Proof.," *BuzzFeed News*, July 23, 2019, https://www .buzzfeednews.com/article/emilyhoerner/police-facebook-racist-violent-posts -comments-philadelphia; U.S. Department of Justice, Civil Rights Division, and U.S. Attorney's Office, Western District of Kentucky, Civil Division, "Investigation of the Louisville Metro Police Department and Louisville Metro Government" (Washington, DC: U.S. Department of Justice, March 8, 2023), 1, 50–51, https://www.justice.gov/opa/press-release/file/1573011/download.

16. Ariel White, "Misdemeanor Disenfranchisement? The Demobilizing Effects of Brief Jail Spells on Potential Voters," *American Political Science Review* 113, no. 2 (May 2019): 311–24, https://doi.org/10.1017/S000305541800093X; Amy E. Lerman and Vesla M. Weaver, *Arresting Citizenship: The Democratic Consequences of American Crime Control* (Chicago: University of Chicago Press, 2014); Kristin Turney, "Depressive Symptoms Among Adolescents Exposed to Personal and Vicarious Police Contact," *Society and Mental Health* 11, no. 2 (July 2021): 113–33, https://doi.org/10.1177/2156869320923095; Kristin Turney and Dylan B. Jackson, "Mothers' Health Following Youth Police Stops," *Preventive Medicine* 150 (September 2021): 106693, https://doi.org/10.1016/j .ypmed.2021.106693; Sarah Brayne, "Surveillance and System Avoidance: Criminal Justice Contact and Institutional Attachment," *American Sociological Review* 79, no. 3 (June 2014): 367–91, https://doi.org/10.1177/0003122414530398; Devah Pager, "The Mark of a Criminal Record," *American Journal of Sociology* 108, no. 5 (March 2003): 937–75, https://doi.org/10.1086/374403.

17. Mark Fathi Massoud, "The Price of Positionality: Assessing the Benefits and Burdens of Self-Identification in Research Methods," *Journal of Law and Society* 49, no. S1 (2022): S64–86, https://doi.org/10.1111/jols.12372.

INDEX

Abbott, John, 95
abolitionist approach, to policing, xii,
    12; Kaba on, 239; Vitale on, 238. *See
    also* police defunding
Abt, Thomas, 237
accessible firearms, of public, 128, 164,
    225, 240
accountability. *See* discipline and
    accountability
Ahrens, Lorne, 94
ambush, 154; Canterbury on, 152–53;
    FBI, ODMP and GVA data on,
    4; of Liu and Ramos by Brinsley,
    1–2, 142, 153; NLEOMF on, 118;
    parking strategy to prevent, 177;
    police concerns for, x, 117–18, 155,
    162, 177, 180, 225; touch of car trunk
    to prevent, 179–80, 246, 247
American Sniper (film), about Kyle, 75
Ames, Fisher, 60
Anderson, Elijah, 15, 221
Annual Peace Officers' Memorial
    Service, George W. Bush speech
    at, 102
anonymization, in fieldwork, 249–50

anti-police brutality activists: Dallas
    protest by, 94–98; PBA on, 2
archetypes, of policing, 9–10, 12
Arradondo, Medaria, xiii

Back the Blue Act, FOP lobbying for, 231
ballistic vest, 257; discomfort of, 258–59;
    5.7×28mm cop killer cartridge with
    armor-piercing rounds, 126, 299n13
Banks, Willie Ray, xii
Barrientos, Jorge, 95
batons: as nonlethal weapon, xii, xiii,
    31, 62, 63, 148, 149, *204*; in police
    academy training, 62, 63; violent
    policing using, xii, xiii, 148, 149
battle dress uniforms (BDUs), for
    SWAT teams, 10
beanbag munitions, violent policing
    using, xiii
behavioral indicators, for violence
    threat, 43
Biden, Jill, 99
Biden, Joe: at Dallas memorial service,
    99; on policing and prevention
    programs, xv

BJA. *See* Bureau of Justice Assistance

Black criminality: Anderson on iconic ghetto and, 15, 221; UCR on, 15

Black Lives Matter, vii, 94, 168; of Dallas protest and officer shrine, *99*; "The Danger of 'Black Lives Matter' Movement" by MacDonald on, 122; police concern over activists of, 16; violent crime increases and, 122

Blacks: racial disparities for stops, search, arrests of, 7, 18, 227, 282n75; talk of parents for police encounters, xi–xii

bladed interview stance, as preventive method, 177, 225, 246

Blasio, Bill de, 2

Blue H.E.L.P., on officer suicides, 112–13

Blue Lives Matter, xv–xvi; Trump alignment with, x

body-worn cameras (BWCs), police academy discretionary training on, 32–33

Bourgois, Philippe, 288n23

Boyd, John, 59

B pillar stand, at traffic stops, 178

Brannan, Andrew Howard, 35–39

Bratton, Bill, 123, 153

Brayne, Sarah, 138

Brinsley, Ismaaiyl, 1–2, 142, 153

Brown, Michael: Ferguson protests at killing of, vii, xi, 10, 170, 245; public response to murder of, 2–3, 170; Wilson death of, vii, 245

Bulletproof Mind, KRG on, 53, 54

Bulletproof Vest Partnership program, 3

Bulletproof Warrior seminar, Castile shooting by officer after attending, 236

bureaucratic routine, policing and, ix–x

Bureau of Justice Assistance (BJA), VALOR Initiative "Survive and Thrive" training, 232

Bureau of Labor Statistics, on violent injury rate of policing, 4

Bush, Barbara, 99

Bush, George H. W., 81, 102

Bush, George W., 99; at Annual Peace Officers' Memorial Service, 102

BWCs. *See* body-worn cameras

California Peace Officers' Memorial, 297n36

Cannon, Lee, 95

Canterbury, Chuck: on danger and violence against police, 152–53; as FOP president, 3; on police killings as hate crime, 3

Castile, Philando, xii, 94, 236, 258, 294n26

CAT. *See* Combat Application Tourniquet

"Catalog of Unique, Concealed & Disguised Weapons, Concealments, Escape Techniques, Tactics & Tradecraft" (Chesbro), 125

Census of Law Enforcement Training Academies, on weapons/defensive tactics training in police academy, 31

Centurions, EPD academy class logo of, 50

Chauvin, Derek: Arradondo criticism of actions of, xiii; Floyd death by, xii, xiv; MPD report with violent policing absence, xiv; murder conviction of, xiii; previous internal departmental investigations for, xiv

Chesbro, Michael, 125

Christensen, Loren, 53, 75

CITF. *See* Correctional Intelligence Task Force

civilians, killed by police: Banks, xii; Brown by Wilson, vii, xi, 2–3, 10, 170, 245; Castile by Yanez, xii, 94, 236, 258, 294n26; Floyd by Chauvin, xii, xiv; Garner by Pantaleo, vii, 2–3, 170; Grant by Mehserle, 167–69, 307n22; Hamilton, 154; Mbegbu, xii; Rice by Garmback and Loehmann, 2–3, 169–75; Small, 93; Sterling, 93–94; Valenzuela, xii

civilians, killing of police: of Ahrens, Krol, Thompson, Michael Smith and Zamarippa by Johnson, 94; ambush of Liu and Ramos by Brinsley, 1–2, 142, 153; Canterbury on hate crime for, 3; of Dinkheller by Brannan, 35–41, 146; of Holder by Howard, 123; of Patterson in ambush, 84–85, 102–4; of Randolph and Daiyo, 83–84, 88–91; Trump on death penalty for, xi

Clark, David A., 3

clearance rate calculations: UCR data on, 300n24; WPD on, 301n24

Clinton, Hillary, 157

code 2 1/2 high-speed driving, 183–85

code 3 high-speed driving, 182–85

color-blind policing, 161, 261–63; danger, race and, 14–19; history of, 14–15; officers white supremacy links and, 17–18; racial bias language

removal in, 19; racial inequality naturalization by, 17–18, 226–27. *See also* tactical color-blindness

Combat Application Tourniquet (CAT), 166

command presence, of officers: described, 187–88; drive for dominance and, 225; IACP on, 189; killology and, 56; unintended consequences of, 187–94, 225

commemoration, of fallen officers, 25–26, 77–78; cultural artifacts for, 79; EPD award ceremony and, 110–14; EPD commemorative poem displayed, *108*, 108–9; flags at half-mast for, 93; funeral pamphlets for, *100*, 100–101; memorial services for, 80–81, 99–100, 102; memorial walls for, 79, 224; mourning bands for, 93, 98, 103; National Law Enforcement Memorial, 81; ODMP and, 4, 101–2; patriotic symbolism and artifacts, 84–85, 101–9, *108*; Peace Officers Memorial Day on May 15, 80; through personal effects, 85–91, *99*; police comradery and, 91; within police departments, 83–85, 88–91; police suicides omission from, 112–14; of SPD for Patterson, 84–85, 102–4; Washington, DC annual memorial service, 80–81; of WPD for Randolph and Daiyo, 83–84, 88–91

community: Anderson on iconic ghetto in, 15, 221; local challenges in, 33; need for direct investments in, 241; physical structure changes for future policing, 239; social inequality and, ix, 19, 226, 240

community policing: elements of, 29;
EPD failed implementation of, ix;
EPD philosophy of, 29, 246; Office
of Community Oriented Policing
Services funding of, 29; origins in
1960s of, viii; Twenty-First Century
Policing Task Force on, viii; warrior
officer policing and, 10–11
Congriff, Chris, 101–2
consensual encounters, reasonableness
and, 218–19
conspiracy of safety, Dave Smith on, 30
control of policing violence-centric,
fear-based training, 232–33; of
Grossman warrior officer training
and, 234; local-level intervention
for, 236; proposed restrictions for,
235; public fund removal for, 236;
reforms for, 236–37; by state-level
POST bodies, 236; of Street Cop
Training on social media, 234, 235
Conway, Gerry, 48
Correctional Intelligence Task Force
(CITF), 144
crime: Black criminality, 15, 221;
Black Lives Matter and increases
in violent, 122; Canterbury on
police killings as hate, 3; hot
sheet printout of prior shift, 26,
130–36; lineup information on
recent incidents of, 224; racialized
schema of, 226–27; scientific
discourse on, 15; -suppression
detail, 46; Trump tough-on-crime
policies, xi; UCR data on incident
records, 300n23
crime reduction units (CRUs), 124
crime-suppression detail, 46

criminal justice reform, violence
against police and, 122–23; FOB
Gamaldi criticism of, 230–31
criminal legal system, viii; policing
expansion and, 16; tough-on-crime
policies of Trump, xi
criminal victimization, 7
crisis intervention training, of EPD,
33–34
Crisis Response Vehicle (CRV), 1–2
CRUs. See crime reduction units
CRV. See Crisis Response Vehicle
cultural artifacts, for commemoration,
79
cultural capital, fieldwork and, 255–56
cultural frame, of danger imperative,
127–28
cultural influences, on policing inertia,
228–29
culture: Parsons download model of,
11–13, 298n3; socialization and,
298n3; violence shaping of, 6–8

Daiyo, Timothy, 83–84, 88–91
Dallas attack on police, during
protest (July 2016): Ahrens, Krol,
Thompson, Michael Smith and
Zamarippa murder by Johnson,
94–95; anti-police brutality activists
at, 94–98; five police officer deaths,
nine wounded during, 94–98;
funeral pamphlets from, 100, 100;
government officials at memorial
service for, 99–100, 102; Johnson
shooting rampage during, 94–96;
memorial service for, 99–100, 102;
misinformation on, 97; response of
police departments to, 97–98; Salda,

Rocha, McBride, Cannon, Wells, Shaw, Abbott, Reitana, Barrientos wounding by Johnson, 95; shrine outside Dallas Police Department headquarters, 98–99, *99*
danger and violence, against police: ambush of Liu and Ramos by Brinsley, 1–2, 142, 153; bureaucratic routine and, ix–x; Canterbury on, 152–53; criminal justice reforms and, 122–23, 230–31; everyone is trying to murder feature, of police academy, 41–43; FBI, ODMP and GVA data on, 4; Moskos on survival concerns, 6; Dave Smith on, 30; violent injury rate of, 4. *See also* civilians, killing of police; Dallas attack on police; police, killing of
danger imperative: EPD focus on, ix; Giddens on, 187; governing institutional frame of, 9; as officer attention to violence and potential death, 8; officer socialization within police department on, 8; police and public relationship damage from, 160; on policing racial inequalities, 13–14; re-creation through routine operations, 13, 224–25; as soul of policing, 9, 28, 223–28; unconstitutional policing and, x–xi, 27, 226; violence preoccupation and, 13. *See also* survival
"Danger of the 'Black Lives Matter' Movement, The" (MacDonald), 122
Danielson, Gary, 93
de-escalation training: of EPD, 33–34; police academy minimal, 31; public demand for, 33

defensive tactics training: in police academy, 25, 31; POST lesson plan, 55, 290n45
Deluca, Andrew, 110
Department of Homeland Security (DHS), on fusion center transmission of threats, 138, 302n35
Detectives Endowment Association of NYPD, on alleged restaurant poisoning of officers, 229
DHS. *See* Department of Homeland Security
DiIulio, John, 157–58
Dinkheller, Kyle, 146; video of murder by Brannan of, 35–41
discipline and accountability, police: Chauvin absence of violent policing in MPD report, xiv; for code 3 unauthorized high-speed driving, 182–85; for excessive force, 40; for line-of-duty killings, 229–30; for racism and violence, 123–24; for violent policing, xiii, xiv, 14, 123–24
discretionary design, of police academy, 34; on BWCs, 32–33; Census of Law Enforcement Training Academies on weapons/defensive tactics, 31; for local challenges, 33; minimal de-escalation training, 31; on nonlethal weapons training, 31–32; POST oversight of, 32; subject hours in, 32; weapons and defensive tactics attention in, 25, 31
Do Not Resist (film), 54
download model of culture: Parsons and, 298n3; in police academy training, 11–13

drive for dominance: command
presence and, 225; example of, 191;
Grossman, 235; in police-public
interactions, 291n46
driver-side approach, 146, 173, 178,
309n36
drug enforcement, SWAT team as tool
for, 10

Elgin, Don, 111–12
Elmont Police Department (EPD):
award ceremony of, 110–14;
Centurions academy class logo, 50;
commemorative poem displayed
at, 108, 108–9; community policing
philosophy of, 29, 246; crisis
intervention and de-escalation
training of, 33–34; danger and
violence focus of, ix; description of,
77–79; discretionary training topic
examples, 33; failed community
policing implementation by, ix;
graduation ceremony of, 292n61;
homicide rate decline, 158; lineup
at, 116; officer safety focus of, ix,
246; police academy training hours
of, 32; portraits of officers killed
on duty, 78–79, 82; PRISim virtual
shoot/don't shoot simulators at,
71–74; racial disparities in stops,
searches, arrests, 282n75; ride-along
policy of, 248; social inequality and,
ix; street gangs list outside, 298n5;
two-person patrol cars at, 159
empathy, in fieldwork, 257–59
enemies, threat network on, 122–24;
street gangs and, 120–21, 154–56, 244,
298n5

EPD. See Elmont Police Department
ethnographic interviews, in fieldwork,
20–21
everyone is trying to murder you
feature, of police academy, 41–43;
behavioral indicators for violence
threat, 43; reality-based scenario
training, 42–43, 224
Explorer youth programs, ride-alongs
for, 248

misinformation by police unions, on
alleged restaurant poisoning of
officers, 229
fatality rates, for policing, 4
FBI. See Federal Bureau of
Investigation
fear-based training, control of, 232–37
Federal Bureau of Investigation
(FBI): "LEOKA Officer
Safety Awareness Training" of,
231–32; National Situational
Information Report of, 142;
officer definition by, 283n83;
violence against police data of, 4;
on white supremacist infiltration
of police, 17
federal government, policing inertia
and: BJA VALOR Initiative
training, 232; of FBI "LEOKA
Officer Safety Awareness Training,"
231–32
Ferguson, Missouri, x; Brown killing
protests and, vii, xi, 10, 170, 245;
Barack Obama Twenty-First
Century Policing Task Force and,
viii; war on cops after Brown killing
in, xi, 4, 152

fieldwork: anonymization in, 249–50; author identity characteristics, 260–61; city characteristics, *21*, 21–22; cultural capital and, 255–56; data collected, *20*; decision for study direction, 243–47; demographic characteristics of officers in, 251; department characteristics, *21*, 21–22; department divisions and units, 22; empathy and, 257–59; ethnographic interviews in, 20–21; IRB approval for, 248; methodological appendix for, 243–65; officer pseudonyms used, 249; police department ride-alongs, 20, 247–48, 258–59; police department selection, 250; rapport with officers in, 252–54; reflexivity, positionality, inference, 259–65

fight for your life drill, for survival skills, 64–66; physical combat and, 74–75

firearms: accurate and concealable, 125, 126, 231; 5.7×28mm cop killer cartridge with armor-piercing rounds, 126, 299n13; improvised slap guns, 140; need for regulations of, 240; officers use in suicides, 113; readily accessible, 128, 164, 225, 240; safe storage laws for, 240; tactical imagination and, 163–66, 225; threat of, 19, 27, 133, 165

fitness, police academy on importance of, 45

5.7×28mm cop killer cartridge, armor-piercing rounds ability of, 126, 299n13

flags at half-mast, for commemoration, 93

Flo Block street gang, 154–56

Floyd, George: Frazier phone recording of death of, xiv; murder by Chauvin, xii

Flynn, Ed, 152

FOP. *See* Fraternal Order of Police

FOPA. *See* Fraternal Order of Police Auxiliary

Fraternal Order of Police (FOP): Canterbury as president of, 3; Gamaldi criticism of criminal legal reform, 230–31; lobbying efforts funding by, 231; Trump endorsement by, xi, 231; on war on cops, 230–31; Washington DC memorial service and, 80–81

Fraternal Order of Police Auxiliary (FOPA), Washington DC memorial service and, 80–81

Frazier, Darnella, xiv. *See also* Chauvin, Derek; Floyd, George

funeral pamphlets, for commemoration, *100*, 100–101

funeral services, for commemoration, 106

fusion centers, officer safety bulletins distribution by, 26, 136–45, *141*, *143*, 302n35

future, of policing: abolitionist approach, 238–39; addressing police task of violence solutions, 239–40; change from punishment to empowerment for, 239; community physical structure changes for, 239; direct investments for community and, 241; Manning

future (*continued*)
on, 238; non-police interventions, 240; police defunding proponents and, 238; reform and, 237; safe firearm storage laws and, 240; Vitale on reduction of policing harms, 238

Gamaldi, Joe, 230–31. *See also* Fraternal Order of Police.
Garmback, Frank, 2–3, 169–75
Garner, Eric, xii; Pantaleo killing of, vii; public response to murder of, 2–3, 170
gender imbalance, in policing, 23–24
Get Off the X adage, in tactical training, 177, 309n33
Giddens, Anthony, 187
graduation, from police academy, 74–76
Graham v. Connor (1989), objective reasonableness in, 70, 207, 208, 292n59
Grant, Oscar, 167–69, 307n22
Grossman, Dave, 75; predator language in training course of, 55–56; as KRG founder, 53–56; online training of, 235; on righteous violence, 53–54; violent ideology of, 54–55; on warrior officers, 54–56, 234
gun homicides, 164
gun violence: author research on, 245; National Network for Safe Communities on, 245; Project Longevity for reduction in, 244
Gun Violence Archive (GVA), violence against police data of, 4

Hahn, George, Jr., 297n36
Hamilton, Dashawn, 154

handcuffs, 52, 149, 198–99, 207; during vehicle searches, reasonableness and, 211, 214–15, *215*
hate crimes, Canterbury on police killings as, 3
Hemingway, Ernest, 47
high-risk traffic stops, 209–12, *210*
high-speed driving, of officers, 186, 225; code 2 1/2, 183–85; code 3 unauthorized, 182–85
Hinton, Elizabeth, xi
history, of color-blind policing, 14–15
Holder, Randolph, 123
Homeland Security Intelligence Network (HSIN), 138
homicides: EPD decline in rate of, 158; gun, 164; police defunding and increase of, xv; SCSD Mattison and, 52, 290n40
hot sheet printout, of prior shift crimes, 26, 130–36
Howard, Tyrone, 123
HSIN. *See* Homeland Security Intelligence Network
hypervigilance, tactical imagination and, 162

IACP. *See* International Association of Chiefs of Police
iconic ghetto, Black criminality and, 15, 221
ILEETA. *See* International Law Enforcement Educators and Trainers Association
inertia, of policing: misinformation, 229–30; from federal government, 231–32; at national level, 230–31; from police unions, 229–30; from

political, operational, cultural influences, 228–29

innocent suspects, mistaken arrest of, 205–8

In Search of Respect (Bourgois), 288n23

insignia: Punisher skull, 47–48, *49*; of thin blue line, 48, *49*, 50

Institutional Review Board (IRB) approval, for fieldwork, 248

instructors in police academy, as violence expert, 43, 46–47; on fitness, 45; tactical training and, 44

International Association of Chiefs of Police (IACP), 3; on command presence, 189; crisis intervention and de-escalation training recommendation by, 33

International Law Enforcement Educators and Trainers Association (ILEETA), extreme violence plan to overthrow U.S. government by, 16

interventions: crisis intervention training, 33–34; local-level for control of policing violence-centric training, 236; non-police, 240

IRB. *See* Institutional Review Board

January 6, 2020 insurrection, Proud Boys and Oathkeepers Punisher skulls display at, 289n36

Johnson, Micah Xavier, 94–97

justice, police righteous violence in pursuit of, 47

Kaba, Mariame, 239

Kennedy, David, 244

Kennedy, John F., 80

killology: command presence and, 56; Grossman as inventor of, 53–56, 235; proposed audit of, 235; restrictions for attending seminars of, 235

Killology Research Group (KRG): on Bulletproof Mind, 53, 54; Grossman as founder of, 53

kneeling officer image, 297n36

Koch, Harry, 106–7

KRG. *See* Killology Research Group

Krol, Michael, 94

Kyle, Chris, 289n32; *American Sniper* film about, 75; Punisher admired by, 47–48

Lahren, Tomi, 234

Law Enforcement Leaders to Reduce Crime and Incarceration, 122–23

Law Enforcement Officers Safety Reform Act, FOP lobbying funding for expansion of, 231

Law Officer policing website, 236

Lazarus game, 142, *143*

legislation: Back the Blue Act funding by FOP, 231; Law Enforcement Officers Safety Reform Act expansion, 231; OODA, 59; Protect and Serve Act funding by FOP, 231; Thin Blue Line Act funding by FOP, 231; Violent Crime Control and Law Enforcement Act, 157

"LEOKA Officer Safety Awareness Training," of FBI, 231–32

line-of-duty killings, police discipline and accountability for, 229–30

lineup, danger signals during, 115–17, *116*, 130–36; use of recent violent crime incidents, 224; video use in, 145–51

Liu, Wenjian, 1–2, 142, 153
lobbying efforts, FOP funding for:
    for Back the Blue Act legislation,
    231; on Law Enforcement Officers
    Safety Reform Act expansion, 231;
    Protect and Serve Act legislation,
    231; for Thin Blue Line Act
    legislation, 231
Loehmann, Timothy, 2–3, 169–75
Lynch, Patrick, 230

MacDonald, Heather, 122
Manning, Peter, 238
Martienza, Franklin, 110
Martinelli, Ron, x
mass incarceration, viii
Mattison, Scott, 52, 290n40
Mbegbu, Balantine, xii
McBride, Misty, 95
Meares, Tracey, 244
Mehserle, Johannes, 167–69, 307n22
memorial bracelets, as commemoration,
    86–88, 91; of NLEOMF, 86–87
memorial services: Annual Peace
    Officers' Memorial Service, 102;
    for police in Dallas attack, 99–100,
    102; Washington, DC annual,
    80–81
memorial walls, as commemoration,
    79, 224
methodological appendix, for
    fieldwork, 243–65
militarized police tactics and
    equipment, 16; protests response
    with, vii, 10–11, 245
Minneapolis Police Department
    (MPD), Floyd death report missing
    violent policing, xiv

mistakes and burden of error, in
    survival-centric policing, 214,
    226; innocent suspect and
    mistaken arrest, 205–8; vehicle
    misidentification mistake, 209–13
"Monument, The" (Hahn), 297n36
morality, of violence, 19, 25, 31, 51
Moskos, Peter, 6
mourning bands, for commemoration,
    93, 98, 103
MPD. See Minneapolis Police
    Department

National Law Enforcement Memorial
    Fund (NLEOMF): on ambushes,
    118; George H. W. Bush on, 81, 102;
    memorial bracelets of, 86–87; name
    etching of Patterson on, 103; on
    on-duty car crashes, 182
national level policing inertia, FOP
    Gamaldi criticism of criminal legal
    reform and, 230–31
National Network for Safe
    Communities, on gun violence, 245
National Situational Information
    Report, of FBI, 142
Naval Criminal Investigative Service
    (NCIS), 144–45
New England Journal of Medicine,
    on violent policing and beanbag
    munitions, xiii
New York Police Department
    (NYPD): commemorative patriotic
    symbolism for 9/11 deaths of,
    104–6; Detectives Endowment
    Association of, 229; PBA of, 229,
    230; SBA of, 229; unconstitutional
    stop-and-frisk tactics, x–xi; union

misinformation and antipolice violence messages, 229

NLEOMF. *See* National Law Enforcement Memorial Fund

nonlethal weapons: batons as, xii, xiii, 31, 62, 63, 148, 149, *204*; OC spray as, 31, 61–64, 149, 151, 197–99, *204*; training on, 31–32, 62–63. *See also* Taser

non-police interventions, 240

NYPD. *See* New York Police Department

Oathkeepers, Punisher skulls display on January 6, 289n36

Obama, Barack: at Dallas memorial service, 99, 102; policing reform policies of, xi; Twenty-First Century Policing Task Force of, viii

Obama, Michelle, 99

objective reasonableness, in *Graham v. Connor*, 70, 207, 208, 292n59

Observe, Orient, Decide Act (OODA) loop, of Boyd, 59

OC. *See* oleoresin capsicum

ODMP. *See* Officer Down Memorial Page

Office of Community Oriented Policing Services, U.S., community policing funded by, 29

Officer Down Memorial Page (ODMP): commemoration and, 4, 101–2; Congriff as founder of, 101–2; violence against police data of, 4

officers: command presence of, 56, 187–94, 225; concept of warrior, vii, 10–12, 16, 46, 54–56, 223–24, 234, 245; danger imperative as attention to

violence and potential death by, 8; pseudonyms used for, 249; FBI definition of, 293n83; minority, 23; raceless tactics and individual responsibility discourse, 26; safety-enhancing strategies of, 14; suicides of, 112–14; tactical color-blindness, 26, 167–75, 225, 307n22; tactical imagination of, 26, 161–66, 225; Twenty-First Century Policing Task Force on safety of, 3; violence preoccupation and safety of, 8; as white nationalists, 17

officer safety bulletins: CITF and, 144; FBI National Situational Information Report of, 142; fusion centers distribution of, 26, 136–45, *141*, *143*, 302n35; on Lazarus game, 142, *143*; from NCIS, 144–45

oleoresin capsicum (OC) spray exposure, 149, 151, 197–99, *204*; as nonlethal weapon, 31; for survival skills, 61–64

On Combat (Christensen and Grossman), 53, 75

on-duty car crashes, NLEOMF on, 182

online training: of Grossman, 235; of Policer, 235; of Street Cop Training, 235. *See also* social media platform

On the Blue Water (Hemingway), 47

OODA. *See* Observe, Orient, Decide Act

Pantaleo, Daniel, vii, 2–3, 170. *See also* Garner, Eric

Papachristos, Andrew, 244

paramilitary police units (PPUs), 10, 12. *See also* SWAT

Parsons, Talcott, 298n3

"Part of America Died, A" (Koch), 106–7

passenger-side approach, 309n36

patriotic symbolism, in commemorations: commemorative poem at EPD, 84–85, *108*, 108–9; in funeral services, 106; ODMP and, 4, 101–2; "A Part of America Died" poem and, 106–7; Patterson example of, 84–85, 102–4; of police killed in 9/11 terror attacks, 104–6

patrol cars, preventive measures with, 176, 225, 246; EPD two-person, 159; parking strategy to prevent ambush, 177

Patterson, Harold, 84–85, 102–4

PBA. *See* Police Benevolent Association

Peace Officers Memorial Day on May 15, Kennedy proclamation of, 80

Peace Officers Research Association of California (PORAC), against public police disciplinary records, 230

Peel, Robert, 285n1

Peelian principles, 285n1

pepper spray. *See* oleoresin capsicum

personal effects, commemoration through, 85; of memorial bracelets, 86–88; of shrines, 90–91, 98–99, *99*; of tattoos, 91

Peterson, Jordan, 51–52

Pew Research Center, on public perception of war on cops, 4–5

Pirone, Tony, 168. *See also* Grant, Oscar; Mehserle, Johannes

POI. *See* position of interrogation

police: ambush concerns by, x, 117–18, 155, 162, 177, 180, 225; antifascist groups and Black Lives Matter activists concerns by, 16; Black parent talk on encounters with, xi–xii; comradery for commemoration, 91; discipline and accountability for violent policing by, xiii, xiv, 14, 123–24; EPD on officer safety focus, ix, 246; FBI on white supremacist infiltration of, 17; public sentiment shift toward, vii–viii; Punisher paraphernalia, 49; social problem mediation by, 5; state violence distribution by, 7; as targets of prejudice and distrust, 257; as thin blue line between order and anarchy, 47–48, *49*, 50, 57, 80, 224

police, civilian killing by: of Banks, xii; of Brown by Wilson, vii, xi, 2–3, 10, 170, 245; of Castile by Yanez, xii, 94, 236, 258, 294n26; of Floyd by Chauvin, xii, xiv; of Garner by Pantaleo, vii, 2–3, 170; of Grant by Mehserle, 167–69, 307n22; of Hamilton, 154; of Mbegbu, xii; of Rice by Garmback and Loehmann, 2–3, 169–75; of Small, 93; of Sterling, 93–94; of Valenzuela, xii. *See also* Ferguson, Missouri

police, civilian killing of: Ahrens by Johnson, 94; ambush of Liu and Ramos by Brinsley, 1–2, 142, 153; Canterbury on hate crime for, 3; Dinkheller by Brannan, 35–41, 146; Holder by Howard, 123; Krol by Johnson, 94; Patterson in ambush, 84–85, 102–4; Randolph and Daiyo,

83–84, 88–91; Michael Smith by Johnson, 95; Thompson by Johnson, 95; Trump on death penalty for, xi; video of Brannan murder of Dinkheller, 35–41, 224; Zamarippa by Johnson, 94–95. *See also* Dallas attack on police

police academy, 29–32; batons in training at, 62, 63; defensive tactics training at, 25, 31; discretionary design of, 31–34; download model of culture in training of, 11–13, 298n3; everyone is trying to murder you feature of, 41–43, 223–24; on fitness importance, 45; graduation, 74–76; instructors as violence experts in, 43–47; killology in, 53–56; PRISim virtual shoot/don't shoot simulators at, 25, 66, *67*, 68–74, *69*, 224; on proof of peril, 34–41; Punisher narrative and, 47–53; reality-based scenario training at, 42–43, 224; on righteous violence, 224; on science of violence, 56–60; showing of graphic videos, 34–35, 224; socialization within, 11, 13, 25; stress-based training, 60–64; on survival skills, 60–74; training hours for, 286n7; warrior officer training in, 11–12, 223–24; weapons training in, 25, 31, 66–74

Police Benevolent Association (PBA), of NYPD: on alleged restaurant poisoning of officers, 229; on death of Liu and Ramos, 2; against public police disciplinary records, 230

police brutality, viii, 12; anti-police brutality activists, 2, 94–98; author absence of observation of, 256, 261,

263; Dallas July 2016 protest against, 94–98; protests against, 168, 170; racial justice and, xi

police defunding, xii; homicide increase after, xv; proponents of, 238

police department police danger signals: hotsheets at daily lineup meetings, 26, 130–36; officer safety bulletins, 26, 136–45, *141*, *143*; threat network of local, state, federal agencies, 26, 138–39; YouTube, social media, and policing websites on, 26, 35, 51, 145–46, 234–36, 290n37

police departments: commemoration of fallen officers within, 83–85, 88–91; fieldwork on characteristics of, *21*, 21–22; officer socialization to danger imperative within, 8; response to Dallas attack on police, 97–98; ride-along program, 247–48; selection for fieldwork, 250. *See also specific police department*

police department units: CRUs, 124; fieldwork and, 22, 250; PPUs, 10, 12; SWAT teams, 10, 12, 16, 22, 83, 90–91, 170; undercover, 41–42, 98

police legitimacy: crisis of, vii, 187–88, 247; damage to, 27, 193–94, 225

Police Officer Standards and Training (POST): defensive tactics lesson plan and, 55, 290n45; minimum standards of, 32, 286n7; police academy standards oversight by, 32; Psychology of Survival approved course of, 55, 56, 290n45; state-level control of violence-centric, fear-based training, 236

police organizations, Trump
endorsement by, xi
police-public interactions, drive for
dominance in, 291n46
Policer: Academy platform topics, 235;
online training of, 235
police trainings, audit and oversight
for, 235
police unions: misinformation , 229–30;
policing inertia from, 229–30;
against public police disciplinary
records, 230
policing: abolitionist approach to, xii,
12, 238, 239; archetypes of, 9–10,
12; Joe Biden on, xv; bureaucratic
routine and, ix–x; Bureau of Labor
Statistics on violent injury rate
of, 4; capabilities and structure of,
312n51; control of, 232–37; criminal
legal system and expansion of, 16;
danger imperative as soul of, 9, 28,
223–28; fatality rates for, 4; future
of, 237–41; gender imbalance in,
23–24; inertia of, 228–32; lack of
racial representation in, 23; 1960s
justification for expansion of, 15–16;
Barack Obama reform efforts on,
xi; racial inequalities in, 13–14, 16–17;
reform for, xvi; social inequality
and structural racism impacted by,
17; surveillance technology hiding
bias in, 18–19; survival and daily
production of, 9. *See also* violent
policing
PORAC. *See* Peace Officers Research
Association of California
position of interrogation (POI), of
police, 178, 225

POST. *See* Police Officer Standards
and Training
PPUs. *See* paramilitary police units
Preventing Violence Against Law
Enforcement and Ensuring Officer
Resilience and Survivability
(VALOR Initiative), "Survive and
Thrive" training course, 232
prevention programs, Joe Biden on, xv
preventive measures, in survival-
centric policing: bladed interview
stance and, 177, 225, 246; command
presence of officers and, 56, 187–94,
225; driver-side approach and, 146,
173, 178, 309n36; patrol cars and,
176–77, 225, 246; POI and, 178;
seating at places like restaurants,
176, 225; during traffic stops, 178–80,
209–12, 210, 246, 247
PRISim virtual shoot/don't shoot
simulators, at weapons training, 25,
66, 67, 68–74, 69, 224
prison gangs, 298n5
Project Longevity: for gun violence
reduction, 244; of David Kennedy,
244; Meares and Papachristos of,
244; police audits by, 244–45
proof of peril training, in police
academy, 36–41; graphic videos
in, 34–35; *Law Enforcement Today*
videos, 35
Protect and Service Act, FOP lobbying
for, 231
protests: for Brown killing in Ferguson,
vii, xi, 10, 170, 245; extreme force
by police use in, xii; militarized
response to, vii, 10–11, 245; against
police brutality, 94–98, 168, 170;

violent policing during, xii–xiii. *See also* Dallas attack on police
Proud Boys, Punisher skulls display on January 6, 289n36
Psychology of Survival, POST approved course, 55, 56, 290n45
public sentiment: on Brown, Garner, Rice murders, 2–3, 170; danger imperative damage to police-public relationship, 160; for de-escalation training, 33; drive for dominance and police-public interactions, 291n46; Pew Research Center on war on cops and, 4–5; shift toward police, vii–viii
Punisher: as criminal, 48; Kyle and, 47–48; police academy and, 47–53; police paraphernalia of, 49; Proud Boys and Oathkeepers January 6 display of skulls of, 289n36; skull insignia of, 47–48, *49*

race: color-blind policing and, 14–19; policing lack of representation in, 23; street gangs and, 120–21. *See also* color-blind policing; white supremacy
racial bias: color-blind policing removal of language for, 19; minorities unconstitutional policing stops and, 263
racial disparities, for Blacks and stops, searches, arrests, 7, 18, 227, 282n75
racial inequality, viii; color-blind policing naturalization of, 17–18, 226–27; Hinton on, xi; in policing, 13–14, 16–17, 227
racialized schema, of crime, 226–27

racial justice, police brutality and, xi
racism, police discipline and accountability for, 123–24
Ramos, Rafael, 1–2, 142, 153
Randolph, Emmanuel, 83–84, 88–91
rapport with officers, in fieldwork, 252–54
reality-based scenario training, 42–43, 224
reasonableness: consensual encounters and, 218–19; danger and corruption of, 214–22; *Graham v. Connor* objective approach of, 70, 207, 208, 292n59; handcuffing during vehicle searches and, 52, 149, 198–99, *204*, 207, 211, 214–15, *215*; subjective objectivity, 214
recovery, of firearms, 94, 110, 112, 124, 126
recruit training, 291n54
red man drill, in survival skills training, 65–66
reforms: criminal justice, 122–23, 230–31; for fear-based training control, 236–37; for future of policing, 237; for policing, xi, xvi; policy changes and, 27–28
Regional Information Sharing System (RISS) program, 138–39
regulations, need for firearms, 240
Reitana, Jesus, 95
restaurant: PBA on alleged officer poisoning at, 229; preventive measure of seating at, 176, 225
retaliatory violence, 154
Rice, Tamir: Garmback and Loehmann killing of, 169–75; public response to murder of, 2–3, 170

ride-alongs: author preparation for, 258–59; background checks for prevention of, 248; during fieldwork, 20, 247–48, 258–59; as part of Explorer youth programs, 248; for recruitment, 247–48

righteous violence, of police, 25, 224; to ensure survival, 31; Grossman, 53–54; in pursuit of justice, 47

RISS. See Regional Information Sharing System

RISSNET. See RISS Secure Cloud

RISS Officer Safety Website, 138

RISS Secure Cloud (RISSNET), 138

Rocha, Gretchen, 95

routinization, of violence, 130–36

Rubinstein, Jonathan, 57

safe storage laws, for firearms, 240

safety-enhancing strategies, of officers, 14, 27, 224

Safir, Howard, 3

Salda, Ivan, 95

SBA. See Sergeant's Benevolent Association

science of violence: emotional reactions and, 58–59; OODA loop of Boyd on, 59; Rubinstein on, 57; understanding of stress, 57–58

scientific discourse, on crime, 15

SCSD. See Swift County Sheriff's Department

seat belt policy, for officers, 184–86, 225, 246, 247

security threat groups, 298n5

September 11 terror attacks, commemorations of, 104–6

Sergeant's Benevolent Association (SBA), of NYPD, about antipolice violence, 229

Shaw, Brian, 95

shrines, as commemoration, 90–91, 98–99, 99

skull insignia, of Punisher, 47–48, 49

slap guns, improvised, 140

SLTT. See State, Local, Tribal and Territorial

Small, Delrawn, 93

Smith, Dave "JD Buck Savage": on conspiracy of safety, 30; on danger and violence against police, 30

Smith, Michael, 95

social inequality: Abt on, 237; community and, ix, 19, 226, 240; policing impact on, 17

socialization: culture and, 298n3; in police academy, 11, 13

social media platform, 26; of Law Officer, 236; Street Cop Training and, 234, 235; of #thinblueline, 51, 290n37

social problems, police mediation of, 5

soul of policing: danger imperative as, 9, 28, 223–28; Swidler on ethos, 9

SPD. See Sunshine Police Department

special weapons and tactics (SWAT) teams, 16, 22, 83, 90–91, 170; BDUs for, 10; as drug enforcement tool, 10; warrior officer in, 10, 12.. See also paramilitary police units

State, Local, Tribal and Territorial (SLTT), threat-related information from, 138

state violence: culture shaping of, 8; police distribution of, 7

Sterling, Alton, 93–94
stop-and-frisk tactics of NYPD, as unconstitutional policing, x–xi
Stoughton, Seth, 11, 46
"Street Academy" seminar, Street Cop Training, 234
Street Cop Training, on social media, 234; online training of, 235
street gangs, 121, 244; EPD list of, 298n5; Flo Block, 154–56; SPD and WPD on, 120-1
stress, physiological understanding of, 57–58
stress-based training, in police academy: OC spray exposure in, 61–64; physical exercise, 60–61
structural racism, policing impact on, 17
subjective objectivity, reasonableness and, 214
suicides, of officers: Blue H.E.L.P. on, 112–13; commemorations omission of, 112–14; firearms use for, 113
Sunshine Police Department (SPD), ix, xv; on BWCs, 32–33; commemoration of Patterson at, 84–85, 102–4; fight for your life drill, in police academy of, 74–75; police academy combat-related topics of, 34; police academy training hours of, 32; PRISim virtual shoot/don't shoot simulators at, 66, 67, 68–71, 69; ride-along policy of, 248; on street gangs, 120
superpredator thesis, of DiIulio, 157–58
surveillance technology, policing bias hidden by, 18–19
survival: Moskos on concerns of police focus on, 6; police academy core lessons on, 30; police academy on skills for, 60–74; police righteous violence to ensure, 31; policing daily production and, 9
survival-centric policing, 227–28; command presence and unintended consequences, 187–94, 225; danger and reasonableness corruption, 214–22; high-speed driving, 182–86, 225; mistakes and burden of error, 205–14; NLEOMF on on-duty car crashes, 182; physical violence use during calls, 194–203, 204; preventive measures, 176–81; problem solving service calls and, 194–203; safety-enhancing behaviors of officers, 181–87; seat belt policy, 184–86, 225, 246, 247; tactical color-blindness, 167–75, 224, 307n22; tactical imagination, 161–66, 225
survival skills training, at police academy: fight for your life drill, 64–66, 224; on hand-to-hand combat, 224; red man drill, 65–66; stress-based training, 60–64; weapons training, 66–74
"Survive and Thrive" training, of VALOR Initiative, 232
SWAT. See special weapons and tactics
Swidler, Anne, 9
Swift County Sheriff's Department (SCSD), Mattison on homicides and, 52, 290n40

tactical color-blindness, 26, 225; Mehserle accidental killing of Grant and Taser confusion, 167–69,

tactical color-blindness (*continued*)
307n22; Rice killing by Garmback
and Loehmann, 169–75; training
issues and, 168–69

tactical imagination 26; hypervigilance
and, 162; for life-or-death
encounters, 162; response imagined
and rehearsed in, 161–62; uncertainty
and firearms for, 163–66, 225

tactical training: Get off the X adage
in, 177, 309n33; in police academy,
44; tactical equipment examples, 44

Taser, 129, 148, *204*, 206, 238, 258;
Mehserle accidental killing of
Grant and confusion with, 167–69,
307n22; as nonlethal weapon, 32;
training, 32, 62, 291n54; WPD policy
on use of, 313n59

tattoos, as commemoration, 91

Tennessee v. Garner, 207

thin blue line, police as, 47, 57, 80, 224;
insignia of, 48, *49*, 50

Thin Blue Line Act, FOP lobbying
for, 231

#thinblueline social media platform, 51,
290n37

Thompson, Brent, 95

threat network: ambush concerns
and, x, 117–18, 155, 162, 177, 180, 225;
amplification of danger signals in,
118–19; on enemies, 120–24, 154–56,
244, 298n5; fusion centers and office
safety bulletins, 138–45, *141*, *143*,
224–25, 302n35; hot sheet printout
of prior shift crimes, 26, 130–36;
HSIN on, 138; lineup and danger
signals, 115–17, *116*, 130–36, 145–51;
of local, state, federal agencies,

26, 138–39; officer safety bulletins
and, 26, 136–45, *141*, *143*; RISS
program, and RISSNET database,
138–39; routinization of violence
and, 130–36; violence against one
of department officers, 151–56; on
weapons, 124–30, 225, 231

touch of car trunk, at traffic stops,
179–80, 246, 247

tough-on-crime policies, of Trump, xi

tourniquet, for uniforms and
equipment, 149, 166, *204*

traffic stops: B pillar stand at, 178;
high-risk, 209–12, *210*; probability
of violence during, 177–78; touch of
car trunk at, 179–80, 246, 247

training: control of fear-based, 232–37;
crisis intervention, of EPD, 33–34;
de-escalation, 31, 33–34; defensive
tactics, 25, 31, 55, 290n45; nonlethal
weapons, 31–32, 62–63; online, 235;
proof of peril, 34–41; reality-based
scenario, 42–43, 224; recruit, 291n54;
shadow phase of police field, 309n31;
Street Cop Training, 234, 235;
stress-based, 60–64; survival skills,
60–74, 224; tactical, 44, 177, 309n33;
Taser, 32, 62, 291n54; virtual, 25, 66,
67, 68–74, *69*, 224; warrior officer,
11–12, 223–24; weapons, 31–32, 62–63.
See also police academy; reform, for
control of fear-based training

Trump, Donald: on death penalty for
police killing, xi; FOP endorsement
of, xi, 231; police organizations
endorsement of, xi; tough-on-crime
policies of, xi; war on cops narrative
support by, x–xi

Twenty-First Century Policing
  Task Force, of Barack Obama:
  on Bulletproof Vest Partnership
  program, 3; on community policing,
  viii; on officer safety and wellness,
  3; Voices from the Field panel of, 3;
  Zakhary and Canterbury testimony
  at, 3

UCR. *See* Uniform Crime Reports
uncertainty: tactical imagination and,
  163–66, 225; violence probability
  and, 233
unconstitutional policing, 218; danger
  imperative and, x–xi, 27, 226;
  NYPD stop-and-frisk tactics, x–xi;
  perpetuation of, 222; stops of racial
  minorities as, 263
undercover narcotics work, 41–42, 98
Uniform Crime Reports (UCR):
  arrests and crime incidents records
  data, 300n23; on Black criminality,
  15; clearance rate calculations data,
  300n24
uniforms and equipment: ballistic vests,
  126, 257–59, 299n13; batons, xii, xiii,
  31, 62, 63, 148, 149, *204*; BDU, 10;
  BWCs and, 32–33; handcuffs, 52,
  149, 198–99, *204*, 207, 211, 214–15, *215*;
  OC spray, 31, 61–64, 149, 151, 197–99,
  204; tourniquet, 149, 166, *204*. *See
  also* Taser
unintended consequences, of command
  presence, 187–94, 225

Valenzuela, Fermin Vincent, xii
VALOR Initiative. *See* Preventing
  Violence Against Law

Enforcement and Ensuring Officer
  Resilience and Survivability
vapor lock, 163, 306n10
vehicle misidentification, mistake of,
  209–13
Ventura, Jesse, 289n32
videos, of violence against police: of
  Dinkheller murder by Brannan,
  35–41, 224; *Law Enforcement Today*
  hosted, 35; police academy showing
  of graphic, 34–35; *Police* and *Police
  Magazine* website for, 35; use in lineup
  training, 145–51; websites for, 145–46
violence: behavioral indicators for
  threat of, 43; Black Lives Matter
  and increase in, 122; culture shaped
  by, 6–8; danger imperative and
  preoccupation with, 13; morality
  of, 19, 25, 31, 51; Project Longevity
  and police knowledge of, 244–45;
  retaliatory, 154; righteous, 25, 31, 47,
  53–54, 224; routinization of, 130–36;
  science of, 56–60; uncertainty and
  probability of, 233
Violent Crime Control and Law
  Enforcement Act (1994), 157
violent policing: beanbag munitions
  and, xiii; as consequence of past, xii;
  police discipline and accountability
  for, xiii, xiv, 14, 123–24; during
  protests, xii–xiii; using batons, xii,
  xiii, 148, 149
virtual training, in police academy, 25,
  66, *67*, 68–74, *69*, 224
Vitale, Alex, 238

Wake Forest Police Department
  (WFPD): memorial of, 79, 292n1

war on cops, xv–xvi, 16; after Brown
    killing in Ferguson, xi, 4, 152; Clark
    on, 3; FOP on, 230–31; lack of
    data support for, 4, 247; Lahren
    proponent of narrative of, 234;
    MacDonald, Heather, 122; Martinelli
    on, x; Pew Research Center on
    public perception of, 4–5; Safir on,
    3; Trump support for narrative on,
    x–xi; *Washington Times* op-ed on, x.
    See also danger and violence, against
    police; police, killing of
war on crime, in 1960s, 16
warrior officer: community policing
    and, 10–11; Grossman on, 54–56,
    234; militarized police tactics and
    equipment of, vii, 10–11, 16, 245;
    police academy training for, 11–12,
    223–24; in PPUs and SWAT teams,
    10, 12; Stoughton on, 46
Washington DC memorial service,
    80–81
Washington Times op-ed, on war on
    cops, x
weapons, threat network on, 127, 130,
    225; concealed and disguised, 125,
    126, 231; reframing mundane objects
    as lethal weapons, 128–29; slap guns
    and, 140; WPD display of recovered
    firearms, 124. *See also* firearms

weapons training: Census of Law
    Enforcement Training Academies
    on, 31; on nonlethal weapons, 31–32,
    62–63; in police academy, 25, 31,
    66–74
Wells, Giovanni, 95
West River Police Department
    (WPD), ix, xv; on clearance
    rate calculations, 301n24;
    commemoration of Randolph
    and Daiyo at, 83–84, 88–91; CRU
    of, 124; lineup at, 115–16, *116*;
    memorial wall at, 82–84; police
    academy combat-related topics of,
    34; recovered firearms display at,
    124; ride-along policy of, 248; on
    street gangs, 120; Taser use policy,
    313n59
white supremacists, FBI on infiltration
    of police by, 17
Willis, Brian, 55–56
Wilson, Darren, vii, xi, 2–3, 10, 170, 245
WPD. *See* West River Police
    Department

Yanez, Jeronimo, xii, 94, 236, 258,
    294n26

Zakhary, Yousry "Yost," 3
Zamarippa, Patrick, 94–95

Printed in the USA
CPSIA information can be obtained
at www.ICGtesting.com
LVHW090950170424
777329LV00005B/13

9 780231 198479